W9-CMP-814

Introduction to Programming Languages

Introduction to Programming Languages

W. WESLEY PETERSON

Department of Information and Computer Sciences University of Hawaii

Prentice-Hall, Inc.
Englewood Cliffs, N.J.

Library of Congress Cataloging in Publication Data

Peterson, William Wesley
Introduction to programming languages.

Bibliography: p.
1. Programming languages (Electronic computers)
I. Title.
QA76. 7. P49 001.6′424 74-2468
ISBN 0-13-493486-5

Englewood Cliffs, N. J.

10 9

Printed in the United States of America

PRENTICE-HALL INTERNATIONAL, INC., *London*
PRENTICE-HALL OF AUSTRALIA, PTY. LTD., *Sydney*
PRENTICE-HALL OF CANADA, LTD., *Toronto*
PRENTICE-HALL OF INDIA PRIVATE LIMITED, *New Delhi*
PRENTICE-HALL OF JAPAN, INC., *Tokyo*

Contents

PREFACE ix

CHAPTER 0 *INTRODUCTION* 1

Programming Style *3*
Debugging *6*
Backus-Naur Form *8*

PART I *SCIENTIFIC COMPUTATION* 11

CHAPTER 1 *BASIC* 11

Introduction *13*
Examples of BASIC Programs *14*
BASIC Language *24*

CHAPTER 2 *FORTRAN FOR SCIENTIFIC PROGRAMS* 31

FORTRAN Examples *33*
FORTRAN Language *42*

CHAPTER 3 *ALGOL* 59

Introduction *59*
Examples of ALGOL Programs *61*
ALGOL Language *68*
Recursive Procedures *80*

CHAPTER 4 *PL/I FOR SCIENTIFIC PROBLEMS* 85

Examples of PL/I Programs *87*
PL/I Language *95*

CHAPTER 5 *APL* 117

Introduction *117*
Scalar Expressions in APL *119*
Procedure Definition *122*
Arrays in APL *126*

PART II *DATA PROCESSING* 133

CHAPTER 6 *PL/I FOR DATA PROCESSING* 135

On-conditions *135*
Picture Specifications *143*
Structures *146*
Record I/O *148*
Fixed-Decimal Variables *150*
Data-processing Program Examples *154*

CHAPTER 7 *COBOL* 171

COBOL Examples *174*
COBOL Language *187*
Procedure Division *196*

PART III *CHARACTER-STRING PROCESSING* 209

CHAPTER 8 *PL/I FOR CHARACTER-STRING PROCESSING* 211

Character String Functions and Operations *211*
Examples of PL/I Character String Processing *216*

CHAPTER 9 *SNOBOL* 231

Introduction to SNOBOL4 Language *232*
Patterns and Pattern Matching Statements *236*
Indirect Reference *244*
Function Definition in SNOBOL4 *246*

PART IV *LIST PROCESSING* 253

CHAPTER 10 *LIST PROCESSING IN PL/I* 255

Based Storage *255*
List Processing Concepts *259*

CHAPTER 11 *LISP* 287

APPENDIX A *SUGGESTED REFERENCES* 305

APPENDIX B *REVISED REPORT ON THE ALGORITHMIC LANGUAGE ALGOL60* 309

APPENDIX C *COMPUTER PROGRAMMING PROBLEMS* 327

APPENDIX D *TYPICAL COMPUTER RUNS* 335

APPENDIX E *IMPLEMENTATION OF RECURSIVE PROCEDURES* 343

APPENDIX F *LANGUAGE PROCESSOR AVAILABILITY* 351

INDEX 353

Preface

This book is the outgrowth of a course taught during the past six years at the University of Hawaii. The students are expected to know one computer language when they start, and thus are familiar with programming concepts. In the course of one semester they do 11 computer programming assignments —one per chapter. It is hard work, but it is also a gratifying experience to get a first-hand acquaintance with such varied languages and techniques, and the students do it enthusiastically. From the start, the problem was teaching material, which is available, but spread in many books and not practical for every student to purchase. This book provides the student with the essentials, presented in a manner that takes advantage of the fact that he already knows programming. Of course, not everything can be put in one book—or one semester, for that matter. The students will need supplementary reference materials, but, one hopes, only occasionally.

The notes that preceded this book frequently found another use, which I hope the book will also serve. For an experienced programmer who wants to acquaint himself with a new language, the essential ideas are presented in this book concisely and in a style appropriate for his background.

My participation in two software research projects at the University of Hawaii, one sponsored by the National Science Foundation, and the other by the U.S. Army Research Office in Durham, North Carolina, has had a positive influence on my ideas on software and hence on this book.

I would like to express my sincere appreciation for much support and cooperation to our Department of Information and Computer Sciences and our Computing Center. Specifically, the excellent typing done by Sharon Tanaka, Tamerlene Mark, and Rhonda Kubota on the original and many revisions has made my work much easier. I received some valuable suggestions and encouragement from Ralph E. Griswold. I owe most of all to my many students, with whom and from whom I have learned almost everything I know about computer programming.

W. Wesley Peterson
University of Hawaii

Everyone who specializes in computer science must know computer languages. Knowing a language means more than simply having read about it and having heard about it—one must use a language to know it. There are so many programming languages that it certainly isn't possible for one person to have experience with all of them. A few very important languages representative of a variety of styles and application areas are presented in this book, in enough detail so that you can use them and gain introductory experience with them. The importance of actual experience with a language cannot be overemphasized—in order to learn to swim one must get in the water. The purpose of this book is to facilitate and encourage the student of computer science to gain experience with a variety of programming languages.

This book is divided into four sections according to the applications area, and each section has chapters on each of several languages, according to the following outline:

Scientific Computation

1. BASIC
2. FORTRAN IV
3. ALGOL60
4. PL/I
5. APL

Introduction Chapter 0

Data Processing
6. PL/I
7. COBOL

String Processing
8. PL/I
9. SNOBOL4

List Processing
10. PL/I
11. LISP

Of these languages FORTRAN was the earliest, with development starting about 1954. FORTRAN was well-established when development started on ALGOL60 in about 1957. LISP and COBOL developed concurrently with ALGOL, but just a little later. These three languages were quite well-established by about 1962, and APL, SNOBOL4, PL/I, and BASIC were developed during the mid-1960's. More historical detail is given in the introduction of each chapter. Further detail on history, as well as endless other information on these and many other languages, can be found in Sammet's very excellent book, *Programming Languages: History and Fundamentals*.†

Generally, each chapter starts with a brief description of the characteristics of the language and several examples of programs. The goal is familiarity and understanding. The description is followed by more detailed explanations that should be adequate for writing simple programs. Occasional reference to more detailed manuals or books may be necessary, and some suggested references are given in Appendix A.

Although a comparison of languages is not the primary purpose of this book, comparing the languages can certainly give you a better perspective on programming languages as a whole. To that end, a set of example programs was selected for each section, and those examples are presented for each language. You should also seriously consider choosing one problem for each section and programming and running that same problem in each language.

In thinking about a language and comparing it with other languages, there are a number of ideas that you should bear in mind. Above all, a language should always be evaluated in the context of its intended purpose.

1. Is the language effective for its intended purpose?
2. Is it aesthetically pleasing? Does it have unity in its design, or chaos?
3. Is the language simple and easy to learn, or is it complex?

†Jean E. Sammet, *Programming Languages: History and Fundamentals* (Englewood Cliffs, N.J.: Prentice-Hall, Inc., 1969).

4. Is the language capable of doing sophisticated jobs? Is its scope narrow or broad?
5. Is the language definition clear, precise, and unambiguous?
6. Is good documentation available on both the language and on the compilers that make its use possible on computing systems?
7. Are apparent weaknesses actually inherent in the language, or are they weaknesses of the particular implementation being used? Can you even determine which is the case?
8. Is the language implemented on various machines in reasonably compatible manners?
9. Is debugging particularly easy or difficult?
10. Is the object program efficient? What features of the language may make an efficient compiler and object program particularly easy or difficult to achieve?

It is in no way the purpose of this book to answer these questions for you, although occasional discussions of some of these points are included.

Anyone who is going to study programming languages seriously will be writing programs in many of these languages. He will be able to use all the help he can get in debugging those programs. The next two sections are included for that reason.

Programming Style

In the use of natural language there is a great difference between grammatically correct use of the language and really good, effective writing or speaking. It is possible to write or say something which is true and accurate and grammatically correct but which is difficult to understand and is easily misunderstood. Generally, this is undesirable, and one should strive to speak and write in a clear, accurate, easily understood style. Obviously, the same is true of the use of computer languages.

The most serious problem and the biggest challenge to the computer industry today is, in the opinion of many, software reliability. Long after a large program is supposed to be completely free of errors, occasional annoying errors seem to have a way of appearing. Often new errors are introduced in the process of correcting old errors or making minor modifications in a software system. Good programming style can contribute a great deal to avoiding errors in the first place, finding errors during program check-out, and avoiding errors when a program is modified. In fact, my own personal experience and my experience with students has convinced me that even for short programs, and even if one is concerned only with getting a given job done as quickly as possible without regard for how much computer time he may waste in the process of debugging, one can finish the job most quickly if he takes adequate time initially to plan the program carefully and write it clearly and neatly in good programming style.

Much of the detail of programming style depends on the language being used, but there are a number of general principles that apply to every language.

Plan carefully. The plan should be as clear and simple and as straightforward as possible. It is generally better to use a simple method and simple logic even if it makes the program a little longer. There are exceptions, but they should be carefully justified and carefully documented.

A written plan is essential for all except the most trivial programs. Since the written plan is traditionally a flowchart, every programmer must be familiar with flowcharts. Although the flowchart is the best form for the plan of many programs, it is not for all programs and all programming languages. Some form of outline is better suited to some people, problems, and programming languages. For example, I claim that the following plan cannot be expressed as clearly or simply as a flowchart. (This is an outline plan for the first example in the next chapter.)

A. Start at the center of the interval and set the step size equal to half the interval size.

B. Repeat the following until the step size is negligible (e.g., <0.000001):

1. Halve the step size.
2. If $3x > e^x$, move one step left. Otherwise, move one step right.

C. Print x and e^x.

The flow of control in a program should be as simple and clear as possible. Conforming to the following rules will help you avoid some kinds of complicated program logic:

A. The program should be divided into segments of modest length in as natural a way as possible. Comments should explain the purpose of each segment.

B. Those segments should be made modular with respect to the rest of the program by having a clearly defined relationship with the program as a whole.

C. In particular, such segments should be entered only at their beginning. A jump into the middle of a segment from outside should not be allowed.

D. Flow of control should procede upward in a program *only* from the end of a loop to the beginning of that loop, and both ends of the loop should be clearly identified. Loops also should be entered only at their beginning.

One way to implement B and C is to make each segment a separate subroutine or procedure.

If the above rules are followed, then flow is always forward in the program except for well-defined loops. This fact, in combination with good comments, can in many cases make flowcharts completely unnecessary as part of the documentation of such a program.

Last, but not least, a checking and debugging plan must be a part of the initial plan. The initial plan must assure that it is possible to get enough information printed so that the programmer can check whether or not the program has followed his plan properly and gotten correct results at key check points along the way. This is best accomplished by inserting print statements for the specific purpose of providing information for checking and debugging.

An extremely useful technique for large programs is to make these debugging print statements a permanent part of the program and to provide a simple way to turn them on and off. For example, one way is to introduce a new variable, perhaps called DEBUG, and set it to one for runs on which the debugging printing is desired, to zero when the information is not desired. Then, statements of the following type would be inserted at key points:

```
IF DEBUG=1 THEN PUT EDIT('ENTER PROC.SS',X,Y,Z)(A,3 E(14,6));
```

(This example is PL/I. Examples in each language we study are given in their respective chapters.)

It is essential that the printing identify which debugging print statement caused it to be printed, as is done in the above example. During the debugging process, flow of control may not be as the programmer intended, and deviations must be made clear by the printed information.

Placement of debugging statements requires careful thought. It is good practice to place print statements following each statement that reads data from cards, tape, or disc to confirm that that point was reached and that the data actually entered the machine properly. It is often useful to place print statements at the beginning and/or end of subroutines to confirm that they were entered and to show the parameter values and/or returned values. At early stages in debugging, print statements may be needed inside most loops. Later they may be placed between loops to confirm that loops were completed and that the results are correct. Note that print statements placed in loops may theoretically cause thousands of pages or printing. On modern computing systems, however, one can easily specify a limit on printing. If a limit of about 500 lines or 10 pages is specified, plenty of useful information will be printed, and yet debugging print statements can be placed freely even inside loops without concern about wasting too much paper or printing time.

The program and comments should be carefully and neatly written, and they should provide as complete a documentation as possible.

1. At the beginning of the program and at the beginning of each major segment of code and each procedure or subroutine definition, a brief but clear explanation of what that section does should be given.

2. The programmer should use names that suggest the meaning of a variable.

3. A list of variable names and a brief explanation of their use should be included at the beginning of the program. If a name is used only in a subroutine or procedure, its meaning should be explained at the beginning of that subroutine or procedure.

4. Other comments should be included as necessary, but obvious or redundant comments should be avoided. Thus, for a statement `X=X+1`, the comment "`ADD ONE TO X`" not only is a waste but also will tend to make useful comments less conspicuous.

5. Make sure that the beginning and end of loops or other natural segments of code can be clearly seen. If a loop consists of only a few statements, this can be done by a combination of blank lines and/or indenting. For a long loop or segment of code, there should be a comment at each end, for example, `BEGINNING OF INTEGRATION LOOP` and `END OF INTEGRATION LOOP`.

For our study of programming languages, the examples will necessarily be short. All the rules are much more important in long programs. Some don't really apply to short programs. Nonetheless, these rules will be followed in the examples in this book, and you are strongly encouraged to follow them in the programs you write.

Debugging

Errors fall into four categories:

1. The language was used incorrectly. For example,

```
X = (A+B)C
```

is invalid because a multiplication sign (usually *) is needed:

```
X = (A+B)*C
```

An error message will be printed during compilation, and the program won't run.

2. The language may have been used correctly, but the computer was instructed to do something that it cannot do, for example, to divide by zero.

The program will compile and start to run, but when it reaches this point, it will stop and print an error message.

3. The programmer may have used the language correctly and instructed the computer to do something it can do, but for some reason it may not do what the programmer really intended it to do. For example, the program may run in a normal manner with no error messages, but it may print no answer or print incorrect answers, or the program may exceed the time limit specified because there is an infinite (never-ending) loop.

4. The computer may have done what the programmer intended, but it may nevertheless not give correct results because the method or algorithm chosen by the programmer for solving this problem is incorrect.

The error messages given by various compilers for (1) and (2) vary from completely clear to completely obscure, and there is little one can do except keep an open mind and use considerable imagination. Bugs of the third and fourth types are the most demanding of the programmer—there is no alternative to his contributing some mental effort. Type (2) errors also are sometimes quite demanding—e.g., the message "zero divide" may be printed in a long computation with many divides. Which divide caused the trouble? What do you do?

If the suggestions in the preceding section on planning for checking and debugging have been followed, the computer will print the information needed to locate the error, whether it is type (2), type (3), or type (4). Printed information will tell which parts of the program have executed and whether or not they have given correct results. In the case of a zero-divide or similar problem, it will be possible to narrow the problem to a few statements. In the case of an infinite loop, if there happened to be a print statement in the loop, it should be evident why the loop is not doing what was intended. If not, at least it should be possible to determine which loop, and at worst a print statement can be inserted and the problem run once again.

If, however, the program at least started to execute and if the problem cannot be isolated to a few statements, the debugging plan was inadequate. If it is not clear, with the exception of the last few statements, which statements were executed and which were not, adequate debugging printing has not been provided. We can expect the beginning programmer to complain, "My program ran and there weren't any errors, but no answers were printed." The experienced programmer will very, very seldom find himself in that plight.

Some languages have debugging aids such as "trace" and "snapshot" built in. Occasionally, they may offer advantages over your own inserted print statements. More often programmers use them as a substitute for thinking and planning the debugging process, for which there is no real substitute. In any case, for the purpose of this book, in which we study many languages, it is not feasible to study special debugging aids for each language as well. It is best to rely on the print statements of the language.

Backus-Naur Form

Backus-Naur Form, or simply BNF, is a method for describing syntax precisely. It was devised for the description of ALGOL60 (see Appendix B). Of the several systems commonly used, BNF is the most widely used. It is precise, simple, and clear enough to be practical and fairly easily understood by humans and at the same time easily processed by computers.

In general, in these notes we describe syntax by a combination of English and examples. At points where the syntax is especially complicated or especially interesting, a description in BNF is also included. Thus, although an understanding of BNF is not a prerequisite for reading the rest of this book it can enhance your understanding and appreciation of computer languages.

In BNF there are two special marks, ::= (read "is defined to be") and | (read "or"). The first is used to separate the name of the syntactical unit being defined from its definition. The name is placed on the left, the definition on the right. Names of syntactical categories are enclosed in the symbols < and >. Anything else stands for itself. For example, the statement

```
<digit> ::= 0 | 1 | 2 | 3 | 4 | 5 | 6 | 7 | 8 | 9          (1)
```

states that the syntactical category called <digit> may be one of the symbols 0, 1, 2, 3, 4, 5, 6, 7, 8, or 9. Then the statement

```
<a> ::= <digit> | <digit> <digit>
```

defines <a> to be any one- or two-digit number. If the first term, <digit>, is chosen, it can be replaced by any digit 0 through 9. If the second term, <digit> <digit>, is chosen, then each of the <digit>'s can be replaced by any digit.

Frequently, a definition of a syntactical unit involves that same syntactical unit, either directly or indirectly. Such a definition is called *recursive*. For example,

```
<unsigned integer> ::= <digit> | <unsigned integer> <digit>(2)
```

This states that a <digit> is an <unsigned integer> and also that placing a <digit> at the right of any <unsigned integer> makes another <unsigned integer>. Thus, 7 is a <digit> and hence an <unsigned integer>. Since 5 is a <digit> and 7 an <unsigned integer>, 75 is an

<unsigned integer>. Since 8 is a <digit> and 75 an <unsigned integer>, 758 is also an <unsigned integer>. Since 0 is a <digit> and 758 an <unsigned integer>, 7580 is an <unsigned integer>, etc.

The rules for <digit> and <unsigned integer> are part of the definition of ALGOL60. Here are a few more:

```
<decimal fraction> ::=  . <unsigned integer>                      (3)
<unsigned number>  ::= <unsigned integer> | <decimal              (4)
            fraction> | <unsigned integer> <decimal fraction>
```

Note that this allows numbers with or without a decimal point, but that if there is a decimal point, there must be at least one digit to its right.

```
    <letter> ::=a|b|c| . . . |z                                    (5)
 <identifier> ::=<letter> |<identifier> <letter>
                 | <identifier> <digit>                            (6)
```

This states that an <identifier> can be formed by starting with a letter and adding as many letters and/or digits as desired on the right. The <identifiers> are used as names for variables, functions, and procedures, and as labels in the programs.

It is instructive to see how syntax for arithmetic expressions can be expressed in BNF. Here is a part of the ALGOL60 BNF sufficient for generating ordinary expressions with exponentiation (A^B, expressed as A↑B in ALGOL-60) and the ordinary arithmetic operations, but with subscripted variables, functions, and some other features omitted for simplicity. (The complete ALGOL60 BNF is included in Appendix B.)

```
<variable> ::= <identifier>                                        (7)
<adding operator> ::= + | -                                        (8)
<multiplying operator> ::= * | /                                   (9)
<primary> ::= <unsigned number> | <variable> |
              ( <arithmetic expression> )                          (10)
<factor> ::= <primary> | <factor> ↑ <primary>                      (11)
<term> ::= <factor> | <term> <multiplying operator>                (12)
           <factor>
<arithmetic expression> ::= <term> | <adding operator>
           <term> | <arithmetic expression> <adding
           operator> <term>                                        (13)
```

Note that (11), (12), and (13) are each recursive in a manner very similar to

(2). Thus, (11) states that one can form a <factor> by starting with a <primary> and adding on the right as many times as desired a ↑ symbol followed by another <primary>. Then, (12) states that you may make a <term> by starting with a <factor> and adding on the right, as many times as desired, a * or / symbol followed by another <factor>. Finally, (13) states that <arithmetic expression> is formed by starting with a <term>, preceded by + or - sign if desired, and adding on the right, as many times as desired, a + or - sign followed by another <term>.

Rule (10) is recursive in a deeper way. One way to form a <primary> is to form an <arithmetic expression> and then enclose it in parentheses. But the definition of <arithmetic expression> involves <primary> indirectly through (11), (12), and (13).

As an example of the meaning and use of this BNF, a derivation follows for the expression

```
A ↑ B * (A + B * C)
```

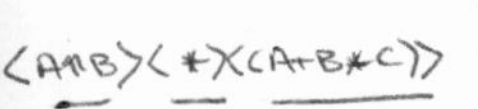

```
<arithmetic expression> → <term>                                    by (13)
  → <term> <multiplying operator> <factor>                          by (12)
  → <term> * <factor>                                               by  (9)
  → <term> * <primary>                                              by (11)
  → <term> * ( <arithmetic expression> )                            by (10)
  → <term> * ( <arithmetic expression> <adding
                 operator> <term> )                                 by (13)
  → <term> * ( <arithmetic expression> + <term> )                   by  (8)
  → <term> * ( <arithmetic expression> + <term>
                 <multiplying operator> <factor> )                  by (12)
  → <term> * ( <term> + <term> * <factor> )                         by  (9)
  → <factor> * ( <factor> + <factor> * <factor> )                   by (12)
  → <factor> ↑ <primary> * ( <factor> + <factor> *
                 <factor> )                                         by (11)
  → <primary> ↑ <primary> * ( <primary> +
                 <primary> * <primary> )                            by (11)
  → <variable> ↑ <variable> * ( <variable> +
                 <variable> * <variable> )                          by (10)
  → <identifier> ↑ <identifier> * ( <identifier>
                 + <identifier> * <identifier> )                    by  (7)
  → <letter> ↑ <letter> * ( <letter> + <letter>
                 * <letter> )                                       by  (6)
  →  A ↑ B * ( A + B * C )                                          by  (5)
```

PART

SCIENTIFIC COMPUTATION I

Electronic computers were first applied to scientific problems, and higher-level computer languages, the subject of this book, also started in scientific applications. Computers are best known for their wide use in science, and a substantial portion of computers today, including the most powerful, are doing primarily scientific work. Therefore, it seems fitting to start our study of computer languages in this area.

Science is broad, and scientific applications of computers involve every known computational technique, but those covered in Part I are the bread and butter of scientific computation. By the same token, every computer user will at least occasionally want to do some computation sufficiently complicated so that it really falls in this category. For example, one is likely to think of business data processing as almost the opposite of scientific computation, and yet there is a growing use in business of such techniques as operations analysis, linear programming, optimization, and statistical analysis and prediction, all of which require programming techniques of scientific computation.

Introduction

BASIC language was created in 1965 at Darthmouth College for use in a time-sharing system being developed there primarily for student use. Ease of learning and ease of use were emphasized in the design. The Dartmouth time-sharing system was one of the most successful early time-sharing systems, and BASIC language has also succeeded, gradually increasing in popularity until now it is very widely available on machines of a number of manufacturers. Although BASIC was designed for time-sharing use, in which the program and data are entered and run interactively from a teletype keyboard-printer or similar terminal, the language itself is also well-suited for conventional batch use, in which the program and data are punched in cards and submitted to the computing center to be run and returned with results after a "turn-around time" that may range from a few minutes to a number of hours. A number of modern systems make BASIC available in both modes. (There is a brief discussion of time-sharing and batch operation with examples in Appendix D.)

BASIC programs are divided into lines. Each line starts with a line number, and the line numbers of successive lines are in sequence. Following the line number is a key word that indicates the type of statement, and that is followed by the rest of the statement. For example, in the statement

BASIC Chapter 1

```
100 PRINT X, Y, Z
```

the key word PRINT orders the computer to print the values of X, Y, and Z. The statement

```
200 LET X = Y + Z
```

orders the computer to calculate Y + Z and assign the result as the new value of X.

Examples of BASIC Programs

On the following pages five examples of BASIC programs are given, with some explanations of the language. Following these is a more detailed and general explanation of BASIC language. Even if you are not familiar with BASIC, you should be able to understand the examples to a large extent, and having become familiar with the examples you should be able to understand the further explanation of BASIC. You may find it helpful to review the examples after you have read the entire chapter.

The first example is a program to find by trial and error a root of the equation $3X = e^X$. Note that if $X = 0$, the left side has the value of 0 and the right side has the value 1; therefore, the right side is greater. On the other hand, if $X = 1$, then the value of the left side is 3 and the value of the right side is $e^1 = e = 2.71828$; therefore, the left side is greater. For some value of X between zero and one they must be equal. (See Fig. 1.1.) The strategy of

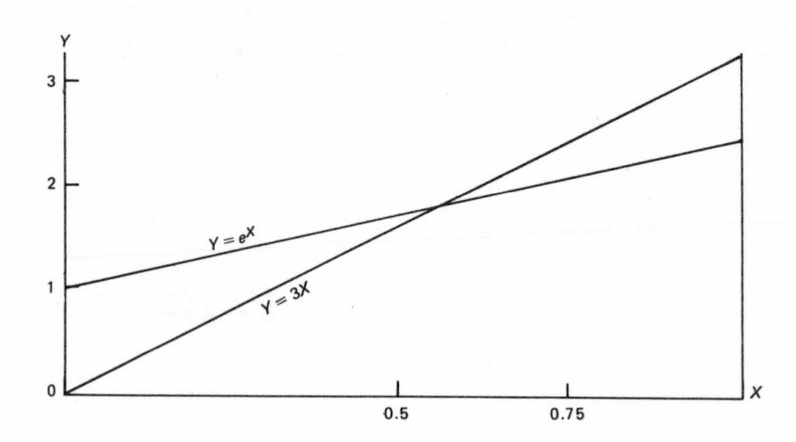

Figure 1.1 Graph of $Y = e^X$ and $Y = 3X$.

the program is to narrow the search at each step by checking at the middle of the interval. The first step tests at $X = 0.5$ whether it is the left side or the right side that is greater. It turns out to be the right side, which shows that the solution lies between $X = \frac{1}{2}$ and $X = 1$. Next, a check is made at the middle of this interval, i.e., at $X = \frac{3}{4}$. It turns out that here the left side is greater, and thus the root must lie between $X = \frac{1}{2}$ and $X = \frac{3}{4}$. Then the middle of this interval is tested, and so on, until the interval size is so small that any point in the interval is a satisfactory approximation to the root. The program prints out the midpoint of that interval as the value of the root.

Here are the BASIC program and results:

```
50    REM EXAMPLE PROGRAM NO. 1
51    REM CALCULATION OF A ROOT OF THE EQUATION EXP(X) = 3X BY
52    REM TRIAL AND ERROR. X IS THE LOCATION TO TRY NEXT, AND
53    REM WE WILL MOVE LEFT OR RIGHT A DISTANCE D AND CUT D IN
54    REM IN HALF AT EACH STEP. T IS SET NON-ZERO FOR TESTING,
55    REM ZERO FOR A PRODUCTION RUN.
56    LET T = 1
57
100   LET X,D = 0.5
102
110   REM --THIS IS THE MAIN LOOP, REPEATED UNTIL D IS NEGLIGIBLE.
115   LET D = D*0.5
120   IF 3*X>EXP(X) THEN 135
124   REM --GO RIGHT
125   LET X = X+D
130   GO TO 140
134   REM --GO LEFT
135   LET X = X-D
140   LET D = D*0.5
142   IF T=0 THEN 145
143   PRINT X,D,3*X,EXP(X),'  A'
145   IF D>=0.000001 THEN 120
146   REM END OF MAIN LOOP
147
150   PRINT X,EXP(X),3*X
155   END

RUN
EXECUTION STARTED

 0.75             0.125             2.25              2.117000016613  A
 0.625            0.0625            1.875             1.868245957432  A
 0.5625           0.03125           1.6875            1.75505465696   A
 0.59375          0.015625          1.78125           1.810766072119  A
 0.609375         0.0078125         1.828125          1.839281488542  A
 0.6171875        0.00390625        1.8515625         1.853707152046  A
 0.62109375       0.001953125       1.86328125        1.860962356705  A
 0.619140625      0.0009765625      1.857421875       1.857331211797  A
 0.6181640625     0.00048828125     1.8544921875      1.855518297141  A
 0.61865234375    0.000244140625    1.85595703125     1.856424533166  A
```

```
0.618896484375 0.000122070313 1.856689453125 1.856877817142  A
0.619018554688 0.000061035156 1.857055664063 1.857104500633  A
0.619079589844 0.000030517578 1.857238769531 1.857217852755  A
0.619049072266 0.000015258789 1.857147216797 1.857161175829  A
0.619064331055 0.000007629395 1.857192993164 1.857189514076  A
0.61905670166  0.000003814697 1.85717010498  1.857175344899  A
0.619060516357 0.000001907349 1.857181549072 1.857182429474  A
0.619062423706 9.53674316E-07 1.857187271118 1.857185971772  A
0.619062423706 1.857185971772 1.857187271118

LINE 155 -- NORMAL END
56 LET T = 0
RUN
EXECUTION STARTED

 0.619062423706 1.857185971772 1.857187271118

LINE 155 -- NORMAL END
```

In the program, X is the midpoint of the interval to be tested next, and D is half the interval size. If 3X > EXP(X), the root is on the left and the next midpoint is X - D, but if 3X < EXP(X), the root is on the right and the next midpoint is X + D. In either case, the interval size must be tested, and if it is not yet small enough, it must be cut in half and another step taken. Note the form of the IF statement. There is a line number following the word THEN, and control procedes to that line if the predicate is true, to the next line following the IF statement if it is false. The answer is printed by line 150. Although the printing format is simple, it is not very flexible. Ease of use was considered primary in the design of BASIC.

Statement 143 is for debugging purposes. It prints X, D, 3*X, and EXP(X) each time through the loop, and from this information it can be seen very clearly whether or not the program is actually carrying out the proposed plan properly. This statement prints the letter A to identify its output. If there were other debugging print statements, each would print its own unique identifier. Also, although again it is not needed in so simple a program, the technique of providing an easy way of turning debugging printing is illustrated here. Statement 142 will cause the print statement 143 to be executed if T is not zero, but will skip by it if T is zero. T is set in statement 56. In a complicated program, many debugging statements could be simultaneously turned on or off with one very trivial change in the program using this technique. The printed results actually show two runs. A run was made with $T = 1$, and hence with the debugging information printed. Then line 56 was changed to read LET T = 0, and another run was made on which only the final answers were printed.

The second example illustrates the function-type subroutine. The subroutine calculates the square root of its argument using Newton's method. Successive approximations to the square root of X are found by the formula

$$R_{n+1} = \frac{X + R_n^2}{2R_n}$$

This program uses X as the value of the first approximation R_0. Thus, for example, for $X = 2$,

$$R_0 = 2$$

$$R_1 = \frac{2 + 2^2}{2 \cdot 2} = \frac{6}{4} = 1.5$$

$$R_2 = \frac{2 + (1.5)^2}{2 \cdot (1.5)} = \frac{4.25}{3} = 1.417$$

$$R_3 = \frac{2 + (1.417)^2}{2 \cdot (1.417)} = 1.414$$

$$R_4 = \frac{2 + (1.414)^2}{2 \cdot (1.414)} = 1.414$$

which is accurate to three decimal places.

In the program, R is the previous approximation and S is the new one. Until they differ by a negligible amount, the procedure is repeated. In BASIC, variable names consist of either a single letter or a letter followed by a digit. User-defined function names consist of the letters FN followed by a single letter. Note that the returned value is assigned to the function name before returning—the statement LET FNS = S states that S is to be returned as the function value. The statement FNEND actually causes return to the main program. The main program shown simply tests the subroutine for values of A read from the DATA statement as long as any data remains in that statement. The next execution of the READ statement after the last card is read will terminate the program. This is a perfectly acceptable way to terminate execution.

```
1      REM BASIC     SAMPLE PROBLEM #2
2      REM
3      LET T = 0
100    REM THE SUBROUTINE SQR(X) CALCULATES THE SQUARE ROOT
102    REM OF X BY THE COMMONLY USED ITERATIVE METHOD.
103    REM HERE ALSO WE HAVE INSERTED A DEBUGGING PRINT STATEMENT
104    REM THAT WILL CAUSE EXTRA PRINTING IF T IS NOT ZERO.
105
106
200    DEF FNS(X)
201       REM --S IS THE NEXT APPROXIMATION, R THE PREVIOUS ONE.  WE
202       REM TAKE X AS THE FIRST APPROXIMATION.
210       LET R = X
215
216       REM BEGINNING OF LOOP
```

```
220      LET S = (X+R*R)/(2*R)
224      IF T=0 THEN 230
225      PRINT X,R,S
230      IF ABS(S-R)<=0.000001 THEN 260
240      LET R = S
250      GO TO 220
255      REM END OF LOOP
260      LET FNS = S
280   FNEND
290
291
300   REM THIS IS A SHORT MAIN PROGRAM FOR TESTING FNS(X).
310   READ X
320   PRINT X,FNS(X)
330   GO TO 300
340   DATA 0.5,1.44,2.0,4
999   END

RUN
EXECUTION STARTED

0.5               0.707106781187
1.44              1.2
2                 1.414213562373
4                 2.

LINE 310 -- OUT OF DATA
```

The third example gives another example of the use of IF statements and illustrates a technique in BASIC for writing a subroutine. This program calculates the greatest common divisor of two numbers using the Euclidean division algorithm. The idea is to divide the larger number by the smaller one and keep the remainder. If the remainder is zero, the smaller number is the greatest common divisor. Otherwise, the process is repeated throwing away the larger number and using the remainder. For example, to find the greatest common divisor of 1651 and 1079, first we divide 1651 by 1079. The quotient is 1 and the remainder is $1651 - 1079 = 572$. Since this is not zero, we repeat the process, dividing 1079 by 572, which gives quotient 1 and remainder 507. The computation continues as follows:

$$1651 \div 1079 = 1 \text{ remainder } 572$$

$$1079 \div 572 = 1 \text{ remainder } 507$$

$$572 \div 507 = 1 \text{ remainder } 65$$

$$507 \div 65 = 7 \text{ remainder } 52$$

$$65 \div 52 = 1 \text{ remainder } 13$$

$$52 \div 13 = 4 \text{ remainder } 0$$

The greatest common divisor is the smaller number in the last division, i.e., 13.

In the main program, N1 is the larger of the two numbers, N2 is the smaller, and N3 is the remainder. If N3=0, then N2 is the answer. Otherwise, N2 is taken as the new value of N1, N3 as the new value of N2, and another division is done. In this program, after the greatest common divisor for two numbers is found, the statement 190 GO TO 110 causes another pair of numbers to be read and another calculation done, as long as any input is supplied. (Input to an INPUT statement comes from cards in a batch BASIC compiler and comes from the time-sharing terminal in a time-sharing system.)

The subroutine, starting at line 200, calculates the remainder after dividing N1 by N2 and stores it as N3. The calculation is done by subtracting over and over until the result is less than N2. The statement 135 GOSUB 200 causes control to go to 200 and causes the number of the next line, 140, to be saved. Then the RETURN statement causes control to return to the next statement following the last previous GOSUB, i.e., to statement 140 in this case.

```
100  REM BASIC SAMPLE PROBLEM #3
101
102  REM --THIS PROGRAM READS N1 AND N2 AND CALCULATES THEIR
103  REM GREATEST COMMON DIVISOR USING THE EUCLIDEAN ALGORITHM.
104  REM AGAIN THERE IS A DEBUGGING PRINT STATEMENT, 131,
105  REM WHICH WILL PRINT KEY INFORMATION IF T IS NOT ZERO.
106
107  LET T = 0
108
109
110  REM --BEGINNING OF READ-COMPUTE-PRINT LOOP
111  INPUT N1,N2
120  PRINT 'GREATEST COMMON DIVISOR OF ';N1;' AND ';N2;
127
129  REM --BEGINNING OF MAIN LOOP
130  IF T=0 THEN 135
131  PRINT N1,N2,N3
135  GOSUB 200
140  IF N3=0 THEN 180
150  LET N1 = N2
160  LET N2 = N3
170  GO TO 130
171  REM --END OF MAIN LOOP
172
180  PRINT ' IS ';N2
190  GO TO 110
191  REM --END OF READ-COMPUTE-PRINT LOOP.
198
199
200  REM --THIS IS A SUBROUTINE THAT CALCULATES THE REMAINDER
201  REM AFTER DIVIDING N1 BY N2, AND PUTS THE RESULT IN N3.
202
210  LET N3 = N1
```

```
220   IF N3<N2 THEN 250
230   LET N3 = N3-N2
240   GO TO 220
250   RETURN
260   END

RUN
EXECUTION STARTED

? 65,39,
GREATEST COMMON DIVISOR OF  65 AND  39 IS  13
? 169,91,
GREATEST COMMON DIVISOR OF  169 AND  91 IS  13
? 65535,4095,
GREATEST COMMON DIVISOR OF  65535 AND  4095 IS  15
? STOP

LINE 111 -- PROGRAM HALTED
```

The fourth example illustrates a kind of problem that will not occur in a very small and simple program but that sometimes occurs in long, complicated programs. This example is short and simple, and, therefore, somewhat artificial. Suppose we wish to calculate water bills. There may be many cases, for example, for home use, commercial, industrial, and government users, and the rate may depend on location inside city limits or outside city limits, for example. There may be many cases and a different formula for each case. We will assume four cases for simplicity:

1. \$5.00 + 50¢ per 1000 gallons.
2. \$20.00 + 40¢ per 1000 gallons.
3. \$1000.00 for first 4,000,000 gallons and 0.25 for each additional 1000 gallons.
4. \$1000.00 if the usage doesn't exceed 4,000,000 gallons.
   \$2000.00 if the usage is greater than 4,000,000 but doesn't exceed 10,000,000 gallons.
   \$3000.00 if usage exceeds 10,000,000 gallons.

This program includes an example of the `ON` statement. The statement `20 ON I GO TO 100, 200, 300, 400` causes control to go to line 100 if $I = 1$, 200 if $I = 2$, 300 if $I = 3$, or 400 if $I = 4$. This program also includes a character string variable. String variable names consist of one letter followed by a dollar sign, or a letter, a digit, and a dollar sign. Character string variables can be used in `READ`, `INPUT`, `PRINT`, `IF`, and `LET` statements, and character string constants can be used in `PRINT`, `IF`, and `LET` statements. It is possible to have arrays of character strings.

```
1     REM --BASIC--SAMPLE PROBLEM #4
2
3     REM CALCULATION OF A WATER BILL WHERE FOUR DIFFERENT
4     REM FORMULAS ARE USED FOR DIFFERENT CUSTOMERS.  THE PARTICULAR
5     REM CASE WHICH APPLIES IS SPECIFIED BY THE VALUE OF "I".
6     REM "N" IS THE NUMBER OF GALLONS, "B" IS THE AMOUNT OF
7     REM THE BILL, AND A$ IS THE NAME.
8
9     REM --BEGINNING OF READ-COMPUTE-PRINT LOOP
10    INPUT A$,I,N
20    ON I GO TO 100,200,300,400
30
100   REM --CASE 1
101   LET B = 5+0.0005*N
102   GO TO 500
103
200   REM --CASE 2
201   LET B = 20+0.0004*N
202   GO TO 500
203
300   REM --CASE 3
301   LET B = 1000
302   IF N<=4000000. THEN 500
303   LET B = 1000+0.00025*(N-4000000.)
304   GO TO 500
305
400   REM --CASE 4
401   LET B = 1000
402   IF N<=4000000. THEN 500
403   LET B = 2000
404   IF N<=10000000. THEN 500
405   LET B = 3000
406
500   PRINT A$;'     BILL=';B
510   GO TO 10
520   REM --END OF READ-COMPUTE-PRINT LOOP
530   END

RUN
EXECUTION STARTED

? GEORGE J. JONES,1,3000
GEORGE J. JONES     BILL= 6.5
? A. B. JOHNSON,2,5000
A. B. JOHNSON     BILL= 22.
? FIRE DEPARTMENT,3,550000
FIRE DEPARTMENT     BILL= 1000
? HAWAIIAN ELECTRIC,4,5000000
HAWAIIAN ELECTRIC     BILL= 2000
? STOP

LINE 10 -- PROGRAM HALTED
```

The fifth example, which we call the money distribution problem, illustrates the use of subscripted variables and loop control with a fixed number of iterations in the loop. Suppose there are four countries, C_1, C_2, C_3, and C_4, in the world, and in year K they have D_{1K}, D_{2K}, D_{3K}, and D_{4K} dollars, respectively. Each year country C_I spends a percentage P_{IJ} of its money in country C_J. The total amount of money is assumed to be constant. Then, the first problem is to find out how much money each country has the next year. Country C_J will have the amount of money it spent in itself, $P_{JJ}D_{JK}$, plus the amount it received from other countries, $P_{IJ}D_{IK}$ ($I \neq J$). Altogether the formulas become:

$$D_{JK} = P_{1J}D_{1(K-1)} + P_{2J}D_{2(K-1)} + P_{3J}D_{3(K-1)} + P_{4J}D_{4(K-1)}$$

Now, let us assume that in year 0 country C_1 has $1,000,000 and the other countries have none. Let us calculate and print the value for year 1. Then, from that value let us calculate and print the value for year 2, etc. Eventually, the distribution of money will stabilize—an equilibrium will occur. Since we wish to know the equilibrium values, we will continue the calculation until we observe that none of the values D_{1K}, D_{2K}, D_{3K}, or D_{4K} changes by as much as 1.0, and then we will stop the computation. The BASIC program follows:

```
LIST

1      REM BASIC   SAMPLE PROBLEM #5
3      REM MONEY DISTRIBUTION PROBLEM
4      REM
5      REM P(I,J) IS THE PERCENT OF MONEY THAT COUNTRY I SPENDS IN
6      REM COUNTRY J EACH YEAR. D(I) IS THE AMOUNT OF MONEY THAT
7      REM COUNTRY I HAS ONE YEAR, E(I) THE AMOUNT THE NEXT YEAR.
8      REM WE START WITH $1000000 IN COUNTRY 1, ZERO IN THE OTHERS,
9      REM AND CONTINUE UNTIL EQUILIBRIUM.  L$ IS USED IN THE TEST.
10     REM IT IS A CHARACTER VARIABLE, AND IS ASSIGNED "TRUE" OR
11     REM "FALSE". K IS THE NUMBER OF THE YEAR.
12
20     MAT READ P
30     DIM P(4,4)
50     DATA 0.80,0.10,0.05,0.05
51     DATA 0.10,0.75,0.10,0.05
52     DATA 0.25,0.00,0.50,0.25
53     DATA 0.00,0.00,0.10,0.90
54
55     LET D(1) = 1000000.
60     FOR I = 2 TO 4
65        LET D(I) = 0
70     NEXT I
```

```
71    LET K = 0
72
74    REM --START OF YEAR-BY-YEAR LOOP
75    LET Y = Y+1
76    FOR J = 1 TO 4
80       LET E(J) = 0
85       FOR I = 1 TO 4
90          LET E(J) = E(J)+D(I)*P(I,J)
95       NEXT I
100   NEXT J
105   FOR J = 1 TO 4
110      PRINT E(J),
115   NEXT J
116   PRINT Y
117
119   REM --TEST FOR EQUILIBRIUM
120   LET L$ = 'FALSE'
125   FOR J = 1 TO 4
130      IF ABS(E(J)-D(J))<=1 THEN 150
140      LET L$ = 'TRUE'
150      LET D(J) = E(J)
160   NEXT J
170   IF L$='TRUE' THEN 75
171   REM --END OF YEAR-BY-YEAR LOOP
172
180   END

RUN
EXECUTION STARTED

 800000.          100000.          50000.           50000.           1
 662500.          155000.          80000.           102500.          2
 565500.          182500.          98875.           153125.          3
 495368.75        193425.          111275.          199931.25        4
 443456.25        194605.625       119741.5625      242196.5625      5
 [illegible]0.953125 190299.84375  125723.8125      279815.390625    6
 230[illegible]   183140.978125    130081.4773437   312987.8445312   7
 230431.62[illegible] [illegible]4734.7035937 133343.1059375 342055.9633203 8
 230429.2977886 [illegible]504102 135843.9310176   367416.1900098   9
 230427.2916381 92177.[illegible] 137802.4609789   389472.5477118   10
 230425.5620715 92175.543967[illegible] [illegible].6578593 408612.1577508 11
 230424.0709566 92174.21418307 147[illegible]523  425193.2656601   12
 230422.7854188 92173.06773297 147464.56[illegible] [illegible]9540.3315815 13
 230421.6771155 92172.0793416  147464.6879404 [illegible]875226   14
 230420.7216116 92171.22721775 147464.7913204 529943.[illegible] [illegible]15
 230419.8978412 92170.49257448 147464.8804476 529944.7291[illegible]
 230419.1876423 92169.85921498 147464.957287  529945.9958558     76
 230418.5753571 92169.31317546 147465.0235327 529947.0879348     77
 230418.0474864 92168.8424173  147465.0806452 529948.0294511     78

LINE 180 -- NORMAL END
STOP
EOF
```

This example illustrates the use of arrays. Line 30 shows a dimension statement. In BASIC, if an array is used but no DIM statement is included, the subscript limits are assumed to be 10. The lower limit 0 is always assumed. The statement FOR I = 1 TO 4 has the obvious meaning: it is the beginning of a loop. The end of the loop is indicated by the statement NEXT I.

In a BASIC time-sharing system, the statement INPUT calls for the program to stop and request input from the time-sharing terminal. After the input is typed on the terminal and the carriage returned, execution continues. The statement READ takes data from DATA statements, starting with the first DATA statement and continuing in sequence. Thus, the five statements 20 to 45 cause the 16 numbers in the DATA statements 50 to 53 to be inserted as the 16 values in the matrix P.

BASIC has no logical variables. The variable L$ used in lines 120, 140, and 170 is a character string variable, and the values "TRUE" and "FALSE" assigned to it are character strings. Statement 170 is an example of a comparison of two character strings.

BASIC Language

The following description of BASIC language is based on Kemeny and Kurtz's *BASIC Programming*.† Various implementations of the language differ in minor respects from this "official" version, partly because the "official" version has changed with time, and partly because of machine differences and differences in the implementors' ideas.

The language uses letters (upper and lower case, if available), digits, and the special characters comma, period, +, -, *, /, ↑, =, parentheses, and quote marks. Blanks may be used, but they are disregarded completely no matter where they are placed in BASIC statements. Identifiers consisting either of a single letter or a single letter followed by a single digit are used as variable names. There are a number of key words used in statements, and all these consist of two or more letters and, therefore, are distinct from identifiers.

A program consists of a number of lines. Each line has a line number which is an integer. Program statements must be in sequence by line number. The line numbers are used in sequence control statements such as GO TO, and also for editing on a time-sharing system. A line may consist of a line number and blanks only. This is a null statement—it does nothing but may be referenced in sequence control statements. Otherwise, immediately following the line number is a key word that indicates the type of statement. For example, remarks may be inserted as statements of the following form:

†John G. Kemeny and Thomas E. Kurtz, *BASIC Programming*, 2nd ed. (New York: John Wiley & Sons, Inc., 1971).

<statement number> REM <remark>

and this statement also does nothing but may be referred to in sequence control statements.

There are only two data types—numerical and string. Numerical data are always represented in floating-point format in the computer. Numerical variables use identifiers as names. Numerical constants are written in the usual form, with or without a decimal point. They may have a scale factor which is a positive or negative integer preceded by the letter E. Examples are:

1, 10, 10.3, 2.75E20, 3.1E140, 2E-3

(2.75E20 means 2.75×10^{20}. 2E-3 means $2 \times 10^{-3} = 0.002$.)

Strings are character strings of arbitrary length. String variables are represented by identifiers followed by a dollar sign. String constants are enclosed in quote marks in a program. String data on input are separated by commas. The reference book does not make clear what conventions apply to the use of commas and quote marks in strings in order to avoid the obvious ambiguities that may occur. Avoiding their use is sufficient.

Numerical or string variables whose names have a single letter may be used as one- or two-dimensional arrays. If they are used in that way with no declaration at all, the subscripts are assumed by the program to run from 0 to 10. For any other range, a statement DIM must be included to indicate how many subscripts and their maximum value. The minimum value is assumed to be zero. For example:

```
DIM A(12), B(12,12), C$(21)
```

declares A to be a list of numbers with subscript range from 0 to 12, B is a two-dimensional list with each subscript ranging from 0 to 12, and C$ is a list of character strings with subscript range from 0 to 21. When the variables are used in expressions and assignment statements, the subscripts are enclosed in parentheses and separated by commas.

In BASIC, exponentiation is represented by ↑, i.e., A↑B represents A^B, and implementations on machines on which the ↑ is not available use the FORTRAN symbol ** in its place. The usual BASIC built-in functions are shown in Table 1.1.

The BASIC assignment statement for numerical variables has the forms

<statement number> LET <variable> = <expression>

where <variable> may be either an ordinary variable or a subscripted variable with subscripts in parentheses. For string variables,

TABLE 1.1. BASIC Built-in Functions

SQR(X)	Square root
SIN(X)	Sine (angle in radians)
COS(X)	Cosine (angle in radians)
TAN(X)	Tangent (angle in radians)
ATN(X)	Arctangent (angle in radians)
LOG(X)	Natural logarithm
EXP(X)	e^x
ABS(X)	Absolute value
SGN(X)	$\text{SGN}(X) = 0$ if $X = 0$, 1 if $X > 0$, -1 if $X < 0$
INT(X)	Integer part (INT(X) = greatest integer that is smaller than X)
RND	Random number

```
<statement number> LET <string variable> = <string>
```

where

```
<string> :: = <string variable> | <string constant>
```

The GO TO statement has the form

```
<statement number> GO TO <statement number>.
```

There is a computed GO TO statement also. It has the form

```
<statement number> ON <expression> GO TO <statement number
          list>,
```

where the statement number list is simply a list of statement numbers separated by commas.

The BASIC numerical IF statement has the form

```
<statement number> IF <expression> <relational operator>
          <expression>
  THEN <statement number>
  <relational operator> ::= < | <= | = | > | >= | <>
```

Note that < > means "less than or greater than," i.e., "not equal." If the relation is true, control will go to the given statement number. Otherwise, control will proceed to the next statement.

BASIC has a pair of special statements for making loops. The first has the forms:

```
<statement number> FOR <simple variable> = <expression>
          TO <expression>
```

or

```
<statement number> FOR <simple variable> = <expression>
            TO <expression>
                         STEP <expression>
```

Here <simple variable> means that no subscripts are allowed. If the STEP <expression> is omitted, step size 1 is assumed. The expressions are not limited to integer values. Furthermore, BASIC even allows negative step size. If the step size is positive and the limit is lower than the initial value, or if the step size is negative and the limit is higher than the initial value, the loop is not done even once.

The end of the loop is indicated by the other loop-control statement, which has the form

```
<statement number> NEXT <simple variable>
```

where the variable name matches the name in the FOR statement. FOR loops must be properly nested; if two loops overlap, one must be entirely inside the other. Thus, the following is forbidden:

```
100 FOR X = 1 TO 10

200 FOR Y = 0.1 TO 10 STEP 0.1
    ____________

    ____________
600 NEXT X

700 NEXT Y
```

The statement STOP stops execution and returns control to the system. The statement END must appear as the last statement of every program.

For output there is a statement PRINT, which consists of the word PRINT followed by a list of real expressions or string variables or constants. The items may be separated by commas or semicolons. Punctuation may be omitted before or after a character string constant. If the comma is used, the number or string is printed in an even multiple of 15 spaces. If the semicolon is used, or if punctuation is omitted, the number or string is printed in as small a space as possible. If there is no comma or semicolon at the end of the line, the next PRINT statement starts on a new line, but otherwise the next PRINT statement continues from where this one left off.

There are two input statements, consisting of the keyword READ or INPUT followed by a list of names of numerical and/or string variables separated by commas. READ calls for data from DATA statements. In a time-sharing system, an INPUT statement causes the computer to stop and wait for data to be typed in at the terminal. In a background system, the data for an INPUT statement is read from cards. In either case, the data to be read consist of numbers (in any form acceptable in the program) and/or strings separated by commas. Note that because commas separate the data items, the string data must not contain commas.

The DATA statements consist of a statement number followed by the word DATA followed by a list of numbers and/or strings. READ statements use items from DATA statements in order, one READ statement starting from where the previous one left off. There is a statement RESTORE, which causes the next READ statement to start again at the beginning of the first DATA statement.

There is another statement, which has the form

```
<statement number> LINPUT <string variable>
```

and which causes the computer to accept a complete line from the time-sharing terminal or card from the card reader as the new value for the string variable. This statement allows strings containing commas and quote marks to be read easily.

There are two kinds of function definition. A *one-line function definition* has the form

```
<statement number> DEF FN <letter> (<formal parameter
           list>) = <expression>
```

For example,

```
23 DEF FNR(X,Y) = SQR(X*X+Y*Y+A*A)
```

In the *multi-line function definition*, the first line has the form

```
<line number> DEF FN <letter> (<formal parameter list>)
```

and the last statement is simply

```
<line number> FNEND
```

Between these is a program in which the function value is assigned to the function name. Here is an example:

```
213 DEF FNS (X)
217 FNS = 0
```

```
223 IF X<0 THEN 247
231 FNS = 1
247 FNEND
```

For either function definition, when the function is used, the formal parameters are replaced by expressions, and the expression values are used in evaluating the function. Variables that appear in the function definition but are not formal parameters assume their current values when the function is evaluated.

There is a simple but crude kind of subroutine linkage available in BASIC. One statement has the form

```
<statement number> GOSUB <statement number>
```

This has the effect of (1) placing the number of the statement following this one on a list or "stack" and (2) going to the specified statement and proceeding from there. The other statement is RETURN, which has the effect of (1) going to the statement whose number was last placed on the stack and (2) removing that number from the stack. Used in the simplest way, if GOSUB is used to branch control to a set of statements, RETURN at the end of this list of statements will cause return to the next statement after the GOSUB. But in this group of statements it is possible to GOSUB to another group of statements and return, etc.

BASIC also has some simple matrix operations built into the language. They allow reading or writing a matrix, adding, subtracting, multiplying, or inverting matrices, but with only one operation per statement. The following examples illustrate these statements:

```
100 DIM A(5,5), B(5,5), C(5,5)
200 MAT INPUT A, B
300 MAT READ C
400 MAT PRINT A, B
500 MAT C = B
600 MAT C = A + B
700 MAT A = B * C
```

```
800  MAT B = (K) * A

900  MAT C = INV(B)

1000 MAT A = TRN(C)

1100 MAT A = ZER

1200 MAT B = CON

1300 MAT C = IDN
```

In addition, A = A + B is allowed, but in multiplication A = A * B is not allowed, and inversion does not allow A = INV(A). Statement 800 illustrates multiplying a matrix by a scalar. Statement 1000 gives the matrix transpose, 1100 a matrix of all zeros, 1200 a matrix of all one's, and 1300 the identity matrix.

Matrices and arrays may be redimensioned at any point in the program, provided that no more space is required than was required in the original declaration. Matrices may be redimensioned as in the following examples:

```
100 MAT INPUT A(4,4)
200 MAT B = ZER(3,5)
```

Also, if the result of a matrix operation has different dimensions from the variable to which it is assigned, that matrix is redimensioned. For example,

```
100 DIM A(4,4), B(4,4), C(5,5)
200 MAT C = A + B
```

will redimension C to 4 × 4.

FORTRAN was the first higher-level computer language to receive wide acceptance, and it is still the most widely used computer language for scientific applications, with no apparent successor in sight.

At the time the FORTRAN project was undertaken almost all programs were written in assembly language, a language very much like the one the computer itself uses. Every program must be in machine language before it is run, and assembly language has the advantage of being easy to translate into machine language, but it also has the disadvantage of being so unlike English and algebra—the way humans usually communicate ideas related to computing—that most people found assembly language awkward and difficult to use. Several predecessors of FORTRAN demonstrated clearly that it was feasible to write programs in a language using algebraic expressions and English words and to use the computer itself to translate or "compile" them into machine language. However, they were not widely accepted. One important reason was that no computer had on its printer the characters required for representing formulas in a natural way, and thus awkward substitutions were required. The result was programs that were more difficult to read than assembly language. Another important reason why they were not accepted was that the early compilers produced inefficient machine language programs, and therefore, in addition to requiring extra time for compiling, they

Chapter 2
FORTRAN for Scientific Programs

required considerably more time for execution than a good program written in assembly language. The computer community was not ready to accept that exchange of computational efficiency for the programmer's efficiency and convenience. It is interesting to note that some of the most widely used compilers today produce programs that probably are on the average one-third as fast as a good program in assembly language, but everyone accepts this more readily now than they ought to.

In 1954 IBM undertook to develop FORTRAN for the IBM 704 in a bold and ambitious project for that time. The 704, which was in the final stages of development, was equipped with a printer having math symbols. Considerable effort was made to develop a compiler that would translate the FORTRAN programs to efficient machine language programs. The project received IBM's full support. FORTRAN was made available to IBM customers early in 1957 and soon received wide acceptance.

In mid-1958 a new version, FORTRAN II, was released. The important additions were the ability to write functions and subroutines in FORTRAN language, the ability to include assembly-language subroutines and functions rather easily, the use of common storage, and the ability to compile subroutines and main program separately and thus make libraries of compiled subroutines.

IBM released FORTRAN compilers for machines other than the 704 and its successors as early as 1958, and by 1961 compilers for machines of other manufacturers began to appear. The first compilers included some highly machine-dependent statements. For this and other reasons the various versions of FORTRAN were not completely compatible. SHARE, the organization of users of large IBM computers, issued a report describing a version that became FORTRAN IV. In it, most of the machine-dependent statements were dropped, and logical, double-precision, and complex variables were incorporated. The logical `IF` statement and the `DATA` statement were introduced.

In 1962 the American National Standards Institute, ANSI (then known as the American Standards Association), undertook to produce a standard version of FORTRAN. In 1966 standards were approved that included a description of FORTRAN which corresponds roughly to FORTRAN IV and a subset, Basic FORTRAN, which corresponds roughly to FORTRAN II. Most implementations now include one or the other as a subset, but they include language extensions. In particular, most manufacturers other than IBM have tried to assure simple conversion from IBM compilers to their own, but they usually include language extensions that make conversion in the other direction very difficult. Thus, in spite of much effort, compatibility has not been achieved.

In spite of incompatibilities, it is possible to write FORTRAN programs that can be run on many different computers simply by using simple standard

FORTRAN statements and carefully avoiding features that differ from one implementation to the next. Especially to be avoided are the so-called "language extensions," the often very convenient and attractive features offered by a manufacturer to make his FORTRAN better than the others. They are anything but convenient and attractive when one wants to convert this program for use on another machine.

The compatibility problem makes any presentation of FORTRAN difficult. Since the purpose of this book is to acquaint the reader with FORTRAN, the presentation will concentrate on a subset of the language that shows its main features and not on the details that vary from one implementation to the next.

FORTRAN Examples

The same five examples that appear in Chapter 1 in BASIC are presented here in FORTRAN. A good study plan is to read them to become familiar with the language, then to study the rest of the chapter, which describes the language in much more detail, and finally to study the examples once more, this time paying attention to details.

A FORTRAN program consists of a list of statements, and each new statement starts on a new card. A statement may have a statement number which may be used to refer to that statement in other statements. Comments are included on separate cards with a C in column 1. The end of a program is indicated by a statement consisting only of the word END.

The first example is the program to find by trial and error a root of the equation $3X = e^X$. Note that if $X = 0$, the left side has the value 0 and the right side has the value 1; therefore, the right side is greater. If, however, $X = 1$, then the value of the left side is 3 and the value of the right is $e^1 = e = 2.71828$; therefore, the left side is greater. For some value of X between zero and one they must be equal. The strategy of the program is to narrow the search at each step by checking at the middle of the interval and determining whether the root is at the right or at the left. The problem and method of solution are the same as in Chapter 1 and are described in more detail there.

```
C     EXAMPLE 1--CALCULATE A ROOT OF EXP(X)=3X BY TRIAL AND ERROR.
C     X IS THE NEXT LOCATION TO TRY, AND WE WILL MOVE LEFT OR RIGHT
C     A DISTANCE D AND CUT D IN HALF AT EACH STEP.
C
C     DEBUGGING PRINTING WILL BE DONE IF THE VALUE OF ITEST
C     IS NOT ZERO.
C
      READ(5,2)ITEST
    2 FORMAT(I1)
```

```
C
      X = 0.5
      D = 0.5
C
C
C     THIS IS THE MAIN LOOP, WHICH WE DO UNTIL D IS NEGLIGIBLE.
   10 D = D*0.5
      IF (3.0*X.GT.EXP(X)) GO TO 12
C     GO RIGHT
      X = X+D
      GO TO 11
C     GO LEFT
   12 X = X-D
C
   11 IF (ITEST.NE.0) WRITE(6,3)X, D
    3 FORMAT(' CHECK OF X AND D. ',2E14.6)
C
      IF (D.GT.0.000001) GO TO 10
C     END OF LOOP
C
C
      Y = EXP(X)
      Z = 3*X
      WRITE (6,1) X, Y, Z
      STOP
    1 FORMAT(' X=',F10.6,'  EXP(X)=',F10.6,'  3X=',F10.6)
      END
```

PRINTED OUTPUT:

```
X=  0.619061  EXP(X)=  1.857184  3X=  1.857184
```

In the program, X is the midpoint of the interval to be tested next, and D is half the interval size (after statement 10 is executed). If 3X > EXP(X), the root is on the left, and the next midpoint is X - D; if 3X < EXP(X), the root is on the right and the next midpoint is X + D. In either case, the interval size must be tested; if it is not yet small enough, it must be cut in half and another step taken.

Note the form of the IF statement. This is the FORTRAN IV type IF statement. If the logical expression in the parentheses is true, the single statement following it is executed. Otherwise, control procedes to the statement following the IF statement. At the time FORTRAN IV was created, the symbols >, < were not standard print characters, and the designers of FORTRAN IV chose .GT. , .LT. , etc., to represent these symbols. More detail is included later in this chapter.

In the WRITE statements, the word WRITE is followed by two numbers in parentheses. The first is the device number, and it is traditional to use 6 for the printer. The second is the number of a FORMAT statement (format items are discussed in some detail later in this chapter). Here F in statement 1 means fixed-point printed format, I in statement 2 means integer format, and E in statement 3 means floating-point printed format. FORMAT statements 2 and 3 also show how to insert alphabetic information into printed lines. Note that there is a list of variable names in the WRITE statements. In FORTRAN, unlike BASIC, constants and expressions are not allowed in the WRITE statement.

The second example illustrates the function-type subroutine. The subroutine calculates the square root of its argument by using Newton's method. Successive approximations to the square root of X are found by the formula

$$R_{n+1} = \frac{X + R_n^2}{2R_n}$$

This program uses X as the value of the first approximation R_0, just as the corresponding example did in Chapter 1.

Note that the function definition starts with a statement consisting of the word FUNCTION followed by the name of the function, followed by a list of parameters enclosed in parentheses. The definition ends with the END statement, and the main program follows. Actually, either the function or the main program may come first. The statement RETURN causes return from the function program to the main program.

```
      FUNCTION SQR(X)
C
C     THIS FUNCTION CALCULATES SQUARE ROOT BY NEWTON'S METHOD.
C     S IS THE NEXT APPROXIMATION, R THE PREVIOUS ONE.
C
      S = X
C
C     START OF ITERATION LOOP
    1 R = S
      S = (X+R*R)/(2*R)
      IF (ABS(S-R).GT.0.000001) GO TO 1
C     END OF LOOP
C
      SQR = S
      RETURN
      END


C     THIS MAIN LOOP MERELY READS A FROM A CARD, CALCULATES SQUARE
C     ROOT OF A, AND PRINTS IT, TO TEST THE FUNCTION SQR.
C
    2 READ(5,1)A
      B = SQR(A)
      WRITE(6,1)A,B
      GO TO 2
```

```
      1 FORMAT(2F10.5)
        END
```

```
PRINTED OUTPUT:


0.50000    0.70711
1.44000    1.20000
2.00000    1.41421
4.00000    2.00000
```

The third example illustrates further use of IF statements and illustrates integer arithmetic and a subroutine. This program calculates the greatest common divisor of two numbers using the Euclidean division algorithm. The idea is to divide the larger number by the smaller one and keep the remainder. If the remainder is zero, the smaller number is the greatest common divisor. Otherwise, the process is repeated, throwing away the larger number and using the remainder.

```
      SUBROUTINE MD(I,J,K)
C
C     THIS SUBROUTINE CALCULATES AND ASSIGNS TO K THE REMAINDER
C     AFTER DIVIDING I BY J.  IT IS DONE BY OVER-AND-OVER SUBTRACTION.
C
      K = I
C
C     SUBTRACTION LOOP
    1 IF (K.LT.J) RETURN
      K = K-J
      GO TO 1
C     END OF LOOP
C
      END
C     THIS MAIN PROGRAM READS NA AND NB AND CALCULATES THEIR GCD BY
C     EUCLIDS ALGORITHM.  N1, N2, AND N3 ARE THE NUMBERS USED AT EACH
C     STEP IN THE ITERATIVE PART OF THE ALGORITHM.
C
C     DEBUGGING PRINTING WILL BE DONE IF ITEST IS NOT ZERO.
C
      READ(5,13)ITEST
C
C
C     START OF READ-CALCULATE-PRINT LOOP
C
C
    1 READ (5,13)NA,NB
      N1 = NA
```

```
      N2 = NB
C
C
C     LOOP USING EUCLID'S ALGORITHM
    3 IF(ITEST.NE.0)WRITE(6,12)N1,N2,N3
   12 FORMAT(' TEST PRINT--',3I10)
      CALL MD(N1,N2,N3)
      IF (N3.EQ.0) GO TO 2
      N1 = N2
      N2 = N3
      GO TO 3
C     END OF LOOP FOR EUCLID'S ALGORITHM
C
C
    2 WRITE (6,13)NA,NB,N2
   13 FORMAT(3I10)
      GO TO 1
C     END OF READ-CALCULATE-PRINT LOOP
C
      END
```

PRINTED OUTPUT:

```
TEST PRINT--        91       169         0
TEST PRINT--       169        91        91
TEST PRINT--        91        78        78
TEST PRINT--        78        13        13
        91       169        13
TEST PRINT--     65535     31767         0
TEST PRINT--     31767      2001      2001
TEST PRINT--      2001      1752      1752
TEST PRINT--      1752       249       249
TEST PRINT--       249         9         9
TEST PRINT--         9         6         6
TEST PRINT--         6         3         3
     65535     31767         3
TEST PRINT--        73        99         0
TEST PRINT--        99        73        73
TEST PRINT--        73        26        26
TEST PRINT--        26        21        21
TEST PRINT--        21         5         5
TEST PRINT--         5         1         1
        73        99         1
TEST PRINT--       100        20         0
       100        20        20
TEST PRINT--        20       100         0
TEST PRINT--       100        20        20
        20       100        20
```

The program includes a subroutine MD(I,J,K) that calculates the remainder after dividing I by J and assigns that remainder as the value of K. The remainder is calculated by assigning the value of I to K and then subtracting J from K over and over until K is less than J. (There is actually a built-in function MOD(I,J) that does this more efficiently.) Note that a subroutine is invoked in the main program by a CALL statement. The subroutine definition has the same format as the function definition except that the word SUBROUTINE replaces the word FUNCTION.

In the main program, N1 is the larger of the two numbers, N2 is the smaller, and N3 is the remainder. If N3 = 0, then N2 is the answer. Otherwise, N2 is taken as the new value of N1, N3 as the new value of N2, and another division is done. In this program, after the greatest common divisor for two numbers is found, the GO TO 1 statement causes another pair of numbers to be read and another calculation done, as long as any input cards remain.

Ordinarily, FORTRAN programs use two distinct types of variables, called real and integer. Real variables are represented internally in floating point and may store very large and very small values, e.g., from about 10^{-79} to 10^{+75} in the IBM/360-370. Integers are whole numbers, and the maximum value is more limited, e.g., about two billion in the IBM/360-370. Integers are more efficient for simple counting and for list and array subscripts. Normally, variables and functions whose names begin with I, J, K, L, M, or N are stored as integers. All others use the floating-point representation. Thus, in the greatest common divisor program, all variables use the integer representation.

The fourth example is the water bill problem, with four different formulas for calculating the bill depending on which of four cases occurs:

1. \$5.00 + 50¢ per 1000 gallons.
2. \$20.00 + 40¢ per 1000 gallons.
3. \$1000.00 for first 4,000,000 gallons and 0.25 for each additional 1000 gallons.
4. \$1000.00 if the usage doesn't exceed 4,000,000 gallons.
   \$2000.00 if the usage is greater than 4,000,000 but doesn't exceed 10,000,000 gallons.
   \$3000.00 if usage exceeds 10,000,000 gallons.

We will assume that the input is a card with the account name in the first 20 columns, followed by the case number in column 21 and the number of gallons in columns 22–30. For simplicity, we will read a card, calculate the amount, and print a line only. This will suffice to illustrate the technique involved.

```
C     EXAMPLE 4-- THE WATER BILL PROBLEM.  NAME IS THE CUSTOMER
C     NAME, I IS THE CASE NUMBER FOR HIM, AND NGAL IS HIS USAGE.
C     B IS HIS CALCULATED BILL.
C
      DIMENSION NAME(5)
```

```
C
C
C      START OF READ-COMPUTE-PRINT LOOP
    1 READ(5,10)NAME,I,NGAL
   10 FORMAT(5A4,I1,I9)
      GO TO (21,22,23,24), I
C
CASE 1
   21 B = 5.00 + 0.0005*NGAL
      GO TO 2
C
CASE 2
   22 B = 20.00 + 0.0004*NGAL
      GO TO 2
C
CASE3
   23 B = 1000.00
      IF(NGAL.GT.4000000)B = B+0.00025*(NGAL-4000000)
      GO TO 2
C
CASE 4
   24 B = 1000.00
      IF(NGAL.GT.4000000)B = 2000.00
      IF(NGAL.GT.10000000)B = 3000.00
C
    2 WRITE(6,11)NAME,I,NGAL,B
   11 FORMAT(' ',5A4,I1,I9,F10.2)
      GO TO 1
C      END OF READ-CALCULATE-PRINT LOOP.
      END
```

```
PRINTED OUTPUT:


JONES, GEORGE E.     1      3000       6.50
JOHNSON, A. B.       2      5000      22.00
FIRE DEPARTMENT      3    550000    1000.00
HAWAIIAN ELECTRIC    4   5000000    2000.00
```

The statement `GO TO (21,22,23,24),I` will cause control to proceed to statement 21 if `I = 1`, to 22 if `I = 2`, to 23 if `I = 3`, and to 24 if `I = 4`. This "computed `GO TO`" statement is more convenient (and also executes faster) than four `IF` statements. If there were 100 cases, it would still be better than 100 `IF` statements, but it would be awkward. This problem is discussed further in the chapter on ALGOL.

The fifth example, the money distribution problem, illustrates the use of subscripted variables and loop control with a fixed number of iterations in the loop. Suppose that there are four countries, C_1, C_2, C_3, and C_4, in the world, and in year K they have D_{1K}, D_{2K}, D_{3K}, and D_{4K} dollars, respectively. Each year country C_I spends a percentage P_{IJ} of its money in country C_J. The total amount of money is assumed to be constant. Then, the first problem is to find out how much money each country has the next year. Country C_J will have the amount of money it spent in itself, $P_{JJ}D_{JK}$, plus the amount it received from other countries, $P_{IJ}D_{IK}$ $(I \neq J)$. Altogether, the formulas become:

$$D_{JK} = P_{1J}D_{1(K-1)} + P_{2J}D_{2(K-1)} + P_{3J}D_{3(K-1)} + P_{4J}D_{4(K-1)}$$

Now let us assume that in year 0, country C_1 has \$1,000,000 and the other countries have none. Let us calculate and print the value for year 1. Then, from that value let us calculate and print the value for year 2, etc. Eventually, the distribution of money will stabilize—an equilibrium will occur. Since we wish to know the equilibrium values, we will continue the calculation until we observe that none of the values D_{1K}, D_{2K}, D_{3K}, or D_{4K} changes by as much as 1.0, and then we will stop the computation. The FORTRAN program follows:

```
C     EXAMPLE 5--THE MONEY DISTRIBUTION PROBLEM.  P(I,J) IS THE
C     PERCENT OF MONEY THAT COUNTRY I SPENDS IN COUNTRY J EACH
C     YEAR. D1(I) IS THE AMOUNT OF MONEY THAT COUNTRY I HAS ONE
C     YEAR, D2(I) THE AMOUNT THE NEXT YEAR. WE START WITH COUNTRY
C     1 HAVING $1000000, THE REST NONE, AND CONTINUE UNTIL
C     EQUILIBRIUM IS REACHED. T IS USED IN THE TEST FOR EQUILIBRIUM.
C     WE CONSIDER THAT EQUILIBRIUM HAS BEEN REACHED WHEN NO
C     COUNTRY'S AMOUNT CHANGES BY AS MUCH AS $1.
C
C
      LOGICAL T
      DIMENSION P(4,4), D1(4), D2(4)
C
C     INITIALIZATION
C
      READ(5,10)P
      N = 0
      D1(1) = 1000000.
      DO 1 I= 2,4
    1    D1(I) = 0.
C
C
C     THE MAIN LOOP--ONCE PER YEAR-- STARTS HERE.
C     THESE TWO NESTED DO-LOOPS CALCULATE NEXT YEAR FROM THIS YEAR
C
    4 DO 2 J = 1,4
         D2(J) = 0.
         DO 2 I = 1,4
    2       D2(J) = D2(J) + P(I,J)*D1(I)
C
C     NEXT IS THE CHECK FOR EQUILIBRIUM--T WILL BE FALSE IF
```

```
C     EQUILIBRIUM HAS BEEN REACHED.
C     THE STATEMENT "D1(J) = D2(J)" MAKES THE NEW VALUE THIS YEAR
C     BECOME THE OLD VALUE FOR THE NEXT YEAR.
C
      T = .FALSE.
      DO 3 J = 1,4
      T = T .OR. (ABS(D2(J)-D1(J)).GE.1.0)
    3 D1(J) = D2(J)
      N = N+1
      WRITE(6,11)N,D1
      IF (T) GO TO 4
C     END OF YEAR-BY-YEAR LOOP
C
C
      STOP
C
   10 FORMAT(16F5.4)
   11 FORMAT (I6,4F13.5)
      END
```

The statement LOGICAL T declares that T is a logical variable. It may have the value .TRUE. or .FALSE. The statement T = .FALSE. sets T to the constant ".FALSE." The statement T = T .OR. (ABS(D2(J) -D1(J)).GE.1.0) sets T to .TRUE. if either T was .TRUE. or if ABS(D2(J) -D1(J)).GE.1.0. The statement IF(T) GO TO 4 will go to statement 4 if T is true; if it is not true, it will proceed in sequence. Logical variables and operators were introduced into FORTRAN when FORTRAN IV was created.

The statement DIMENSION P(4,4), D1(4), D2(4) defines P to be a 4 by 4 array of numbers and D1 and D2 each to be a list of four numbers. The number in the Ith row and Jth column of P is denoted P(I,J) in the program.

The statements down to and including statement 1 set up initial conditions. The statements from there to statement 2 do the actual calculation. First, D2(J) is set to zero, and then the four terms in the equation are added one by one by statement 2. The next three statements check whether or not the new values differ from the old by more than one. If any one differs by more than one, then the logical variable T becomes TRUE. Otherwise, T remains FALSE. Then, the new value D2(J) replaces the old value D1(J) in the preparation for another iteration if it is necessary. The statements following statement 3 update the count of iterations, print the results for this iteration, and then test T and go to statement 4 to do another iteration if T is TRUE.

There are several examples of the DO statement, which corresponds to the BASIC FOR statement. Note that in FORTRAN the end of the DO loop is indicated by including the statement number of the last statement in the DO statement. In FORTRAN, the initial value, the final value, and the step size, if included, must be integer constants or variables; real variables and expressions are not allowed.

FORTRAN Language

The description here is based on ANSI Standard FORTRAN (1966).† It includes the most important features but not all of ANSI FORTRAN. Most present-day compilers include all these features (in fact, all of ANSI FORTRAN) and often extensions. At several points non-standard commonly implemented features are discussed.

The character set for FORTRAN includes the capital letters, the digits, and the special symbols +, -, *, /, (,), =, comma, period, and blank. The asterisk (*) is used as a multiplication sign and the slash (/) for division. The period is used only in decimal constants and in logical operators. The comma is used for punctuation in various statements, especially in lists of variables. Blanks are used for appearance only and are disregarded completely in processing. In other words, blanks are always optional, but no other symbol is optional. Whenever a comma is specified it must be present, and if it is not specified it must not be present.

There are a number of words used as operators in FORTRAN that have special meanings. Examples are READ, WRITE, DO, IF, DIMENSION. Identifiers, used as names for variables, functions, and subroutines, may be chosen to be any string of one to six letters or numbers, of which the first must be a letter. Standard FORTRAN allows identifiers to be the same as operator names. Thus, IF or IF3 are allowed as identifiers. (This convention is not followed in all compilers.) These conventions make statement analysis and clear error messages more difficult for the compiler. For example, both the following are valid FORTRAN statements

```
DO2K = 1

DO2K = 1,10
```

the first being a simple assignment statement to assign 1 to a variable named DO2K. The second is a DO statement.

A program is divided into statements. A statement may have a statement number, which is from one to five decimal digits. Each statement must start on a new card. The statement number, if any, is punched in columns 1 through 5. The rest of the statement starts in column 7 and may extend through column 72. If the statement will not fit on one card, it may be continued on a "continuation card" that has columns 1 through 5 blank, column 6 any character except a blank, and the statement continuing from column 7.

The original FORTRAN had only two data types, integer and real. The integer variables were represented in the computer by fixed-point integers and originally were restricted to the range −32767 to +32767. The real vari-

†FORTRAN American National Standard X3.9-1966.

ables were represented in floating point in the computer, and in the original implementation they ranged in absolute value from about 10^{-39} to 10^{+39} with about eight significant decimal digits. The range of both integer and real variables, being machine-dependent, varies considerably from one implementation to another, and this is one incompatibility that usually causes no serious problem but occasionally causes subtle problems when a program is converted from one machine to another. The original FORTRAN had sufficiently flexible FORMAT statements so that well-formatted printed reports could be made without using alphanumeric data. Later implementations included more data types, and standard FORTRAN includes the following data types and allows expressions of each type and expressions with certain combinations of more than one of these.

1. Real
2. Double precision
3. Complex
4. Integer
5. Logical
6. Hollerith

In order to keep these notes of reasonable length, we have chosen to discuss only REAL, INTEGER, LOGICAL, and Hollerith data. The LOGICAL variables each store the values of either .TRUE. or .FALSE. which actually requires only one binary digit. Alphanumeric or character data types were not introduced, but it is possible to read alphanumeric data into real or integer variables and even make comparisons on it. This is explained in more detail in the discussion of input/output.

Any variable whose name starts with I, J, K, L, M, or N is assumed to be an integer variable, and all others are assumed to be real. There was no explicit declaration of variable types originally. Obviously, more is needed now in FORTRAN, and some examples are given in the following paragraphs. The above convention, however, is the usual way of determining variable types and applies unless an explicit declaration overrides it.

A list or array is represented in FORTRAN by a variable with one, two, or three subscripts. For these arrays the size must be declared. In FORTRAN, each subscript is assumed to start with one, and the upper limit and number of subscripts are declared in a DIMENSION statement, as in the following example:

```
DIMENSION X(5,10),VAL(17), MM(7,7,7)
```

Here X is declared to have two subscripts with maximum values 5 and 10, respectively. Thus, X represents a 5 by 10 array of real numbers, 50 numbers in all. VAL is a list of 17 real numbers. MM is a 7 by 7 by 7 array of integers, 343 numbers in all.

When there are explicit declarations, the dimensions may be declared at the same time. Some examples follow.

```
INTEGER A, B, T(17)
```

declares A and B to be integer variables and T to be a list of 17 integer variables.

```
DOUBLE PRECISION X(10, 10), Y, Z
```

declares X to be a 10 by 10 array of double-precision real variables, and Y and Z to be double-precision real variables.

There is also an "implicit" declaration:

```
IMPLICIT INTEGER (A - D), DOUBLE PRECISION (X - Z)
```

declares that all variables whose names start with A, B, C, or D are to be integer variables and all starting with X, Y, or Z are double-precision real.

In standard FORTRAN, the declarations can appear anywhere, but in some compilers they must appear at the beginning of the program. The safest plan is to place them at the beginning of the program, implicit declarations first, then other declarations, DIMENSION statements, and finally one-line function definitions before the rest of the program.

In FORTRAN, expressions are formed in much the same way they are in algebra. The form of constants is indicated by the following examples:

```
  1
511
  0.7112
871.2
  1.6E-19
    3E10
```

1.6E-19 (meaning 1.6×10^{-19})

3E10 (meaning 3×10^{10})

If a constant has neither a decimal point nor an E, it is assumed to be integer; otherwise, it is real.

Here are some examples of expressions. (A**B means A^B.)

```
(X + 17.)*A2*K/3.2
A**3 + B**1.73
X + 17 + I
(N + 1)*3
N + 1
N
17
```

The ANSI FORTRAN and ANSI Basic FORTRAN both prohibit "mixed expressions," i.e., expressions containing both real and integer variables (for example, the third example above). Most implementations of FORTRAN, however, allow these expressions. Expressions containing only integer variables and constants are integer expressions, but expressions containing real variables or constants give a computed real-type value. The action taken by the compiler in the case of mixed expressions, which varies from compiler to compiler, is sometimes not what the programmer expects and causes some incompatibility and subtle program bugs. For example, in IBM compilers, within a mixed expression the calculation is generally carried as far as possible in integer arithmetic with integer intermediate results, and conversion to real is done only when necessary. For example, in the statement

```
Y = (1/6) * X
```

the "1" is divided by the "6" in integer arithmetic, giving an integer intermediate result, which is always zero, because dividing one by six gives a zero quotient and remainder one in integer arithmetic. Thus, the value `0*X = 0` is always assigned to `Y`. Some compilers convert all variables and constants to real before doing any computation, and such a compiler will give a different result in this case.

Built-in functions vary from one implementation to the next (see Table 2.1).

TABLE 2.1 Standard ANSI Built-in Functions

SQRT(X)	Square root
ALOG(X)	Natural logarithm
ALOG10(X)	Common logarithm
EXP(X)	Exponential function e^X
SIN(X)	Sine function (argument in radians)
COS(X)	Cosine function (argument in radians)
ATAN(X)	Arctangent (answer is principal value in radians)
TANH(X)	Hyperbolic tangent
ABS(X)	Absolute value (real argument and value)
IABS(X)	Absolute value (integer argument and value)
MOD(N1,N2)	Remainder after dividing N1 by N2 (integer argument and value)
AMOD(N1,N2)	Same, but real argument and value
AMAX0(N1,N2,...)	Maximum value of arguments (integer argument and real value)
AMAX1(X1,X2,...)	Maximum (real argument and real value)
MAX1(X1,X2,...)	Maximum (real argument and integer value)
MAX0(N1,N2,...)	Maximum (integer argument and integer value)
AMIN0(N1,N2,...)	Minimum value of arguments (integer argument and real value)
AMIN1(X1,X2,...)	Minimum (real argument and real value)
MIN1(X1,X2,...)	Minimum (real argument and integer value)
MIN0(N1,N2,...)	Minimum (integer argument and integer value)
FLOAT(N)	Convert integer to real
FIX(X)	Convert real to integer
SIGN(A1,A2)	Sign of A2 times ABS(A1) (real argument and value)
ISIGN(N1,N2)	Same (integer argument and value)
DIM(A1,A2)	A1—AMIN(A1,A2) (real argument and real value)
IDIM(N1,N2)	N1—MIN(N1,N2) (integer argument and integer value)

Functions are written with the argument(s) in parentheses, separated by commas if there are more than one. The arguments may be expressions, for example,

```
SQRT(A*A + B*B)
EXP(-A*T)*(SIN(B*T) + COS(B*T))
```

Dimensioned variables are written with the subscripts in parentheses, separated by commas if there are more than one. ANSI FORTRAN allows only very simple integer expressions, for example,

```
A(2*I + 1)*A(2*I) + B(I - 7)
```

Most implementations allow subscripts to be integer or real expressions and convert to an integer value if necessary by truncating the number, i.e., dropping the part to the right of the decimal point.

ANSI FORTRAN also has logical variables and expressions. Actually, in practice, logical variables are seldom used, and generally, only simple logical expressions are used in conditional statements. The BNF is given here for logical expressions:

```
<relational operator> ::= .EQ. | .NE. | .LT. | .LE. | .GT. |
          .GE.
<logical primary> ::= .TRUE. | .FALSE. | <logical variable>
          | <expression> <relational operator> <expression>
          | ( <logical expression> )
<logical term> ::= <logical primary> | .NOT. <logical
          primary> |<logical term> .AND. <logical primary>
          | <logical term> .AND. .NOT. <logical primary>
<logical expression> ::= <logical term> | <logical
          expression> .OR. <logical term>
```

Examples:

`X.GT.Y` is true if `X` is greater than `Y`, false otherwise

`X.GT.0.AND.I.NE.100` is true if `X` is greater than zero and simultaneously `I` is not equal to 100.

`A.AND..NOT.B.OR.C` has the following "truth table":

A	B	C	Expression Value
False	False	False	False
False	False	True	True
False	True	False	False
False	True	True	True
True	False	False	True
True	False	True	True
True	True	False	False
True	True	True	True

Assignment statements have the following form:

```
<assignment statement> ::=

    <real variable> = <real expression> |
    <integer variable> = <integer expression> |
    <real variable> = <integer expression> |
    <integer variable> = <real expression> |
    <logical variable> = <logical expression>
```

In every case, the value of the expression on the right side of the equal sign is calculated, and this value is assigned as the new value of the variable on the left. In the third case, the integer result is converted to floating-point format before the assignment takes place, and in the fourth case, the value is converted to an integer by truncation before assignment. Examples:

```
Y = A*A + B*B + 17.
X = 17.
N = N + 1
X = N
N = 17.881
A = X.GT.17.2
```

In the second example, X is assigned the value 17. In the third example, N + 1 is calculated and assigned as the new value of N, i.e., N is increased by one. In the fourth example, N is converted to floating point and assigned as the new value for X. In the fifth case, the value 17.881 is truncated to 17, which is assigned as the new value for N. In the last example, the logical variable A is assigned the value TRUE if X is greater than 17.2, FALSE if X is less than or equal to 17.2.

FORTRAN has a simple GO TO statement that consists of the words GO TO followed by a statement number. This simply causes the statement whose number is given to be executed next. There are two GO TO statements that are in fact used much less than the simple GO TO, and yet they are important in certain problems that contain complicated logic. The *computed* GO TO is useful in situations in which there are many cases and the case number is given as the value of a variable. The form of this statement is illustrated by the following example:

```
GO TO (17, 31, 5, 19, 31), I
```

Here I is the name of the variable that designates the case number. If the value of I is 1, statement 17 will be executed next; if I = 2, statement 31 will be executed next, etc. If the value of I is out of range (less than 1 or greater than 5 in this case), the statement following this GO TO statement will be executed.

The other GO TO statement is the *assigned* GO TO. It provides what programmers often refer to as a "switch." Actually, there are two related statements. The first has the form

```
ASSIGN <statement number> TO <integer variable>
```

For example,

```
ASSIGN 17 TO J
```

The second statement has the form

```
GO TO <integer variable>, ( <list of statement numbers> )
```

For example,

```
GO TO J, (17, 31, 2, 500, 11)
```

Every statement number assigned to J must be included in the list. Then control will go to the statement whose number was last assigned to the variable. In the above examples, the ASSIGN statement sets the switch J to the value 17. If after that (but before another value is assigned to J) the GO TO statement is executed, statement number 17 will be executed next.

In FORTRAN, there are two conditional statements. The original FORTRAN has an *arithmetic* IF *statement* of the form

```
IF (<expression>) <statement number>, <statement number>,
        <statement number>
```

Control goes to the statement whose number is given first if the value of the expression is negative, to the second if the value is zero, and to the third if the value is positive. For example,

```
IF (I + J - K) 13,31,11
IF (X - SQRT (Y)) 10,10,17
```

The first of these goes to statement 13 if the value of the expression is negative, to statement 31 if it is zero, or to statement 11 if it is positive. In the second example, statement 17 will be executed next if the value of the expression is positive; otherwise statement 10 will be executed.

The *logical* IF *statement* was introduced with FORTRAN IV and is included in ANSI FORTRAN but not in ANSI Basic FORTRAN. It has the form

```
IF (<logical expression>) <simple statement>
```

in which <simple statement> means any executable statement except an IF statement or a DO statement. If the logical expression has the value TRUE, the statement will be executed. If it is FALSE, the control will proceed to the statement following the IF statement. Unless the <simple statement> is a GO TO statement, control will pass after it is executed to the statement following the IF statement. For example, consider the following statements:

```
IF (X.GT.7.2) I = I + 1

IF (X.LE.0.) GO TO 35

J = J + 1
```

If X is greater than 7.2, I will be increased by 1. In any case, the next IF statement will be executed next. If X is less than or equal to zero, statement 35 will be done next. Otherwise, control will proceed to the statement J = J + 1.

FORTRAN has one special statement for loop control, the DO statement. It has the following format:

```
DO <statement number> <integer variable> = <integer>,
        <integer>, <integer>
```

in which `<integer>` means either an integer variable or an integer constant, but not any other expression; the values of `<integer>` must be greater than zero. These three values are a lower limit, an upper limit, and a step size. (Actually, the step size and the preceding comma may be omitted; if they are omitted, the value one is assumed for the step size.) The `DO` statement means that the statements from this one down to and including the target statement (i.e., the statement whose number is given) are to be done once for each value of the integer variable from the lower limit to the upper limit, incrementing each time by the step size. For example,

```
DO 17 I1 = 1, 13, 2
```

means that the statements from this one through the one numbered 17 should be done seven times, with the values 1, 3, 5, 7, 9, 11, and 13, respectively, for `I1`. In FORTRAN, each value not exceeding the upper limit is used; thus,

```
DO 17 I1 = 1, 14, 2
```

gives exactly the same results as the preceding example. Moreover, the first value is used even if it exceeds the upper limit:

```
DO 17 I1 = 23, 14, 2
```

will be done once, for `I1` = 23, even though 23 exceeds the upper limit 14.

One subtle problem occurs with `DO` statements. Occasionally, there doesn't seem to be an appropriate statement to use as a termination for a `DO` loop. For example, suppose `A(I)` is a list of 100 numbers, and the sum of only the positive numbers in the list is required. Consider the following program:

```
1   SUM = 0
2   DO n I = 1, 100
3   IF (A(I)) n, n, 4
4   SUM = SUM + A(I)
5   WRITE (6, 7) SUM
```

What is the correct statement number to use for `n`? It is incorrect to use `n` = 4 because statement 4 should be done only if `A(I)` is positive. Using n = 5 will result in printing the value of SUM 100 times. This problem is solved in FORTRAN by introducing a statement that does nothing, the CONTINUE statement.

```
1   SUM = 0
2   DO 5 I = 1, 100
3   IF (A(I)) 5, 5, 4
4   SUM = SUM + A(I)
5   CONTINUE
6   WRITE (6, 7) SUM
```

Some programmers like to use a CONTINUE statement to mark the end of every DO loop because it seems to make the limits of the loop easier to see.

The rules of FORTRAN language prohibit the use of GO TO, DO, or IF statements as the last statement of a DO loop. There is a logical reason for each case except the logical IF. It is possible to write a logically correct program in which the logical IF statement appears as the target statement of a DO loop. Some compilers will accept such a program, but others will not.

Input/output in FORTRAN is complicated. There are two types, formatted and unformatted. All input from cards or output to the printer must be formatted, but tape and disc I/O may be of either type. Since unformatted I/O is simpler, it is described first. Statements consist of the word READ or WRITE, followed by a data-set number in parentheses, followed by a list of variables. For example,

```
READ (17) X, Y, Z, I, J
```

means to read the next available data from data-set or data file 17 and use it as the new values for X, Y, Z, I, and J, respectively. The relation between the data-set number and a real file is established by the operating system and will vary greatly from one implementation to the next. On the IBM/360–370, the relation of a real file to data-set 17 is established by describing the file on a DD job control card with the DD name FT17F001. But the details are outside the scope of this book.

The list may be a little more complicated. If one of the variables on the list is dimensioned, but only the name is given, all its values will be read or written. If the subscripts are given, only the single value will be read or written. Thus,

```
DIMENSION A(3, 3)
READ (17) A
WRITE (18) A(1, 1)
```

will read the nine value of A, in the following order:

```
A(1, 1), A(2, 1), A(3, 1), A(1, 2), A(2, 2), A(3, 2),
A(1, 3), A(2, 3), A(3, 3)
```

The second statement will write only the value A(1, 1). The following statements are also possible:

```
WRITE (18) ((A(I, J), I = 1, 3), J = 1, 3)
WRITE (18) (A(I, J), I = 1, 3)
```

The first has exactly the same effect as WRITE (18) A. The second writes A(1, J), A(2, J), and A(3, J).

The information is divided into *records*. Each time a write statement starts, a new record is started. On reading, each read starts a new record and must use precisely one record. Since no conversion is done, care must be taken so that the variable types match in the WRITE and READ statements.

For formatted I/O all input data is in the form of characters and is converted according to a format statement. Similarly, output variables are converted to characters suitable for printing. This usually involves binary-to-decimal conversion also. The format specification is made up of format items. The most important types are described below.

I <width> converts an integer variable to decimal and puts out the number of characters specified by the width. The number is placed at the right, with blanks inserted at the left if necessary. For example, if item I10 is used to convert a number whose value is 144, seven blanks will be inserted at the left to make a total of ten characters.

F <width>.<decimal places> converts a real number, using the specified number of places to the right of the decimal point and inserting blanks to the left if necessary. Note that the width for output must exceed the number of decimal places by at least three, to make room for a sign, at least one digit to the left of the decimal point, and the decimal point. For example, if the format specification F11.4 is used to print a variable whose value is 17.25, four blanks will be inserted to the left of 17.2500 to produce a total of eleven characters.

E <width>.<decimal places> converts a real variable, using the specified number of decimal places to the right of the decimal point, one place to the left, and a scale factor that is the power of ten which this must be multiplied by. For example, if 1732500 is printed using the format item E13.5, the printed characters will be 1.73250E+06 with two blanks at the left to make a total of thirteen characters. Note that 1732500 equals 1.73250×10^6.

These items have been described for output. In general, if the input data are arranged according to the same rules, they will be read properly. There is a little extra freedom, however. For example, if the decimal point on the input data doesn't agree with the format specification, the one on the card is used. It is not even necessary to use a decimal point on the card, and thus the format item F1.0 can be used to convert a single card column to a variable value, even though this specification is illegal on output.

<width> X simply skips characters on input, or inserts blanks on output. For example, 17X will skip over 17 characters on input, or insert 17 blanks on output.

A <width> reads characters into the variable on input and writes from the variable on output, *without conversion*. If fewer characters are specified than the variable will hold, then blanks are inserted at the right. If more are specified than the capacity of the variable, the excess characters are lost. Since the number of characters per variable varies from machine to machine, there are incompatibilities. The capacity of an ordinary variable is four characters on the IBM/360-370, six characters on the IBM 7090 or UNIVAC 1100 series of DEC PDP10, ten characters on the CDC 6000 series and Cyber 70 series.

There are two ways to insert character information (for labels, titles, etc.) in printed lines by including a format item. The first is the Hollerith constant, which consists of an integer followed by H, followed by exactly the number of characters (including blanks) indicated by the integer. For example,

```
100 FORMAT (17HTHE VALUE OF X IS, X)
```

Many FORTRAN compilers (but not ANSI FORTRAN) allow a character string to be enclosed in apostrophes, for example,

```
100 FORMAT ('THE VALUE OF X IS', X)
```

The latter is generally preferable—it seems that many programmers cannot count accurately beyond 10, and an incorrect count in the Hollerith constant almost always causes an error.

The format statement consists of a statement number, the word FORMAT, and a list of format items in parentheses. For example,

```
11 FORMAT (I3, F6.2, E14.6, E14.6)
```

The format statement number is included in parentheses with the data-set reference number in a READ or WRITE statement. The simplest format statement would list one item per variable in the READ or WRITE statement. Thus, the above format statement could be used with the following statements:

```
READ (5, 11) I, X, Y, Z
WRITE (6, 11) N, A, B, C
```

There are some refinements. First, a repeated item can be abbreviated by putting a repetition number in front of the item. Thus, the above format could be written

```
11 FORMAT (I3, F6.2, 2E14.6)
```

Next, a group can be repeated by putting it in parentheses with a repetition number in front. Thus,

```
12 FORMAT (3I3, 2(F6.1, 3E14.5))
```

is equivalent to

```
12 FORMAT (3I3, F6.1, 3E14.5, F6.1, 3E14.5)
```

Parentheses, however, can be inserted no deeper than in the above example.

Output and input are divided into records. In particular, on the printer one line is a record, and on the card reader one card is a record. Every time a new statement is started, it starts a new record. Every time the end of a format statement is reached, a new record is started. Finally, new records can be started at any point by inserting a slash (/) in the format statement. (When there is at least one slash, the comma is unnecessary.) If the format specification indicates a record longer than the maximum allowed (80 for IBM cards, approximately 130 for most printers), an error condition results which, on the IBM/360–370 at least, causes the job to be terminated.

Finally, the number of items in the format statement does not have to match the number of variables in the I/O statement. If there are fewer variables than format items, the rest of the format items are disregarded. If there are more variables than format items, the machine goes back to the rightmost left parenthesis in the format statement and starts from there again, using the repetition number if there is one, and starting a new record.

Data read in by an A-format item can be compared by using an IF statement. Since it will be compared as ordinary numbers, the comparison is dependent to some extent on the machine code for characters. In general, the comparison will turn out correctly whether integer variable or real variable names are used, and A < B < 1 < 9, etc. If, however, characters stored with a real variable name are compared to characters stored with an integer variable name, then the machine, thinking that one is a real number and the other an integer, will convert the "integer" to "real," with unpredictable results. Thus, it is good practice always to use one type, say integer, for storing character data.

In the original FORTRAN, there was a one-line function definition that showed the function name and parameters on the left side of an equals sign and the formula for the function value on the right. For example,

```
TT(A, B) = A*A + B*B + C*C + 17.0
```

defines a function named TT which has two arguments, A and B. TT may then be used in expressions, with expressions replacing A and B, e.g.,

```
X = 23.0 + TT(2.0, X + Y)
```

When the function TT is evaluated in this expression, A is replaced by 2.0, B by X + Y, and the current value of C is used.

This function definition is limited to functions that can be defined by expressions. It excludes functions that require power series and functions similar to the "step function"

$$\begin{aligned} u(t) &= 0 \text{ for } t < 0 \\ &= 1 \text{ for } t \geqq 0 \end{aligned}$$

which have discontinuities. In FORTRAN II, two additional subroutines were introduced, and all three remain in ANSI FORTRAN. One is a more general function definition. It starts with the statement FUNCTION followed by the name of the function and a parenthesized parameter list. Following this statement is the program to calculate the function value. Somewhere in the program a statement must appear that has the function name on the left of an equals sign and the value on the right, and after that the statement RETURN. The statement END must appear at the end of the function definition. For example, for the unit-step function the program might look as follows:

```
FUNCTION U(T)
U = 0
IF (T.GE.0) U = 1
RETURN
END
```

The entire function definition must either precede the main program or follow it.

The subroutine is similar except that it defines a calculation, not a function. Consider the following example:

```
SUBROUTINE SS(R, S, T)
R = S * S + T * T
RETURN
END
```

This subroutine is invoked by a statement CALL in the main program. For example,

```
X = 2.0
Y = 3.0
CALL SS(Z, X, Y)
```

would cause the value $2 * 2 + 3 * 3 = 13$ to be stored as the new value of Z.

Unlike the one-line function definition, both the FUNCTION and SUBROUTINE subprograms are compiled completely separately from the main program, and variables defined in one cannot be used in the other. For example, suppose that a variable named C, not a parameter, is used in a FUNCTION or SUBROUTINE subprogram and that there is also a variable named C in the main program. Then, normally these are two different variables, and assigning a value to C in the main program has no effect on the C in the subroutine and vice versa.

Sometimes, however, it is useful to allow the subroutines access to some of the variables that appear in the main program or other subroutines without the inconvenience of naming them as parameters written explicitly. For that reason COMMON storage was introduced into FORTRAN. Variables named in a COMMON statement in the main program or any subroutine are stored in the same area as those named in a COMMON statement in any other program. The simplest way to use the COMMON statement is to use identical COMMON statements in each program that must access these variables. For example, the statement

```
COMMON A, B, C, D(100), E(10, 10)
```

defines the variables A, B, C, D, and E as being in COMMON storage. A, B, and C are unsubscripted variables (unless they appear in a DIMENSION statement) and D and E are subscripted as shown (with no DIMENSION statement needed). The variables are stored in the order shown, with A at the beginning of COMMON storage. If identical COMMON statements are included in the main program and/or one or more subroutines, each can access A, B, C, D, and E by those names without their appearing in the parameter list of the function or subroutine.

In FORTRAN, in linking both subroutines and functions to the calling program, the locations of the variables in the main program are passed to the subroutine or function. Thus, no additional storage is needed in the subroutine, and the subroutine can change the values of these variables. Although this can be very useful, it can also cause subtle errors. Thus, if the subroutine MD in the third example were written

```
      SUBROUTINE MD(I, J, K)
1     IF (I < J) GO TO 2
      I = I - J
      GO TO 1
2     K = I
      RETURN
      END
```

the value of the first parameter in the main program, N1 in this case, would be changed when MD is executed. In that particular program it happens that no error will result, but if this subroutine were used in another situation in which the first parameter is used after MD is called, erroneous results could occur.

ALGOL Chapter 3

Introduction

Largely as an outgrowth of wide interest in unifying programming languages to improve communication among programmers and users of different organizations, in 1957 a number of meetings were held with representatives from the ACM (Association for Computing Machinery) from GAMM (German Association for Mathematics and Mechanics), and from a number of large user groups including SHARE, an organization of users of large IBM computers. As an outgrowth of this, a report describing a proposed new language known as ALGOL58 was prepared and circulated. Several organizations immediately started implementing it, but a number of weaknesses became evident. About that time John Backus presented a paper on a new method for describing programming language syntax which has come to be known as Backus-Naur Form or BNF. In subsequent months, many very distinquished scholars in the computing field participated in preparing a new report describing ALGOL60. Still, a few ambiguities and difficulties persisted, and in 1962 the report was revised. This revised report is the basis for most of the present implementations of ALGOL60. It is reprinted as Appendix B in this book. (An entirely new language called ALGOL68 evolved recently in much the same manner, but so far it is unclear whether or not it will achieve wide usage.)

ALGOL60 has a unique place among programming languages in several respects. It was the first language—and ALGOL60 and COBOL are the only ones of great importance—developed by groups not oriented primarily to a single computer, manufacturer, or user organization. The language has been widely used, especially in Europe. It is the first language whose design included consideration of its use as a documentation language, and it has been widely used for that purpose. Many new ideas in computer language syntax were introduced with ALGOL60, and its influence on modern languages is evident. The introduction of BNF in the language description was a milestone in language design and has given impetus to theoretical research on programming languages.

Yet ALGOL60 never achieved wide use in the United States, probably because it was never enthusiastically supported by IBM, which chose to back FORTRAN and PL/I, its own creations. ALGOL60 has two outstanding weaknesses as a computer language for today. First, it included no way to process character strings (neither did the early versions of FORTRAN, of course, and even present-day versions are very weak in this area). Second, instead of making input/output a part of the language, the language designers left it to be implemented by external subroutines (or procedures, as they are called in ALGOL60). Philosophically there is nothing wrong with this, but since these procedures were not standardized, there is great incompatibility in input/output between versions of ALGOL60.

The example programs in this chapter are run using the official IBM/360–370 version of ALGOL60. It is a very accurate implementation of the language described in the ALGOL60 report. In particular, it has no character string handling capability. It includes a set of procedures for input/output that are very awkward to use. Since these procedures are not part of the ALGOL60 language, we have chosen not to explain them.

There are ALGOL dialects that are alive and healthy now. Two examples are the Burroughs ALGOL and Stanford University's ALGOL W, each of which has character string handling extensions. Each has good input/output facilities, Burroughs' in the form of a good set of procedures and ALGOL W's in the form of language extensions. Each has other extensions, a couple of which are discussed later in the chapter. Each is reputed to be very adequate and, in fact, a pleasure to work with as a general-purpose modern computing language.

Unlike FORTRAN and BASIC, ALGOL60 is not card or line oriented. Card or line boundaries have no meaning in the language: one statement may occupy more than one card, and more than one statement may appear on one card. The language definition considers key words and identifiers as distinguishable, but it doesn't specify how the computer is to distinguish between them. In the ALGOL60 report, and in this book, key words are printed in boldface. The implementors of IBM/360–370 ALGOL60 chose to enclose all key words in single quotes.

In ALGOL60, all variables must appear in declaration statements that define their data type. The statement structure is significantly more complicated in ALGOL60 than in FORTRAN and BASIC. It is explained more fully later in the chapter, but briefly, one statement can be a part of a larger statement in several ways. (There is one example of this in FORTRAN in the logical IF statement.) For example, the form of the ALGOL60 **if** statement is

if L **then** S_1 **else** S_2

where L is a logical expression and S_1 and S_2 are other statements. Another example is the compound statement, which has the form

begin S_1; S_2; ...; S_n **end**

where S_1, S_2, ..., S_n are statements. The compound statement is a group of statements that acts as a single statement; for example, the S_1 or S_2 in the **if** statement may be a compound statement. There is also a block, which is similar to a compound statement but contains declarations. A program is defined as a compound statement or a block, and thus a program starts with the key word **begin**.

Examples of ALGOL Programs

The same five problems given as examples of BASIC and FORTRAN programs in the preceding chapters are presented here rewritten in ALGOL. Only very brief restatements of the problems are given here. Again, it is a good plan to read the examples first only for familiarity, and then again more thoroughly after studying the rest of the chapter.

The first problem was a trial-and-error solution of $e^X = 3X$. The variable X is the present position being checked, and D is the step size. At each step a step is taken either to the left or the right, depending on whether $3X$ is greater than or less than e^X, and the step size is halved. This is continued until the step size is negligible, and the final value of X is taken as the answer.

```
'BEGIN'
  'COMMENT'--A PROGRAM TO FIND THE ROOT OF F(X)=3X-EXP(X) THAT
LIES BETWEEN 0 AND 1. NOTE THAT F(0)<0 BUT F(1)>0. WE EXAMINE
THE MIDDLE OF THE INTERVAL AND DETERMINE WHETHER THE CROSSING IS
AT THE LEFT OR THE RIGHT. THEN WE STEP TO THE MIDDLE OF THAT
HALF, ETC. X IS THE NEXT POINT WE EXAMINE, AND D IS THE STEP SIZE;
```

```
   'REAL' X, D;

   X := D := 0.5;

   'FOR' D := D*0.5 'WHILE' D>0.000001 'DO'
      'IF' 3*X-EXP(X)>0 'THEN' X := X-D
      'ELSE' X := X+D;

   OUTREAL(1,X);
'END'
```

```
PRINTED OUTPUT:


+6.190624'-01
```

Note that this program, run with the IBM ALGOL60 compiler, has quote marks enclosing key words. The declaration **real** X,D declares X and D to be real variables. Note the use of the assignment symbol := as distinct from the equals sign = which is used when two numbers are being compared. The **for** statement is a kind of generalized FORTRAN DO statement. Here the meaning is (1) make the assignment (D = D*0.5), (2) do the test (D>0.000001), and (3) if the test is true, do the single statement following the **do** and repeat from (1), but if the test is false proceed to the next statement. The single statement following **do** is the **if** statement: If the condition (3*X>EXP(X)) is true, the statement following **then**, (X:=X-D), will be executed; if it is false, the statement following **else**, (X:=X+D), will be executed. Note that input and output are not part of the language, but are done by procedures, OUTREAL in this case. The exact form of I/O procedures depends on the implementation and will not be discussed in this book.

The second example shows how a procedure is written. The procedure calculates the square root of X by Newton's iterative method. At each step R is the old approximation and S is the new approximation. The program calculates S, compares to R, and if the difference is not negligible, it assigns the value of S to R and repeats. All this is done by the **for** statement, which always follows the sequence (1) assign value to **for** variable, (2) perform test, (3) if test is true, do statement following **do** and repeat, otherwise proceed to the next statement.

The main program simply reads in a value of A and prints A and SQR(A).

```
'BEGIN'
   'COMMENT'--THE PROCEDURE SQR(X) CALCULATES THE SQUARE ROOT
OF X BY THE COMMONLY USED ITERATIVE METHOD;
```

```
'REAL' 'PROCEDURE' SQR(X);
   'REAL' X;
   'BEGIN'
      'COMMENT'--R IS THE OLD APPROXIMATION, S THE NEW.
      WE TAKE X AS THE FIRST APPROXIMATION;

      'REAL' R, S;

      R := X;

      'COMMENT'--NEXT STATEMENT ALONE IS THE MAIN LOOP;

      'FOR' S := (X+R*R)/(2*R) 'WHILE' ABS(S-R)>0.000001 'DO'
         R := S;

      SQR := S;   'COMMENT'--RETURNED VALUE;
'END' SQR;


'COMMENT'--A SHORT MAIN PROGRAM FOR TESTING SQR FOLLOWS;
   'REAL' A;

Q: INREAL(0,A);
   OUTREAL(1,A);
   OUTREAL(1,SQR(A));
   'GOTO' Q

'END' MAIN PROGRAM


PRINTED OUTPUT:


+2.000000'+00   +1.414213'+00   +4.000000'+00   +2.000000'+00   +5.000000'+00
+7.071067'-01   +1.439999'+00   +1.199998'+00
```

The third program calculates the greatest common divisor of two numbers, N1 and N2, read from cards and prints N1, N2, and the answer. The method, as explained in Chapter 1, uses the Euclidean algorithm. The procedure MOD (I, J) calculates the remainder after dividing I by J by simply repeatedly subtracting J from I until the result becomes negative, then adding J to I to give the answer. This is done by a single **for** statement, and in fact, following the **do** there is a null statement, i.e., a statement with nothing to do. The computation in the main program is also in one **for** statement. First N2 is assigned to N1. Then the test is made, and if N3 is not zero, N3 is assigned to N2 and a new value of N3 is computed by MD. Then the **for** loop is repeated.

```
'BEGIN'
   'COMMENT'--THIS PROGRAM READS N2 AND N3 AND CALCULATES
THEIR GREATEST COMMON DIVISOR USING THE EUCLIDEAN ALGORITHM.
AT EACH STEP N1 IS DIVIDED BY N2 AND THE REMAINDER IS N3. WHEN
N3 BECOMES ZERO, N2 IS THE GCD. OTHERWISE N2 IS MOVED TO N1,
N3 TO N2, AND ANOTHER STEP IS DONE. NOTE THAT DEBUGGING INF-
ORMATION WILL BE PRINTED IF TEST IS NOT ZERO;


   'INTEGER' N1, N2, N3, TEST;


   'COMMENT'--THE PROCEDURE MD(I,J,K) CALCULATES THE REMAINDER
AFTER DIVIDING I BY J AND ASSIGNS THE REMAINDER TO K;

   'PROCEDURE' MD(I,J,K);
      'INTEGER' I,J,K;
      'BEGIN'
         K := I+J;
         'FOR' K := K-J 'WHILE' K>=J 'DO';
      'END' OF PROCEDURE MD;



 'COMMENT'--MAIN PROGRAM;
    ININTEGER(0,TEST);

 START:
    ININTEGER(0,N2);
    ININTEGER(0,N3);
    OUTINTEGER(1,N2);
    OUTINTEGER(1,N3);

    'FOR' N1 := N2 'WHILE' N3¬=0 'DO'
       'BEGIN'
          N2 := N3;
          MD(N1,N2,N3);
          'IF' TEST¬=0 'THEN' 'BEGIN'
             OUTSTRING(1,'('TEST PRINT')');
             OUTINTEGER(1,N1);
             OUTINTEGER(1,N2);
             OUTINTEGER(1,N3);
             SYSACT(1,14,1); 'COMMENT'--SPACE TO NEW LINE;
          'END'
       'END';


     OUTINTEGER(1,N2);
     'GOTO' START

  'END' OF MAIN PROCEDURE
```

```
PRINTED OUTPUT:

     +65535        +4095   TEST PRINT      +65535        +4095         +15
TEST PRINT      +4095           +15             0
        +15          +91          +169   TEST PRINT          +91          +169
        +91
TEST PRINT       +169           +91           +78
TEST PRINT        +91           +78           +13
TEST PRINT        +78           +13             0
        +13          +73        +65535   TEST PRINT          +73        +65535
        +73
TEST PRINT     +65535           +73           +54
TEST PRINT        +73           +54           +19
TEST PRINT        +54           +19           +16
TEST PRINT        +19           +16            +3
TEST PRINT        +16            +3            +1
TEST PRINT         +3            +1             0
         +1         +120          +720   TEST PRINT         +120          +720
       +120
TEST PRINT       +720          +120             0
       +120
```

The fourth example illustrates programming a problem in which there are many cases, the particular case being specified by an integer I. The problem involves calculation of water bills in which different formulas are used for different customers.

```
'BEGIN'
   'COMMENT'--THE WATER BILL PROBLEM, WITH FOUR RATE FORMULAS.
   "I" INDICATES WHICH FORMULA, "NGAL" IS THE NUMBER OF
   GALLONS USED, AND "BILL" IS THE CALCULATED BILL;

   'REAL' I, NGAL, BILL;
   'SWITCH' S := A, B, C, D;

    'COMMENT'--START OF READ-CALCULATE-PRINT LOOP;
 START:
    INREAL(0,I);
    INREAL(0,NGAL);
    'GOTO' S(/I/);

'COMMENT'--CASE 1;
A:
    BILL := 5+0.0005*NGAL;
    'GOTO' L;
```

```
'COMMENT'--CASE 2;
B:
   BILL := 20+0.0004*NGAL;
   'GOTO' L;

'COMMENT'--CASE 3;
C:
   'IF' NGAL>4'6 'THEN' BILL := 1000+0.00025*(NGAL-4'6)
      'ELSE' BILL := 1000;
   'GOTO' L;

'COMMENT'--CASE 4;
D:
   BILL := 'IF' NGAL>10'6 'THEN' 3000
      'ELSE' 'IF' NGAL>4'6 'THEN' 2000
      'ELSE' 1000;

'COMMENT'--END OF CASES;
L:
   OUTREAL(1,I);
   OUTREAL(1,NGAL);
   OUTREAL(1,BILL);
   SYSACT(1,14,1); 'COMMENT'--SPACE TO NEW LINE;
   'GOTO' START; 'COMMENT'--END OF READ-COMPUTE-PRINT LOOP;

'END' OF MAIN PROCEDURE


PRINTED OUTPUT:


+1.000000'+00   +3.000000'+03   +6.500000'+00
+2.000000'+00   +5.000000'+03   +2.200000'+01
+3.000000'+00   +5.500000'+05   +1.000000'+03
+4.000000'+00   +5.000000'+06   +2.000000'+03
```

In this program the variable S is called a switch designator, and it is a one-subscript variable with four values—S(1) = A, S(2) = B, S(3) = C, S(4) = D, where A, B, C, and D are statement labels. The statement **go to** S(I) will cause the control to go to the statement labeled A if I is 1, B if I is 2, etc.

The statement labeled D illustrates an unusual feature of ALGOL, the use of **if** clauses in expressions. Here BILL will take the value 3000 if NGAL $> 10^7$, 2000 if $10^7 \geq$ NGAL $> 4 \times 10^6$, and 1000 otherwise.

There is a statement called a **case** statement that is implemented in some versions of ALGOL and some PL/I-like languages. In both Burroughs Extended ALGOL and ALGOL W it has the following form:

case <integer expression> **of** <compound statement>

The integer expression is evaluated and then the one statement in the compound statement corresponding to the value of the expression is executed. For example, using the case statement, the main loop of the preceding example could be written as follows:

```
F:
read I and NGAL;
case  I   of begin
        BILL:= 5 + 0.0005 * NGAL;
        BILL:= 20 + 0.0004 * NGAL;
        if NGAL > 4000000 then BILL:= 1000 + 0.00025 *
                      (NGAL - 2500)
              else  NGAL:= 1000;
        BILL:= if NGAL > 10000000  then 3000
              else  if NGAL > 000000  then 2000
                    else   1000
end ;
write answer;
go to  F;
```

This program is simpler and easier to read. The **case** statement should be a part of all modern ALGOL and PL/I-like languages.

The fifth example illustrates subscripted variables. Country i is assumed to have D_{1i} dollars and to spend each year a fraction P_{ij} in country j. The question is, how will the money redistribute itself over a period of many years. The program differs so little from the corresponding FORTRAN program that no further explanation seems necessary here. Note that there are a number of minor improvements in notation. Note also that the function of the **for** statement is the same as the DO statement in FORTRAN, but the structure differs a little. Here, for each value assigned to the **for** variable, the single statement following the **do** is executed. However, following the **do** in some cases is a **begin**. This causes the statements enclosed by this **begin** and the matching **end** to be treated as a single compound statement.

```
'BEGIN'
   'COMMENT'--THE MONEY DISTRIBUTION PROBLEM.
   D1(I) IS THE AMOUNT OF MONEY IN COUNTRY IN ONE YEAR, D2(I)
   THE AMOUNT THE NEST YEAR, AND P(I,J) IS THE AMOUNT OF MONEY
   SPENT BY COUNTRY I IN COUNTRY J EACH YEAR. THESE AMOUNTS ARE
   CALCULATED FROM YEAR TO YEAR UNTIL EQUILIBRIUM IS REACHED.
   THE LOGICAL VARIABLE L IS USED IN CHECKING WHETHER ANY ONE
   COUNTRYS MONEY CHANGED MORE THAN ONE DOLLAR IN A YEAR;
   'INTEGER' N,I,J;
   'ARRAY' D1(/1:4/), D2(/1:4/), P(/1:4,1:4/);
   'BOOLEAN' L;

   'COMMENT'--INITIALIZE;
   INARRAY(0,P);
   D1(/1/) := 1000000;
   'FOR' I := 2 'STEP' 1 'UNTIL' 4 'DO'
      D1(/I/) := 0;

   'COMMENT'--YEAR-BY-YEAR LOOP;
A:
   'FOR' J := 1 'STEP' 1 'UNTIL' 4 'DO'
      'BEGIN'
         D2(/J/) := 0;
         'FOR' I := 1 'STEP' 1 'UNTIL' 4 'DO'
            D2(/J/) := D2(/J/) + D1(/I/)*P(/I,J/);
      'END';
   OUTARRAY(1,D2);

   'COMMENT'--CHECK WHETHER CHANGE THIS YEAR IS NEGLIGIBLE;
   L := 'FALSE';
   'FOR' J := 1 'STEP' 1 'UNTIL' 4 'DO'
      'BEGIN'
         L := L | ABS(D2(/J/)-D1(/J/))>1.0;
         D1(/J/) := D2(/J/);
      'END';
   'IF' L 'THEN' 'GOTO' A;
   'COMMENT'--END OF YEAR-BY-YEAR LOOP;
'END' OF MAIN PROCEDURE
```

ALGOL Language

ALGOL60 is defined by the revised ALGOL60 report, and ALGOL60 syntax is concisely and precisely defined. Since your purpose in reading this book is to learn about computer languages, you should take this opportunity to learn to use the Backus-Naur Form definitions of ALGOL60 syntax and to consider whether or not BNF has advantages of syntax definition in a reference manual, or at least for language design. The ALGOL60 report is included as Appendix B, and when BNF is used here, the report paragraph number is indicated.

ALGOL60 was defined without a particular machine in mind. It turns out that any implementation will deviate in minor ways. For example, although the language allows both upper and lower case letters, most computers have no lower case letters, and thus, their compilers cannot accept lower case. The ALGOL60 report describes a "reference language," and accompanying any compiler there must be a brief list showing the differences between the reference language and that representation. The reference language is described here.

The symbols in ALGOL60 include the following.

1. Letters: upper and lower case, and other characters having no other meaning may be included
2. Digits: 0 through 9
3. Delimiters

Delimiters consist of special characters and words. The special characters include arithmetic operators (+, −, ×, /, ÷, ↑), relational operators (<, ≤ =, ≥, >, ≠), logical operators [≡, ⊃, ∨ (or), ∧ (and), ¬ (not)], parentheses, square brackets, quote marks, period, comma, colon, semicolon, $_{10}$, ␣, and :=. The words are **true, false, go to, if, then, else, for, do, step, until, while, comment, begin, end, own, Boolean, integer, real, array, switch, procedure, string, label, value.** Blanks are disregarded completely, and there is no significance to the beginning or end of a line.

Identifiers, used as labels, function and procedure names, and variable names, consist of strings of one or more letters or digits, of which the first must be a letter. Identifiers and delimiter words are considered to be different. For example, there may be an identifier end and it is different from the delimiter **end.** In this book delimiter words are printed in boldface.

Numbers are written in the usual way, with two exceptions. In place of the "E" used in FORTRAN, ALGOL60 uses a small 10. ALGOL does not allow a decimal point unless it is followed by at least one digit. For example 1, 10, 10.56, 10.0, $5_{10}23$ ($=5\times10^{23}$), and $2.71_{10}-7$ ($=2.71\times10^{-7}$) are all acceptable.

The variable types include **integer, real, Boolean,** and **switch. Boolean** variables may have the value **true** or **false.** The **switch** variables have statement labels as values and are used in computed **go to** statements. Character strings may be used as parameters in a procedure call, but only a procedure coded in some language other than ALGOL60 could use such a parameter. The important application of this feature is sending headings to an output procedure to be printed.

Every variable used in a program must be declared. In addition, a procedure definition is considered to be a declaration of the procedure name. There are four kinds of declarations: type declaration, array declaration, switch declaration, and procedure declaration. The type declaration may declare a variable to be integer, real, or Boolean, for example,

```
integer p, q, s
Boolean A, B
real x, y
```

The array declaration shows the lower and upper limit for each subscript separated by a colon, as in the following examples:

```
array X[1:10,0:100]
integer array n1, n2, n3[-5:5], m[1:10]
Boolean array C[1:100]
```

For a real array, the word **real** may be included or omitted. Thus, X is a real array with two subscripts. The three variables n1, n2, and n3 are one-dimensional arrays whose subscripts range from −5 to 5.

Any statement may be preceded by a label. A label may be either an integer or an identifier. A colon is used as a delimiter between the label and the statement. Labels are used in **go to** statements.

The following is an example of a switch declaration:

```
switch s := a, b, f1, a17
```

Here s is a switch variable and a, b, f1, and a17 are labels of statements. The variable s is used with a subscript. Thus s[1] has the value a, s[2] has the value b, etc. Switch variables are used in **go to** statements.

The procedure declaration will be explained later.

Arithmetic expressions are much the same as in FORTRAN, with the following important exceptions:

1. Mixed expressions—using integer and real variables in the same expression—are specifically permitted.
2. Parentheses are used to enclose function arguments and square brackets enclose array subscripts. (IBM uses (/ and /) in place of brackets.)
3. Exponentiation is designated by the special symbol ↑. For example, X↑n means X^n. (But the IBM implementation uses **.)
4. There is a kind of **if** clause allowed in expressions, as illustrated in the fourth example program, the water bill calculation.
5. Distinct symbols, / and ÷ respectively, are used to designate real number division and integer division.

Boolean expressions are formed in the obvious manner. The **if** clause is allowed in this case also. Here are some examples of Boolean expressions:

```
(X<Y)∨(Z=0)

if B then (X=Y) else A∧(X=0)
```

The first has the value **true** if X<Y or if Z=0; otherwise it is **false**. If B is **true**, the second expression is **true** if X=Y, **false** if X≠Y, but if B is **false** this expression is **true** if X=0 and A is **true**; otherwise it is **false**.

Designational expressions (switch expressions) are defined to be

```
<designational expression> ::=
          <simple designational expression> |
          <if clause> <simple designational expression>
           else <designational expression>
```

and a simple designational expression is either a switch, a label, or a designational expression enclosed in parentheses (3.5.1).† Here is an example:

```
if A then (if B then a1 else a2) else a3
```

Assignment statements use the symbol := instead of the equal sign to emphasize that they are not equations, and the fact that := is different from the relational operator = simplifies syntax analysis. Here are some examples:

```
X := X + 1

Y := A*sin(t)

M := N:= 1
```

In the third, both M and N will be set equal to 1. The variables on the left of an assignment may be real, integer, or Boolean, and if there are more than one they must be of the same type. If the variable is real, the right side expression must be integer or real, and in the former case the proper conversion will be done. Similarly, if the left side is integer, the right must be integer or real, and in the latter case the result will be rounded and converted. If the left side is Boolean, the right must also be.

Conditional statements have one of three forms (4.5.1):

†This is the paragraph number in the ALGOL60 report, Appendix B.

<if clause> ::= **if** <Boolean expression> **then**

<if statement> ::= <if clause> <unconditional statement>

<conditional statement> ::= <if statement> |

<if statement> **else** <statement> |

<if clause> <for statement>

Here are some examples:

if a = b **then** X := 1

if X ≧ 0 **then** Z := 1 **else** Z := 0

if B **then for** n := 1 **step** 1 **until** 10 **do** X = X + Y(n)

In the first and last examples, the statement following the **then** will be done if the Boolean expression is true. If not, the statement following this statement will be done next. In the second example, if X ≧ 0, then Z will be set to the value 1, but if X < 0 Z will be set to the value 0. In either case, the statement following this one will be done next.

The **go to** statement consists simply of the word **go to** followed by a designational expression. In particular, a designational expression may simply be a label, and this case gives a simple **go to** to the statement with that label. The designational expression may be a switch, which results in a statement like the FORTRAN calculated GO TO. Here are some examples:

switch s := a, b, f1, a17

go to a17

go to s(n)

go to if B **then** a **else** b

In the first, if a17 is a label, control will proceed to the statement with that label. In the second, control will proceed to a if $n = 1$, b if $n = 2$, f1 if $n = 3$, a17 if $n = 4$. The third statement will cause control to proceed to a if B is true and to b otherwise. This statement is equivalent to **if** B **then go to** a **else go to** b.

Procedure statements, corresponding to FORTRAN subroutine calls, consist simply of the procedure name followed by the parameter list in parentheses and separated by commas. For example, invert(a,b) is a complete statement in which invert is the name of a procedure and a and b are parameters.

ALGOL60 has one special statement for loop control like the FORTRAN DO statement, but with a number of other features. Let us study the syntax in detail (4.6.1).

```
<for list element> ::= <arithmetic expression> |
          <arithmetic expression>
          step <arithmetic expression>
          until <arithmetic expression> |
          <arithmetic expression> while <Boolean expression>
```

Thus, there are three types of <for list element>'s. Here are some examples:

First type:

```
2

2.78

n

n + 2
```

Second type:

```
1 step 1 until 100

0.1 step 0.01 until 2.73

0 step n1 until n2

i step i/10 until 5 * i + 17
```

Third type:

```
X + 2 while Z > 0
```

Next, a <for list> is simply a list of <for elements> separated by commas. A <for clause> has the form **for** <variable> := <for list>

do and a <for statement> is simply a <for clause> followed by any statement, and possibly preceded by one or more labels. Here are examples of complete **for** statements:

```
for i := 1, 2, 17 do X := X + Y[i]

for i := 1 step 2 until 17 do X := X + Y[i]

for i := 0 step 1 until 10, 12 step 2 until 20, 23, 25, 2 * i while
      i < 1000 do px(i)
```

The first does the statement X := X + Y(i) three times with the three values 1, 2, and 17 substituted for i. The second does the same statement with i = 1, 3, 5, 7, 9, 11, 13, 15, and 17. The third executes the procedure px(i) successively with the values 0, 1, 2, 3, 4, 5, 6, 7, 8, 9, 10, 12, 14, 16, 18, 20, 23, 25, 50, 100, 200, 400, 800.

Both ALGOL W and Burroughs Extended ALGOL include a very useful, simpler **while** statement with the syntax

```
<while statement> ::= while <Boolean expression> do <statement>
```

The Boolean expression is evaluated, and if it is false, control proceeds to the statement following the **while** statement. If it is true, the <statement> is executed, and then the **while** statement is repeated from the start. Thus, for example, the repeated subtraction of J from K in the third example could be written more simply with the **while** statement as follows:

```
K := J;

while K ≧ J do K := K - J
```

Statements can be combined into groups of statements that will be treated as a single statement in two ways. The simpler is called a <compound statement> and the other is called a <block>. A compound starts with the word **begin** followed by any number of statements, followed finally by the word **end**. Statements are separated by semicolons, but no semicolon follows the word **begin** or precedes the word **end**. A block is the same, except that it also includes declarations, and all declarations must precede all statements. Declarations also are delimited by semicolons. Thus, the general form for a compound statement is

```
begin S; S; ... S; S end
```

and for a block

```
begin D; D; ... D; S; ... S; S end
```

where S represents a statement and D a declaration. The only difference in syntax between a statement and a block is that a block has at least one declaration. Here are simple examples of a compound statement and a block:

```
begin X := 0; Y := 2; for Y := Y/2 while Y > 0.0001
            do X := X + Y end
begin real X; if Y > 0 then X := Y else X = 0; Z = Y - X end
```

The important feature of a block is that any variable declared in a block has significance in the block but not outside it. The same is true of labels that occur in a block. Consider the following example:

```
a: begin real X, Y, Z;
   . . .
   . . .
     b: begin real s, t, Z;
        . . .
        . . .
          c: begin real V, Y, Z;
             . . .
             . . .
          end c;
     end b;
end a;
```

The variable V has meaning only in block c. The variables s and t have meaning in both blocks b and c. The variable X has meaning in all three blocks. The variable Y is declared in both a and c, and in c this is interpreted to mean a new variable Y unrelated to the other. Thus, the variable Y declared in a has meaning in a and b, but any reference to Y in c will be interpreted to mean a reference to the new variable Y declared in c. Similarly, there are three separate variables Z defined in a, b, and c, respectively.

Presumably, a sophisticated compiler and system would allocate storage on entry to a block for all variables declared in that block and free it upon exit. Thus, if a value is assigned to a variable declared in a block, after exit and reentry to the block that variable will not have the value—it will be undefined. In some cases it may be desirable to have the memory allocated permanently and never freed. This can be requested by preceding the declaration by the word **own**, for example, **own real** X, Y, Z.

It is possible to **go to** a labeled statement inside a compound statement from outside, but this is not permitted with blocks. It is permitted to jump out of either.

Note that either a compound statement or a block is treated as a statement—in fact, an unconditional statement—and thus may occur in **if** and **for** statements and other blocks or compound statements. Note also that in a block, all declarations precede all statements. Of course the statements may include blocks with declarations.

The use of semicolons in ALGOL differs from their use in PL/I and is sometimes confusing. Semicolons separate statements and declarations in compound statements and blocks. (They are used in procedure declarations also, but this is the only other use.) No semicolon follows **begin** or precedes **end**. In ALGOL, however, a statement consisting of no symbols (called a null statement) is allowed. Thus, in fact, it is syntactically correct to write either

begin X := 1; Y := Y + 1 **end**

or

begin; X := 1; Y := Y + 1; **end**.

Grammatically, they are different—the latter has a null statement following the word **begin** and another preceding the word **end**. Execution, of course, will produce identical results. Therefore, in this context, inserting a semicolon has no effect.

In other cases, inserting a semicolon can change the meaning entirely. For example,

if X < 0 **then** I := 1; **else** I := -1

is *wrong* syntactically—the semicolon is simply not permitted.

```
begin
    I := 0;
    for J := 1 step 1 until 100 do
      I := I + J;
end
```

In this program, we calculate 1 + 2 + 3 + . . . + 100 by executing the statement I := I + J for each value of J from 1 to 100. Now, if we insert a semicolon following the word **do**, the result is entirely wrong. The semicolon is considered to end completely the **for** statement, and thus the interpretation is made that the statement following the **do** is a null statement. The statement I : = I + J is executed only once, for J = 101.

Comments may be included in three ways:

The sequence of basic symbols	is equivalent to
; **comment** <any sequence not containing;>;	;
begin **comment** <any sequence not containing;>;	**begin**
end <any sequence not containing **end** or; or **else** >	**end**

There is also a subtle way to make errors here. Consider the following lines extracted from example 3:

```
for N1:=N2 while N3¬=0 do
   begin N2:=N3; MD(N1,N2,N3); end;
OUTINTEGER(1,N2);
go to START;
```

If the semicolon following the key word **end** is omitted, everything up to the next semicolon, i.e., OUTINTEGER(1,N2), will be treated as a comment, and hence not executed. There should be a semicolon after the **end** to separate the **for** statement and the procedure call OUTINTEGER(1,N2) because they are separate statements in a block.

A program is defined to be either a compound statement or a block, but usually it will be a block because it will have declarations. Note that the program examples given early in this chapter have the form of blocks.

Finally, let us consider procedure declarations (5.4.1).

```
<formal parameter> ::= <identifier>
<formal parameter list> ::= <formal parameter> |
          <formal parameter list> <parameter
          delimiter> <formal parameter>
<formal parameter part> ::= <empty> | (<formal
          parameter list>)
```

The formal parameter part may be empty or it may consist of a list of identifiers separated by delimiters and enclosed in parentheses. The delimiters may have one of two forms—one is simply a comma and the other will not be discussed here. The formal parameters are the parameters of the procedure.

```
<identifier list> ::= <identifier> | <identifier list>,
          <identifier>
<value part> ::= value <identifier list>; | <empty>
```

The list of parameters in the value part must be one or more of the formal parameters. Ordinarily, parameters in ALGOL procedures are "passed by name," which means that the ALGOL procedure uses the actual variables named when the procedure is used, and if a value is assigned to such a parameter, it becomes the value of that variable outside the procedure. If, however, a parameter Y is shown in the **value** list, it will be passed by value, which means that the procedure does not actually use the main program variable but instead has a new variable within itself, and the value of the main program variable is assigned to the new variable on entry to the procedure. Then the procedure cannot affect that main program variable. The following illustrates this.

```
'BEGIN'
   'INTEGER' 'PROCEDURE' P(J); 'INTEGER' J;
      'BEGIN'
         J := J-11;
         OUTINTEGER(1,J)
      'END';
   'INTEGER' 'PROCEDURE' Q(J); 'VALUE' J; 'INTEGER' J;
      'BEGIN'
         J := J-11;
         OUTINTEGER(1,J)
      'END';
```

```
'INTEGER' N;

N := 55;
OUTINTEGER(1,N);
P(N);
OUTINTEGER(1,N);
Q(N);
OUTINTEGER(1,N)

'END'
```

```
PRINTED OUTPUT:


+55           +44           +44           +33           +44
```

In the main program, 55 is assigned to N and N is printed. Thus, the first printed value is 55. Then procedure P is called with N named as a parameter. Since it is called by name, N in the main program is the same variable as J in the procedure. Thus, in the procedure, when 11 is subtracted from J, it is really N that changes. Hence, the value of J printed in the procedure and the value of N printed after returning are both 44. Next, Q is called, but since this is call by value, the J in Q is a different variable, and the value of N is assigned to it. Thus, when 11 is subtracted from this J, it should not affect N. Thus, when this J is printed, the value is 33, but when N is printed after return to the main program now, N is still 44.

<specifier> ::= **string** | <type> | **array** | <type> **array** | <label> |
    <switch> | <procedure> | <type> **procedure**

<specification part> ::= <empty> | <specifier> <identifier
        list> ; |
    <specification part> <specifier> <identifier list> ;

The specification part must specify from among the above listed choices what the nature of each formal parameter is.

Thus, the specification part must contain the same number of items as the formal parameter list. In particular, it is empty if, and only if, the formal parameter part is empty.

```
<procedure heading> ::= <procedure identifier> <formal
            parameter part>  ; <value part>
    <specification part>
<procedure body> ::= <statement> | <code>
```

The procedure body may be either a single ALGOL statement (or a compound statement or block, of course) or some other kind of code, for example, assembly language.

```
<procedure declaration> ::= procedure <procedure heading>
            <procedure body> | <type> procedure
            <procedure heading> <procedure body>
```

Here, for a procedure that will be called by a procedure statement the `<type>` is not needed, but for a procedure used as a function, the function value type must be specified as **real**, **integer**, or **Boolean**.

In a function-type procedure, the value returned must be assigned to the procedure name as in FORTRAN. Thus, the procedure must include an assignment statement with the procedure name as its left part, and this statement must be executed every time the procedure is used.

A procedure acts like a block in that the formal parameters have meaning in the procedure and no relation to any variable outside the procedure, but any variable that has meaning in the block that contains this procedure declaration has meaning in the procedure provided that no formal parameter has the same name. No **go to** into the procedure body is allowed, but a **go to** out is allowed. Note the punctuation. The formal parameter list, if there is any, is enclosed in parentheses. The **value** part, if there is any, is followed by a semicolon. The specification part, if there is any, is followed by a semicolon. This is followed by a single statement. Ordinarily, this single statement will be a block or compound statement and thus have a **begin** and **end**, but this is not always true. For example, here is a declaration for the step function, `s(t)`, which has the value 0 if $t < 0$, 1 if $t \geqslant 0$:

```
real procedure s(t); real t; s:= if t < 0 then 0 else 1
```

Recursive Procedures

A procedure that calls itself is called recursive. It is also possible to have two or more procedures that call each other. For example, procedure A may call procedure B and B may call A. Procedures like these are called co-routines and are considered recursive. ALGOL60 procedures may be recursive.

Recursive procedures are not usually the best way to solve a problem. Usually, they are slow and require more memory than conventional methods. Occasionally, however, they are a very effective tool, and every serious student of computer science should be familiar with this concept.

As a simple illustration of a recursive procedure, let us consider binomial coefficients, the numbers that appear in Pascal's triangle (Fig. 3.1). Each

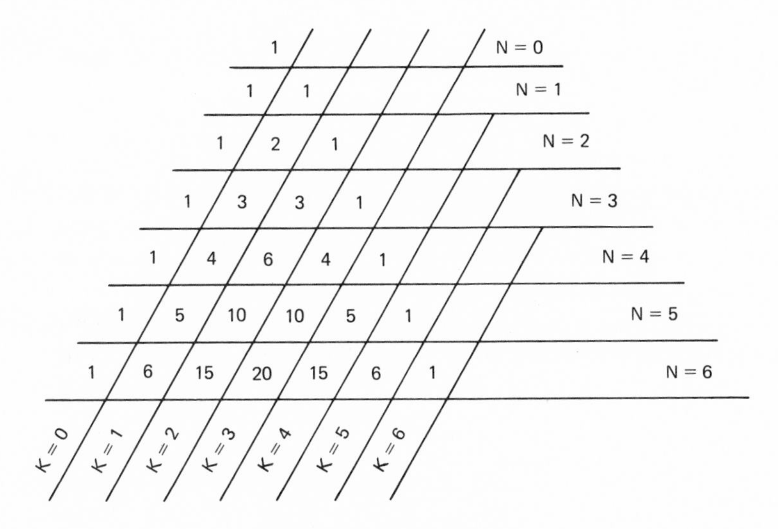

Figure 3.1 Pascal's Triangle.

number on the border of the triangle is a 1, and each number in the inside is the sum of the two numbers above it. We number the horizontal rows $N = 0$, $N = 1, N = 2, \ldots$ and the slanting columns $K = 0, K = 1, K = 2, \ldots$ from the left, and we call the number in the Nth row and Kth column $B(N, K)$. Thus, $B(3, 1) = 3$, $B(5, 2) = 10$, and $B(6, 3) = 20$. Now we may describe how Pascal's triangle is formed mathematically by the following three formulas:

For all N, $B(\mathrm{N}, 0) = 1$ (left border)

and $B(N, N) = 1$ (right border)

For $0 < K < N$, $B(N, K) = B(N-1, K-1) + B(N-1, K)$ (inside)

Here is the corresponding procedure written in ALGOL60:

```
'BEGIN'
   'COMMENT' THE FOLLOWING PROCEDURE CALCULATES BINOMIAL
   COEFFICIENTS USING THE PRINCIPLE OF PASCAL'S TRIANGLE;

   'INTEGER' 'PROCEDURE' B(N,K);
      'INTEGER' N, K;

      B := 'IF' N=K | K=0 'THEN' 1 'ELSE' B(N-1,K-1) + B(N-1,K);

   'COMMENT'--THE FOLLOWING IS THE MAIN PROCEDURE FOR TESTING;
   OUTINTEGER(1,B(5,3))
'END'
```

In order to learn how a recursive procedure works, let us rewrite the above procedure and have it print what it does. We will print a line each time we enter, showing the parameter values. We will print a line each time we return, showing parameter values and returned value. It will be well worth your while to study the printed output until you are satisfied that you understand exactly what is happening. Note that each time the procedure B calls itself it is for a simpler case—a case that is higher on the triangle. Eventually, it will reach the border of the triangle and call itself no more. Thus, eventual conclusion is assured. This is the key to writing recursive procedures.

```
'BEGIN'
   'COMMENT' THE FOLLOWING PROCEDURE CALCULATES BINOMIAL
   COEFFICIENTS USING THE PRINCIPLE OF PASCAL'S TRIANGLE;


   'INTEGER' 'PROCEDURE' B(N,K);
      'INTEGER' N, K;

      'BEGIN'
         'INTEGER' B1;

         OUTSTRING(1,'('ENTER B WITH N=')');
         OUTINTEGER(1,N);
         OUTSTRING(1,'(' AND K =')');
         OUTINTEGER(1,K);
         SYSACT(1,14,1); 'COMMENT'--SKIP TO NEXT LINE;

         B1 := 'IF' N=K | K=0 'THEN' 1 'ELSE' B(N-1,K-1) + B(N-1,K);
         B := B1;

         OUTSTRING(1,'('RETURN WITH B=')');
         OUTINTEGER(1,B1);
         OUTSTRING(1,'(' FOR N=')');
         OUTINTEGER(1,N);
         OUTSTRING(1,'(' AND K=')');
         OUTINTEGER(1,K);
```

```
        SYSACT(1,14,1); 'COMMENT'--SKIP TO NEXT LINE;

      'END' OF PROCEDURE B;

   'COMMENT'--THE FOLLOWING IS THE MAIN PROCEDURE FOR TESTING;
   OUTINTEGER(1,B(5,3))
'END'
```

PRINTED OUTPUT:

```
ENTER B WITH N=           +5   AND K =        +3
ENTER B WITH N=           +4   AND K =        +2
ENTER B WITH N=           +3   AND K =        +1
ENTER B WITH N=           +2   AND K =         0
RETURN WITH B=           +1   FOR N=        +2   AND K=          0
ENTER B WITH N=           +2   AND K =        +1
ENTER B WITH N=           +1   AND K =         0
RETURN WITH B=           +1   FOR N=        +1   AND K=          0
ENTER B WITH N=           +1   AND K =        +1
RETURN WITH B=           +1   FOR N=        +1   AND K=         +1
RETURN WITH B=           +2   FOR N=        +2   AND K=         +1
RETURN WITH B=           +3   FOR N=        +3   AND K=         +1
ENTER B WITH N=           +3   AND K =        +2
ENTER B WITH N=           +2   AND K =        +1
ENTER B WITH N=           +1   AND K =         0
RETURN WITH B=           +1   FOR N=        +1   AND K=          0
ENTER B WITH N=           +1   AND K =        +1
RETURN WITH B=           +1   FOR N=        +1   AND K=         +1
RETURN WITH B=           +2   FOR N=        +2   AND K=         +1
ENTER B WITH N=           +2   AND K =        +2
RETURN WITH B=           +1   FOR N=        +2   AND K=         +2
RETURN WITH B=           +3   FOR N=        +3   AND K=         +2
RETURN WITH B=           +6   FOR N=        +4   AND K=         +2
ENTER B WITH N=           +4   AND K =        +3
ENTER B WITH N=           +3   AND K =        +2
ENTER B WITH N=           +2   AND K =        +1
ENTER B WITH N=           +1   AND K =         0
RETURN WITH B=           +1   FOR N=        +1   AND K=          0
ENTER B WITH N=           +1   AND K =        +1
RETURN WITH B=           +1   FOR N=        +1   AND K=         +1
RETURN WITH B=           +2   FOR N=        +2   AND K=         +1
ENTER B WITH N=           +2   AND K =        +2
RETURN WITH B=           +1   FOR N=        +2   AND K=         +2
RETURN WITH B=           +3   FOR N=        +3   AND K=         +2
ENTER B WITH N=           +3   AND K =        +3
RETURN WITH B=           +1   FOR N=        +3   AND K=         +3
RETURN WITH B=           +4   FOR N=        +4   AND K=         +3
RETURN WITH B=          +10   FOR N=        +5   AND K=         +3
        +10
```

What must a procedure do to work when called recursively? It must use a last-in, first-out stack, and every time it is entered, the parameter values, the return address, and any local or temporary variables must be placed on top of a stack. Each time there is an exit from the procedure, the top of the stack is discarded, and the procedure is left in the same condition as before that entry. The compiler takes care of all this detail. If you are interested in more detail, however, see Appendix E, in which there is a procedure for recursive calculation of binomial coefficients with the stacking of variables coded explicitly in PL/I using concepts explained in Chapter 10.

PL/I is the most modern widely used language. It combines an impressive collection of facilities and capabilities into one well-integrated language. For applications that require more than one special facility, there is often no other widely available language that can compare to PL/I. It appears now that PL/I will become the most important programming language in the next decade.

In October, 1963, a committee was formed within SHARE, the organization of users of large IBM computers, to specify a programming language with the following goals:

1. To serve the needs of an unusually large group of programmers. In particular, the committee constantly attempted to encompass among its users the scientific, commercial, real-time and systems programmers and to allow both the novice and expert to find facilities at their own level.
2. To take a simple approach which would permit a natural description of programs so that few errors would be introduced during the transcription from the problem formulation into NPL.†

†NPL (New Programming Language) was an early name for PL/I.

PL/I for Scientific Problems Chapter 4

3. To provide a programming language for contemporary (and perhaps future) computers, monitors, and applications. As a frequent benchmark, the committee chose not the familiar "can we write NPL in NPL?" but "can we write, in NPL, a real-time operating system to support NPL programs?"†

The original committee consisted of three IBM employees and three people associated with IBM customers' computing centers. The original expectation apparently was that the new language would be an extension of FORTRAN. The committee, however, took a broader and more ambitious view of its task. A first version was presented early in 1964. The committee changed somewhat, and several drastic revisions were made. The first IBM manual on PL/I appeared early in 1965, and the end result was a language that bears a close resemblance to ALGOL but is much broader in scope, simpler in some respects, and more closely oriented to real computers—particularly the IBM/360-370—than ALGOL.

Currently, acceptance of PL/I among IBM customers is gradually increasing. PL/I gives the programmer facilities and conveniences available in no other language, and many users want these facilities. On the negative side, I quote some comments made by Saul Rosen late in 1964 while PL/I was being developed:

> I cannot seriously question the right of IBM (or SHARE) to allocate its efforts as it sees fit. I can nevertheless deplore the methods by which programming languages, which will almost inevitably become standards for the computing field, are developed. IBM is reported to have spent many years and hundreds of millions of dollars in the design of the 360. The design of a New Programming Language, which could turn out to be more important to the computer industry, was undertaken as a crash project, to be completed in just a few months by a committee of six men, some of whom had other responsibilities at the same time. Considering the number of people involved, and the amount of time they could devote to the project, their accomplishment was very impressive.††

Professor Rosen's remarks are still appropriate. The nature of the project made attention to details difficult, and many special cases and exceptions to rules exist. Some have been or are being cleared up, but most are so inherently a part of the language that they could be cleaned up only by defining a new language. This situation, together with the fact that they could not

†G. Radin and H. P. Rogoway, "Highlights of a New Programming Language," *Comm. of the ACM*, VIII, No. 1 (1965), 9-17. Reprinted in S. Rosen, *Programming Systems and Languages* (New York: McGraw-Hill Book Company, 1967).

††Review No. 7275 on Report II of the SHARE Advanced Language Development Committee. *Computing Reviews* VI No. 2 (1965).

participate in the development of PL/I, has caused other manufacturers of computers to be very reluctant to produce PL/I compilers. By now, however, the growing acceptance of PL/I in the IBM community is forcing the other manufacturers to produce PL/I compilers in order to remain competitive.

Professor Rosen's last comment is still appropriate. PL/I does integrate into one language, in a fairly natural way, an impressive variety of facilities, and on the whole it is a good programming language. Considering the total effort put into the language design, the committee's accomplishment was indeed impressive.

The PL/I facilities for scientific programs, corresponding roughly to FORTRAN, are described here. Additional facilities to support data processing, character-string processing, and list processing are described in Chapters 6, 8, and 10, respectively.

Examples of PL/I Programs

The same five examples presented in Chapters 1, 2, and 3 are presented here. Again, the best plan is to read them first without trying to understand every detail, then to read the more detailed discussion of PL/I, and finally to reread the examples attempting to understand them completely.

A PL/I program—main program or subroutine—is called a procedure; it starts with a label and the word PROCEDURE and ends with the word END. The first statement in any program must be the PROCEDURE statement for the main program, and any subroutines are placed anywhere within the main procedure. Compound statements, called DO groups, start with the word DO and end with the word END and are treated in every way as a single statement. Blocks begin with the word BEGIN and end with the word END. In any program there is an END for each PROCEDURE, DO, or BEGIN, and only for these. Each statement, including each PROCEDURE statement, DO, BEGIN, and END, is followed by a semicolon which is considered part of the statement.

The first example again calculates by trial and error the root of $f(x) = 3x - e^x$ that lies between zero and one. The method is precisely the same as that used in previous programs. The word SOLVE is a label, and a label on a PROCEDURE statement serves as a name for the procedure. Note that comments are delimited by the symbol pairs /* and */. The statement `X, D = 0.5;` serves to set both X and D to the value 0.5. The statement `DO WHILE (D > 0.000001);` causes the test to be made, and if it is true, the statements down to the matching END are done and the test repeated, etc. When the test is false, control procedes to the statement following the matching END statement. The IF statement is like ALGOL except for punctuation: If the condition is true, the statement following THEN is done, and otherwise the ELSE clause is done. In either case, control then procedes to the statement following the ELSE clause. PUT DATA (X) causes X to be printed in a reasonable format, much in the way PRINT does in BASIC, but with the variable name also printed.

```
SOLVE: PROCEDURE OPTIONS (MAIN);
/*************************************************************************/
/*                                                                       */
/*        A PROGRAN TO FIND THE ROOT OF F(X) = 3*X - EXP(X)  THAT        */
/*    LIES BETWEEN 0 AND 1. NOTE THAT F(0)<0, BUT F(1)>1. X IS THE       */
/*    NEXT POINT TO BE EXAMINED,  AND D IS THE SIZE  OF  THE  NEXT       */
/*    STEP.                                                              */
/*                                                                       */
/*************************************************************************/

  DECLARE (X,D) DECIMAL FLOAT(6);

  X, D = 0.5;

  DO WHILE (D>0.000001);
     D = D*0.5;
     IF 3*X-EXP(X) > 0 THEN X = X-D;
        ELSE X = X+D;
  END;  /* OF DO WHILE  */

  PUT DATA (X);

END;

PRINTED OUTPUT:

X= 6.19061E-01;
```

The second example illustrates a function procedure. The function is square root, calculated by Newton's iterative method. In the SQR procedure, the DO WHILE statement requires that the test be made before anything else is done in the loop, and, therefore, both R and S must be assigned values before the loop is entered. If R = X = 1, the loop is never executed, but S = 1 is the correct answer. Otherwise the program procedes in the usual manner. Note that the returned value is indicated in the RETURN statement.

The statement DO WHILE (2 + 2 = 4); will repeat forever, because 2 + 2 = 4 is always true. However, when there are no more data cards to be read by the GET LIST statement, execution will be terminated by a system interrupt; this is a perfectly acceptable way to write a program. To illustrate the power of sequence control statements in a good modern computer language, we have made a point of writing all the PL/I programs (except the water bill problem) without using GO TO statements. The statement ON ENDFILE(SYSIN) STOP; gives the computer information on what it should do when there are no more data on file SYSIN, which is the card reader. There is a comprehensive system in PL/I for handling exceptional conditions; it is discussed in Chapter 6.

```
M: PROCEDURE OPTIONS (MAIN);

SQR: PROCEDURE (X) RETURNS(DECIMAL FLOAT(6));

  DECLARE (X,R,S) DECIMAL FLOAT(6);

/***********************************************************************/
/*                                                                     */
/*       THIS PROCEDURE CALCULATES THE SQUARE ROOT OF X  BY  THE       */
/*   COMMONLY   USED   ITERATIVE    METHOD.   R  IS  THE  PREVIOUS     */
/*   APPROXIMATION AND S IS THE NEXT APPROXIMATION.                    */
/*                                                                     */
/***********************************************************************/

  R = X;
  S = 1;

  DO WHILE (ABS(S-R)>0.000001);
     R = S;
     S = (R*R+X)/(2*R);
  END;

  RETURN (S);

END;  /*  OF  SQR  */

/***********************************************************************/
/*                                                                     */
/*       THE FOLLOWING IS A SHORT TEST PROGRAM.                        */
/*                                                                     */
/***********************************************************************/

  DECLARE A DECIMAL FLOAT(6);
  ON ENDFILE(SYSIN) STOP;

  DO WHILE (2+2=4);   /* REALLY, UNTIL NO MORE DATA CARDS  */
     GET LIST (A);
     PUT LIST (A, SQR(A));
  END;  /* OF DO WHILE  */

END;  /* OF MAIN PROCEDURE  */
```

The third example is the calculation of the greatest common divisor using the Euclidean division algorithm. In PL/I, as in FORTRAN, undeclared variables whose names start with I, J, K, L, M, or N are assumed to be integer, and variables whose names start with other letters are assumed to represent real (floating-point) variables. In the IBM/360–370, however, the undeclared integer variables are made length 15 and thus can represent only numbers less than $2^{15} = 32768$. The declarations in this program indicate 31 digits + sign for each variable. In this program, printing is done by PUT EDIT statements, which include a format list similar to those used in FORTRAN at the end of the statement. The only other new idea in this program is the statement PUT SKIP; that causes the printer to terminate a line and start the next PUT statement on a new line. Similarly, GET SKIP causes the new data read by a GET statement to come from a new card, whereas normally each GET statement starts where the last left off. Note that the symbol ¬ is used to mean "not."

Note that a debugging statement is included in this program. The printed results are for a run in which TEST was set to 1 and hence printing was done.

```
A: PROCEDURE OPTIONS(MAIN);

/*************************************************************************/
/*                                                                       */
/*        THIS PROCEDURE READS  N2  AND  N3,   CALCULATES  THEIR         */
/*   GREATEST COMMON DIVISOR BY  THE  EUCLIDEAN  ALGORITHM,    AND       */
/*   PRINTS,  AND THEN REPEATS AS LONG AS ANY DATA CARDS  REMAIN.        */
/*   AT EACH STEP N1 IS DIVIDED BY N2,  AND THE REMAINDER PUT  IN        */
/*   N3. IF N3 IS NOT ZERO, THEN N2 IS MOVED TO N1, N3 TO N2, AND        */
/*   THE STEP REPEATED. IF N3 IS ZERO, THEN N2 IS THE ANSWER.            */
/*                                                                       */
/*************************************************************************/

  DECLARE (N1,N2,N3,TEST) FIXED BINARY(31);
  ON ENDFILE(SYSIN) STOP;
  GET LIST(TEST);



  MD: PROCEDURE(I,J,K);

/*************************************************************************/
/*                                                                       */
/*                                                                       */
/*        IF TEST¬=0 THEN DEBUGGING PRINTING WILL BE DONE.               */
/*        THIS PROCEDURE CALCULATES THE REMAINDER AFTER  DIVIDING        */
/*************************************************************************/

     DECLARE (I,J,K) FIXED BINARY(31);

     K = I;

     DO WHILE(K>=J);
        K = K-J;
     END;

  END;  /*  OF  MD  */


  DO WHILE(2+2=4);  /*  REALLY UNTIL NO MORE DATA CARDS  */

     GET LIST(N2,N3);
     PUT SKIP EDIT('THE GCD OF', N2, ' AND',N3)(A,F(6),A,F(6));
```

```
      DO WHILE(N3¬=0);
         N1 = N2;
         N2 = N3;
         CALL MD(N1,N2,N3);
         IF TEST¬=0 THEN PUT SKIP EDIT
            ('CHECK N1,N2,N3--',N1,N2,N3)(A,3 F(6));

      END;  /*  OF DO WHILE(N3¬=0)  */

      PUT EDIT(' IS',N2)(A,F(6));

   END;  /*  OF DO WHILE(2+2=4)  */

END;  /*  OF MAIN PROCEDURE  */

PRINTED OUTPUT:


THE GCD OF  4095 AND   169
CHECK N1,N2,N3--  4095   169    39
CHECK N1,N2,N3--   169    39    13
CHECK N1,N2,N3--    39    13     0 IS    13
THE GCD OF    91 AND   120
CHECK N1,N2,N3--    91   120    91
CHECK N1,N2,N3--   120    91    29
CHECK N1,N2,N3--    91    29     4
CHECK N1,N2,N3--    29     4     1
CHECK N1,N2,N3--     4     1     0 IS     1
THE GCD OF     6 AND    73
CHECK N1,N2,N3--     6    73     6
CHECK N1,N2,N3--    73     6     1
CHECK N1,N2,N3--     6     1     0 IS     1
```

The fourth example, the calculation of the water bills, illustrates several more features of PL/I. First, the LABEL variable S is declared to have one subscript with range from 1 to 4. LABEL variables have labels as values and are typically used in GO TO statements. The INITIAL key word indicates the designation of initial values, in this case the labels A, B, C, and D. In PL/I, as in FORTRAN on the IBM/360-370, unless variables are specifically assigned initial values, garbage from the previous program is left in them. Note also that NAME is declared to be a character variable of 20 characters.

```
WB: PROCEDURE OPTIONS (MAIN);
/**********************************************************************/
/*                                                                    */
/*        A PROGRAM TO CALCULATE WATER BILLS ACCORDING TO ONE  OF     */
/*   FOUR DIFFERENT FORMULAS INDICATED BY THE VARIABLE I. NAME IS     */
/*   THE CUSTOMER'S NAME, NGAL IS THE NUMBER OF GALLONS, AND BILL     */
/*   IS THE CALCULATED WATER BILL.  S IS A LABEL  VARIABLE  WHOSE     */
/*   VALUES ARE THE LABELS OF THE FOUR FORMULAS.                      */
/*                                                                    */
/**********************************************************************/
```

```
 DECLARE S(4) LABEL INITIAL (A, B, C, D),
         I FIXED BINARY(15),
         (NGAL,BILL) DECIMAL FLOAT(6),
         NAME CHARACTER(20);
 ON ENDFILE(SYSIN) STOP;


 /*  START OF READ-COMPUTE-PRINT LOOP  */
 DO WHILE(1);  /* REALLY UNTIL NO MORE CARDS  */

    GET EDIT (NAME, I, NGAL) (A(20), F(1), F(5)); GET SKIP;
    GO TO S(I);

 /*  CASE 1  */
    A: BILL = 5 + 0.0005*NGAL;
    GO TO L;

 /*  CASE 2  */
    B: BILL = 20 + 0.0004*NGAL;
    GO TO L;

 /*  CASE 3  */
    C: IF NGAL>4E6 THEN BILL = 1000 + 0.00025*(NGAL-4E6);
       ELSE BILL = 1000;
    GO TO L;

 /*  CASE 4  */
    D: IF NGAL>10E6 THEN BILL = 3000;
       ELSE IF NGAL>4E6 THEN BILL = 2000;
       ELSE BILL = 1000;

 L:  /*  END OF CASES  */
       PUT EDIT (NAME, I, NGAL, BILL)(A(20), F(1), F(5), F(5,2));
       PUT SKIP;

 END;  /* READ-COMPUTE-PRINT LOOP  */

END;  /*  OF MAIN PROCEDURE  */
```

```
PRINTED OUTPUT:


JOHN A JONES        1 1000 5.50
BILL JOHNSON        2 200020.80
FIRE DEPARTMENT     3 900000.00
```

Note again that this program could be written more clearly and concisely if the case statement were implemented. This is one example of an idea that has developed since PL/I was designed, but it fits so well into the language that it ought to be incorporated even now. The case statement is implemented in XPL†, which is a PL/I-like language, in the following way. At the beginning is a statement

```
DO CASE <expression> ;
```

and at the end is a matching `END;`. The expression is evaluated, and if its value is n, the nth statement in the enclosed group is done. That part of the program would look like this in XPL:

```
DO CASE I;
/*  CASE 1  */
BILL = 5 + 0.0005*NGAL;
/*  CASE 2  */
BILL = 20 + 0.0004*NGAL;
/*  CASE 3  */
DO;
IF NGAL>4E6 THEN BILL = 1000 + 0.00025*(NGAL-4E6);
ELSE BILL = 1000;
END;
/*  CASE 4  */
DO;
IF NGAL>10E6 THEN BILL = 3000;
ELSE IF NGAL>4E6 THEN BILL = 2000;
ELSE BILL = 1000;
END;
END;
```

The fifth example is the calculation of the distribution of money among a group of four countries. It illustrates matrix calculations. Again, the program is so similar to the FORTRAN and ALGOL programs that discussion of

†W. M. McKeeman, J. J. Horning, and D. B. Wortman, *A Compiler Generator* (Englewood Cliffs, N.J.: Prentice-Hall, Inc., 1970).

the details seems unnecessary. In PL/I, logical variables are considered to be bit strings of length 1, hence the declaration for L. The '1'B used in the INITIAL clause and in the IF statement designates a binary bit string of length 1 and value 1. "True" is represented by 1, "false" by 0.

```
MDP: PROCEDURE OPTIONS (MAIN);   /* MONEY DISTRIBUTION PROBLEM   */

/*********************************************************************/
/*                                                                   */
/*      D1(I) IS THE AMOUNT OF MONEY THAT COUNTRY I HAS IN  ONE      */
/*   YEAR,  D2(I) THE AMOUNT THE NEXT YEAR,   AND   P(I,J)   IS  THE */
/*   PERCENT COUNTRY I SPENDS IN COUNTRY J IN ANY YEAR.  WE START    */
/*   WITH COUNTRY 1 HAVING $1,000,000 AND THE OTHERS HAVING NONE,    */
/*   AND CALCULATE YEAR-BY-YEAR UNTIL EQUILIBRIUM IS REACHED. THE    */
/*   VARIABLE L IS USED IN THE TEST FOR EQUILIBRIUM.                 */
/*                                                                   */
/*********************************************************************/

  DECLARE D1(4), D2(4), P(4,4) DECIMAL FLOAT(6),
          (I,J) FIXED BINARY(15),
          L BIT(1) INITIAL('1'B),
          TRUE BIT(1) INITIAL('1'B),
          FALSE BIT(1) INITIAL('0'B);

  /* INITIALIZE  */

  GET LIST(P);
  PUT LIST (P); PUT SKIP;
  D1(1) = 1000000;
  DO I = 2 TO 4;
     D1(I) = 0;
  END;

  /*  START OF YEAR-BY-YEAR LOOP   */
  DO WHILE (L);

     DO J = 1 TO 4;
        D2(J) = 0;
        DO I = 1 TO 4;
           D2(J) = D2(J) + D1(I)*P(I,J);
        END;
     END;

     PUT LIST (D2); PUT SKIP;

  /*  TEST FOR EQUILIBRIUM  */

     L = FALSE;

     DO J = 1 TO 4;
        L = L | ABS(D2(J)-D1(J))>1.0;
        D1(J) = D2(J);
     END;
  END;  /* OF DO WHILE(L)  */
END;  /* OF MAIN PROCEDURE */
```

PL/I Language

This description of PL/I is based primarily on the IBM PL/I Language Reference Manual†, a book of over 400 pages. There seems to be no more authoritative source. Clearly, in this chapter only a small part of the complete definition of the language can be included, but enough can be included to give a representative idea of what kind of language PL/I is.

PL/I uses a set of 60 characters, including capital alphabetic characters, the digits, and 24 special characters. The $, #, and @ are treated as alphabetic characters. There is an official 48 character set, with official substitutes for certain special characters, but the appearance of the program suffers.

Identifiers consist of a string of one or more letters or digits, of which the first must be a letter. The "break" character _ is also allowed, for example, `RATE_OF_PAY` is an acceptable identifier. There are approximately two hundred key words. They are not reserved, i.e., even though `END` is a key word, the same word `END` may also be used as an identifier.

Blanks are not allowed in identifiers or constants (except character string constants), in key words, or in the middle of certain two-symbol operators such as ** or <=, but they may be otherwise used freely to improve readability. Furthermore, if there is no other operator or delimiter separating two identifiers, constants, or key words, then they must be separated by one or more blanks.

Comments are delimited by the character-pairs /* at the beginning, */ at the end. A comment is equivalent to a blank and may be placed in a program anywhere in place of a blank. A comment, of course, may extend over several cards.

In a PL/I program, the statements are delimited by semicolons. Each statement has a semicolon as its last character. There is no meaning to a card—there may be more than one statement on one card or one statement may extend to any number of cards. There is a null statement that consists simply of a semicolon. Assignment statements can be distinguished from other kinds of statements by the fact that they contain equal signs. All other kinds of statements start with a key word. Any statement may have one or more labels, and labels are delimited from what follows by a colon, e.g., `A:B:GO TO C;`.

The PL/I designers' philosophy on data types was that the users should declare various attributes, and the compiler will choose a suitable internal representation. Thus, the language seems not to have well-defined data types. Following is an outline of some of the attributes that may be declared:

Arithmetic Data

1. `BINARY`

†OS *PL/I Checkout and Optimizing Compilers: Language Reference Manual* 2nd Ed. SC33-0009-1 New York: IBM Corporation.

2. DECIMAL
3. FIXED
4. FLOAT
5. COMPLEX
6. PICTURE

Character String Data
1. CHARACTER
2. VARYING
3. PICTURE

Bit String Data
1. BIT
2. VARYING

Program Control
1. LABEL
2. EVENT
3. TASK
4. POINTER
5. OFFSET
6. AREA

Attributes are declared in DECLARE statements:

```
DECLARE X DECIMAL FLOAT;
```

The attributes may be arranged in any order. Array bounds may consist of a single integer for each subscript, in which case this is taken as the upper limit and 1 is taken as the lower limit. Or they may consist of two integers, the lower and upper limits, separated by a colon. The array bounds are separated by commas if there are more than one dimension, enclosed in parentheses, and follow the array name. After the attributes BINARY and DECIMAL there may appear one or two integers in parentheses. If the attribute FLOAT is not specified, the first integer is the length of the number, and the second is the number of digits to the right of the decimal point. If there is no second number, zero is assumed. If the variable is declared to be FLOAT, then one integer enclosed in parentheses is allowed, and it specifies the number of significant digits. The attributes CHARACTER and BIT must be followed by an integer in parentheses which specifies length. Here are some examples:

```
DECLARE  A  CHARACTER (20);
DECLARE  B  BIT(4), C(10) BIT (1);
DECLARE  (X,Y,Z) DECIMAL FLOAT (7),
         (C,D,E)   (-10:10,-10:10) BINARY (12);
```

Here A is declared to be a character variable of length 20 characters, and B and C are bit string variables of length 4 and 1 binary digits, respectively. C is a one-dimensional list with subscript range from 1 to 10. X, Y, and Z are declared to be DECIMAL FLOAT of seven digits precision, and C, D, and E are declared to be three two-dimensional arrays with each subscript ranging from −10 to 10. Each value is declared to be 12 binary digits plus sign.

The following are also possible:

```
DECLARE F;
DECLARE G, H, I  DECIMAL FIXED(5);
```

If no attributes are assigned by the programmer, PL/I assigns "default" attributes, short decimal float in the case of F. In the second statement, parentheses are absent, in contrast to the preceding examples, and the attributes DECIMAL FIXED(5) apply only to I. G and H become short decimal float.

Unlike ALGOL60, declarations can be placed in a program anywhere any kind of statement can be placed. They apply in the smallest block or procedure declaration that contains them.

In contrast to the philosophy of the designers of PL/I, it is best if the programmer is aware of the internal representation of numeric data. In the IBM/360–370, the following correspondence holds:

Declaration		Internal Representation
DECIMAL FLOAT(n)	$1 \leqq n \leqq 6$	Short hexadecimal float
	$7 \leqq n \leqq 16$	Long hexadecimal float
	$17 \leqq n \leqq 33$	Extended hexadecimal float
BINARY FLOAT (n)	$1 \leqq n \leqq 21$	Short hexadecimal float
	$22 \leqq n \leqq 53$	Long hexadecimal float
	$54 \leqq n \leqq 109$	Extended hexadecimal float
FIXED BINARY(n)	$1 \leqq n \leqq 15$	Fixed binary 15 bits + sign
	$16 \leqq n \leqq 31$	Fixed binary 31 bits + sign
FIXED DECIMAL(n, k)	$n \leqq 15$, odd	Fixed decimal (n, k)
	$n \leqq 14$, even	Fixed decimal (n + 1, k)
PICTURE		Character

The declared precisions will affect certain operations, for example, conversions from one data type to another.

Knowing what kinds of internal representations are possible, it is probably best simply to decide what internal representation you want and choose a declaration that gives it to you. It is good programming practice to declare all variables, and then to check the list of variables produced by the compiler to make certain that they were given suitable attributes, and to catch misspellings.

Any correct FORTRAN expression is a correct PL/I expression, but in PL/I much more freedom is allowed in mixing variable types in expressions. If one data type appears where meaning is defined for another, a conversion automatically takes place. For instance, character string variables can be used in arithmetic expressions, and an attempt will be made to interpret the character string as a number. In addition to the ordinary arithmetic operators used in FORTRAN, ALGOL, and BASIC, there are comparison operators and logical operators. Comparison operators can be used to compare arithmetic quantities or bit or character strings, and if you try to compare two dissimilar quantities, one will be converted, with conversion always forward in the sequence (binary, decimal, floating, bit, character). If lengths are not compatible on strings, zeros are added to the end of bit strings, blanks to character strings. The result of a comparison is a bit string of length one, with "true" represented by 1, "false" by 0.

The logical operators are & for "and," | for "or," and ¬ for "not," and they are supposed to operate on bit strings. Operations are done bit-by-bit on the entire bit strings. Thus, if `X` and `Y` are bit strings of length 8, and if `X` = 11110000 and `Y` = 11001100, then `X & Y` = 11000000, `X|Y` = 11111100, and `¬X` = 00001111. There is one more operation, concatenation, for which the symbol || is used, for both bit strings and character strings. It will be discussed further in Chapter 6.

Precedence of operations is given in the following:

1. **, prefix +, prefix — (i.e., +A, —A), ¬
2. *, /
3. infix +, infix — (i.e., A + B, A — B)
4. ||
5. <, <=, =, >=, >
6. &
7. |

Of course, these rules apply in the absence of parentheses, and any expression in parentheses is always completed before the result is used in further computation. (It is always good practice in programming to use parentheses when you have any doubt about how procedence rules apply.)

There are, of course, many examples of expressions in the program examples. Here are examples of unusual things that can be done in PL/I:

```
M = (X = Y) + (X < Z);
N = (I|J) + (I & J);
X = Y = Z;
```

M will have the value 0 if X≠Y and X≥Z, it will have the value 1 if X = Y and X≥Z or if X≠Y and X<Z; it will have the value 2 if X = Y and X < Z. Assuming I, J, and N are fixed binary of length 15, I and J will be converted to bit strings of length 15, the sign having been omitted. Then I & J and I|J will be computed as logical operations on bit strings. Finally, the results will be converted to fixed binary of length 15, added, and assigned to N. In the third example, Y is compared to Z, the result being a bit string of length 1, and the result is assigned to X, after conversion if it is needed. Thus, very complicated mixed expressions are possible in PL/I, and the necessary conversions are done automatically. The conversion rules, however, are very complicated and in some cases quite arbitrary, with the result that very subtle errors very frequently occur. This is discussed further at the end of this chapter.

Array expressions are also possible. Two arrays of the same dimensions may be connected by an infix operator, or an array may be preceded by a prefix operator. For example, if A and B are arrays, then A + B is an array in which each element is the sum of corresponding elements in A and B. A*B is an array in which each element is the product of corresponding elements in A and B. A < B is an array of bit strings of length one which has a one in a certain position if the corresponding element of A is less than the corresponding element of B. Also, one operand may be a single element and the other an array. For example, 5*A is an array in which each element is five times the corresponding element in A.

The ordinary form for an assignment statement is

```
<assignment statement> ::= <variable> = <expression>
```

where the variable may be an ordinary variable or one element of an array, with subscripts indicated. If the left and right sides are different data types, a conversion will be done automatically. Multiple assignments are possible, as shown in the first example program, with the variables separated by commas. Finally, the left side may be an array variable and the right side an array expression of the same dimensions. For example, if A, B, and C are declared as follows

```
DECLARE (A,B,C)(10,10) DECIMAL FLOAT (6);
```

then they are matrices, and

```
C = A + B;
```

means that each element of C is to be assigned the value of the sum of corresponding elements of A and B. This is ordinary matrix addition. However,

```
C = A * B;
```

means that each element of C is the product of corresponding elements of A and B, which is *not* the same as ordinary matrix multiplication.

The IF statement is much the same as in ALGOL:

```
IF <expression> THEN <statement> ELSE <statement>
```

There are semicolons only at the ends of the included statements. The expression is converted to a bit string, if necessary, and if at least one bit in the bit string is a 1, the THEN clause will be done. Otherwise, the ELSE clause will be done. In either case, unless the clause that is done results in a GO TO to somewhere else, the statement following the IF statement will be done next. There is one difference in logic between PL/I and ALGOL: In PL/I, the THEN clause may be an IF statement. Thus, the following is acceptable:

```
IF X = Y THEN IF Y < Z THEN N = 2; ELSE N = 0;
```

Now it is not obvious which IF statement the ELSE clause belongs to, but PL/I defines it to be the nearest one. Thus, the ELSE N = 0; here will be done if and only if X=Y and Y $\geq$ Z. However in the statement

```
IF X = Y THEN IF Y < Z THEN N = 2; ELSE; ELSE N = 0;
```

the first ELSE with the null statement belongs to the second IF, and the clause ELSE N = 0; belongs to the first IF. Thus, ELSE N=0; will be done if and only if X $\neq$ Y. Here is an alternative way to achieve the same result:

```
IF X = Y THEN DO; IF Y < Z THEN N = 2; END; ELSE N = 0;
```

The GO TO statement consists of the words GO TO or GOTO followed by either a statement label or a label variable. Examples of both kinds appear in the fourth program example. As in ALGOL, it is not permitted to jump into a BEGIN block. It is possible to jump out of a block, and in that case the block is deactivated in the same way as in a normal exit from a block, i.e., storage allocated upon entry to the block will be freed. If control leaves a procedure used as a function in an expression (by a GO TO statement), then evaluation of the expression is discontinued. There is one more rule: A GO TO statement cannot transfer control from outside a DO group to a statement inside a DO group if the DO group specifies iterative execution, unless the GO TO terminates a procedure or on-unit invoked from within the DO group.

PL/I has two loop-control statements. The first has the form

```
DO WHILE ( <expression> );
```

and the end of the loop is indicated by a matching END statement. The expression is converted to a bit string if necessary, and if at least one bit is a 1, the statements in the loop are executed. Then, the test is repeated, and the loop repeated if the expression yields a non-zero bit string, etc. When the expression is zero, control proceeds to the statement following the matching END statement.

The second loop-control statement is similar to the ALGOL **for** statement but differs in minor respects. First, let us define a <specification>. One form is

```
<specification> ::= <expression> TO <expression> BY
          <expression> WHILE ( <expression> )
```

Of the three parts, each consisting of a key word followed by an expression, any one, two, or even all three parts may be omitted to give other forms of <specifications>. Furthermore, the BY part may precede the TO part. The complete loop-control statement has the form

```
<specification list> ::= <specification> | <specification
          list> , <specification>
<iterative DO statement> ::= DO <variable> =
          <specification list> ;
```

i.e., it consists of the key word DO followed by a variable name, an equals sign, a list of one or more specifications separated by commas, and a semicolon. The meaning is as follows:

If there is neither a TO part nor a BY part, a <specification> specifies one value to be used in the DO loop, the value given by the <expression>.

If either a TO part or a BY part appears, then an iteration is implied. The first <expression> gives the initial value. The BY part gives the step size; if it is omitted, step size one is assumed. The TO part gives an upper limit, but if it is omitted, no upper-limit test is done. The loop will continue until terminated in some other way. The initial value, step size, and limit are calculated when a <specification> is met, and those same values of step size and limit are used until that <specification> is completed. Negative step size is allowed. If the initial value is beyond the limit, this <specification> doesn't even cause one calculation of the loop.

If there is a WHILE part, it implies a test each time through the loop with that specification, and if ever the logical expression in the WHILE part is false, that <specification> is terminated.

If there are several <specification>'s, they are used in succession. After the last <specification> control proceeds to the statement following the END; that matches the DO;.

Here are some examples:

```
DO I = 1 TO 100 WHILE (X < Y);
```

means to do the statements from this one down to the matching END; for I = 1, 2, 3, . . . either up to 100 or until X $\geq$ Y, whichever occurs first.

```
DO I = 1 BY 0.1 WHILE(Y < 0);
```

means to do the loop for I = 1, 1.1, 1.2 . . . until Y $\geq$ 0.

```
DO X = 100 WHILE(Z > 1);
```

means to do the "loop" for X = 100 provided Z > 1. Actually, then, it will be done at most once, so it isn't really a loop.

```
DO I = 1, 2, 4, 10 TO 50 BY 10, 100 WHILE (X < 0);
```

will result in execution for I = 1, 2, 4, 10, 20, 30, 40, 50, and if X < 0 for I = 100 also. In this example, 1, 2, 4, 10 TO 50 BY 10, and 100 WHILE (X < 0) are each specifications. Finally, here is one example actually run on the computer with results:

```
MAIN: PROCEDURE OPTIONS(MAIN);
  DECLARE I FIXED BINARY(15);
  I = 31;
  DO I=1, I+3, I+17, 1 TO 5*I BY I, I+10;
     PUT SKIP LIST(I);
  END;
END;  /*  OF MAIN  */

PRINTED OUTPUT:

         1
         4
        21
         1
        22
        43
        64
        85
       116
```

Note that the values of the expressions in each <specification> are evaluated at the time it is started. Thus, in evaluating I + 3, I is 1, giving 4 as the new value. In evaluating 5*I and I, the previous value 21 is used. For this iterative specification, the sixth time, the value 85 + 21 = 106 is assigned to I, and since this exceeds 5*I = 105, the PUT LIST is not done. But it is this value that I retains; hence I + 10 = 116.

There are two different types of I/O: stream I/O, which uses the statements GET for input and PUT for output, and record I/O, which uses READ for input and WRITE for output. READ and WRITE will be discussed in Chapter 6, GET and PUT here. It isn't feasible to describe more than a fraction of the available features.

The stream I/O statements have the following form: First is the key word GET or PUT. Next, a file name may be specified by the key word FILE with the file name in parentheses. (For the IBM/360–370 implementations, the file name is the DD name, and there must be a DD statement with that name somewhere among the job control language.) If the file name is omitted, the card reader, i.e., file name SYSIN, is assumed on input and the printer, i.e., file name SYSPRINT, is assumed on output. Next comes another key word, LIST, DATA, or EDIT, followed by a data list, and in the case of EDIT a format list.

For GET LIST, the data list is a list of variable names separated by commas. Subscripted variables may have the subscripts indicated or not, and if they are not, the whole array will be read in. For example, in the statements

```
DECLARE A(2,2) DECIMAL FLOAT (6);
GET LIST (A(1,2));
GET LIST (A);
```

the first GET LIST reads just one number, and the second one reads four numbers in the following order:

```
A(1,1), A(1,2), A(2,1), A(2,2)
```

On the input medium (cards, for example) the data may be in any form acceptable as a constant in a PL/I program, with items separated by a comma and/or one or more blanks.

For PUT LIST, the data items in the list may be ordinary expressions or array expressions, and they are printed in a reasonable format with no format specification.

For GET DATA and PUT DATA, the data lists may contain ordinary variable names. Array names may be used in PUT DATA data lists, but they may not be used in GET DATA statements. For PUT DATA, the data are printed in an easily readable format with each item identified by having its name printed. For example,

```
PUT DATA (I,J,K);
```

results in a printed line of the form

```
I = 10, J = 100, K = 1000;
```

Note that individual items are separated by commas and that a semicolon follows the last data for one statement. A similar form is required for input. One difference is that one or more items may be omitted. In this case their values do not change. For example, if a card punched as follows

```
X = 10, Z = 1000;
```

is read with the statement

```
GET DATA (X,Y,Z);
```

X will be assigned the value 10, Y will not be changed, and Z will be assigned the value 1000.

PUT EDIT is similar to FORTRAN I/O in that format lists are used. The principal format items are the following:

1. F(w,d) or F(w) for fixed-point numbers, where w is the total number of characters and d is the number of places to the right of the decimal point (assumed to be zero if omitted).
2. E(w,d) for floating-point numbers, where w is the total number of characters and d is the number of places to the right of the decimal point.
3. A(w) for character strings, where w is the length.
4. B(w) for bit strings, where w is the length.
5. X(w) causes w characters to be skipped on input or w blanks to be inserted on output.

Unlike FORTRAN, in PL/I, if one GET statement does not use all the data from one card, the next continues from where the previous one left off. Similarly, if one PUT statement doesn't use all of a line on the printer (or a record more generally), the next starts where the previous one left off. This is called "stream" input-output because the data is treated as a stream without regard for card or line boundaries.

The word SKIP inserted at the end of any GET or PUT statement causes a skip to the next record, i.e., card or line, *before* data transfer takes place. An expression in parentheses can be used to skip more than one record. The statements GET SKIP; and PUT SKIP; may be used. The word PAGE may be used similarly to cause the printer to skip to the next page. For example, the statement

```
GET LIST (X,Y,Z) SKIP;   or   GET SKIP LIST (X,Y,Z);
```

is equivalent to

```
GET SKIP; GET LIST (X,Y,Z);
```

Either one causes the machine to go to the next card and read X, Y, and Z starting from it whether or not any data had been used on the previous card. On the other hand,

```
GET LIST (X,Y,Z); GET SKIP;
```

causes X, Y, and Z to be read starting from the current card and then causes a skip to the next card after the one on which Z was found.

A function or subroutine is called a procedure and starts with a PROCEDURE statement that contains the following items in this order:

1. One or more labels used as entry names.
2. The keyword PROCEDURE.
3. A formal parameter list, with parameter names separated by commas and enclosed in parentheses. This is omitted if there are no formal parameters.
4. If this is the main procedure, the key word OPTIONS and the word MAIN enclosed in parentheses.
5. The key word RECURSIVE if it is desired to make this procedure recursive.
6. The keyword RETURNS, followed by a list of attributes to be declared for the form into which the returned value should be placed before it is returned. If this is not included, default values are assigned according to the procedure name, i.e., FIXED BINARY (15) if the name starts with I, J, K, L, M, or N and DECIMAL FLOAT (6) otherwise.

The procedure then consists of all statements from the procedure statement to its matching END statement. Examples are included among the program examples. A procedure declaration can be placed anywhere any statement may be placed and acts like a declaration in that it will be skipped and not executed if met in a list of statements. It can be executed only by a procedure call. A procedure is defined only within the block in which it is defined.

In a procedure, the statement RETURN causes return to the calling program. Also, if execution proceeds to the procedure's END statement, control will return to the calling program. If a value is to be returned, i.e., if the procedure is used as a function, the value to be returned is placed in the form of an expression in parentheses following the key word RETURN. A function procedure is called by simply using it as a function in an expression.

A subroutine procedure is invoked by a statement consisting of the key word CALL followed by the function name, which is followed by the parameter list in parentheses, if there are parameters.

There is a declaration (at least by default) within a procedure that declares attributes for each formal parameter and for the returned value. In PL/I, it is possible to write an "external procedure," put it in a library, and then use it in another program. In that case, it is necessary to include information with the program to tell the compiler what attributes are required for parameters. This is done by using an ENTRY declaration. If this is not done, the calling program will do no conversion on parameters and will assume the default attributes of the procedure name for the returned value. The form of the ENTRY declaration is

```
DECLARE (<procedure name>) EXTERNAL ENTRY (<attribute list>)
        RETURNS (<attributes>);
```

If the procedure has n formal parameters, then the <attribute list> contains n sets of attributes, one for each formal parameter, separated by commas. The <attributes> following the key word RETURNS are those for the returned value. Following is an example of a complete declaration:

```
DECLARE SAM EXTERNAL ENTRY (FIXED BINARY (31), DECIMAL
        FLOAT (6)) RETURNS (FIXED BINARY (31));
```

This declaration in the main procedure is suitable for an external procedure declared as follows:

```
SAM:  PROCEDURE (X,Y) RETURNS (FIXED BINARY (31));
      DECLARE X FIXED BINARY (31), Y DECIMAL FLOAT (6);
```

None of this is redundant.

The newer IBM PL/I optimizing compiler allows the ENTRY declaration only for external procedures and normally determines the attributes of parameters of internal procedures from the procedure declaration. Its predecessor, the PL/I F compiler, does not check whether parameters and returned value attributes declared in and outside a procedure match even for internal procedures, and it is good practice to make an ENTRY declaration (with the word EXTERNAL omitted) for every internal procedure as well as every external procedure for that compiler.

Ordinarily, if a variable is used as a formal parameter, the address is passed, and the procedure can change the value of the parameter in the calling procedure. If this "call by name" is not desired, "call by value" can be caused by enclosing the parameter in parentheses. Also, if an ENTRY declaration is made and if a conversion is required for any parameter, a temporary location is created for the converted parameter; if the parameter is changed in the procedure, it is the temporary location that is changed so that this in effect causes call by value.

It was mentioned that recursive procedures are possible. Here is an example, the calculation of binomial coefficients using the method of Pascal's triangle:

```
M: PROCEDURE OPTIONS(MAIN);

  B: PROCEDURE(N,K) RECURSIVE RETURNS(FIXED BINARY(31));

/*********************************************************************/
/*                                                                   */
/*        THIS IS A RECURSIVE PROCEDURE TO CALCULATE THE BINOMIAL    */
/*   COEFFICIENT B(N,K) BY THE METHOD OF PASCAL'S TRIANGLE.          */
/*                                                                   */
/*********************************************************************/

     DECLARE (N, K) FIXED BINARY(31);

     IF N=K | K=0 THEN RETURN(1);
     ELSE RETURN(B(N-1,K-1) + B(N-1,K));

  END;  /*  OF B  */

/*********************************************************************/
/*                                                                   */
/*        THE FOLLOWING IS A SHORT TEST PROGRAM.                     */
/*                                                                   */
/*********************************************************************/

  DECLARE FINAL_ANSWER FIXED BINARY(31);
  FINAL_ANSWER = B(6,3);
  PUT SKIP EDIT('FINAL ANSWER IS ',FINAL_ANSWER)(A,F(3));

END;  /*  OF MAIN PROCEDURE  */
```

```
PRINTED OUTPUT:


FINAL ANSWER IS  20
```

PL/I blocks and compound statements are almost identical in concept to those in ALGOL. In PL/I, a compound statement starts with the keyword DO and ends with the key word END. A block starts with the key word BEGIN and ends with the key word END. Any declarations inside a block, including procedure declarations, have no meaning outside that block. The examples of variables declared in nested blocks and the scopes of their declarations given for ALGOL also apply identically to PL/I. Although blocks can be entered only at their beginning, it is permissible to jump into the middle of a compound statement. It is permissible to jump out of either from any point. Procedures act like blocks with respect to declarations—any declarations inside have no meaning outside that procedure.

It is possible in PL/I to label a BEGIN, DO, or PROCEDURE statement, and then put the same label in the matching END statement:

```
A:  DO I = 1 TO 100;
    ______

    ______

B:  DO J = 2 TO 10;
    ______

    ______

    END A;
```

Any BEGIN, DO, or PROCEDURE occurring after A is also ended at the statement END A; thus, no END is needed in the above example for the DO labeled B. At first sight, this seems like a good idea. However, it hides errors. Suppose in the above example you forgot to put in an END for the DO labeled B, and suppose you did not intend that it be immediately preceding the END A. Without the A in the END statement you will get an error message at the end of your program saying that one END is missing. With the A in the end statement you get execution and wrong results and quite possibly no error message. The error may be extremely difficult to find. It is definitely best never to use this feature.

Now, let us consider expressions and assignment statements again.

```
DECLARE (I,J)FIXED BINARY(15),
        (A,B)CHARACTER(5),
        (X,Y)DECIMAL FLOAT(6);
Y = (X + I) + (A + J);
```

Here there are several variable types in one expression, and some conversions are needed. There are partial results, and each must be of some data type. The optimum set of rules for choosing data attributes is not obvious. The designers of PL/I worked out a set of rules to cover every case. These rules seem quite reasonable when you examine them, but under certain circumstances they result in answers that are very much in conflict with what you would want or expect. It would be inappropriate to give the detailed rules here, for, in my opinion, they are so complicated and arbitrary that if in writing a program you depend on details of these results of conversion, the program will be difficult to debug and difficult to understand. Thus, in my opinion, most conversions of this type should be avoided. We need to look at the problem a little closer to determine exactly what we should avoid.

In the above statement `Y = (X + I) + (A + J)`, in order to add `A` and `J`, `A` must be converted. Since PL/I does not look beyond its immediate task, the obvious thing would be to convert `A` to fixed binary and add as fixed binary, and keep the intermediate result in fixed binary. PL/I proceeds in this way, one operation at a time without looking ahead, until the expression is completely evaluated. Only then is the left side of the equals sign considered, and a final conversion is done if necessary. Furthermore, since certain conversions require intermediate results, intermediate results occur sometimes for a simple assignment statement with a variable on the right.

The most difficult problem in choosing conventions for partial results occurs with fixed-point numbers. For example,

```
DECLARE P FIXED DECIMAL (15,5),
        Q FIXED DECIMAL (15,10),
        R FIXED DECIMAL (15,8);
R = P + Q;
```

What should be the declaration for the intermediate result? Clearly, the only completely safe choice would be `FIXED DECIMAL (20,10)` because `P` has 10 digits to the left of the decimal point and `Q` has `10` to the right. (Even then, overflow could occur out of the tenth position.) However, the maximum number of digits allowed is 15. Should you assume that you need all the precision at the right and chop off at the left or should you assume that you need all the capacity and chop off at the right? IBM generally chose the former, with the result that overflow often occurs unexpectedly in expression evaluations. The above is only one example. You must consider multiplication, division, and operations on fixed binary and on one fixed binary with one fixed decimal number.

Thus, the most serious problems seem to be (a) intermediate results, especially in fixed-point arithmetic and (b) implicit conversions. What is the solution? Simply completely avoid intermediate results and implicit conversions except in circumstances in which you know that they are safe. The best way to do that is to restrict yourself to a subset of PL/I which can do what you want to do but which is safe. It is unfortunate that PL/I allows such error-prone statements. It is a consequence of the way PL/I was designed. Nonetheless, if the programmer is willing to discipline himself, he can quite effectively avoid these problems.

For most scientific computation, the best and safest plan is to declare all variables floating decimal. After all, floating-point arithmetic was invented precisely to relieve the programmer of responsibility for keeping track of the decimal point. Floating-point intermediate results are quite safe. It is best to declare all to be of the same length. Using floating-point variables even for array subscripts is certainly acceptable. It will make a program a little slower, but in most cases that loss is made up in the simplicity of having only one type of numeric data and consequently fewer bugs.

Constants in programs are fixed decimal unless they are written with an E and an exponent. A constant written with an E is treated as floating-point with precision equal to the number of digits preceding the E. Since in the IBM/360–370 floating-point numbers with precision 1 to 6 are represented as single-precision floating hexadecimal, and those with precision 7 to 16 are represented as double-precision floating hexadecimal, 3.1416E0 (for example) will be single precision and 3.141592E0 will be double precision.

When two fixed-point operands are combined by an operation, the calculation is done in fixed point. If a fixed-point and a floating-point operand are combined, the fixed-point operand is converted to floating point, to the same precision as the other operand. Here are some examples:

```
DECLARE (X,Y,Z) FLOAT DECIMAL(16);
Y = 12*X + 3.1416*Z + 11.2;
Y = X*(12 + 3.1416/6);
Y = X**(1E0/3);
```

In the first assignment statement, each time a constant is used, it is immediately combined with a FLOAT DECIMAL(16) variable or intermediate result, and thus is converted to FLOAT DECIMAL(16) with the result that the entire calculation is accurate. In the second assignment statement, the calculation in parentheses is done using fixed-point decimal arithmetic, and as innocent as it looks, the result is not correct. (It is included in the program on page (113).) In the third assignment statement, for the calculation of 1E0/3, 1E0 becomes FLOAT DECIMAL(6) and the calculation is done to that precision. Then the final result can be no more precise.

A simple way to insure accuracy is simply to avoid having two constants enter into an operation. Thus, the safest plan for scientific computation is to follow this rule:

Rule A: Pure Floating-Point Arithmetic

Declare all variables decimal float, all of the same precision. Do not allow any arithmetic operation on two constants.

In scientific computations it is very common to use some integer-valued variables. For these, floating-point variables may still be used. Fixed-binary variables will give slightly faster arithmetic and require less storage space, but using them is more error-prone than using floating-point variables. The following rule is quite safe:

Rule B: Combined Floating-Point and Integer Arithmetic

Declare all variables either `FLOAT DECIMAL` (all of the same precision) or `FIXED BINARY` (with enough digits to assure no overflow). Allow no operation on two constants. Allow no operation on a fixed binary operand and a constant unless the constant is written as an integer with no decimal point. Allow no division operation on two fixed-point operands unless it is the last operation in the calculation of an expression *and* immediately assigned to a fixed-binary variable.

Addition or multiplication of two integers produces an integer result, and if there is no overflow, there will be no problem. For division, however, the result may not be integer, and the precision is governed by a machine-dependent rule. If the result is immediately assigned to a fixed-binary variable, it will be truncated to an integer and hence easily predictable.

For the IBM/360–370 compilers, the rule for precision for fixed binary division states that for the special case of a `FIXED BINARY(31)` denominator, the result of fixed binary division is an integer. (Note that 31 is a magic number associated with the IBM/360–370. That machine does all fixed binary operations with 31-bit-plus-sign precision.) Thus for the IBM/360–370 the following rule may be used:

Rule C: Combined Floating-Point and Integer Arithmetic

Declare all variables either `FLOAT DECIMAL` (all of the same precision), or `FIXED BINARY(31)`. Do not allow any operation between two constants and use only constants with no decimal places in operations with fixed-binary variables or fixed-binary intermediate results and even then never as the denominator of a division.

Of course, either Rule B or Rule C may be used for calculations involving only integers.

There appears to be virtually no need to use fixed-binary arithmetic with digits to the right of the binary point. Fixed-decimal arithmetic with decimal places is useful in business data processing and similar problems, but it must be used with great caution; it is discussed in Chapter 6. Methods of safely converting between numbers and character strings are also discussed in Chapter 6.

The following program shows some examples of what may happen if care is not taken:

```
P: PROCEDURE OPTIONS(MAIN);

  ON ZERODIVIDE PUT EDIT('ZERODIVIDE--')(A);
  ON FIXEDOVERFLOW PUT EDIT('OVERFLOW--')(A);
  ON SIZE PUT EDIT('SIZE ERROR--')(A);

  DECLARE STMT CHARACTER(1),
          X DECIMAL FLOAT(6),
          (I,J,K) FIXED BINARY(15),
          (LL,M,N) FIXED BINARY(31);

  STMT = 'A';
  X = 1.000000*1.000000*1.000000;
  PUT EDIT('STATEMENT ',STMT,X)(A,A,F(10,5));
  PUT SKIP;

  STMT = 'B';
  X = 12 + 3.1416/6;
  PUT EDIT('STATEMENT ',STMT,X)(A,A,F(10,5));
  PUT SKIP;

  STMT = 'C';
  X = 12 + 3.1416E0/6;
  PUT EDIT('STATEMENT ',STMT,X)(A,A,F(10,5));
  PUT SKIP;

  STMT = 'D';
  X = (1+1+1+1+1+1+1+1+1+1+1+1+1+1+1)/4;
  PUT EDIT('STATEMENT ',STMT,X)(A,A,F(6,2));
  PUT SKIP;

  STMT = 'E';
  I = 1;
  X = I+0.1;
  PUT EDIT('STATEMENT ',STMT,X)(A,A,F(10,5));
  PUT SKIP;

  STMT = 'F';
  LL = 7;
  M = 3;
```

```
X = LL/M;
PUT EDIT('STATEMENT ',STMT,X)(A,A,F(10,5));
PUT SKIP;

STMT = 'G';
I = 7;
J = 3;
X = I/J;
PUT EDIT('STATEMENT ',STMT,X)(A,A,F(10,5));
PUT SKIP;

STMT = 'H';
I = 7;
J = 3;
X = (I/J)*(I/J);
PUT EDIT('STATEMENT ',STMT,X)(A,A,F(10,5));
PUT SKIP;

STMT = 'I';
LL = 7;
M = 3;
X = (LL/M)*(LL/M);
PUT EDIT('STATEMENT ',STMT,X)(A,A,F(10,5));
PUT SKIP;

STMT = 'J';
DO N = 1 TO 10/2;
   PUT EDIT(' DONE FOR N = ',N)(A,F(3));
END;
PUT EDIT('STATEMENT ',STMT,N)(A,A,F(3));
PUT SKIP;

DECLARE A BIT(1) INITIAL(1),
        B BIT(1);

IF A THEN PUT LIST('A IS TRUE.');
     ELSE PUT LIST('A IS FALSE.');
PUT SKIP;

B = 1;
IF B THEN PUT LIST('B IS TRUE.');
     ELSE PUT LIST('B IS FALSE.');
PUT SKIP;


DECLARE JJ CHARACTER(5);

JJ = 12345;
PUT EDIT('JJ IS ',JJ)(A,A);
I = 12345;
JJ = I;
PUT EDIT('--NOW JJ IS ',JJ)(A,A);
PUT SKIP;
```

```
JJ = '11.33';
X = JJ;
PUT EDIT('FIRST X =',X)(A,F(7,3));
X = JJ + JJ;
PUT EDIT('--NOW X =',X)(A,F(7,3));
PUT SKIP;


L: PROCEDURE(I); RETURN(I); END;
I = 2;
X = 2;
PUT EDIT('L(2)=',L(2))(A,F(10));
PUT SKIP;
PUT EDIT('L(X)=',L(X))(A,F(10));
PUT SKIP;
PUT EDIT('L(I)=',L(I))(A,F(10));
PUT SKIP;

END;
```

```
OVERFLOW--STATEMENT A     0.00000
OVERFLOW--STATEMENT B     2.52360
STATEMENT C  12.52360
STATEMENT D  3.00
STATEMENT E   1.06250
STATEMENT F   2.00000
STATEMENT G   2.33333
OVERFLOW--STATEMENT H     0.44442
STATEMENT I   4.00000
STATEMENT J  1
A IS FALSE.
B IS FALSE.
JJ IS     12--NOW JJ IS      1
FIRST X = 11.330--NOW X = 22.000
L(2)=       11264
L(X)=       16672
L(I)=           2
```

Statements A and B and D are problems with fixed-decimal intermediate results. Because C is done completely in floating point it is all right. In E, the problem is again intermediate results. In F, the result is the integer quotient of 7/3, i.e., 2. But G has an intermediate result that is not integer. Again, in H, the problem is intermediate results, which in this case are not integer-valued. Since I uses FIXED BINARY (31), the intermediate results of division are FIXED BINARY (31) and are all right. The problem in J, again, is the incompatibility of the intermediate result of 10/2 with the declaration for N, which results in an incorrect conversion.

The results "A IS FALSE" and "B IS FALSE" come from the conversion of "1," which is assumed to be fixed decimal, to a bit string—again an intermediate result problem. The next two are the same problem: intermediate results in conversion from numbers to strings, this time character strings.

This program was run using the PL/I F compiler, and therefore, the absence of an entry declaration results in no conversions of either parameters or returned value. Thus, the parameter in L(2) is assumed to be fixed decimal, but the returned value is assumed to be integer (the default for identifiers starting with I, J, K, L, M, or N). Thus, the fixed-decimal number 2 is printed using fixed-binary conversion rules. The problem with L(X) is analogous, but X is floating hexadecimal in the computer. L(I) prints correctly.

These problems with parameter and returned value conversion would not have occurred with the optimizing compiler with an internal procedure like this. Since they would, however, with an external procedure, it is, therefore, important to use entry declarations for all procedures in PL/I F and for all external procedures with the optimizing compiler.

None of the examples in this program is a compiler or other implementation error. Each example conforms to the language specifications given by IBM, and some of the examples are the same as or very similar to examples given in the IBM manuals. If you consider them errors, you must consider them errors in language design. The necessity for using the rules stated here is unfortunate but certainly clear. Fortunately, the problems are associated with details, and by following a few simple rules we can avoid these problems and thus effectively take advantage of the broad scope and power that is available only in PL/I among the widely-available languages.

Programming style suggestions for PL/I are summarized on page 154 of Chapter 6, which includes further discussion of PL/I problems.

Introduction

In his book, *A Programming Language*†, Ken Iverson describes his ideas on a new language that has some very interesting features. A large subset of this language, which came to be called APL, was implemented at IBM's Watson Research Center on an IBM360/50 dedicated to that project alone in 1966 under the direction of Iverson. The language found many enthusiastic backers and users, and eventually, the implementation was modified to make it compatible with operating systems and made available to all users of large IBM/360–370 systems. Versions have been implemented on a number of other computers.

APL/360 is a time-sharing system. It communicates with the user in a conversational style that affects the language in much the same way that conversational English differs from written English. It is the language itself that concerns us primarily, not the conversational style. Yet, we can hardly study APL as a computer language in any other context. Therefore, I want to discuss computer conversational style first so that we can distinguish it

†Kenneth E. Iverson, *A Programming Language*, Wiley (New York), 1962.

APL Chapter 5

from the language itself. Conversational style probably began with the JOSS time-sharing system developed at the RAND Corporation about 1963, and it has gradually evolved. The style in APL/360 is probably the best in general use. The style itself is surprisingly language-independent—it could be implemented easily with any of the languages presented in this book—and it can be described with surprising conciseness.

The user sits at a typewriter console or equivalent and types an order. The computer then types a reply. Then another order is typed and the computer returns another reply, etc.

If the user types an expression, the computer types the value of the expression. This is its ordinary use. Here are some examples. In APL/360, the user's typing is indented five spaces, but the computer starts at the left margin.

```
      2+2
4
      12+5×7
47
      3.1416÷4
0.7854
```

Next, the user may type an assignment statement. In this case, the expression is calculated and assigned to the variable and saved but not typed. Here are some examples: (Note that APL uses the symbol ← for assignment.)

```
      A←3.1416
      B←4
      X←3+5×4
      X
23
      A÷B
0.7854
      X-5×B
3
      Y←X-5×B
      Y
3
      A+B+Y
10.1416
```

The user may also define procedures that may be used as functions or subroutines. After these definitions are entered, the functions may be used in expressions or a subroutine may be invoked merely by typing its name.

Finally, there are miscellaneous commands, for example, *ERASE* to erase procedures or variables, *FNS* to list defined functions, or *OFF* to terminate a session. A typical session illustrating some of the most useful commands is included in Appendix D.

Clearly, these concepts are language-independent. They could be implemented with any language.

Scalar Expressions in APL

Identifiers in APL consist of any number of letters and digits of which the first must be a letter. APL uses many special symbols. They are most commonly made available by using a time-sharing terminal containing an IBM Selectric typewriter and using the special golf-ball-shaped type element that contains APL characters. Thus, +, -, ×, and ÷ are used for ordinary arithmetic. The * means exponentiation: $A{*}B$ means A^B. Parentheses are used in the conventional manner. If, however, parentheses are not used, operations are done from right to left. APL does not give precedence to any operation. Thus, by $A \times B + C$ we usually mean that multiplication should be done first, i.e., $A \times B + C = (A \times B) + C$. APL, however, works strictly from right to left and interprets this as $A \times (B + C)$. If parentheses are inserted, then APL does everything inside the parentheses first.

The simplicity of the syntax for APL scalar expressions shows clearly in the BNF:

```
<primary> ::= <variable> | <constant> | ( <expression> )
<expression> ::= <primary> | <monadic operator> <expression>
              | <primary> <dyadic operator> <expression>
```

Here are some examples that continue from the previous section with $A = 3.1416$, $B = 4$, $X = 23$, and $Y = 3$. Two different minus signs are used: Negative numbers are indicated by a raised minus sign, ¯3. The ordinary minus sign is an operator meaning subtract:

```
      5×7+12
95
      (5×7)+12
47
      5×(7+12)
95
      X÷X×B-Y
1
      X÷(X×(B-Y))
1
      5-3-2
4
      (5-3)-2
0
      2-6
¯4
      B-X
¯19
      ¯23+5
¯18
      -23+5
¯28
```

In the last case, the operator –, which operates on only one number, means "change the sign." Operators that operate on two variables are called dyadic functions; those that operate on a single variable are called monadic functions. Functions do not operate on more than two variables (although we will see later that the variables may be vectors, which provides a way around this restriction). Most symbols have different meanings as monadic functions and as dyadic functions. The various available scalar functions are summarized in Table 5.1.

TABLE 5.1. APL Scalar Functions

```
SCALAR DYADIC FUNCTIONS

X + Y   X PLUS Y
X - Y   X MINUS Y
X × Y   X TIMES Y
X ÷ Y   X DIVIDED BY Y
X ⋆ Y   X TO THE YTH POWER
X ⌈ Y   LARGER OF X AND Y
X ⌊ Y   SMALLER OF X AND Y
X ⍟ Y   BASE X LOGARITHM OF Y
X ! Y   BINOMIAL COEFICIENT (Y over X) = NUMBER OF COMBINATIONS OF
          Y THINGS TAKEN X AT A TIME

TRIGONOMETRIC AND HYPERBOLIC FUNCTIONS

0 ○ Y   √(1 - Y²)
1 ○ Y   SIN Y      ¯1 ○ Y   SIN⁻¹ (Y)
2 ○ Y   COS Y      ¯2 ○ Y   COS⁻¹ (Y)
3 ○ Y   TAN Y      ¯3 ○ Y   TAN⁻¹ (Y)
4 ○ Y   √(1 + Y²)
5 ○ Y   SINH Y     ¯5 ○ Y   SINH⁻¹ (Y)
6 ○ Y   COSH Y     ¯6 ○ Y   COSH⁻¹ (Y)
7 ○ Y   TANH Y     ¯7 ○ Y   TANH⁻¹ (Y)

COMPARISON OPERATORS HAVE THE VALUE 1 IF THE RELATION HOLDS,
  0 OTHERWISE: X < Y, X ≤ Y, X = Y, X ≥ Y, X > Y, X ≠ Y

LOGICAL OPERATORS ARE DEFINED BY THIS TABLE
```

X	Y	X ∨ Y	X ∧ Y	X ⍱ Y	X ⍲ Y
0	0	0	0	1	1
0	1	1	0	0	1
1	0	1	0	0	1
1	1	1	1	0	0

TABLE 5.1. APL Scalar Functions *(cont'd)*

SCALAR MONADIC FUNCTIONS

+Y	Y
-Y	0 - Y
×Y	SIGN OF Y = 0 IF Y = 0, -1 IF Y < 0, +1 IF Y > 0
÷Y	RECIPROCAL OF Y
⋆Y	e^Y WHERE e = 2.71828 = BASE OF NATURAL LOGARITHM
⌈Y	SMALLEST INTEGER NOT LESS THAN Y
⌊Y	GREATEST INTEGER NOT LARGER THAN Y
∣Y	ABSOLUTE VALUE OF Y
⍟Y	NATURAL LOGARITHM OF Y
!Y	FACTORIAL OF Y (OR MORE GENERALLY Γ [(Y + 1)]
○Y	π TIMES Y
~Y	LOGICAL FUNCTION "NOT" Y
?Y	A RANDOM INTEGER BETWEEN 1 AND Y

As a simple example of an expression using other scalar functions, consider the following:

```
          X←3
          0⌈X⌊2-X
0
          X←1.5
          0⌈X⌊2-X
0.5
          X←0.5
          0⌈X⌊2-X
0.5
          X←¯1
          0⌈X⌊2-X
0
```

Since APL works from the right, first 2 - X is calculated; then the smaller of 2 - X and X is taken. Finally, the larger of 0 and that result is taken as the value of Z. The same result might be achieved as follows in ALGOL or PL/I:

```
IF X < 2 - X THEN Z = X; ELSE Z = 2 - X;
IF Z < 0 THEN Z = 0;
```

APL is conspicuously more concise, but which one can be understood more easily? You might compare the other examples presented with the same question in mind.

Procedure Definition

Procedures may have zero, one, or two parameters. They may or may not return a function value. Thus, there are six cases (see Table 5.2). (The restriction to two parameters is not too serious, since a parameter may be a vector with many values, as we shall see later.)

TABLE 5.2. APL Procedure Definition Statements

Case	Parameters	Returned value	Name	Definition statement	Example of use
1	None	None	*F*	∇ *F*	*F*
2	*X*	None	*F*	∇ *F X*	*F X*
3	*X*,*Y*	None	*F*	∇ *X F Y*	*X F Y*
4	None	*Z*	*F*	∇ *Z* ← *F*	*W* ← *F*
5	*X*	*Z*	*F*	∇ *Z* ← *F X*	*W* ← *F X*
6	*X*,*Y*	*Z*	*F*	∇ *Z* ← *X F Y*	*W* ← *X F Y*

The example programs that follow include several of these six cases. The procedure definition includes the definition statement followed by one or more statements, followed finally by the symbol ∇ to indicate the end of the definition. The statements are numbered sequentially, with the definition statement considered to be 0 and the succeeding statements 1, 2, 3, etc. Any statement may have a label, an identifier followed by a colon. If, for example, a statement labeled *L* happens to be statement number 17, then *L* is given the value 17 and may be used in expressions. Then, the symbol → means "GO TO." A statement →*L* would result in the execution of the statement labeled *L* next, and →17 would result in executing statement 17 next. The right side of the → operator may be an expression. The statement → 0 causes return from the procedure.

Here is a program to solve for a root of $3x - e^x$.

```
        ∇ SOLVE
[1]      X←0.5
[2]      D←0.5
[3]     L:D←0.5×D
[4]      Y←(3×X)-*X
[5]      X←X+D-2×D×Y>0
[6]      →(D>1E¯6)/L
[7]      X
        ∇
[8]      ∇
         SOLVE
0.61906147
         Y
1.299346591E¯6
```

The definition statement is of the first type—no parameters and no returned value. Note that $Y > 0$ has the value 1 if $Y > 0$, 0 if $Y \leq 0$, and thus $X = X + D$ if $Y \leq 0$, while $X = X + D - 2D = X - D$ if $Y > 0$.

The statement $\rightarrow A/B$ will cause a "GO TO B" if $A = 1$, but it will continue in sequence if $A = 0$. An attempt to continue in sequence past the last statement in a program will cause return to the calling program to occur. Thus, statement six causes a branch to L if $D > 10^{-6}$; otherwise statement seven is executed. Statement seven causes X to be printed, and after that the return occurs, in this case to the system.

The procedure is made to execute simply by typing the word *SOLVE*. It types the answer for X and stops. Note that the value for Y, for example, is still stored and can be printed now.

In the second example, the square-root function is calculated using Newton's method. The function definition is of the fifth type, with one parameter and a returned value. The parameter R following the semicolon is a local variable. If other local variables are required, they are separated by semicolons. Thus, in ∇A ← B F C;D;E;G, F is the function name, A the returned value, B and C parameters, and A, B, C, D, E, and G are all local variables.

Following the function definitions are some examples of the use of the function *SQR* in expressions:

```
          ∇ S←SQR X;R
[1]         S←X
[2]         SSS:R←S
[3]         S←((R×R)+X)÷2×R
[4]         →SSS×1E¯6<|R-S
[5]         ∇
            SQR 2
1.414213562
            SQR 1.44
1.2
            SQR (3×3)+(4×4)
5
```

For the third example, previous programs in FORTRAN, ALGOL, and PL/I used three parameters in the subroutine MD. Since three parameters cannot be used in APL, the closest we can come is to define *MD* to operate on the three variables *N*1, *N*2, *N*3, storing as *N*3 the remainder after dividing *N*1 by *N*2, as was done in the BASIC program:

```
        ∇ MD
[1]     N3←N1
[2]     →(N3<N2)/0
[3]     N3←N3-N2
[4]     →2
[5]     ∇
        N1←27
        N2←5
        MD
        N3
2
        N1←27
        N2←10
        MD
        N3
7
```

The procedure *GCD* uses the sixth type of definition statement, with two parameters and a returned value. Otherwise, there are no new ideas. Note the examples of its use following its definition.

```
        ∇K←N1 GCD N2;N3
[1]     MD
[2]     →(N3=0)/E
[3]     N1←N2
[4]     N2←N3
[5]     →1
[6]     E:K←N2
[7]     ∇
        12 GCD 21
3
        91 GCD 169
13
        31 GCD 31
31
        31 GCD 32
1
```

Although the water bill problem is ill-suited to APL, we include it to illustrate the use of the computed GO TO. Note that statement four will cause go to statement 5 if $I = 1$, go to statement 7 if $I = 2$, go to statement 9 if $I = 3$, and go to statement 11 if $I = 4$.

The other new symbol introduced in this program is the window ⎕. If the window appears in an expression, the calculation is interrupted and a window is typed on the typewriter. At that point the user is expected to type input that will be used as the value of the window in the expression. If some value is assigned to the window, it is typed immediately.

In this program, it is also seen that a character string can be assigned to a variable. A variable may be real or character, depending on what was last assigned to it.

```
     ∇ WB
[1]     NAME←⎕
[2]     I←⎕
[3]     NGAL←⎕
[4]     →(2×I)+3
[5]     BILL←5+0.0005×NGAL
[6]     →E
[7]     BILL←20+0.0004×NGAL
[8]     →E
[9]     BILL←1000+(NGAL>4000000)×0.00025×NGAL-4000000
[10]    →E
[11]    BILL←1000+((NGAL>4000000)×2000)+((NGAL>10000000)×2000)
[12]  E:⎕←NAME
[13]    ⎕←I,NGAL,BILL
[14]    →1
     ∇
[15]    ∇
        WB
⎕:
        'PETERSON, W. W.'
⎕:
        4
⎕:
        5E6
PETERSON, W. W.
4  5000000  3000
⎕:
        'JOHNSON, J. J.'
⎕:
        3
⎕:
        6E6
JOHNSON, J. J.
3  6000000  1500
⎕:
        →
```

Functions in APL may be recursive. Here is a function definition for the binomial coefficients $B(N,K)$ using the Pascal triangle principle, as was done for ALGOL60 and PL/I:

```
     ∇ B1←N B K
[1]    B1←1
[2]    →((K=N)∨(K=0))/0
[3]    B1←((N-1) B(K-1))+((N-1) B K)
     ∇
[4]    ∇
       6 B 3
20
       4 B 2
6
```

Arrays in APL

Some languages have more elaborate and powerful methods than APL does for storing arrays and data structures, but no other language includes comparable facilities for processing arrays.

A variable becomes a vector in APL when a list of values is assigned to it.

```
      V1←2 5 11 17
      V1
2  5  11  17
      V2←V1
      V2
2  5  11  17
```

The scalar operators can be used with vectors, in which case they are done component by component.

```
      V3←1 2 3 4
      V1×V3
2  10  33  68
      V1-V3
1  3  8  13
      V1 ≥ 9 10 11 12
0  0  1  1
```

With a dyadic operator or two-parameter procedure, one operand may be a scalar and the other a vector:

```
      2×V1
4  10  22  34
      V1≤8
1  1  0  0
      V3*2
1  4  9  16
      2*V3
2  4  8  16
```

Individual elements of a vector can be referenced by putting the subscript in brackets. If a vector is used as a subscript, the result is a new vector, with elements taken from the old vector corresponding to the elements of the subscript vector:

```
      V1[3]
11
      V1[1]+V1[2]×V1[3]
57
      V1[4 3 2 1 3]
17  11  5  2  11
```

When a character string is assigned to a variable, it is treated as a vector with one letter per element:

```
              DDD←'NOW IS THE TIME'
              DDD[3]
        W
              DDD[1 5 8 10 6]
        NITES
```

Vectors can be concatenated, the comma serving as the concatenation symbol:

```
         V1
    2 5  11  17
         V1,V1,31
    2 5  11  17  2  5  11  17  31
         (V1,3)+3,V1
    5 7  16  28  20
         DDD,' FOR ALL'
    NOW IS THE TIME FOR ALL
```

The symbol iota (ι) used as a monadic operator gives a vector of successive integers:

```
         ι7
   1  2  3  4  5  6  7
         V1+ι4
   3  7  14  21
```

The symbol iota is also used as a dyadic operator on vectors. $A\iota B$ means search vector A for each value in B and give the index in A for the first occurrence of each. If the value is not found, the index returned is one greater than the last index of A.

```
         V1ι11
   3
         V1ι23
   5
         V1ι2 5 11 55 5 2
   1  2  3  5  2  1
         V1ιV3
   5  1  5  5
```

There are special operators for sorting vectors. The value is the list of indices of the largest element, next largest element, etc., in the original vector.

```
          V1←7 5 6 2 4 9
          V2←⍒V1
          V2
6   3   1   2   5   4
          V1[V2]
9   8   7   5   4   2
          V3←⍋V1
          V3
4   5   2   1   3   6
          V1[V3]
2   4   5   7   8   9
```

Up to this point we have discussed vectors, i.e., one-dimensional arrays. In APL, it is possible to have any number of subscripts, and operations on multi-dimensional arrays will be discussed next. Of course, they apply to vectors as a special case and also provide further facilities for processing vectors.

First, the array form must be declared—the equivalent of the dimension statement in FORTRAN or BASIC. In APL, the initial values must also be declared. The operator ρ is used for this purpose as a dyadic operator. On the left is a vector that gives the upper limit of the subscripts. On the right is a scalar or vector, and it is used, repeatedly if necessary, to furnish values. Here are some examples:

```
      3 4 ρ 0
0 0 0 0
0 0 0 0
0 0 0 0
      M←2 5 ρ 1 2 3
      M
 1   2   3   1   2
 3   1   2   3   1
      10ρ1 0 ¯1
1   0  ¯1   1   0  ¯1   1   0  ¯1   1
      3 4 ρ ⍳4
 1   2   3   4
 1   2   3   4
 1   2   3   4
```

As in the case of vectors, arrays of the same shape can be combined with an operator, and the operation is done on corresponding elements. Also, as in the case of vectors, scalar operators may be used and they operate element by element:

```
      MA←2 5ρ3 4 2 1 5 1 2 3 4 5
      MA
3   4   2   1   5
1   2   3   4   5
      M+MA
4   6   5   2   7
4   3   5   7   6
      M×MA
  3    8    6    1   10
  3    2    6   12    5
      MA+7
 10   11    9    8   12
  8    9   10   11   12
```

Also, individual elements can be referenced by placing the subscripts in brackets separated by semicolons. Note the use of vectors as subscripts.

```
      MA[2;3]
3
      MA[1 2;2 3 4]
 4  2  1
 2  3  4
      MA[2 1;4 3]
 4  3
 1  2
```

The operator ρ as a monadic operator gives the dimensions of an array:

```
      ρV1
6
      ρM
2  5
```

An extremely important concept is *reduction*. It is written with an operator followed by / followed by an array; for a vector, it means to apply that operator to all the elements, as if that operator were placed between each pair of elements. Thus, +/*V* means the sum of all elements in *V*, and ⌈/*V* means the largest element in *V*. Other operators may not have such simple interpretations.

```
      V1
7  5  8  2  4  9
      +/V1
35
      ⌈/V1
9
      ⌊/V1
2
      -/V1
3
```

On a multi-dimensional array, the operation is done on the last subscript, unless the subscript is specified by a number in brackets following the reduction sign:

```
      M×MA
   3   8   6   1  10
   3   2   6  12   5
      +/M×MA
28  28
      +/[1]M×MA
6  10  12  13  15
      ⌈/M×MA
10  12
      ⌊/M×MA
1  2
```

Conventional matrix product is written A+.×B, a notation that allows substitution of other dyadic operators for + and × to give other, occasionally useful, computations. For example, if C = A∧.>B, then C[I,J] = 1 if and only if every element in the Ith row of A is greater than the corresponding element in the Jth column of B. If A and B are vectors and OP1 and OP2 are two operators, then A OP1 . OP2 B is the same as OP1/A OP2 B.

```
          AAA←3 3ρ1 3 5 2 3 1 3 5 4
          BBB←3 3ρ1 2 1 3 1 1 4 1 3
          AAA
      1  3  5
      2  3  1
      3  5  4
          BBB
      1  2  1
      3  1  1
      4  1  3
          AAA+.×BBB
      30  10  19
      15   8   8
      34  15  20
          AAA∧.≥BBB
    1 0 1
    0 1 0
    1 1 1
```

"Outer product," written A ∘.OP B, requires operation OP to be applied to each element of A with each element of B, to produce an array with a higher dimension:

```
             1 3 5 ∘.× 2 4 6
         2   4   6
         6  12  18
        10  20  30
             HH←1 0 1 0∘.∨0 0 1 1
             HH
      1 1 1 1
      0 0 1 1
      1 1 1 1
      0 0 1 1
```

Compression has the form A/B where A and B are vectors of the same length, and A is composed of zeros and ones. The elements of B corresponding to zeros are simply eliminated. Compression can be applied to higher-dimension arrays, in which case it is applied to the last subscript or to a subscript indicated in brackets following the compression sign.

```
          V1
 7  5  8  2  4  9
          1 1 1 0 0 1/V1
 7  5  8  9
          AAA
  1  3  5
  2  3  1
  3  5  4
          1 0 1/AAA
  1  5
  2  1
  3  4
          CCC←1 0 1/[1]AAA
          CCC
  1  3  5
  3  5  4
          1 0 1/[2]AAA
  1  5
  2  1
  3  4
```

Expansion has the form $A \backslash B$ where B is a vector and A is a vector of zeros and ones, with the number of ones matching the number of elements of B. It produces a vector whose length equals the length of A, and which has the elements of B in the positions where A had ones, zeros where A had zeros. Again expansion can be applied to arrays of any number of dimensions.

```
          V2←1 1 0 0 1 1 0 0 1 1\V1
          V2
 7  5  0  0  8  2  0  0  4  9
          1 0 1 0 1\AAA
  1  0  3  0  5
  2  0  3  0  1
  3  0  5  0  4
          1 0 1 0 1\[1]AAA
  1  3  5
  0  0  0
  2  3  1
  0  0  0
  3  5  4
```

A complete list of the array functions is given in Table 5.3.

To conclude this chapter, here is the fifth program example, the money distribution, done in APL.

```
      P←4 4⍴.8 .1 .05 .05 .1 .8 .1 0 0 .1 .8 .1 .1 .1 0 .8
      P
0.8              0.1              0.05             0.05
0.1              0.8              0.1              0
0                0.1              0.8              0.1
0.1              0.1              0                0.8
```

```
      ∇ MDP
[1]     N←0
[2]     D2← 1000000 0 0 0
[3]     D1←D2
[4]     N←N+1
[5]     D2←D1+.×P
[6]     ⎕←D2,N
[7]     →3×∨/1<|D2-D1
      ∇
[8]     ∇
        MDP
800000   100000   50000   50000   1
655000   170000   90000   85000   2
549500   219000   121750   109750   3
472475   253300   146775   127450   4
   055   277310   166373.75   140261.25   5
      05   294117   181632.75   149649.125   6
25679      05881.9   193447.9562   156612.6312   7
256692.539      33   202549.4306   161837.7762   8
256614.7374   333      09526.0507   165799.9372   9
256557.8011   333318.         8.6477   168832.1489   10
256516.2608   333322.6003            171170.6695   11
256486.0535   333325.8202   23076          985.4275   12
256464.1669   333328.0742   230765.449          43   13
256448.3719   333329.6519   230768.375   17945
256437.0229   333330.7563   230770.0838   179462.13
256428.9076   333331.5294   230770.9938   179468.5692   34
256423.136   333332.0706   230771.3933   179473.4001   35
256419.0558   333332.4494   230771.4785   179477.0162   36
256416.1912   333332.7146   230771.3806   179479.7136   37
256414.1958   333332.9002   230771.1855   179481.7185   38
256412.8185   333333.0302   230770.9482   179483.2031   39
256411.8781   333333.1211   230770.7025   179484.2983   40
256411.2445   333333.1848   230770.468   179485.1028   41
```

The matrix P is defined here outside the procedure *MDP*. In the procedure, the fifth statement does the actual computation as a special case of matrix multiplication—the vector $D1$ is multiplied by the matrix P and the result is assigned to $D2$ and to the window, i.e., to be printed. The 7 th statement

1. Subtracts $D1$ from $D2$ (as vectors—four answers).
2. Takes absolute value of each element.
3. Compares each to 1.0, giving four answers (1 = true, 0 = false).
4. Does the "or reduction," the answer being a single zero if all answers to step 3 were 0, otherwise 1.
5. Multiplies by 2.
6. Goes to that statement, either 0 or 2.

Part of the results are shown.

This problem clearly shows APL's power for handling arrays.

TABLE 5.3. Array Operations

#/Y[†]	THE # REDUCTION OF Y ALONG THE LAST DIMENSION
#/[Z]Y	THE # REDUCTION OF Y ALONG THE Z^{TH} DIMENSION
X/Y	COMPRESSION ACCORDING TO X OF Y ALONG THE LAST DIMENSION
X/[Z]Y	COMPRESSION ACCORDING TO X OF Y ALONG THE Z^{TH} DIMENSION
X\Y	EXPANSION ACCORDING TO X OF Y ALONG THE LAST DIMENSION
X\[Z]Y	EXPANSION ACCORDING TO X OF Y ALONG THE Z^{TH} DIMENSION
X+.×Y	ORDINARY MATRIX PRODUCT OF X AND Y
X#.#Y	GENERALIZED INNER PRODUCT OF X AND Y
X∘.#Y	GENERALIZED OUTER PRODUCT OF X AND Y
XρY	RESHAPE Y TO HAVE DIMENSIONS X
ρY	DIMENSION OF Y
X[Y]	THE ELEMENTS OF X AT LOCATIONS Y
XιY	THE LOCATIONS OF Y WITHIN X
ιY	THE FIRST CONSECUTIVE Y INTEGERS
X∊Y	EACH ELEMENT OF X IS A MEMBER OF Y
X⊤Y	REPRESENTATION OF Y IN NUMBER SYSTEM X
X⊥Y	VALUE OF THE REPRESENTATION Y IN NUMBER SYSTEM X
X?Y	X INTEGERS SELECTED RANDOMLY WITHOUT REPLACEMENT FROM ιY

†# denotes any standard operation.

TABLE 5.3. Array Operations (*cont'd*)

XΦY	ROTATION BY X OF Y ALONG LAST DIMENSION
XΦ[Z]Y	ROTATION BY X OF Y ALONG Z^{TH} DIMENSION
ΦY	REVERSAL OF Y ALONG LAST DIMENSION
Φ[Z]Y	REVERSAL OF Y ALONG Z^{TH} DIMENSION
X⍉Y	TRANSPOSE BY X OF Y
⍉Y	ORDINARY TRANSPOSE OF Y (I.E., LAST TWO COORDINATES)
X,Y	Y CONCATENATED TO X
,Y	MAKE Y INTO A VECTOR
X↑Y	TAKE THE FIRST (OR LAST) X ELEMENTS OF Y
X↓Y	LEAVE THE FIRST (OR LAST) X ELEMENTS OF Y

PART

DATA PROCESSING II

Business and government data processing account for the bulk of the computer business. Not only are the majority of computers and computer programmers employed in this area, but it is growing rapidly and thus accounts for the greatest opportunities in the computer field. Beyond that, every computer programmer, no matter what his field of specialization, can expect at least occasionally to be faced with large quantities of data, and hence with the need to know about data-processing techniques.

PL/I for Data Processing Chapter 6

PL/I is a comprehensive language that has many facilities. Chapter 4 described its general characteristics and the features most commonly used in scientific calculations. This chapter describes additional features of PL/I that are particularly useful in processing large or complex files of data. More features are described in Chapters 8 and 10. The features described here are (1) ON-conditions, for handling exceptional situations, (2) picture specifications, which in particular, handle printing of decimal points, commas, and dollar signs effectively, (3) data structures, for describing the arrangement of data in data records, (4) record input-output, and (5) fixed-decimal arithmetic.

ON-conditions

ON-conditions are signals that may be turned on when certain exceptional conditions occur. Some of the more important are

```
CONVERSION

ENDFILE
```

```
FIXEDOVERFLOW
OVERFLOW
UNDERFLOW
ZERODIVIDE
ENDPAGE
SIZE
SUBSCRIPTRANGE
```

CONVERSION occurs when an impossible data conversion of a character string is required, as for example, by

```
DECLARE X FIXED BINARY(15);
X = 'ABC';
```

because X must be given a numeric value and ABC simply has no numeric value.

ENDFILE occurs when an attempt is made to read a data card or record and there are no more. The file name enclosed in parentheses must follow the word ENDFILE.

FIXEDOVERFLOW and OVERFLOW occur when a result of an arithmetic operation exceeds the capacity of the type of variable used to store it. For FIXED BINARY(15), this is $2^{15} - 1 = 32767$. For FIXED BINARY(31), it is $2^{31} - 1$, which is a little more than two billion. For FIXED DECIMAL(n,k), there are $n - k$ places to the left of the decimal point and this determines the limit. For floating point, the limit is about 10^{75} in the IBM/360-370. For example, in the program

```
DECLARE X DECIMAL FLOAT(6) INITIAL(1.0), I FIXED BINARY(15);
DO I = 1 TO 100;
X = X*10;
END;
```

X will eventually exceed 10^{75} (at $I = 76$), and at that point the OVERFLOW condition will be raised. Normally, execution will be interrupted and an error message printed.

UNDERFLOW means the occurrence as a result of an arithmetic operation of a floating-point number that is smaller than the machine capacity (10^{-79} for the IBM/360-370) but not zero. Thus, the following program would cause an underflow at I = 80:

```
DECLARE X DECIMAL FLOAT(6),
        I FIXED BINARY(15);
X = 1;
DO I = 1 TO 100;
   X = X*0.1;
END;
```

ZERODIVIDE occurs when an attempt is made to divide by zero.

ENDPAGE occurs when an attempt is made to print a line after a page is full. The file name enclosed in parentheses must follow the word ENDPAGE.

SIZE occurs when a value exceeding the capacity of a variable is assigned to a variable or when a value is printed using PUT EDIT and a format specification that does not allow the full number to be printed. For example, the following will raise the SIZE condition:

```
DECLARE I FIXED BINARY(15);
I = 50000;
PUT EDIT(250000)(F(4));
```

Here I, being FIXED BINARY(15), cannot store a number exceeding $2^{15} - 1 = 32767$, and the six-digit number 250000 cannot be printed in four characters on the printer. Normally, the SIZE condition is disabled, and the high-order digits are simply lost. The binary representation of 50000 is 1100001101010000. The statement I = 50000; will assign the last 15 of these to I, i.e., 100001101010000, which has the value 17232 = 50000 − 32768. The statement PUT EDIT(250000)(F(4)); will print the last four digits of 250000, i.e., 0000. SIZE is normally disabled.

SUBSCRIPTRANGE means going outside the subscript range on a subscripted variable. For example,

```
DECLARE X(10) DECIMAL FLOAT(6);
X(100) = 1;
X(-1) = 0;
```

will raise the SUBSCRIPTRANGE condition. Normally, it is disabled, and statements above can cause unpredictable errors. It is disabled to save time.

An ON-condition can be enabled to do something other than the standard system action by a statement of the following format:

```
ON <ON-condition> <ON-unit>
```

when <ON-unit> may be a single simple statement or a BEGIN block. RETURN is not allowed as the single statement, and RETURN is not allowed in the BEGIN block if it returns to some place outside the block. Here are examples:

```
ON ENDFILE(SYSIN) GO TO EE;
ON ENDFILE(JANE) GO TO ANN;
ON CONVERSION BEGIN;
    PUT EDIT('ERROR IN CARD NO.',N)(A,F(3));
    GO TO R;
END;
ON SIZE PUT EDIT ('SIZE ERROR')(A);
ON UNDERFLOW;
```

The first of these statements will cause GO TO EE when the ENDFILE condition occurs on the card reader. The second refers to the input file named JANE. The statement ON SIZE PUT EDIT ('SIZE ERROR'); causes the words 'SIZE ERROR' to be printed, and then execution will proceed from where it was interrupted. Similarly, ON UNDERFLOW; will do nothing, but control will proceed from where it was interrupted, i.e., it is as if the underflow interrupt were simply disabled.

For OVERFLOW, UNDERFLOW, FIXEDOVERFLOW, SIZE, and ZERODIVIDE, on return from an ON-unit, the operation that caused the problem is not retried. For example, in the statement ON SIZE PUT EDIT ('SIZE ERROR') (A) when a SIZE error occurs, the words SIZE ERROR will be printed and then execution will be continued immediately after the point at which the error occurred. For CONVERSION, however, the conversion is retried after return. For example, the statement ON CONVERSION PUT EDIT ('CONVERSION ERROR')(A) when a CONVERSION error occurs will cause the words 'CONVERSION ERROR' to be printed. Then execution will be resumed by retrying the conversion. In this case, since the source of the error has not been corrected, the conversion will fail again, and this time execution will be terminated. Thus, the ON-unit for an ON CONVERSION must either contain a GO TO or STOP statement or correct the character string being converted.

An ON-statement must be executed before it has any effect. There may be any number of ON-statements referring to the same condition, and the last one executed is in effect. The effect of an ON-statement executed in a procedure or block is cancelled when that procedure or block is exited.

Unless an ON-unit that specifies otherwise has been executed, the standard system action will be taken when a condition is enabled. In most cases, this means printing an error message and stopping execution. The only exceptions among the on-conditions discussed here are ENDPAGE, which simply skips to a new page, and UNDERFLOW, which prints an error message and continues execution.

An ON-condition may be enabled or disabled by a "condition prefix." One or more ON-conditions, possibly preceded by the letters NO with no intervening space, are listed in parentheses and followed by a colon. This precedes a statement, as for example,

```
(CONVERSION, NOUNDERFLOW): A: Z = X + Y;
```

means that in executing the following statement, CONVERSION is to be enabled and UNDERFLOW disabled. These prefixes apply only to a single statement, except when they precede a PROCEDURE statement or a BEGIN block, in which case they apply to the entire procedure or block. When a condition prefix precedes an IF statement, it applies only to the evaluation of the predicate but not to the THEN or ELSE clause. When it precedes a DO, it applies only to the first semicolon, not to the statements in a compound statement. Of the conditions listed, ENDPAGE and ENDFILE cannot be disabled.

Although it is out of place in this chapter, the following is an example of the use of a condition prefix. Pseudorandom numbers are used in many computer applications, especially in the scientific area. Here is a procedure for generating pseudorandom numbers by the commonly used power-residue method. The method finds each random number from the preceding one by multiplying by A, using fixed binary, and keeping only the low-order digits of the result. Here A is taken to be $1162261467 = 3^{19}$. In the statement I = I*1162261467, the multiplication produces more than 31 binary digits and only the low-order 31 are kept, because I has only 31 digits. This is what we want. Normally, the computer signals FIXED OVERFLOW, but we want to simply proceed. Multiplication by $2^{-31} = 0.46466$ gives the resulting number distributed uniformly between 0 and 1. Note that 31 is a machine-dependent number associated with the IBM/360–370, and so this procedure is machine-dependent.

```
TESTR: PROCEDURE OPTIONS (MAIN);

  RAND: PROCEDURE RETURNS (DECIMAL FLOAT(6));
```

```
/***************************************************************************/
/*                                                                         */
/*       THIS PROCEDURE GENERATES PSEUDO-RANDOM NUMBERS  BY  THE           */
/*   USUAL POWER-RESIDUE METHOD.  A NEW NUMBER X IS  GOTTEN  FROM          */
/*   THE PREVIOUS ONE BY MULTIPLYING  THE  OLD  X  BY  3**19  AND          */
/*   KEEPING ONLY THE LOW 31 BINARY DIGITS OF  THE  RESULT.  THE           */
/*   MACHINE NORMALLY DOES JUST THAT WHEN USING FIXED  BINARY(31)          */
/*   NUMBERS, BUT IT NORMALLY SIGNALS OVERFLOW. HENCE WE TURN OFF          */
/*   THE FIXEDOVERFLOW SIGNAL FOR THIS ONE  STATEMENT.  THEN  WE           */
/*   CONVERT TO FLOATING POINT AND NORMALIZE THE NUMBERS  TO  LIE          */
/*   IN THE INTERVAL FROM ZERO TO ONE.                                     */
/*                                                                         */
/***************************************************************************/

     DECLARE I STATIC FIXED BINARY(31) INITIAL (1162261467);

     (NOFIXEDOVERFLOW):  /*  SO HIGH ORDER DIGITS OF        */
     I = I*1162261467;   /*  PRODUCT WILL BE NEGLECTED      */
     RETURN (I*0.4656613E-9); /*  0.46566 = 2**-31  NORMALIZES  */
  END;  /*  OF  RAND  */

/***************************************************************************/
/*                                                                         */
/*        THIS   IS   A   SHORT   TEST   ROUTINE   TO   GENERATE   100     */
/*   PSEUDO-RANDOM NUMBERS.                                                */
/*                                                                         */
/***************************************************************************/

  DECLARE (I,J) FIXED BINARY(15);

  PUT EDIT('100 UNIFORM PSEUDO-RANDOM NUMBERS:')(A);
  PUT SKIP;

  DO I = 1 TO 10;
     DO J = 1 TO 10;
        PUT EDIT(RAND)(F(7,4));
     END;
     PUT SKIP;
  END;

END;  /*  OF TESTR  */
```

PRINTED OUTPUT:

```
100 UNIFORM PSEUDO-RANDOM NUMBERS:
 0.8135 0.4129 0.2990 0.6322 0.9978 0.9816 0.0156 0.6531 0.9654 0.8668
 0.1411 0.5476 0.4573 0.2931 0.4465 0.8307 0.0516 0.6833 0.5831 0.3484
 0.5331 0.4462 0.4415 0.4998 0.2105 0.7878 0.6431 0.5431 0.0514 0.1701
 0.0400 0.6148 0.5146 0.0449 0.0972 0.0830 0.9519 0.4844 0.0323 0.8624
 0.4549 0.3364 0.5893 0.3155 0.0229 0.5274 0.3184 0.3641 0.9252 0.1391
 0.2404 0.4371 0.1348 0.8840 0.7675 0.8794 0.7064 0.6033 0.7579 0.4465
 0.9753 0.4142 0.5775 0.5096 0.4512 0.1305 0.0449 0.5978 0.2830 0.5810
 0.1342 0.9000 0.1680 0.4522 0.3099 0.3536 0.5823 0.2786 0.3708 0.9437
 0.2057 0.2072 0.6757 0.8382 0.4176 0.1602 0.6274 0.9843 0.7379 0.0205
 0.2892 0.7905 0.0879 0.4667 0.0099 0.5194 0.7472 0.0808 0.9305 0.0173
```

Picture Specifications

Picture specifications were taken over from COBOL as a very convenient way to describe the format of data, especially in data-processing problems. PL/I picture specifications differ in minor but significant ways from COBOL.

Picture specifications are used in two ways: (1) They can be used as a format item in a GET EDIT or PUT EDIT statement to describe the format of data on an input card or printed line. (2) They can be used in a DECLARE statement to describe data format in the computer.

```
PUT EDIT(S)(P'999.99');
DECLARE T PICTURE '999.99';
```

Note that in both cases the picture, 999.99, is enclosed in quotes instead of parentheses, as is the usual case.

In PL/I, there are two distinct picture specifications: character string and numeric. A specification is character string if and only if it contains at least one A or X. Character specifications are the simpler case, and we will discuss them next.

There are only three picture characters for character-string pictures:

X indicates that the corresponding position may contain any character.

A indicates that the corresponding position may contain any alphabetic character or a blank.

9 indicates that the corresponding position may contain any digit or a blank.

Picture characters are put together in a string to describe the format of allowed data. For example, a social-security number consists of three digits, hyphen, two digits, hyphen, and four digits, for example, 575-46-9271. The picture would be 999X99X9999. Suppose that we require a date to be written with three letters for the month, followed by two digits for the day, comma, and four digits for the year, as APR17,1968. The picture would be AAA99X-9999. Repetition factors written in parentheses and preceding a picture character are allowed. Thus, AAA99X9999 could be written (3)A99X(4)9.

Character-string picture specifications and ordinary character specifications differ in only one respect. If data do not match the picture when data are assigned to a picture variable or format item from a source that doesn't have the same picture, the CONVERSION ON-condition is brought up. Thus, certain kinds of errors can be detected. For example, in the program,

```
DECLARE (C,D)CHARACTER(11),
        S PICTURE'999X99X9999';
S = C;
GET EDIT(D)(P'999X99X9999');
```

if C does not match the picture specified for S, then the statement S = C will raise the CONVERSION ON-condition. If the corresponding data on the card do not match the picture, this GET EDIT statement will raise the CONVERSION ON-condition. It is possible then, using the ON-statement, to specify a special action to be taken, for example, printing an error message.

Numeric pictures describe data that are a character string having a numeric value. The simplest numeric picture characters are 9, which indicates a digit, *not blank*, and V, which indicates the assumed position of the decimal point. The picture 9999V99 could be used with character data 007499 and would be considered to have the value 74.99.

There are two leading-zero suppression characters, Z and *. They represent digits, except that when they appear to the left of the most significant digit, Z represents blank and * represents the character *. Following are examples:

Picture	Numeric value	Character-string value
ZZZZ9	0	' 0'
ZZZZ9	1000	' 1000'
ZZZZ9	10	' 10'
****9	1000	'*1000'
****9	0	'****0'
*****	0	'*****'

If any leading-zero suppression character appears to the right of the assumed decimal point V, then all characters to the right of the V must be the same, and the digits to the right of the V will not be suppressed unless they can all be suppressed:

Picture	Value	Character-string
ZZZVZZ	0.01	' 01'
ZZZVZZ	0.00	' '

The numeric picture character Y causes zero to be replaced by a blank, regardless of whether or not it is a leading zero.

The comma, period, slash, and B (representing blank) are called insertion characters. They are inserted in the character-string value, but they do not affect the numeric value. They are replaced by blanks if there are no significant digits to their left.

Picture	Numeric value	Character-string value
Z9/Z9/99	12345	'1/23/45'
Z,ZZZ,ZZZ,ZZZ	1000000000	'1,000,000,000'
Z,ZZZ,ZZZ,ZZZ	1000	' 1,000'
Z,ZZZ,ZZZ,ZZZ	1	' 1'
ZZZV.99	200	' 200.00'
ZZZV.99	0	' .00'

Note that the period inserts a printed decimal point but does not affect the numeric value, while V denotes the position of the assumed decimal point but doesn't cause a decimal point to be printed. Although the V and a period will ordinarily be together, PL/I does not require this.

There are four "drifting" picture characters, $, +, -, and S (meaning sign). They are placed wherever leading zeros are expected and cause leading zeros to be replaced by blanks and one "drifting" character. $ represents itself.

The + means a + character if the value is positive, otherwise a blank. The - means — character if the value is negative, otherwise a blank. The S means a + or — character, whichever is appropriate.

Picture	Numeric value	Character-string value
$$$$9.V99	1000	'$1000.00'
$$$$9.V99	0.01	' $0.01'
SSSSSSS9	1	' +1'
SSSSSSS9	-1	' -1'
-------9	1	' 1'
-------9	-1	' -1'

In using IBM cards, it is common practice (antedating the use of electronic computers) to punch the sign of a number in the same column as one of the digits, usually the right-most digit. PL/I accommodates this kind of data by providing picture characters, T, I, and R, which are equivalent to a 9 picture character except that in the case of T, the sign will be punched or expected over the digit, in the case of I, the sign will be punched if the number is positive, and in the case of R if negative. A combination of a sign and a non-zero digit is also the card code for a letter: + and 1 is A, + and 9 is I, -

and 1 is J, and - and 9 is R. If T, I, or R picture characters are used for printing, the corresponding letter will print. For example, +75 printed with a picture 9T will print as 7E. There are also less useful characters for representing exponents and scale factors.

A variable declared to be a numeric picture variable is stored in the memory as characters and must be converted to some arithmetic form in the IBM/360-370 every time it is used in a calculation. If it is used only once, there is no inefficiency, since one conversion is unavoidable. If it is used many times, the many conversions result in wasted computer time. Thus, for example, if you want to read many numbers from cards and find their total, it is not inefficient to declare the variable for the original numbers to be pictured, but the total should be declared as a fixed decimal.

Structures

Structures allow us to group related data items and refer to the entire structure or certain substructures with a single name. Consider the following example:

```
DECLARE    1 R,
              2 NAME,
                 3 LAST CHARACTER(15),
                 3 FIRST CHARACTER(10),
              2 ADDRESS,
                 3 BUSINESS,
                    4 STREET CHARACTER(20),
                    4 CITY CHARACTER(15),
                    4 STATE CHARACTER(15),
                    4 ZIP PICTURE '99999',
                 3 HOME,
                    4 STREET CHARACTER(20),
                    4 CITY CHARACTER(15),
                    4 STATE CHARACTER(15),
                    4 ZIP PICTURE '99999',
              2 PHONE,
                 3 BUSINESS PICTURE '999X9999',
                 3 HOME PICTURE '999X9999';
```

Now, it is possible to refer to the whole structure by the name R. NAME can be used to reference FIRST and LAST, together, or FIRST or LAST can be referred to individually. The "completely qualified" name for FIRST is R.NAME.FIRST. This is acceptable, as is R.FIRST, NAME.FIRST, or simply

FIRST. In each case there is no ambiguity. If the same name occurs more than once in the same structure or anywhere else in the same block, enough qualification must be included to make the reference unambiguous. For example, since there are two items named STREET, a reference to STREET is ambiguous. It is adequate to reference BUSINESS.STREET and HOME.STREET to distinguish them. There are two items called BUSINESS, and they must be distinguished, for example, by referring to ADDRESS.BUSINESS or PHONE.-BUSINESS. If all names are chosen to be unique, then no qualification is ever necessary; this is, of course, a convenient practice.

It is possible to have arrays of structures and/or arrays in structures:

```
1 A(10),
   2 B FIXED BINARY(15),
   2 C(5),
       3 D DECIMAL FLOAT(6),
       3 E(5)DECIMAL FLOAT(6);
```

In referring to the elements, all subscripts are grouped in parentheses after the name. For example, the following are examples of correct references to elements of this structure:

```
B(I)
A.B(I)
D(I,J)
A.C.D(I,J)
E(I,J,K)
C.E(I,J,K)
```

Assignment statements can apply to elements of a structure, parts of a structure, or entire structures. In

```
W = U
```

W and U may be structures or substructures, provided that they have the same form. More specifically, if we declare

```
1 F(5),
   2 G FIXED BINARY(15),
   2 H(5)DECIMAL FLOAT(6);
```

then we may write

```
A.C(I) = F;
```

or

```
F = A.C(I);
```

or

```
A.C(I,J) = F(J);
```

The last case, for example, is equivalent to assigning G(J) to D(I,J), and the five values H(J,1), H(J,2), . . . , H(J,5) are assigned to E(I,J,1), E(I,J,2), . . . , E(I,J,5).

Record I/O

Record I/O statements have the forms

```
READ FILE ( <file name> ) INTO ( <variable name> );

WRITE FILE ( <file name> ) FROM ( <variable name> );
```

The <file name> indicates what file of data is to be used. In the IBM/360-370, it is the DD-name that appears on a DD card which indicates the name and/or location of the file. The <variable name> can be a variable, array, or structures. *No conversion takes place*, and if invalid data are read into a picture variable, the CONVERSION condition *is not raised*. Thus, if a record is written on tape or disc, it must be read into a variable of identically the same structure, including attributes of the data items. Therefore, the number of characters in the record must equal the number of characters in the variable or structure. In particular, the data read from cards are an 80 character string, and the variable must be compatible with that. Information sent to the printer must likewise be a character string. Either may be a structure, provided every item in the structure is either a PICTURE variable or a CHARACTER variable, not VARYING, and provided the total length of the structure is compatible with the card reader or printer record size.

The file name can also be specified in any stream I/O statement, as in the following example:

```
PUT FILE(JAMES) EDIT(X,Y)(2 F(10));
PUT FILE(JAMES) SKIP;
PUT FILE(JAMES) DATA (A,B,C);
```

In either stream I/O or record I/O, if no file name is specified, the file name

SYSIN referring to the card reader is assumed for input, and the file name SYSPRINT referring to the printer is assumed for output. One file is either stream or record, and thus the same file—even SYSIN or SYSPRINT—cannot be used for both GET or PUT and READ or WRITE in the same program. You may declare file names. In fact, it is probably advisable to do so. The most important attributes in all possible combinations are the following:

```
DECLARE A FILE RECORD INPUT;
DECLARE B FILE RECORD OUTPUT;
DECLARE C FILE RECORD UPDATE;
DECLARE D FILE STREAM INPUT;
DECLARE E FILE STREAM OUTPUT;
DECLARE F FILE STREAM OUTPUT PRINT;
```

File A can be used with READ I/O statements only, file B with WRITE only, file C with READ and WRITE. File D can be used only with GET statements and E and F only with PUT statements.

Actually, most printers use the first byte they receive in each record for carriage control, with a blank meaning normal spacing, 1 skip to a new page, 0 double spacing, and + print over the preceding line. If a file is declared to be a PRINT file, or if it is SYSPRINT used with stream I/O, the PL/I input/output subroutines automatically supply these carriage control characters. For example, if you write

```
PUT FILE(F) PAGE;
```

the next record will have the carriage-control character 1. For record I/O, this is never done for you, and if you use WRITE statements for the printer, you must furnish the carriage-control characters.

Many other attributes, such as buffering and direct-access file characteristics, may be specified in file name declarations, but the handling of direct-access files has little bearing on language and thus is outside the scope of this book.

Files must be "opened" before they are used and "closed" afterward. Opening a file allocates a place for it if it is new, locates it if it is old, and generally prepares for its use. Closing an output file may cause an end of file mark to be written at the end, rewinding if it is a tape, and discarding tables that may no longer be needed. There are explicit statements OPEN and CLOSE, but they are optional in PL/I. The files will automatically be opened when needed and closed at the end of the job if OPEN and CLOSE statements are not put in the program. There are two common uses for OPEN and CLOSE.

1. OPEN causes the positioning of a file to its first record. Thus, a tape or sequential disc file can be "rewound" to its starting position by closing it and opening it again.

2. Certain attributes, among them INPUT, OUTPUT, UPDATE, and PRINT, can be included in the OPEN statement if no conflicting attribute is included in the DECLARE statement. (UPDATE and INPUT conflict, as do PRINT and RECORD, for example.) Thus, it is possible to open a file and read from it, then close, open, and write on it, as follows:

```
DECLARE PETE FILE RECORD;
OPEN FILE(PETE) INPUT;
—
—
READ FILE(PETE) INTO A;
—
—
CLOSE FILE(PETE);
OPEN FILE(PETE) OUTPUT;
—
—
WRITE FILE(PETE);
—
—
CLOSE FILE(PETE);
```

Fixed-decimal Variables

The IBM/360–370 can do actual decimal arithmetic with any odd number of digits from 1 to 15. (You may declare an even number of digits, in which case the 360 will use the next larger odd number.) Decimal variables are declared with the words FIXED and DECIMAL. The number of digits and, if any, the number of digits to the right of the decimal point, are enclosed in parentheses, as in the following examples:

```
DECLARE R FIXED DECIMAL(7);
DECLARE S FIXED DECIMAL(7,0);
DECLARE T FIXED DECIMAL(7,3);
```

In each of these there are seven decimal digits. In the first two, the decimal point is assumed at the extreme right, but in the third, three digits are assumed to the right and four digits are assumed to the left of the decimal point.

In the IBM/360–370 computer, fixed-binary arithmetic is the fastest, and generally, floating-point arithmetic is faster than decimal. Conversion, however, must proceed from character to decimal to fixed binary to floating decimal, and therefore, conversion is simplest and fastest between input and output and decimal. As a general rule, therefore, if many data are read and printed and little calculation is done, as in typical business data processing, decimal arithmetic is preferable. It is also closer to traditional business calculations, but conversion to floating point and back may occasionally cause an error of a penny which may sometimes distress accountants. For scientific calculation, however, the speed of fixed binary and floating point and the wide range of possible values with no worry about decimal points in floating point dictate a strong preference for them over decimal.

As was pointed out in Chapter 4, scaling (i.e., keeping track of decimal points) in fixed-point arithmetic is difficult. That is the reason that floating point arithmetic was invented. For all arithmetic operations—add, subtract, multiply, and divide—the result, if it is to be saved with full accuracy, may require more digits than the operands. Thus, PL/I, which limits its intermediate results to 15 digits maximum, if frequently faced with the choice of whether to truncate digits at the right, with a possible loss of accuracy, or at the left, with the possible loss of high-order digits. For addition, subtraction, and multiplication, PL/I follows the latter course—the FIXEDOVERFLOW condition is raised if non-zero digits are lost. For division, the former course was chosen—overflow (except divide by zero) is impossible, but loss of accuracy may occur. Given the PL/I philosophy (decide on format of intermediate results without looking beyond the operation being done), these choices probably are as good as any that can be made. They probably minimize the frequency of errors and program bugs, but unfortunately, they are not adequate—*the occurrence of problems is frequent enough to be very serious.*

Fortunately, PL/I has built-in functions that allow the programmer to specify the precision of the result:

```
ADD(X,Y,I,J)
MULTIPLY(X,Y,I,J)
DIVIDE(X,Y,I,J)
```

In each case, the operation is done on fixed-decimal numbers X and Y and the result is given with a total of I decimal digits and J digits on the right of the decimal point.

In practice, the rules for addition and subtraction are simple enough that the function ADD is usually unnecessary—if the maximum number of digits to the right of the decimal point in a list of numbers is n, then the sum also has n places on the right. The total number of digits is at most 15 in every case.

Thus, the following rule leads to decimal arithmetic that can be relatively easily understood and debugged by the programmer:

Rule D: General Fixed-Decimal Arithmetic

1. Addition and subtraction may be used freely as long as you bear in mind that the number of decimal digits to the right of the decimal point is the maximum for the numbers added or subtracted and as long as you assure yourself that with a total of 15 digits, overflow won't occur.
2. For multiplication and division, use the MULTIPLY and DIVIDE built-in functions, carefully considering how many places you want on each side of the decimal point in the result.

Numeric picture variables can be used anywhere that corresponding fixed-decimal variables can be used. They are stored in character code, but they are converted to fixed decimal whenever a numeric value is required.

Now let us consider conversion by assignment. If we write a statement X = Y; and if X and Y are different data types, a conversion takes place when the value of Y is assigned to X. If Y is numeric and X is floating point, the conversion is always safe and accurate. (There can be a very small error because, for example, 0.1 has a non-terminating binary or hexadecimal representation just as $\frac{1}{3} = 0.333\ldots$ has a non-terminating decimal representation.) If the left side X is a fixed-binary or fixed-decimal integer variable, the right side is truncated, i.e., any non-integral part is simply thrown away. If the left side is a fixed decimal and the right side is floating point, the right side is converted to decimal, and the specified number of places are kept, both on the right and on the left of the decimal point. If the left side is fixed decimal and the right is a binary integer, the right side will be converted to decimal, and digits truncated and/or zeros added as needed. Similarly, if both sides are fixed decimal, digits will be truncated and/or zeros added on the right and left as needed. In summary, fixed-to-floating conversion is safe and accurate to the precision of the floating-point variable. Floating-to-fixed or fixed-to-fixed conversion is as accurate as can be expected—digits may be lost or zeros inserted at the right or left. If, however, non-zero digits are lost at the left, the SIZE condition (which, incidentally, is normally disabled) is raised.

An assignment "X = Y;" where either X or Y is a character-string variable and the other is not, is subject to complicated rules. The same is true of character-string variables used in expressions in which their context requires that they be converted to a numeric value.

If a character string consists of no more than 15 digits with no decimal point, possibly preceded by a sign and possibly surrounded by blanks, it can safely be used in expressions in which conversion to a numeric value is required. A null string, i.e., a string of zero length, will be interpreted as having the numeric value zero. However, a string with blanks between the sign and digits or a string of all blanks cannot be converted. There seem to be no other difficulties for this simple case, outside the possibility of a SIZE error.

Otherwise, conversions from character to numeric or numeric to character should be done by some method for which the conversion rules are clearly defined and easily understood. There are two good methods:

1. Use a numeric picture variable as an intermediate step, because numeric picture variables have well-defined character and numeric values. For example, the following assignments will be safe:

```
DECLARE (A,B) CHARACTER (6),
        C PICTURE 'ZZZ.V99',
        (D,E) FIXED DECIMAL(5,2);
A = ' 74.99';
C = A;
D = C;
E = 2.5;
C = E;
B = C;
```

They will result in the numeric value 74.99 for D, and character string value ' 2.50' for B.

2. Well-defined conversion can be done by the statements GET STRING and PUT STRING. They work exactly like GET FILE and PUT FILE, except that for GET STRING the source is a character string instead of an input device, and that for PUT STRING the result is put in memory instead of on an output device like a printer. For example,

```
DECLARE S CHARACTER(16),
        X FLOAT DECIMAL(6) INITIAL(3.1416);
PUT STRING(S) EDIT('ANSWER IS', X)(A(10), F(6,4));
```

will result in the string S having the value 'ANSWER IS 3.1416'.

```
DECLARE A CHARACTER(10) INITIAL('1 3 2.5 10');
DECLARE(S,T,U,V) DECIMAL FLOAT(6);
GET STRING(A) LIST(S,T,U,V);
```

will result in assigning the values S = 1, T = 3, U = 2.5, V = 10.

In this chapter and in Chapter 4, there are specific suggestions for programming style for PL/I that will help avoid programming bugs. Here is a summary:

1. Declare all variables, and each time you compile a program, check the list of variables. Remaining undeclared variables probably either are misspelled or have wrong attributes.

2. Carefully indent after each DO, BEGIN, or PROCEDURE statement, and return before each END. This will not only show errors in nesting and forgotten or extra END's, but it will also make the structure of the program clearer.

3. Do not use labels in END statements (i.e., "END A;"). They hide forgotten END statements and can make such errors extremely difficult to find.

4. Use as few data types as you can consistent with effective solution of your problem. This will minimize conversion problems. In particular, use floating point except for calculations that either are entirely on whole numbers or are extremely trivial.

5. Use one of the subsetting rules A, B, C, or D for numerical expressions.

6. Do not use character variables in numeric expressions or in assignment to and from numerical values. Either use numeric picture variables, which have both well-defined numeric and well-defined character values, or else use GET STRING and PUT STRING, for which conversion rules are well-defined and easily understood.

In addition, it is a good idea to enable the SIZE, SUBSCRIPTRANGE, OVERFLOW, FIXEDOVERFLOW, and ZERODIVIDE ON-conditions during debugging and to consider using all but SUBSCRIPTRANGE even in production runs.

Data-processing Program Examples

Data processing typically involves large files of data with large quantities of data coming in and out of the computer, but relatively little actual computation. Accurate, neat reports are demanded, and the input data are likely to contain errors. It can be a real challenge.

In data processing, there are two distinct processing methods in wide use now: on-line processing and batch processing. The older is batch processing. Typically, there is a master file, usually kept on tape, in sequence by key. The key is the record identification, for example, name or social-security number for people, part numbers for an inventory, etc. Processing consists of making changes in the file and producing one or more reports on the changes and/or the status of the file. Input data concerning changes are called transactions. Typically, transactions are collected for some period of time—a day, a week, or a month. Then they are sorted by key, like the master file, and the two files are processed in sequence together. This processing once a day, once a week, or once a month is very efficient, and storage of information on tape is very economical. For some jobs, for example, a weekly payroll, weekly processing is fine. For others, for example, airline reservations, the delays cannot be tolerated.

Modern computers are capable of time-sharing. They can receive and process information from many terminals—units with a keyboard and printer or TV display, such as a teletype unit. The computer processes individual terminals one at a time in turn, but so quickly that even with many terminals, each waits a negligible amount of time. Most modern computers use magnetic-disc files which can store large quantities of information and retrieve any part of it in a fraction of a second. These modern computer systems have made possible on-line systems, in which the master file is stored on disc and the transactions are entered from terminals and processed as they occur. On-line systems are coming into wider and wider use. For example, a batch system is adequate and most economical for department store credit accounts. Yet, there are advantages to an on-line system. The store can in moments check the precise status of an account, both in response to customer inquiries and to prevent new charges on accounts not in good standing or to catch quickly the use of stolen credit cards.

Included here is an example of each type of system: (1) a very simple-minded on-line system for stock price inquiries and (2) a batch-processing system. Since the former is simpler, it is described first.

In our simple-minded system, we allow six types of entries, the type being indicated by the first letter entered:

E New entry: corporation name and brief description.
N Inquiry: corporation name.
P Data entry: price, in dollars and eighths.
Q Inquiry: price quotation.
D Data entry: quarterly dividend, entered as a decimal number.
Y Inquiry: dividend and percent yield.

The transaction type code is followed by a three-letter code for the stock, e.g., GMC for General Motors Corporation. That, in turn, is followed by the input data in the case of data entry. This can best be understood by looking at some results from the program. The following was one session at the terminal, starting with an empty master file. First, data were entered, and then some inquiries were made. Later changes and further inquiries were made. This was run with IBM OS/360-370 TSO (Time-Sharing Option). The lower-case letters were typed by the terminal operator and the upper case letters by the computer. The translation from lower to upper case was done by TSO as a standard operating procedure.

```
STOCK INQUIRY SYSTEM NOW READY

edmtdolemonte corp.--pineapple production & canning
DMT DOLEMONTE CORP.--PINEAPPLE PRODUCTION & CANNING
eomaoutrigger marine, inc.--retail boats & supplies
OMA OUTRIGGER MARINE, INC.--RETAIL BOATS & SUPPLIES
eghbgreat hawaiian bank--complete financial service
GHB GREAT HAWAIIAN BANK--COMPLETE FINANCIAL SERVICE
efbnflybynight airlines--low cost travel
FBN FLYBYNIGHT AIRLINES--LOW COST TRAVEL
eoirouter island resorts, inc.--hotel chain
OIR OUTER ISLAND RESORTS, INC.--HOTEL CHAIN
pdmt35 3
DMT  35 3/8
ddmt00.70
DMT QUARTERLY DIVIDEND  $0.70 YIELD  7.9%
poma52 4
OMA  52 1/2
doma01.20
OMA QUARTERLY DIVIDEND  $1.20 YIELD  9.1%
pghb46 0
GHB  46
dghb00.95
GHB QUARTERLY DIVIDEND  $0.95 YIELD  8.2%
pfbn2 7
FBN   2 7/8
dfbn00.05
FBN QUARTERLY DIVIDEND  $0.05 YIELD  6.9%
poir76 2
OIR  76 1/4
doir01445
OIR QUARTERLY DIVIDEND  $1.45 YIELD  7.6%
nghb
GHB GREAT HAWAIIAN BANK--COMPLETE FINANCIAL SERVICE
qghb
GHB  46
yghb
GHB QUARTERLY DIVIDEND  $0.95 YIELD  8.2%
qdmt
DMT  35 3/8
qfbn
FBN   2 7/8
yfbn
FBN QUARTERLY DIVIDEND  $0.05 YIELD  6.9%
dfbn00.04
FBN QUARTERLY DIVIDEND  $0.04 YIELD  5.5%
yfbn
FBN QUARTERLY DIVIDEND  $0.04 YIELD  5.5%
ygmc
CODE "GMC" NOT IN FILE
xfbn
INVALID CODE
dfbn00.0a
INVALID DATA
```

It is outside the scope of this book to discuss details of input and output with various devices, and particularly disc files. Nevertheless, a brief discussion of disc file operation is needed. The records are stored with keys, and here the three-letter abbreviation for the corporation name is used as a key. On READ, the key is given, and the file is searched for the record with that key. The hardware actually has the capability to search for a record with a given key. On READ and WRITE there is a "00000000" concatenated to the key. This indicates where the search is to start—in this case it is to start always from the beginning of the file. This is inefficient, and for a large real system, it is necessary to use a more sophisticated method of storing and searching, such as "hashed addressing," which, unfortunately, is also outside the scope of this book.[†]

The following program needs little additional explanation. In operating a terminal with TSO, the operator enters a line of information and then returns carriage. It works out best, then, to program the computer also to type a line and then return carriage. PUT SKIP causes a carriage return.

```
STOCK: PROCEDURE OPTIONS(MAIN);
/*************************************************************************/
/*                                                                       */
/*       THIS IS A PROGRAM FOR AN ON-LINE STOCK  DATA  BANK  AND         */
/*   INQUIRY SYSTEM.  "STKLIST" IS A RANDOM-ACCESS FILE IN  WHICH        */
/*   THE THREE-LETTER COMPANY ABBREVIATION CODE, COMPANY NAME AND        */
/*   BRIEF DESCRIPTION,  LATEST  PRICE,  AND  CURRENT  QUARTERLY         */
/*   DIVIDEND RATE ARE STORED.  "IN" AND "OUT" BOTH REFER TO  THE        */
/*   TERMINAL FROM  WHICH  THE  INFORMATION  CAN  BE  ENTERED  OR        */
/*   INQUIRIES MADE.  TERMINAL  INPUT  INFORMATION  MATCHES  THE         */
/*   STRUCTURE "INDATA",  I.  E.  A ONE-LETTER  TRANSACTION  TYPE        */
/*   FOLLOWED BY A THREE-LETTER COMPANY CODE  FOLLOWED  BY  OTHER        */
/*   DATA IF DATA IS BEING ENTERED. THE TYPES ARE                        */
/*                                                                       */
/*       E NEW ENTRY--COMPANY NAME AND BRIEF DESCRIPTION                 */
/*                                                                       */
/*       N INQUIRY--NAME AND DESCRIPTION                                 */
/*                                                                       */
/*       P DATA ENTRY--PRICE ENTERED AS DOLLARS AND EIGHTHS (TWO         */
/*   INTEGERS)                                                           */
/*                                                                       */
/*       Q INQUIRY--PRICE                                                */
/*                                                                       */
/*       D DATA ENTRY--QUARTERLY DIVIDEND ENTERED AS  A  DECIMAL         */
/*   NUMBER                                                              */
/*                                                                       */
/*       Y INQUIRY--DIVIDEND AND PERCENT YIELD                           */
/*                                                                       */
/*       N, Y, AND D ARE USED IN THE YIELD CALCULATION.                  */
/*                                                                       */
/*************************************************************************/
```

[†] An excellent reference is Donald E. Knuth, *Sorting and Searching*, Vol. 3 of *The Art of Computer Programming*, Reading, Mass.: Addison-Wesley Publishing Co. (1973).

```
DECLARE STKLIST FILE RECORD KEYED
            ENVIRONMENT(REGIONAL(2) BLKSIZE(56) KEYLENGTH(3) F),
        IN FILE RECORD INPUT ENVIRONMENT(U BLKSIZE(80)),
        OUT FILE PRINT;

DECLARE 1 STOCKDATA,
            2 DESC CHARACTER(48),
            2 PRICE,
               3 DOLLARS PICTURE '999',
               3 EIGHTHS PICTURE '9',
            2 DIVIDEND PICTURE '99V99';

DECLARE 1 INDATA,
            2 TYPE PICTURE 'A',
            2 CODE PICTURE 'AAA',
            2 DATA CHARACTER(48),
            2 FILLER CHARACTER(28);

DECLARE C(0:7) CHARACTER(4) INITIAL('    ',' 1/8',' 1/4',' 3/8',
            ' 1/2',' 5/8',' 3/4',' 7/8'),
        (N,D,Y) FIXED DECIMAL(8,4);

/*********************************************************************/
/*                                                                   */
/*        THE FOLLOWING TWO  STATEMENTS  CAUSE  THE  FILE  TO  BE    */
/*   CREATED AND INITIALIZED. THEY SHOULD BE  OMITTED  AFTER  THE    */
/*   FIRST TIME THE PROGRAM IS RUN, I. E. WITH AN OLD FILE.          */
/*                                                                   */
/*********************************************************************/

OPEN FILE (STKLIST) OUTPUT DIRECT;
CLOSE FILE (STKLIST);


ON CONVERSION BEGIN;
   PUT FILE(OUT) EDIT('INVALID DATA')(A);
   PUT FILE(OUT) SKIP;
   GO TO READ;
END;

ON KEY(STKLIST) BEGIN;
   IF TYPE='E' THEN PUT FILE(OUT) EDIT(
      'CODE "',CODE,'" ALREADY IN FILE--CANNOT BE INSERTED')(A);
   ELSE PUT FILE(OUT) EDIT('CODE "',CODE,'" NOT IN FILE')(A);
   PUT FILE(OUT) SKIP;
   GO TO READ;
END;

OPEN FILE (STKLIST) UPDATE DIRECT;
PUT FILE(OUT) EDIT('STOCK INQUIRY SYSTEM NOW READY')(A);
PUT FILE(OUT) SKIP(2);

READ:
```

```
 DO WHILE(1);
    DATA = ' ';  /*  IN CASE OF SHORT INPUT LINE  */
    READ FILE(IN) INTO(INDATA);
    IF TYPE='S' & CODE='TOP' THEN STOP; /* OPERATOR TYPED "STOP" */
/*********************************************************************/
/*                                                                   */
/*        ENTER NEW RECORD IN STKLIST FILE.                          */
/*                                                                   */
/*********************************************************************/

    IF TYPE='E' THEN DO;
       DOLLARS = 0;
       EIGHTHS = 0;
       DIVIDEND = 0;
       DESC = DATA;
       WRITE FILE(STKLIST) FROM(STOCKDATA) KEYFROM(CODE||'00000000');
    END;   /*  OF IF TYPE='E'  */

    ELSE READ FILE(STKLIST) INTO(STOCKDATA) KEY(CODE||'00000000');

/*********************************************************************/
/*                                                                   */
/*        ENTER NEW DATA IN STKLIST FILE.                            */
/*                                                                   */
/*        NOTE THAT "GET STRING" IS USED TO CONVERT  THE  NUMERIC    */
/*   DATA IN THE INPUT CHARACTER STRING TO DECIMAL FORMAT.           */
/*                                                                   */
/*********************************************************************/

    IF TYPE='P' THEN GET STRING(DATA) LIST(DOLLARS,EIGHTHS);

    IF TYPE='D' THEN GET STRING(DATA) LIST(DIVIDEND);

    IF TYPE='P' | TYPE='D' THEN
       REWRITE FILE(STKLIST) FROM(STOCKDATA) KEY(CODE||'00000000');

/*********************************************************************/
/*                                                                   */
/*        PRINT INQUIRY OR CONFIRMATION CATA.                        */
/*                                                                   */
/*********************************************************************/

    IF TYPE='Q' | TYPE='P' THEN PUT FILE (OUT) EDIT
       (CODE,DOLLARS,C(EIGHTHS))(A(4),F(3),A(4));

    ELSE IF TYPE='Y' |TYPE='D' THEN DO;
       N = 100*4*DIVIDEND;
       D = DOLLARS + EIGHTHS/8.0;
       Y = N/D;
       PUT FILE (OUT) EDIT (CODE,' QUARTERLY DIVIDEND ',DIVIDEND,
          ' YIELD ',Y,'%')(A,A,P'$$9V.99',A,P'Z9V.9',A);
    END;  /*  OF IF TYPE='Y'  */
```

```
    ELSE IF TYPE='N' | TYPE='E' THEN PUT FILE (OUT) EDIT
       (CODE,DESC)(A(4),A);

    ELSE PUT FILE(OUT) EDIT('INVALID CODE')(A);
    PUT FILE(OUT) SKIP;

  END;  /*  OF DO WHILE(1)  */

END;  /*  OF MAIN PROCEDURE  */
```

In data processing problems, it is well to prepare for all errors (or as many as possible) that may occur in input data. The ON KEY catches errors of trying to read a non-existent record or trying to write two records with the same key. The ON CONVERSION catches invalid numeric data. There is a check for invalid type code. Also, on data entry, the entered data are typed back, which allows the operator to verify.

The second example is a program which I actually use to keep records of students' homework and test scores. There is a master file in which there is a record for each student including his name, social-security number, and his scores. Each time a student turns in an assignment, he turns in a card on which his name, social-security number and the assignment number are punched. When I grade the assignment, I write, and later punch, the grade, and perhaps a remark, into the card. I collect these cards, and once each week I run the program, which updates the master file. At the same time, two reports are produced: one is a list of the week's transactions and the other is a status report showing the total score and all individual scores for each student. In addition, the number of students who have completed each problem and the average total score and average on each problem are given.

On the transaction cards, the social-security number goes in columns 1 to 11 and a code "A" for update, "B" for new student, "C" for deletion is punched in column 12. This is followed by the problem number in columns 13 and 14 and the grade in columns 15 and 16. The name goes in columns 17 to 40 and the rest of the card is available for comments.

Here are the input data and results of the first two runs, starting from an empty master file. (The status report provides for 15 assignments—the right half is cut off.)

```
TRANSACTION INPUT CARDS FOR FIRST RUN:

105-58-3583B    CHANG, ELEANOR
105-58-3583A0157CHANG, ELEANOR
105-66-6566B    BRECK, DONNA MAE
113-27-1520B    ADAMSON, LAURENCE
113-27-1520A0175ADAMSON, LAURENCE
113-27-1520A0286ADAMSON, LAURENCE
132-00-5230B    OSAKI, KENNETH
132-00-5230A0169OSAKI, KENNETH
```

```
132-00-5230A02650SAKI, KENNETH
202-36-8231B     KIM, HENRY
202-36-8231A0145KIM, HENRY
202-36-8231A0290KIM, HENRY              WELL DONE PAPER
202-36-8231A0385KIM, HENRY
513-29-8314B     EL DIEZ, ANNA
749-26-7457B     AKAKA, MEILANI
919-02-2513B     ENDERSON, MILES
995-22-2222A02MLJONES, JOHN T.
UUU-K7-8249B     DOE, JOHN


LIST OF TRANSACTIONS

NAME                SSNO         TYPE       PROB#-GRADE-REMARKS

CHANG, ELEANOR      105-58-3583  INSERTION
CHANG, ELEANOR      105-58-3583  UPDATE    01   57
BRECK, DONNA MAE    105-66-6566  INSERTION
ADAMSON, LAURENCE   113-27-1520  INSERTION
ADAMSON, LAURENCE   113-27-1520  UPDATE    01   75
ADAMSON, LAURENCE   113-27-1520  UPDATE    02   86
OSAKI, KENNETH      132-00-5230  INSERTION
OSAKI, KENNETH      132-00-5230  UPDATE    01   69
OSAKI, KENNETH      132-00-5230  UPDATE    02   65
KIM, HENRY          202-36-8231  INSERTION
KIM, HENRY          202-36-8231  UPDATE    01   45
KIM, HENRY          202-36-8231  UPDATE    02   90   WELL DONE PAPER
KIM, HENRY          202-36-8231  UPDATE    03   85
EL DIEZ, ANNA       513-29-8314  INSERTION
AKAKA, MEILANI      749-26-7457  INSERTION
ENDERSON, MILES     919-02-2513  INSERTION
JONES, JOHN T.      995-22-2222  UPDATE    02   ML   SSNO NOT FOUND
DOE, JOHN           UUU-K7-8249  INSERTION           BAD SSNO OR DATA


STATUS REPORT

NAME                SSNO        TOTAL     1     2     3     4     5

CHANG, ELEANOR      105-58-3583   57     57
BRECK, DONNA MAE    105-66-6566    0
ADAMSON, LAURENCE   113-27-1520  161     75    86
OSAKI, KENNETH      132-00-5230  134     69    65
KIM, HENRY          202-36-8231  220     45    90    85
EL DIEZ, ANNA       513-29-8314    0
AKAKA, MEILANI      749-29-7457    0
ENDERSON, MILES     919-02-2513    0

NUMBER OF STUDENTS                 8      4     3     1

AVERAGES                         71.5  61.5  80.3  85.0
```

```
TRANSACTION INPUT CARDS FOR SECOND RUN:

105-58-3583A0290CHANG, ELEANOR
105-66-6566C     BRECK, DONNA MAE
113-27-1520A0367ADAMSON, LAURENCE
113-27-1520A0480ADAMSON, LAURENCE
132-00-5230A0365OSAKI, KENNETH
132-00-5230A0385OSAKI, KENNETH
132-00-5230A0475OSAKI, KENNETH
147-12-6431B     WONG, DIANA
147-12-6431A0170WONG, DIANA
147-12-6431A02MKWONG, DIANA
147-12-6431A2075WONG, DIANA
202-36-8231A0390KIM, HENRY
466-64-0112A0185DEVON, CRYSTAL
513-29-8314A0169EL DIEZ, ANNA
513-29-8314A0288EL DIEZ, ANNA
513-29-8314A0375EL DIEZ, ANNA
749-26-7457B     AKAKA, MEILANI
749-26-7457A0192AKAKA, MEILANI
749-26-7457A0277AKAKA, MEILANI
```

```
LIST OF TRANSACTIONS

NAME                  SSNO          TYPE       PROB#-GRADE-REMARKS

CHANG, ELEANOR        105-58-3583   UPDATE     02   90
BRECK, DONNA MAE      105-66-6566   DELETION
ADAMSON, LAURENCE     113-27-1520   UPDATE     03   67
ADAMSON, LAURENCE     113-27-1520   UPDATE     04   80
OSAKI, KENNETH        132-00-5230   UPDATE     03   65
OSAKI, KENNETH        132-00-5230   UPDATE     03   85
OSAKI, KENNETH        132-00-5230   UPDATE     04   75
WONG, DIANA           147-12-6431   INSERTION
WONG, DIANA           147-12-6431   UPDATE     01   70
WONG, DIANA           147-12-6431   UPDATE     02   MK   BAD SSNO OR DATA
WONG, DIANA           147-12-6431   UPDATE     20   75   INVALID PROB#
KIM, HENRY            202-36-8231   UPDATE     03   90
DEVON, CRYSTAL        466-64-0112   UPDATE     01   85   SSNO NOT FOUND
EL DIEZ, ANNA         513-29-8314   UPDATE     01   69
EL DIEZ, ANNA         513-29-8314   UPDATE     02   88
EL DIEZ, ANNA         513-29-8314   UPDATE     03   75
AKAKA, MEILANI        749-26-7457   INSERTION            DUPLICATE SSNO
AKAKA, MEILANI        749-26-7457   UPDATE     01   92
AKAKA, MEILANI        749-26-7457   UPDATE     02   77
```

```
STATUS REPORT

NAME                  SSNO          TOTAL      1      2      3      4      5

CHANG, ELEANOR        105-58-3583   147       57     90
ADAMSON, LAURENCE     113-27-1520   308       75     86     67     80
```

```
OSAKI, KENNETH      132-00-5230  294   69    65    85    75
WONG, DIANA         147-12-6431   70   70
KIM, HENRY          202-36-8231  225   45    90    90
EL DIEZ, ANNA       513-29-8314  232   69    88    75
AKAKA, MEILANI      749-26-7457  169   92    77
ENDERSON, MILES     919-02-2513    0

NUMBER OF STUDENTS                 8    7     6     4     2

AVERAGES                       180.6 68.1  82.6  79.2  77.5
```

```
CHECK       105-58-3583    999-99-9999    105-58-3583    CODE=A
CHECK       105-58-3583    105-58-3583    105-66-6566    CODE=A
CHECK       105-66-6566    105-58-3583    105-66-6566    CODE=C
CHECK       105-66-6566    105-66-6566    113-27-1520    CODE=C
CHECK       113-27-1520    105-66-6566    113-27-1520    CODE=A
CHECK       113-27-1520    113-27-1520    132-00-5230    CODE=A
CHECK       113-27-1520    113-27-1520    132-00-5230    CODE=A
CHECK       132-00-5230    113-27-1520    132-00-5230    CODE=A
CHECK       132-00-5230    132-00-5230    202-36-8231    CODE=A
CHECK       132-00-5230    132-00-5230    202-36-8231    CODE=A
CHECK       132-00-5230    132-00-5230    202-36-8231    CODE=A
CHECK       147-12-6431    132-00-5230    202-36-8231    CODE=B
CHECK       147-12-6431    147-12-6431    202-36-8231    CODE=A
CHECK       147-12-6431    147-12-6431    202-36-8231    CODE=A
CHECK       147-12-6431    147-12-6431    202-36-8231    CODE=A
CHECK       202-36-8231    147-12-6431    202-36-8231    CODE=A
CHECK       202-36-8231    202-36-8231    513-29-8314    CODE=A
CHECK       466-64-0112    202-36-8231    513-29-8314    CODE=A
CHECK       513-29-8314    202-36-8231    513-29-8314    CODE=A
CHECK       513-29-8314    513-29-8314    749-26-7457    CODE=A
CHECK       513-29-8314    513-29-8314    749-26-7457    CODE=A
CHECK       513-29-8314    513-29-8314    749-26-7457    CODE=A
CHECK       749-26-7457    513-29-8314    749-26-7457    CODE=B
CHECK       749-26-7457    749-26-7457    919-02-2513    CODE=B
CHECK       749-26-7457    749-26-7457    919-02-2513    CODE=A
CHECK       749-26-7457    749-26-7457    919-02-2513    CODE=A
CHECK       749-26-7457    749-26-7457    919-02-2513    CODE=A
```

The master records could have been made more compact. They were made completely character code to make them completely compatible with the COBOL program in Chapter 7; either program can update a master file produced by the other program. Also, by changing only the job-control cards, we can make a master file on tape, disc, or cards.

When a conversion error is met, no attempt is made to correct and use the data. The transaction is simply rejected.

The beginning and end of this program are a little tricky. You must be very careful to process the first and last record and the first and last transaction properly, and you must be able to insert records before the first or after the last or delete the first or last record. Otherwise, the program logic is not complicated and should be understandable from the listing and its comments.

```
GRADES: PROCEDURE OPTIONS(MAIN);


/*************************************************************************/
/*                                                                       */
/*        THIS IS  A  PROGRAM  FOR  BATCH-PROCESSING RECORDS  OF         */
/*   STUDENT HOMEWORK AND TEST SCORES. IT UPDATES THE INFORMATION        */
/*   IN "OLDMAST" PRODUCING A NEW FILE  "NEWMAST",   USING  INPUT        */
/*   DATA FROM FILE "TRANS".   EACH  FILE  IS  SORTED  BY  SOCIAL        */
/*   SECURITY NUMBER.  TWO  REPORTS  ARE  PRODUCED,  A  LIST  OF         */
/*   TRANSACTIONS, "TRLIST", AND A STATUS REPORT "MREPORT", WHICH        */
/*   INCLUDES THE NUMBER OF STUDENTS AND AVERAGE GRADE,   OVERALL        */
/*   AND FOR EACH ASSIGNMENT.  BESIDES THE OBVIOUS INFORMATION, A        */
/*   TRANSACTION DATA CARD MAY CARRY A REMARK,  WHICH IS  PRINTED        */
/*   AS "REMARKA" IN THE  TRANSACTION  REPORT.  "REMARKB"  THERE         */
/*   HOLDS ERROR MESSAGES                                                */
/*                                                                       */
/*        THE TRANSACTION CODES ARE                                      */
/*                                                                       */
/*        A UPDATE--ENTER ONE SCORE IN THE MASTER FILE                   */
/*                                                                       */
/*        B INSERT A NEW STUDENT'S RECORD                                */
/*                                                                       */
/*        C DELETE A STUDENT'S RECORD                                    */
/*                                                                       */
/*************************************************************************/


  DECLARE OLDMAST FILE RECORD INPUT,
          NEWMAST FILE RECORD OUTPUT,
          TRANS   FILE RECORD INPUT,
          TRLIST FILE RECORD OUTPUT,
          MREPORT  FILE RECORD OUTPUT;


/*************************************************************************/
/*                                                                       */
/*        "MASTER_RECORD" IS THE MASTER RECORD  BEING  PROCESSED,        */
/*   AND "NEXT_RECORD" IS THE NEXT MASTER RECORD TO BE PROCESSED.        */
/*   "TRANSACTION"   IS   THE   TRANSACTION   INPUT   RECORD,            */
/*   "TRANSACTION_REPORT"   ONE  LINE  IN  THE  TRANSACTION  LIST        */
/*   REPORT,  "REPORT" A USUAL LINE IN THE  STATUS  REPORT,   AND        */
/*   "AVERAGES" THE LAST  LINE  IN  THAT  REPORT,   WHICH  HAS  A        */
/*   DIFFERENT FORMAT BECAUSE THE NUMBERS ARE NOT INTEGERS.              */
/*                                                                       */
/*************************************************************************/
```

```
DECLARE 1 MASTER_RECORD,
          2 SSNO CHARACTER(11),
          2 NAME CHARACTER(24),
          2 SCORES(15) PICTURE '999';

DECLARE 1 NEXT_RECORD,
          2 SSNO CHARACTER(11),
          2 NAME CHARACTER(24),
          2 SCORES(15) PICTURE '999';

DECLARE 1 TRANSACTION,
          2 SSNO CHARACTER(11),
          2 CODE CHARACTER(1),
          2 PROBLEM_NUMBER CHARACTER(2),
          2 GRADE CHARACTER(2),
          2 NAME CHARACTER(24),
          2 REMARK CHARACTER(40);

DECLARE 1 TRANSACTION_REPORT,
          2 CARRIAGE_CONTROL CHARACTER(1) INITIAL(' '),
          2 NAME CHARACTER(20),
          2 SSNO CHARACTER(13),
          2 TYPE CHARACTER(9),
          2 PROBLEM_NUMBER CHARACTER(4),
          2 GRADE CHARACTER(4),
          2 REMARK CHARACTER(20);

DECLARE 1 REPORT,
          2 CARRIAGE_CONTROL CHARACTER(1) INITIAL(' '),
          2 NAME CHARACTER(20),
          2 SSNO CHARACTER(11),
          2 TOTAL PICTURE 'ZZZZ9',
          2 SPACE1 CHARACTER(2) INITIAL('  '),
          2 S(15),
            3 SCORES PICTURE 'ZZZZ',
            3 SPACE2 CHARACTER(2) INITIAL((15) (2) ' ');

DECLARE 1 AVERAGES,
          2 TITLE CHARACTER(32) INITIAL('0AVERAGES'),
          2 TOTAL PICTURE 'ZZZZZ.V9',
          2 AVERAGE(15) PICTURE 'ZZZZ.VZ';


/**********************************************************************/
/*                                                                    */
/*       "BLANKS",  "HEAD1",  "HEAD2",  "HEAD3", AND "HEAD4" ARE      */
/*   USED FOR HEADINGS. NOTE THAT CARRIAGE CONTROL CHARACTERS ARE     */
/*   INCLUDED.  "CHECK" IS SET TRUE IF DEBUGGING  INFORMATION  IS     */
/*   DESIRED.  "DELETE"  IS  SET  TRUE  WHEN  IT  IS  FOUND  THAT     */
/*   "MASTER_RECORD" SHOULD BE DELETED. "END_OF_TRANSACTIONS" AND     */
/*   "END_OF_MASTER" ARE SET TRUE ON END OF FILE IN EACH CASE.        */
/*                                                                    */
/**********************************************************************/
```

```
 DECLARE BLANKS CHARACTER(132) INITIAL(' '),
         HEAD1 CHARACTER(132) INITIAL('1STATUS REPORT'),
         HEAD2 CHARACTER(132) INITIAL('0NAME                    SSNO
TOTAL      1     2     3     4     5     6     7     8     9    10     1
1    12    13    14    15'),
         HEAD3 CHARACTER(132) INITIAL('1LIST OF TRANSACTIONS'),
         HEAD4 CHARACTER(132) INITIAL('0NAME                    SSNO
  TYPE       PROB#-GRADE-REMARKS'),
         TRUE BIT(1) INITIAL('1'B),
         FALSE BIT(1) INITIAL('0'B),
         CHECK BIT(1) INITIAL('1'B),
         DELETE BIT(1) INITIAL('0'B),
         END_OF_TRANSACTIONS BIT(1) INITIAL('0'B),
         END_OF_MASTER BIT(1) INITIAL('0'B);

/**********************************************************************/
/*                                                                    */
/*       DATA IS MOVED FROM CHARACTER VARIABLES IN "TRANSACTION"      */
/*   TO   PICTURE   VARIABLES   "TEMPSSNO",   "TEMPNUMBER",   AND     */
/*   "TEMPGRADE" TO  CAUSE  A  CHECK  AND  RAISE  THE  CONVERSION     */
/*   ON-CONDITION ON INVALID DATA. "TEMPTOTAL", "TEMP", AND I ARE     */
/*   USED IN CALCULATING THE INDIVIDUAL  STUDENT'S  TOTAL  SCORE.     */
/*   "COUNT",  "SUM",  "TOTAL_NUMBER",  AND  "GRAND_TOTAL"  ARE       */
/*   TABULATIONS OF NUMBER OF STUDENTS AND TOTAL SCORES  ON  EACH     */
/*   ASSIGNMENT AND ALTOGETHER,  FOR THE SUMMARY AND AVERAGES  IN     */
/*   THE STATUS REPORT.                                               */
/*                                                                    */
/**********************************************************************/

  DECLARE TEMPSSNO PICTURE '999X99X9999',
          TEMPNUMBER PICTURE 'ZZ',
          TEMPGRADE PICTURE 'ZZ',
          TEMPTOTAL FIXED DECIMAL(5),
          TEMP FIXED DECIMAL(5),
          I FIXED BINARY(15),
          COUNT(15) FIXED DECIMAL(5) INITIAL((15) 0),
          SUM(15) FIXED DECIMAL(7) INITIAL((15) 0),
          TOTAL_NUMBER FIXED DECIMAL(5) INITIAL(0),
          GRAND_TOTAL FIXED DECIMAL(9) INITIAL(0);
/**********************************************************************/
/*                                                                    */
/*       SEE NOTE ABOUT '999-99-9999' IN REPORT_LINE PROCEDURE.       */
/*                                                                    */
/**********************************************************************/

  ON ENDFILE(OLDMAST) BEGIN;
     NEXT_RECORD.SSNO = '999-99-9999';
     END_OF_MASTER = TRUE;
  END;

  ON ENDFILE(TRANS) END_OF_TRANSACTIONS = TRUE;

  ON CONVERSION BEGIN;
     TRANSACTION_REPORT.REMARK = 'BAD SSNO OR DATA';
```

```
      GO TO P;
   END;
/***********************************************************************/
/*                                                                     */
/*          WE "GO TO P",  WHERE THE TRANSACTION IS PRINTED, RATHER    */
/*     THAN ATTEMPT TO CORRECT THE DATA AND RETRY THE CONVERSION.      */
/*                                                                     */
/***********************************************************************/
   REPORT_LINE: PROCEDURE;
/***********************************************************************/
/*                                                                     */
/*          THIS PROCEDURE WRITES A NEW MASTER RECORD AND PRINTS  A    */
/*     STATUS REPORT LINE AND DOES THE TABULATION.   NOTE  THAT  IF    */
/*     "DELETE" IS TRUE OR SSNO='999-99-9999',  THE  MASTER  RECORD    */
/*     AND   REPORT   LINE   SIMPLY   ARE  NOT  WRITTEN.   WHENEVER    */
/*     "MASTER_RECORD" OR "NEXT_RECORD" DOES  NOT  CONTAIN  A  REAL    */
/*     RECORD, THE SSNO IS SET TO 999-99-9999.                         */
/*                                                                     */
/***********************************************************************/
      IF MASTER_RECORD.SSNO='999-99-9999' THEN RETURN;
      IF DELETE THEN DO;
         DELETE = FALSE;
         RETURN;
      END;

      WRITE FILE(NEWMAST) FROM(MASTER_RECORD);

      REPORT.NAME = MASTER_RECORD.NAME;
      REPORT.SSNO = MASTER_RECORD.SSNO;
      TEMPTOTAL = 0;
      DO I = 1 TO 15;
         TEMP = MASTER_RECORD.SCORES(I);
         REPORT.SCORES(I) = TEMP;
         IF TEMP¬=0 THEN DO;
            COUNT(I) = COUNT(I)+1;
            SUM(I) = SUM(I)+TEMP;
            TEMPTOTAL = TEMPTOTAL+TEMP;
         END;
      END;
      TOTAL_NUMBER = TOTAL_NUMBER+1;
      GRAND_TOTAL = GRAND_TOTAL+TEMPTOTAL;
      REPORT.TOTAL = TEMPTOTAL;

      WRITE FILE(MREPORT) FROM(REPORT);

   END;  /*  OF REPORT_LINE PROCEDURE  */
   OPEN FILE(OLDMAST);
   OPEN FILE(NEWMAST);
   OPEN FILE(TRANS);
   OPEN FILE(TRLIST);
   OPEN FILE(MREPORT);
```

```
   WRITE FILE(MREPORT) FROM(HEAD1);
   WRITE FILE(MREPORT) FROM(HEAD2);
   WRITE FILE(MREPORT) FROM(BLANKS);
   WRITE FILE(TRLIST) FROM(HEAD3);
   WRITE FILE(TRLIST) FROM(HEAD4);
   WRITE FILE(TRLIST) FROM(BLANKS);

   READ FILE(OLDMAST) INTO(NEXT_RECORD);
   MASTER_RECORD.SSNO = '999-99-9999';
   READ FILE(TRANS) INTO(TRANSACTION);
   TRANSACTION_REPORT.REMARK = TRANSACTION.REMARK;
/*********************************************************************/
/*                                                                   */
/*        NOW ONE TRANSACTION RECORD AND ONE MASTER RECORD ARE IN    */
/*   MEMORY, AND WE MAY START THE MAIN LOOP.                         */
/*                                                                   */
/*        IF THE TRANSACTION IS AN INSERTION, IT MUST BE INSERTED    */
/*   BETWEEN THE CORRECT TWO RECORDS,  WHICH MEANS JUST IN  FRONT    */
/*   OF THE FIRST MASTER RECORD WITH A HIGHER  SSNO.   HENCE  THE    */
/*   FOLLOWING LOGIC:                                                */
/*                                                                   */
/*        IF THE SSNO OF THE NEXT RECORD IS EQUAL TO OR LESS THAN    */
/*   THE SSNO OF THE TRANSACTION,   WE  MUST  WRITE  THE  PRESENT    */
/*   MASTER RECORD,  WRITE A REPORT LINE,  MOVE "NEXT_RECORD"  TO    */
/*   "MASTER_RECORD",  AND READ A NEW "NEXT_RECORD". OTHERWISE WE    */
/*   PROCESS THE TRANSACTION.                                        */
/*                                                                   */
/*********************************************************************/

   DO WHILE(¬(END_OF_TRANSACTIONS & END_OF_MASTER));

      IF CHECK THEN DO; /* PRINT FOR DEBUGGING  */
         PUT EDIT('CHECK',TRANSACTION.SSNO,MASTER_RECORD.SSNO,
            NEXT_RECORD.SSNO,'CODE=',CODE)(4 A(15),A,A);
         PUT SKIP;
      END;

      TEMPSSNO = TRANSACTION.SSNO;
      IF TEMPSSNO<NEXT_RECORD.SSNO & ¬END_OF_TRANSACTIONS THEN DO;

/*********************************************************************/
/*                                                                   */
/*        PROCESS A TRANSACTION.                                     */
/*                                                                   */
/*********************************************************************

         IF TEMPSSNO = MASTER_RECORD.SSNO THEN DO;
            IF CODE='A' THEN DO;
               TEMPGRADE = TRANSACTION.GRADE;
               TEMPNUMBER = TRANSACTION.PROBLEM_NUMBER;
               IF TEMPNUMBER<=15 & TEMPNUMBER>=1 THEN
                  MASTER_RECORD.SCORES(TEMPNUMBER) = TEMPGRADE;
               ELSE TRANSACTION_REPORT.REMARK = 'INVALID PROB#';
```

```
            END;
            ELSE IF CODE='B' THEN TRANSACTION_REPORT.REMARK =
               'DUPLICATE SSNO';
            ELSE IF CODE='C' THEN DELETE = TRUE;
         END;
         ELSE IF CODE='B' THEN DO;
            CALL REPORT_LINE;
            MASTER_RECORD.SSNO = TEMPSSNO;
            MASTER_RECORD.NAME = TRANSACTION.NAME;
            MASTER_RECORD.SCORES = 0;
         END;
         ELSE TRANSACTION_REPORT.REMARK = 'SSNO NOT FOUND';

/**********************************************************************/
/*                                                                    */
/*         PRINT A LINE IN THE TRANSACTION LIST AND READ THE  NEXT   */
/*   TRANSACTION.                                                     */
/*                                                                    */
/**********************************************************************/

P:       TRANSACTION_REPORT.SSNO = TRANSACTION.SSNO;
         TRANSACTION_REPORT.NAME = TRANSACTION.NAME;
         TRANSACTION_REPORT.PROBLEM_NUMBER = TRANSACTION.PROBLEM_NUMBER;
         TRANSACTION_REPORT.GRADE = TRANSACTION.GRADE;
         IF CODE='A' THEN TYPE = 'UPDATE';
         ELSE IF CODE='B' THEN TYPE = 'INSERTION';
         ELSE IF CODE='C' THEN TYPE = 'DELETION';
         ELSE TYPE = 'INVALID';
         WRITE FILE(TRLIST) FROM(TRANSACTION_REPORT);
         READ FILE(TRANS) INTO(TRANSACTION);
         TRANSACTION_REPORT.REMARK = TRANSACTION.REMARK;
      END;

/**********************************************************************/
/*                                                                    */
/*         PROCESS A MASTER RECORD,  PRINTING A LINE IN THE STATUS   */
/*   REPORT, AND READ THE NEXT MASTER RECORD.                         */
/*                                                                    */
/**********************************************************************/

      ELSE DO;
         CALL REPORT_LINE;
         MASTER_RECORD = NEXT_RECORD;
         IF ¬END_OF_MASTER THEN READ FILE(OLDMAST) INTO(NEXT_RECORD);
      END;

   END;  /*  OF DO WHILE(¬(END_OF_TRANSACTIONS & END_OF_MASTER))  */

/**********************************************************************/
/*                                                                    */
/*         PRINT THE FINAL SUMMARY AND AVERAGES.                      */
/*                                                                    */
/**********************************************************************/
```

```
  CALL REPORT_LINE;
  REPORT.NAME = 'NUMBER OF STUDENTS';
  REPORT.SSNO = ' ';
  REPORT.TOTAL = TOTAL_NUMBER;
  REPORT.SCORES = COUNT;
  REPORT.CARRIAGE_CONTROL = '0';
  WRITE FILE(MREPORT) FROM(REPORT);
  AVERAGES.TOTAL = DIVIDE(GRAND_TOTAL,TOTAL_NUMBER,7,1);
  DO I = 1 TO 15;
     IF COUNT(I)=0 THEN AVERAGE(I) = 0;
     ELSE AVERAGE(I) = DIVIDE(SUM(I),COUNT(I),5,1);
  END;
  WRITE FILE(MREPORT) FROM(AVERAGES);

END;  /* OF MAIN PROCEDURE  */
```

COBOL Chapter 7

In May, 1959, a meeting of approximately forty representatives of users, manufacturers, and government installations was called by a member of the Department of Defense to discuss the feasibility of establishing a common business language. This was the beginning of the so-called CODASYL (Conference on Data Systems Languages) committee, which was, according to Sammet,† too loosely organized to deserve the name committee. They appointed a "short-range committee" to examine current business-oriented languages and systems and report on their good and bad features. The committee, however, took upon itself the task of actually defining a new language, and its report was completed before the end of that year. It was published by the Government Printing Office in April, 1960 and implemented in 1960 by RCA and Remington Rand. It was revised somewhat in 1961, and in 1962 the sort and report-writer features were introduced. Another revision was done in 1964–1965 and adopted as American National Standard COBOL by the American National Standards Institute; this revision was also published by the Government Printing Office. Now many corporations and government organizations require computer manufacturers to furnish compilers for standard

†J. E. Sammet, *Programming Languages: History and Fundamentals* (Englewood Cliffs, N.J.: Prentice-Hall, Inc., 1969), p. 330.

COBOL and require that their programmers use it exclusively in an attempt to maintain compatibility and prevent dependence on a single computer manufacturer.

Because of the large volume of business and government data processing, and because most of it is done in COBOL, COBOL now has the distinction of being the most used of all computer languages.

This presentation of COBOL is based largely on the 1968 ANSI Standard for COBOL,† which contains the following:

> Any organization interested in using the COBOL specifications as the basis for an instruction manual or for any other purpose is free to do so. However, all such organizations are requested to reproduce this section as part of the introduction to the document. Those using a short passage, as in a book review, are requested to mention "COBOL" in acknowledgment of the source, but need not quote this entire section.
>
> COBOL is an industry language and is not the property of any company or group of companies, or of any organization or group of organizations.
>
> No warranty, expressed or implied, is made by any contributor or by the COBOL Committee as to the accuracy and functioning of the programming system and language. Moreover, no responsibility is assumed by any contributor, or by the committee, in connection therewith.
>
> Procedures have been established for the maintenance of COBOL. Inquiries concerning the procedures for proposing changes should be directed to the Executive Committee of the Conference on Data Systems Languages.
>
> The authors and copyright holders of the copyrighted material used herein
>
> > FLOW-MATIC (Trademark of Sperry Rand Corporation). Programming for the UNIVAC® I and II. Data Automation Systems copyrighted 1958, 1959, by Sperry Rand Corporation; IBM Commercial Translator Form No. F28-8013, copyrighted 1959 by IBM; FACT, DSI 27A5260-2760, copyrighted 1960 by Minneapolis-Honeywell.
>
> have specifically authorized the use of this material in whole or in part, in the COBOL specifications. Such authorization extends to the reproduction and use of COBOL specifications in programming manuals or similar publications.
>
> This complete USA Standard edition of COBOL may not be reproduced without permission of the USA Standards Institute.

In every COBOL program there are four divisions. The first is the *identification division*. It must include the program name, and it may include other information for documentation purposes. The second is called the *environment division*. It specifies the kind of computer. It also lists the I/O files that the program will use and associates their internal name to an external name:

```
SELECT MARY ASSIGN TO UT-S-ANN
```

†*American National Standard COBOL* X3.23-1968 New York: American National Standards Institute, Inc. (1968).

means that internal name MARY refers to the utility sequential data set ANN. (In the IBM/360–370 system, ANN is the so-called dd-name.)

The third division is the *data division*, which gives further information about each file. COBOL I/O is like PL/I record I/O (or perhaps we should say PL/I record I/O is like COBOL I/O because COBOL is an ancestor of PL/I). No conversion is done while reading. The record format is described by a data structure, and the data record structures, and, in fact, all variables, are declared in the data division. *All variables must be declared* and all are given a level number. Ordinary variables used as intermediate values in computations are ordinarily given the level number 77. All variables are declared with pictures, which are much the same as pictures in PL/I.

The actual computation is described in the *procedure division*. The program is divided into paragraphs with names starting in column 8. Other lines start in column 12. The only complicated statement is PERFORM, which is a kind of combination of PL/I DO and CALL. PERFORM P means to do all the statements in paragraph P and then proceed to the next statement after the PERFORM statement. A paragraph P may be either called as a subroutine by a PERFORM statement or executed as an ordinary program by entering in the normal manner in sequence or by GO TO P. In addition, the PERFORM may specify multiple executions of a paragraph.

Another unique feature of COBOL, designed to make the procedure division easy to read, is the condition name. Under the declaration of an item there may be an item with an 88 level number and a clause giving a value:

```
02 X PICTURE 99.

    88 Y VALUE IS 17.
```

Here Y is a condition name, and in the procedure section, writing

```
IF Y PERFORM A
```

is an abbreviation for

```
IF X IS EQUAL TO 17 PERFORM A
```

that is, Y is a name given to the condition X IS EQUAL TO 17.

One of the principal objectives of COBOL language design was to make the program readable and understandable, even to a non-programmer. This was achieved to a remarkable degree. If the programmer uses suggestive names, for example, RATE-OF-PAY, GROSS-SALARY, etc., for variables, takes some care to organize the program simply and clearly, and keypunches it neatly with good comments, the program can be remarkably easy to understand. Writing a correct COBOL program is another matter, for although a correct program is easy to read, the rules for constructing a correct program are not simple. In the next section we will look at two program examples, satisfying ourselves with understanding what they do and what COBOL looks like. Then, in the following section, we will study COBOL syntax and meaning more deeply. You will probably want to study the examples again after you have read the entire chapter.

COBOL Examples

The same two examples as were studied in Chapter 6 are presented here, written in COBOL, but the problem description will not be repeated here in detail. The first program is an on-line data entry and inquiry system for stocks. A person enters a transaction code and a three-letter stock name abbreviation. If it is data entry, the data follow. The computer then replies with either the requested data or a confirmation for data entry.

Here is an example, run with the COBOL program, using the same disc master file as was used with the PL/I program immediately after the run shown in Chapter 6.

```
STOCK DATA SYSTEM READY
qghb
GHB  46
yghb
GHB QUARTERLY DIVIDEND  $0.95 YIELD  8.3%
noma
OMA OUTRIGGER MARINE, INC.--RETAIL BOATS & SUPPLIES
qoma
OMA  52 1/2
yoma
OMA QUARTERLY DIVIDEND  $1.20 YIELD  9.1%
yfbn
FBN QUARTERLY DIVIDEND  $0.04 YIELD  5.6%
qdmt
DMT  35 3/8
qoir
OIR  76 1/4
ecpfcentral pacific financial corp.--real estate
CPF CENTRAL PACIFIC FINANCIAL CORP.--REAL ESTATE
pcpf8 6
CPF 806
pcpf008 6
CPF    8 3/4
dcpf0025
CPF QUARTERLY DIVIDEND  $0.25 YIELD 11.4%
poma053 5
OMA  53 5/8
dghb0105
GHB QUARTERLY DIVIDEND  $1.05 YIELD  9.1%
```

```
qcpf
CPF   8 3/4
ycpf
CPF QUARTERLY DIVIDEND  $0.25 YIELD 11.4%
qfbn
FBN   2 7/8
```

In the program, the name of the variable used as a key in the random-access file search is specified in the sentence about that file in the file-control section of the environment division. The variable itself is declared in the working-storage section of the data division. It includes the key and a number zero, that number indicating that the search is to be begun at the beginning of the file for every record, just as was done in the PL/I program. Again, for a large file, this would be inefficient, and a more sophisticated method, such as "hashed addressing," should be used, but it, however, is beyond the scope of this book.†

The program with its comments should be adequately self-explanatory for our present purposes. I suggest that for this chapter also you read the two programs, study the rest of the chapter, and then read the programs once again after you have better knowledge of COBOL.

```
IDENTIFICATION DIVISION.
PROGRAM-ID.  STOCK.
REMARKS.
        THIS IS A PROGRAM FOR AN ON-LINE STOCK  DATA  BANK  AND
    INQUIRY SYSTEM.  "STKLIST" IS A RANDOM-ACCESS FILE IN  WHICH
    THE THREE-LETTER COMPANY ABBREVIATION CODE, COMPANY NAME AND
    BRIEF DESCRIPTION,  LATEST  PRICE,   AND  CURRENT  QUARTERLY
    DIVIDEND RATE ARE STORED.  "IN" AND "OUT" BOTH REFER TO  THE
    TERMINAL FROM  WHICH  THE  INFORMATION  CAN  BE  ENTERED  OR
    INQUIRIES MADE.  TERMINAL INPUT INFORMATION HAS A ONE-LETTER
    TRANSACTION TYPE FOLLOWED BY  A  THREE-LETTER  COMPANY  CODE
    FOLLOWED BY OTHER DATA IF DATA IS BEING ENTERED.  THE  TYPES
    ARE
        E NEW ENTRY--COMPANY NAME AND BRIEF DESCRIPTION
        N INQUIRY--NAME AND DESCRIPTION
        P DATA ENTRY--PRICE ENTERED AS DOLLARS AND EIGHTHS (TWO
    INTEGERS)
        Q INQUIRY--PRICE
        D DATA ENTRY--QUARTERLY DIVIDEND ENTERED AS  A  DECIMAL
    NUMBER
        Y INQUIRY--DIVIDEND AND PERCENT YIELD

        THE "EDATA",  "PDATA",  AND  "DDATA"  DATA  STRUCTURES,
    BEING DATA RECORDS FOR THE SAME FILE "DATAIN",  OCCUPY  THE
    SAME PLACE IN MEMORY BUT DESCRIBE  THREE  DIFFERENT  FORMATS
    FOR THE THREE DIFFERENT KINDS OF DATA THAT MAY COME IN.  THE
    TYPE AND THREE-LETTER COMPANY CODE OCCUPY THE SAME PLACE FOR
    ALL THREE,  AND ARE DECLARED,  THEREFORE,  IN "EDATA"  ONLY.
```

†An excellent reference is Donald E. Knuth, *Sorting and Searching*, Vol. 3 of *The Art of Computer Programming*, Reading, Mass.: Addison-Wesley Publishing Co. (1973).

```
    SIMILARLY NPRT, QPRT, AND YPRT ARE THREE STRUCTURES DEFINING
    THREE OUTPUT FORMATS,  WHICH ALSO OCCUPY THE SAME PLACE, AND
    THUS PCODE,  THE THREE-LETTER CODE,  IS DECLARED ONLY IN THE
    FIRST.
         IN WORKING STORAGE, "TEMP1" AND "TEMP2" ARE USED IN THE
    YIELD CALCULATION.  "STOCK-KEY" IS THE RECORD  KEY  USED  IN
    SEARCHING THE DISC FILE.  THE ZERO WITH  IT  INDICATES  THAT
    EVERY SEARCH IS TO START AT THE BEGINNING OF  THE  FILE,   A
    SYSTEM TOO SIMPLE AND SLOW FOR A PRACTICAL LARGE SYSTEM.

ENVIRONMENT DIVISION.
CONFIGURATION SECTION.
SOURCE-COMPUTER. IBM-360-J65.
OBJECT-COMPUTER. IBM-360-J65.

INPUT-OUTPUT SECTION.
FILE-CONTROL.
    SELECT DATAIN ASSIGN TO UT-S-DATAIN.
    SELECT PRTR ASSIGN TO UT-S-PRTR.
    SELECT STKLIST ASSIGN TO DA-D-STKLIST
        ACCESS IS RANDOM
        ACTUAL KEY IS STOCK-KEY.

DATA DIVISION.
FILE SECTION.
FD  DATAIN
    LABEL RECORD IS OMITTED
    RECORDING MODE IS U
    DATA RECORDS ARE EDATA PDATA DDATA.
01  EDATA.
    02 INTYPE PICTURE A.
        88 NEW-ENTRY       VALUE IS 'E'.
        88 PRICE-ENTRY     VALUE IS 'P'.
        88 DIVIDEND-ENTRY VALUE IS 'D'.
        88 NAME-INQUIRY    VALUE IS 'N'.
        88 QUOTE-INQUIRY   VALUE IS 'Q'.
        88 YIELD-INQUIRY   VALUE IS 'Y'.
    02 INCODE PICTURE AAA.
    02 INDESC PICTURE X(48).
01  PDATA.
    02 FILLER PICTURE AAAA.
    02 INDOLLARS PICTURE 999.
    02 FILLER PICTURE X.
    02 INEIGHTHS PICTURE 9.
01  DDATA.
    02 FILLER PICTURE AAAA.
    02 INDIVIDEND PICTURE 99V99.

FD  STKLIST
    LABEL RECORDS ARE STANDARD
    DATA RECORD IS STOCKDATA.
01  STOCKDATA.
    02 DESC PICTURE X(48).
```

```
    02 PRICE.
        03 DOLLARS PICTURE 999.
        03 EIGHTHS PICTURE 9.
    02 DIVIDEND PICTURE 99V99.

FD  PRTR
    LABEL RECORDS ARE OMITTED
    DATA RECORDS ARE NPRT YPRT QPRT.
01  NPRT.
    02 PCODE PICTURE AAA.
    02 B1 PICTURE X.
    02 PDESC PICTURE X(48).
01  QPRT.
    02 FILLER PICTURE AAAA.
    02 PDOLLARS PICTURE ZZ9.
    02 PEIGHTHS PICTURE XXXX.
    02 B2 PICTURE X(37).
01  YPRT.
    02 FILLER PICTURE AAAA.
    02 T1 PICTURE A(19).
    02 PDIVIDEND PICTURE $$9.99.
    02 T2 PICTURE A(7).
    02 YIELD PICTURE Z9.9.
    02 T3 PICTURE X.
    02 B3 PICTURE X(7).

WORKING-STORAGE SECTION.
77  STARTMSG PICTURE X(52) VALUE IS 'STOCK DATA SYSTEM READY'.
77  TEMP1 PICTURE 9999V9999 USAGE IS COMPUTATIONAL.
77  TEMP2 PICTURE 9999V9999 USAGE IS COMPUTATIONAL.
01  STOCK-KEY.
    02 TRACK-NO PICTURE 99999
        USAGE IS COMPUTATIONAL  VALUE IS ZERO.
    02 KEY-CODE PICTURE AAA.


PROCEDURE DIVISION.

    OPEN I-O STKLIST.
    OPEN INPUT DATAIN.
    OPEN OUTPUT PRTR.

    WRITE NPRT FROM STARTMSG.

MAIN-LOOP.
    MOVE SPACES TO INDESC. NOTE IN CASE OF SHORT INPUT LINE.
    READ DATAIN AT END STOP RUN.

    IF INTYPE = 'S' AND INCODE = 'TOP' STOP RUN.
       NOTE  OPERATOR TYPED 'STOP'.

    MOVE INCODE TO KEY-CODE.

    NOTE  NEXT STATEMENTS HANDLE NEW ENTRY.
```

```
    IF NEW-ENTRY MOVE ZEROS TO DOLLARS EIGHTHS DIVIDEND
        MOVE INDESC TO DESC
        WRITE STOCKDATA INVALID KEY PERFORM NO-SPACE

    ELSE READ STKLIST INVALID KEY PERFORM NO-DATA.

    NOTE  NEXT STATEMENTS HANDLE OTHER DATA ENTRY.

    IF PRICE-ENTRY MOVE INDOLLARS TO DOLLARS
        MOVE INEIGHTHS TO EIGHTHS.

    IF DIVIDEND-ENTRY MOVE INDIVIDEND TO DIVIDEND.

    NOTE  NEXT STATEMENTS PRINT INQUIRY OR CONFIRMATION DATA.

    IF PRICE-ENTRY OR DIVIDEND-ENTRY
        WRITE STOCKDATA INVALID KEY PERFORM NO-SPACE.

    MOVE INCODE TO PCODE.
    MOVE SPACES TO B1.

    IF QUOTE-INQUIRY OR PRICE-ENTRY
        MOVE DOLLARS TO PDOLLARS
        MOVE SPACES TO B2
        PERFORM MOVE-EIGHTHS
        WRITE QPRT

    ELSE IF YIELD-INQUIRY OR DIVIDEND-ENTRY
        MULTIPLY DIVIDEND BY 4 GIVING TEMP1
        MULTIPLY 100 BY TEMP1
        DIVIDE 8 INTO EIGHTHS GIVING TEMP2
        ADD DOLLARS TO TEMP2
        DIVIDE TEMP1 BY TEMP2 GIVING YIELD ROUNDED
        MOVE DIVIDEND TO PDIVIDEND
        MOVE 'QUARTERLY DIVIDEND ' TO T1
        MOVE ' YIELD ' TO T2
        MOVE '%' TO T3
        MOVE SPACES TO B3
        WRITE YPRT

    ELSE IF NAME-INQUIRY OR NEW-ENTRY
        MOVE DESC TO PDESC
        WRITE NPRT

    ELSE MOVE 'INVALID CODE' TO PDESC
       WRITE NPRT.

    GO TO MAIN-LOOP.

MOVE-EIGHTHS.
        IF EIGHTHS = 0 MOVE SPACES TO PEIGHTHS
        ELSE IF EIGHTHS = 1 MOVE ' 1/8' TO PEIGHTHS
        ELSE IF EIGHTHS = 2 MOVE ' 1/4' TO PEIGHTHS
        ELSE IF EIGHTHS = 3 MOVE ' 3/8' TO PEIGHTHS
```

```
        ELSE IF EIGHTHS = 4 MOVE ' 1/2' TO PEIGHTHS
        ELSE IF EIGHTHS = 5 MOVE ' 5/8' TO PEIGHTHS
        ELSE IF EIGHTHS = 6 MOVE ' 3/4' TO PEIGHTHS
        ELSE MOVE ' 7/8' TO PEIGHTHS.
NO-DATA.
    MOVE 'NO INFORMATION AVAILABLE FOR THIS CODE.' TO DESC.
    MOVE 'N' TO INTYPE.

NO-SPACE.
    MOVE 'NO MORE SPACE AVAILABLE IN FILE.' TO DESC.
    MOVE 'N' TO INTYPE.
```

The second example is the program for keeping records of students' scores on homework and tests. This program is completely compatible with the corresponding PL/I program; the same transaction cards can be used, and either program can use the master file produced by the other. The reports are almost identical. Here is a third-week's run using the master file produced by the PL/I program in the runs shown in Chapter 6.

```
TRANSACTION INPUT CARDS FOR THIRD RUN:


105-58-3583A0390CHANG, ELEANOR          EXCELLENT WORK
105-66-6566C    BRECK, DONNA MAE
113-27-1520A0585ADAMSON, LAURENCE       GOOD
202-36-8231A0480KIM, HENRY
749-26-7457A0485AKAKA, MEILANI
749-26-7457A04MLAKAKA, MEILANI
749-26-7457Z0482AKAKA, MEILANI
919-02-2513C    ENDERSON, MILES
929-75-IIJOA0239JOHNSON, J. J.
```

```
LIST OF TRANSACTIONS

NAME                SSNO           TYPE      PROB#-GRADE-REMARKS


CHANG, ELEANOR      105-58-3583  UPDATE      3   90 EXCELLENT WORK
BRECK, DONNA MAE    105-66-6566  DELETION           SSNO NOT FOUND
ADAMSON, LAURENCE   113-27-1520  UPDATE      5   85 GOOD
KIM, HENRY          202-36-8231  UPDATE      4   80
AKAKA, MEILANI      749-26-7457  UPDATE      4   85
AKAKA, MEILANI      749-26-7457  UPDATE      4   85 BAD SSNO OR DATA
AKAKA, MEILANI      749-26-7457  INVALID     4   82
ENDERSON, MILES     919-02-2513  DELETION
JOHNSON, J. J.      929-75-IIJO  UPDATE             BAD SSNO OR DATA
```

STATUS REPORT

NAME	SSNO	TOTAL	1	2	3	4	5
CHANG, ELEANOR	105-58-3583	237	57	90	90		
ADAMSON, LAURENCE	113-27-1520	393	75	86	67	80	85
OSAKI, KENNETH	132-00-5230	294	69	65	85	75	
WONG, DIANA	147-12-6431	70	70				
KIM, HENRY	202-36-8231	305	45	90	90	80	
EL DIEZ, ANNA	513-29-8314	232	69	88	75		
AKAKA, MEILANI	749-26-7457	254	92	77		85	
NUMBER OF STUDENTS		7	7	6	5	4	1
AVERAGES		255.0	68.1	82.6	81.4	80.0	85.0

Here is a partial listing of information printed by DISPLAY statements for debugging purposes:

```
TRANSACTION READ
MASTER READ
CHECK  105-58-3583 * 999-99-9999 * 105-58-3583
PRINT REPORT LINE
MASTER READ
CHECK  105-58-3583 * 105-58-3583 * 113-27-1520
TRANSACTION READ
CHECK  105-66-6566 * 105-58-3583 * 113-27-1520
TRANSACTION READ
CHECK  113-27-1520 * 105-58-3583 * 113-27-1520
PRINT REPORT LINE
MASTER READ
CHECK  113-27-1520 * 113-27-1520 * 132-00-5230
TRANSACTION READ
CHECK  202-36-8231 * 113-27-1520 * 132-00-5230
PRINT REPORT LINE
MASTER READ
CHECK  202-36-8231 * 132-00-5230 * 147-12-6431
PRINT REPORT LINE
MASTER READ
CHECK  202-36-8231 * 147-12-6431 * 202-36-8231
PRINT REPORT LINE
MASTER READ
CHECK  202-36-8231 * 202-36-8231 * 513-29-8314
TRANSACTION READ
```

The program listing, with its comments, should be self-explanatory. Note that condition names and the PERFORM statement play an important part in the way the program logic is implemented.

```
IDENTIFICATION DIVISION.
PROGRAM-ID. 'GRADES'.
REMARKS.
        THIS IS  A  PROGRAM  FOR  BATCH-PROCESSING  RECORDS  OF
    STUDENT HOMEWORK AND TEST SCORES. IT UPDATES THE INFORMATION
    IN "OLDMAST" PRODUCING A NEW FILE  "NEWMAST",  USING  INPUT
    DATA FROM FILE "TRANS".  EACH  FILE  IS  SORTED  BY  SOCIAL
    SECURITY NUMBER.  TWO  REPORTS  ARE  PRODUCED,  A  LIST  OF
    TRANSACTIONS, "TRLIST", AND A STATUS REPORT "MREPORT", WHICH
    INCLUDES THE NUMBER OF STUDENTS AND AVERAGE GRADE,  OVERALL
    AND FOR EACH ASSIGNMENT.  BESIDES THE OBVIOUS INFORMATION, A
    TRANSACTION DATA CARD MAY CARRY A REMARK,  WHICH IS  PRINTED
    AS "REMARKA" IN THE  TRANSACTION  REPORT.  "REMARKB"  THERE
    HOLDS ERROR MESSAGES
        "MASTER-RECORD" IS THE MASTER RECORD  BEING  PROCESSED,
    AND "NEXT-RECORD" IS THE NEXT MASTER RECORD TO BE PROCESSED.
    "TRANSACTION"  IS  THE  TRANSACTION  DATA  INPUT  RECORD,
    "TRANSACTION-REPORT"  ONE  LINE  IN  THE  TRANSACTION  LIST
    REPORT,  "REPORT" A USUAL LINE IN THE  STATUS  REPORT,  AND
    "AVERAGES" THE LAST  LINE  IN  THAT  REPORT,  WHICH  HAS  A
    DIFFERENT FORMAT BECAUSE THE NUMBERS ARE NOT INTEGERS.

        THE TRANSACTION CODES ARE

        A UPDATE--ENTER ONE SCORE IN THE MASTER FILE

        B INSERT A NEW STUDENT'S RECORD

        C DELETE A STUDENT'S RECORD

        "HEAD1",  "HEAD2",  "HEAD3",  AND "HEAD4" ARE USED  FOR
    HEADINGS.  FOR THE PURPOSES OF  KEEPING  THE  PROGRAM  LOGIC
    SIMPLE AND CLEAR, "TRUE" IS ASSIGNED THE VALUE 1, "FALSE" 0,
    AND THESE VALUES ARE ASSIGNED TO VARIABLES THAT  KEEP  TRACK
    OF CERTAIN CONDITIONS.  THUS DELETE" IS SET TRUE WHEN IT  IS
    FOUND  THAT  THE  "MASTER-RECORD"  SHOULD  BE  DELETED.
    "END-TRANSACTIONS" AND "END-MASTER" ARE SET TRUE ON  END  OF
    FILE IN EACH CASE. NOTE THE USE OF CONDITION NAMES (LEVEL 88
    ENTRIES) WITH THESE VARIABLES.  "TEMPTOTAL",  "TEMP",  AND I
    ARE USED  IN  CALCULATING  THE  INDIVIDUAL  STUDENT'S  TOTAL
    SCORE.  "PROBLEM-COUNT", "PROBLEM-TOTAL", "TOTAL-COUNT", AND
    "GRAND-TOTAL" ARE TABULATIONS  OF  NUMBER  OF  STUDENTS  AND
    TOTAL SCORES ON EACH ASSIGNMENT  AND  ALTOGETHER,  FOR  THE
    SUMMARY AND AVERAGES IN THE STATUS REPORT.

ENVIRONMENT DIVISION.
CONFIGURATION SECTION.
SOURCE-COMPUTER. IBM-360-J65.
OBJECT-COMPUTER. IBM-360-J65.
SPECIAL-NAMES.
    C01 IS NEWPAGE.
```

```
INPUT-OUTPUT SECTION.
FILE-CONTROL.
    SELECT TRANS        ASSIGN UT-S-TRANS.
    SELECT OLDMAST      ASSIGN UT-S-OLDMAST.
    SELECT NEWMAST      ASSIGN UT-S-NEWMAST.
    SELECT TRLIST       ASSIGN UT-S-TRLIST.
    SELECT MREPORT      ASSIGN UT-S-MREPORT.
DATA DIVISION.
FILE SECTION.
FD  TRANS
    LABEL RECORD IS OMITTED
    DATA RECORD IS TRANSACTION.

01  TRANSACTION.
    02 SSNO.
       03 N1 PICTURE 999.
       03 D1 PICTURE X.
       03 N2 PICTURE 99.
       03 D2 PICTURE X.
       03 N3 PICTURE 9999.
    02 TRANSACTION-CODE PICTURE A.
       88 UPDATE VALUE IS 'A'.
       88 INSERTION VALUE IS 'B'.
       88 DELETION VALUE IS 'C'.
    02 PROBLEM-NUMBER PICTURE 99.
    02 GRADE PICTURE 99.
    02 NAME PICTURE X(24).
    02 REMARK PICTURE X(40).

FD  OLDMAST
    LABEL RECORD IS OMITTED
    DATA RECORD IS NEXT-RECORD.

01  NEXT-RECORD.
    02 SSNO PICTURE X(11).
    02 NAME PICTURE X(24).
    02 SCORES OCCURS 15 TIMES PICTURE 999.

FD  NEWMAST
    LABEL RECORD IS OMITTED
    DATA RECORD IS MASTER-RECORD.

01  MASTER-RECORD.
    02 SSNO PICTURE X(11).
    02 NAME PICTURE X(24).
    02 SCORES OCCURS 15 TIMES PICTURE 999.

FD  TRLIST
    LABEL RECORD IS OMITTED
    DATA RECORD IS TRANSACTION-REPORT.

01  TRANSACTION-REPORT.
    02 CARRIAGE-CONTROL PICTURE X.
    02 NAME PICTURE X(20).
```

```
     02 SSNO PICTURE X(11).
     02 FILLER PICTURE XX.
     02 TRANSACTION-TYPE PICTURE X(9).
     02 PROBLEM-NUMBER PICTURE ZZZ.
     02 GRADE PICTURE ZZZZ.
     02 FILLER PICTURE X.
     02 REMARK PICTURE X(20).
FD   MREPORT
     LABEL RECORD IS OMITTED
     DATA RECORDS ARE REPORT-LINE AVERAGES.

01   REPORT-LINE.
     02 CARRIAGE-CONTROL PICTURE X.
     02 NAME PICTURE X(20).
     02 SSNO PICTURE X(11).
     02 TOTAL PICTURE ZZZZ9.
     02 FILLER PICTURE X(2).
     02 S OCCURS 15 TIMES.
        03 SCORES PICTURE ZZZZ.
        03 FILLER PICTURE XX.

01   AVERAGES.
     02 CARRIAGE-CONTROL PICTURE X.
     02 TITLE PICTURE X(31).
     02 TOTAL PICTURE ZZZZZ.Z.
     02 AVERAGE PICTURE ZZZZ.Z OCCURS 15 TIMES.

WORKING-STORAGE SECTION.
77   HEAD1 PICTURE X(15) VALUE IS ' STATUS REPORT'.
77   HEAD3 PICTURE X(25) VALUE IS ' LIST OF TRANSACTIONS'.
77   HEAD4 PICTURE X(100) VALUE IS ' NAME                          SSNO
-    '      TYPE    PROB#-GRADE-REMARKS'.
77   TRUE PICTURE 9 VALUE IS 1.
77   FALSE PICTURE 9 VALUE IS 0.
77   END-TRANSACTIONS PICTURE 9 VALUE IS ZERO.
     88 END-OF-TRANSACTIONS VALUE IS 1.
77   END-MASTER PICTURE 9 VALUE IS 0.
     88 END-OF-MASTER VALUE IS 1.
77   RECORD-DELETE PICTURE 9 VALUE IS 0.
     88 DELETE-RECORD VALUE IS 1.
77   BAD PICTURE 9 VALUE IS 0.
     88 BAD-DATA VALUE IS 1.
     88 GOOD-DATA VALUE IS 0.
77   TEMP PICTURE 999999 USAGE IS COMPUTATIONAL.
77   TEMPTOTAL PICTURE 999999 USAGE IS COMPUTATIONAL.
77   TOTAL-COUNT PICTURE 9(5) USAGE IS COMPUTATIONAL.
77   GRAND-TOTAL PICTURE 9(5) USAGE IS COMPUTATIONAL.
77   I PICTURE 9(5) USAGE IS COMPUTATIONAL.
01   T.
     02 PROBLEM-COUNT OCCURS 15 TIMES PICTURE 9(5)
        USAGE IS COMPUTATIONAL.
     02 PROBLEM-TOTAL OCCURS 15 TIMES PICTURE 9(5)
        USAGE IS COMPUTATIONAL.
```

```
01  HEAD2.
    02 A PICTURE X(44) VALUE IS
    ' NAME                    SSNO         TOTAL     1 '.
    02 B PICTURE X(44) VALUE IS
    '    2     3     4     5     6     7     8   '.
    02 C PICTURE X(45) VALUE IS
    ' 9     10    11    12    13    14    15       '.

PROCEDURE DIVISION.

INITIALIZATION.

    OPEN INPUT TRANS
    OPEN INPUT OLDMAST
    OPEN OUTPUT NEWMAST
    OPEN OUTPUT TRLIST
    OPEN OUTPUT MREPORT.

    WRITE REPORT-LINE FROM HEAD1 AFTER ADVANCING NEWPAGE.
    WRITE REPORT-LINE FROM HEAD2 AFTER ADVANCING 2 LINES
    MOVE SPACES TO REPORT-LINE
    WRITE REPORT-LINE AFTER ADVANCING 1 LINES.

    WRITE TRANSACTION-REPORT FROM HEAD3 AFTER ADVANCING NEWPAGE
    WRITE TRANSACTION-REPORT FROM HEAD4 AFTER ADVANCING 2 LINES
    MOVE SPACES TO TRANSACTION-REPORT
    WRITE TRANSACTION-REPORT AFTER ADVANCING 1 LINES.

    MOVE ZEROS TO TOTAL-COUNT GRAND-TOTAL
    PERFORM TOTAL-ZEROING VARYING I FROM 1 BY 1
       UNTIL I IS GREATER THAN 15.

    PERFORM TRANSACTION-READ
    PERFORM MASTER-READ
    MOVE '999-99-9999' TO SSNO IN MASTER-RECORD.
    NOTE  SEE NOTE ABOUT 999-99-9999 IN PRINT-REPORT-LINE.

MERGE-LOOP-NOTE.
    NOTE NOW ONE TRANSACTION RECORD AND ONE MASTER RECORD ARE IN
    MEMORY, AND WE MAY START THE MAIN LOOP.

         IF THE TRANSACTION IS AN INSERTION, IT MUST BE INSERTED
    BETWEEN THE CORRECT TWO RECORDS,  WHICH MEANS JUST IN  FRONT
    OF THE FIRST MASTER RECORD WITH A HIGHER  SSNO.   HENCE  THE
    FOLLOWING LOGIC:

         IF THE SSNO OF THE NEXT RECORD IS EQUAL TO OR LESS THAN
    THE SSNO OF THE TRANSACTION,   WE  MUST  WRITE  THE  PRESENT
    MASTER RECORD,  WRITE A REPORT LINE,  MOVE "NEXT-RECORD"  TO
    "MASTER-RECORD",  AND READ A NEW "NEXT-RECORD". OTHERWISE WE
    PROCESS THE TRANSACTION.

MAIN-PROCESSING.
    PERFORM MERGE-LOOP UNTIL END-OF-TRANSACTIONS AND
       END-OF-MASTER.
```

```
FINAL-SUMMARY.
    DISPLAY 'FINAL SUMMARY'
    PERFORM PRINT-REPORT-LINE
    MOVE 'NUMBER OF STUDENTS' TO NAME IN REPORT-LINE
    MOVE SPACES TO SSNO IN REPORT-LINE
    MOVE TOTAL-COUNT TO TOTAL IN REPORT-LINE
    PERFORM COUNT-MOVE VARYING I FROM 1 BY 1 UNTIL I IS GREATER
       THAN 15
    WRITE REPORT-LINE AFTER ADVANCING 2 LINES
    DIVIDE GRAND-TOTAL BY TOTAL-COUNT GIVING TOTAL IN AVERAGES
    PERFORM AVERAGE-CALCULATION VARYING I FROM 1 BY 1
       UNTIL I IS GREATER THAN 15
    MOVE 'AVERAGES' TO TITLE
    WRITE REPORT-LINE AFTER ADVANCING 2 LINES
    STOP RUN.
TOTAL-ZEROING.
    MOVE ZEROS TO PROBLEM-COUNT (I) PROBLEM-TOTAL (I).

COUNT-MOVE.
    MOVE PROBLEM-COUNT (I) TO SCORES IN REPORT-LINE (I).

AVERAGE-CALCULATION.
    IF PROBLEM-COUNT (I) IS GREATER THAN ZERO
       DIVIDE PROBLEM-TOTAL (I) BY PROBLEM-COUNT (I)
       GIVING AVERAGE (I)
    ELSE MOVE ZEROS TO AVERAGE (I).

TRANSACTION-READ.
    DISPLAY 'TRANSACTION READ'
    READ TRANS AT END MOVE TRUE TO END-TRANSACTIONS.
    MOVE SSNO IN TRANSACTION TO SSNO IN TRANSACTION-REPORT
    MOVE NAME IN TRANSACTION TO NAME IN TRANSACTION-REPORT
    MOVE REMARK IN TRANSACTION TO REMARK IN TRANSACTION-REPORT
    MOVE FALSE TO BAD
    IF N1 IS NOT NUMERIC OR N2 IS NOT NUMERIC OR N3 IS NOT
       NUMERIC OR UPDATE AND (PROBLEM-NUMBER IN TRANSACTION
       IS NOT NUMERIC OR GRADE IN TRANSACTION IS NOT NUMERIC)
       MOVE 'BAD SSNO OR DATA' TO REMARK IN TRANSACTION-REPORT
       MOVE TRUE TO BAD
    ELSE MOVE PROBLEM-NUMBER IN TRANSACTION TO PROBLEM-NUMBER
       IN TRANSACTION-REPORT
       MOVE GRADE IN TRANSACTION TO GRADE IN TRANSACTION-REPORT.
    IF UPDATE MOVE 'UPDATE' TO TRANSACTION-TYPE
    ELSE IF INSERTION MOVE 'INSERTION' TO TRANSACTION-TYPE
    ELSE IF DELETION MOVE 'DELETION' TO TRANSACTION-TYPE
    ELSE MOVE 'INVALID' TO TRANSACTION-TYPE
       MOVE TRUE TO BAD.
    MOVE '-' TO D1 D2.
MASTER-READ.
    DISPLAY 'MASTER READ'
    READ OLDMAST AT END MOVE TRUE TO END-MASTER
       MOVE '999-99-9999' TO SSNO IN NEXT-RECORD.
       NOTE THIS MOVE IS DONE ONLY IF END OF FILE--ALSO
       SEE NOTE ABOUT 999-99-9999 IN PRINT-REPORT-LINE.
```

```
MERGE-LOOP.
    DISPLAY 'CHECK  ' SSNO IN TRANSACTION ' * ' SSNO
       IN MASTER-RECORD ' * ' SSNO IN NEXT-RECORD.
       NOTE FOR DEBUGGING PURPOSES.

    IF SSNO IN TRANSACTION IS LESS THAN SSNO IN NEXT-RECORD
       AND GOOD-DATA
       IF SSNO IN TRANSACTION IS EQUAL TO SSNO IN MASTER-RECORD
          IF UPDATE MOVE GRADE IN TRANSACTION TO SCORES IN
             MASTER-RECORD (PROBLEM-NUMBER IN TRANSACTION)
          ELSE IF INSERTION MOVE 'DUPLICATE SSNO' TO
             REMARK IN TRANSACTION-REPORT
          ELSE IF DELETION MOVE TRUE TO RECORD-DELETE
          ELSE NEXT SENTENCE
       ELSE IF INSERTION PERFORM PRINT-REPORT-LINE
          MOVE SSNO IN TRANSACTION TO SSNO IN MASTER-RECORD
          MOVE NAME IN TRANSACTION TO NAME IN MASTER-RECORD
          PERFORM SCORE-ZEROING VARYING I FROM 1 BY 1
             UNTIL I IS GREATER THAN 15
       ELSE MOVE 'SSNO NOT FOUND' TO REMARK IN
          TRANSACTION-REPORT.

    IF SSNO IN TRANSACTION IS LESS THAN SSNO IN NEXT-RECORD
       AND NOT END-OF-TRANSACTIONS
       WRITE TRANSACTION-REPORT AFTER ADVANCING 1 LINES
       PERFORM TRANSACTION-READ

    ELSE PERFORM PRINT-REPORT-LINE
       MOVE NEXT-RECORD TO MASTER-RECORD
       IF NOT END-OF-MASTER PERFORM MASTER-READ.

    NOTE THIS NEXT PARAGRAPH WRITES  A  NEW  MASTER  RECORD  AND
    PRINTS A STATUS REPORT LINE AND DOES THE  TABULATION.  NOTE
    THAT IF "DELETE" IS TRUE OR SSNO='999-99-9999',  THE  MASTER
    RECORD AND REPORT LINE SIMPLY  ARE  NOT  WRITTEN.  NOTE THAT
    WHENEVER "MASTER-RECORD" OR "NEXT-RECORD" DOES  NOT  CONTAIN
    A REAL RECORD, THE SSNO IS SET TO 999-99-9999.

PRINT-REPORT-LINE.
    DISPLAY 'PRINT REPORT LINE'
    IF NOT DELETE-RECORD AND SSNO IN MASTER-RECORD IS NOT
       EQUAL TO '999-99-9999'
       MOVE SSNO IN MASTER-RECORD TO SSNO IN REPORT-LINE
       MOVE NAME IN MASTER-RECORD TO NAME IN REPORT-LINE
       MOVE ZEROS TO TEMP TEMPTOTAL
       PERFORM SUMMING VARYING I FROM 1 BY 1
          UNTIL I IS GREATER THAN 15
       ADD 1 TO TOTAL-COUNT
       ADD TEMPTOTAL TO GRAND-TOTAL
       MOVE TEMPTOTAL TO TOTAL IN REPORT-LINE
       WRITE REPORT-LINE AFTER ADVANCING 1 LINES
       WRITE MASTER-RECORD.
    MOVE FALSE TO RECORD-DELETE.
```

```
SUMMING.
    MOVE SCORES IN MASTER-RECORD (I) TO TEMP
       SCORES IN REPORT-LINE (I)
    IF TEMP IS NOT EQUAL TO ZERO
       ADD 1 TO PROBLEM-COUNT (I)
       ADD TEMP TO PROBLEM-TOTAL (I)
       ADD TEMP TO TEMPTOTAL.

SCORE-ZEROING.
    MOVE ZEROS TO SCORES IN MASTER-RECORD (I).
```

COBOL Language

COBOL uses the following 51 characters: the ten digits, 26 letters, space, the four arithmetic operators +, -, *, and /, and =, <, >, (,), ;, $, period, comma, and a quote mark. Although the specifications for ANSI COBOL call for the usual quote mark ", IBM uses the apostrophe ' in its place.

Words in COBOL are made up of from one to thirty letters or digits or hyphens, but they may not start or end with a hyphen. There are many reserved words. The reserved words of ANSI COBOL are listed in Table 7.1, but a given implementation may have additional reserved words. Reserved words cannot be used as variable names. Names must contain at least one letter to distinguish them from constants.

Space, comma, semicolon, quote mark, and parentheses are used for punctuation. The following rules apply:

1. Where punctuation is shown in the examples in this section, *it is required*.
2. A period, comma, or semicolon *must not* be preceded by a space but *must* be followed by a space.
3. There must not be a space just following a left parenthesis or just preceding a right parenthesis.
4. At least one space must separate any two words or parenthesized expressions.
5. An arithmetic operator must be surrounded by spaces.
6. Commas may separate a series of operands. Commas or semicolons may be used to separate a series of clauses. Semicolons may be used to separate a series of statements.

Numerical constants consist of from one to eighteen digits possibly containing a decimal point and possibly preceded by a minus sign. Character constants are enclosed in quotes. The words ZERO or ZEROS can be used to mean a numeric constant or a character-string constant of all zeros, depending on context. SPACES is a character-string constant.

TABLE 7.1. ANSI Standard COBOL Reserved Words

ACCEPT	ENDING	MEMORY	RF
ACCESS	ENTER	MODE	RH
ACTUAL	ENVIRONMENT	MODULES	RIGHT
ADD	EQUAL	MOVE	ROUNDED
ADDRESS	ERROR	MULTIPLE	RUN
ADVANCING	EVERY	MULTIPLY	SAME
AFTER	EXAMINE	NEGATIVE	SD
ALL	EXIT	NEXT	SEARCH
ALPHABETIC	FD	NO	SECTION
ALTER	FILE	NOT	SECURITY
ALTERNATE	FILE-CONTROL	NOTE	SEEK
AND	FILE-LIMIT	NUMBER	SEGMENT-LIMIT
ARE	FILE-LIMITS	NUMERIC	SELECT
AREA	FILLER	OBJECT-COMPUTER	SENTENCE
AREAS	FINAL	OCCURS	SEQUENTIAL
ASCENDING	FIRST	OF	SET
ASSIGN	FOOTING	OFF	SIGN
AT	FOR	OMITTED	SIZE
AUTHOR	FROM	ON	SORT
BEFORE	GENERATE	OPEN	SOURCE
BEGINNING	GIVING	OPTIONAL	SOURCE-COMPUTER
BLANK	GO	OR	SPACE
BLOCK	GREATER	OUTPUT	SPACES
BY	GROUP	PAGE	SPECIAL-NAMES
CF	HEADING	PAGE-COUNTER	STANDARD
CH	HIGH-VALUE	PERFORM	STATUS
CHARACTERS	HIGH-VALUES	PF	STOP
CLOCK-UNITS	I-O	PH	SUBTRACT
CLOSE	I-O-CONTROL	PIC	SUM
COBOL	IDENTIFICATION	PICTURE	SYNC
CODE	IF	PLUS	SYNCHRONIZED
COLUMN	IN	POSITION	TALLY
COMMA	INDEX	POSITIVE	TALLYING
COMP	INDEXED	PROCEDURE	TAPE
COMPUTATIONAL	INDICATE	PROCEED	TERMINATE
COMPUTE	INITIATE	PROCESSING	THAN
CONFIGURATION	INPUT	PROGRAM-ID	THROUGH } equivalent
CONTAINS	INPUT-OUTPUT	QUOTE	THRU } equivalent
CONTROL	INSTALLATION	QUOTES	TIMES
CONTROLS	INTO	RANDOM	TO
COPY	INVALID	RD	TYPE
CORR	IS	READ	UNIT
CORRESPONDING	JUST	RECORD	UNTIL
CURRENCY	JUSTIFIED	RECORDS	UP
DATA	KEY	REDEFINES	UPON
DATE-COMPILED	KEYS	REEL	USAGE
DATE-WRITTEN	LABEL	RELEASE	USE
DE	LAST	REMARKS	USING
DECIMAL-POINT	LEADING	RENAMES	VALUE
DECLARATIVES	LEFT	REPLACING	VALUES
DEPENDING	LESS	REPORT	VARYING
DESCENDING	LIMIT	REPORTING	WHEN
DETAIL	LIMITS	REPORTS	WITH
DISPLAY	LINE	RERUN	WORDS
DIVIDE	LINE-COUNTER	RESERVE	WORKING-STORAGE
DIVISION	LINES	RESET	WRITE
DOWN	LOCK	RETURN	ZERO
ELSE	LOW-VALUE	REVERSED	ZEROES
END	LOW-VALUES	REWIND	ZEROS

Pictures differ from the pictures defined for PL/I, although the concept is the same. The following are the most important pictures:

A Letter or space.
B Space.
S Indicates that the variable is signed. It must be the leftmost character in the picture, and it is not counted as a character position.
V Indicates the position of the assumed decimal point but does not indicate the presence of a period and, hence, is not counted as a character position.
X Any allowable character.
Z Leading zeros suppressed.
9 Digit, not a blank.
0 A zero to be inserted.
, A comma to be inserted.
. A period both to indicate the position of the decimal point and to be inserted in the character string. It is not permitted to have both a period and a V in one picture. The period is not permitted as the last character in a picture.
+, -, CR, DB These are used to show the sign of variable in its character-string representations. The + or - may be at the extreme right or left. CR or DB must be the rightmost two characters. Only one of the four is allowed. The + will be replaced by + or - depending on the sign of the numeric value. The others, -, CR, or DB, will be inserted if the value is negative or replaced by blanks if the value is positive.
$, *, +, - These are floating symbols that are used much as in PL/I, except that the + will cause either + or - to be printed, depending on the sign of the value.

In contrast to PL/I, repetition factors in COBOL are enclosed in parentheses and follow the picture character. Thus, 99999.99 and 9(5).9(2) represent the same picture.

Data represented by pictures are classified into the following five types. (It is important to know these types because there are rules, which appear later, governing which types may occur in arithmetic and move statements.)

1. An *alphabetic item* has a picture containing only the character A.

2. An *alphanumeric item* uses only the picture characters A, 9, and X, but it cannot be all A's or all 9's.

3. A *numeric item* has a picture consisting only of S, V, and 9's.

4. An *alphanumeric edited item* has a picture using only A, X, 9, B, and 0, but in order to distinguish it from other types it must have at least one of the following combinations: 0 and X, B and X, or 0 and A.

5. A *numeric edited item* is one whose picture contains only B, V, Z, 0, 9, *, +, -, CR, DB, $, comma, or period, but which contains something other than 9 and V.

Here are a few examples.

Picture	Type	Numeric Value	Character value
9999	Numeric	12	'0012'
S9999	Numeric	12	'001B' [1]
S9999	Numeric	−12	'001K' [1]
S99V99	Numeric	12.11	'121A' [1]
A(4)	Alphabetic	None	'ABCD'
X99A	Alphanumeric	None	'021B'
00XX	Alphanumeric edited	None	'005#' [2]
BBA9	Alphanumeric edited	None	' A7' [2]
99,999	Numeric edited	12345	'12,345'
99.999	Numeric edited	12	'12.000'
$$$$.99	Numeric edited	12	' $12.00'
ZZZZ.99	Numeric edited	0	' .00'
ZZZZ.ZZ	Numeric edited	0	' '

[1] The COBOL numeric picture S9999 must correspond to four characters on a card because the S is not counted. In practice, the sign is usually punched in the same column as the last digit. Note that the combination of two punches corresponds to a letter unless the digit is zero. Thus, + over 1 gives A, + over 2 gives B, . . . , + over 9 gives I, - over 1 gives J, - over 2 gives K, and - over 9 gives R. Internal codes may vary from this, but at least on IBM equipment, if a numeric picture with a sign is used for printed output, the letter is printed in the last digit position.

The practice of punching the sign over one digit is extremely common in data processing, and it is the usual practice in business data processing.

[2] The 0 and B are insertion characters. If '5#' is moved to a variable with the picture 00XX, the zeros are inserted, and the result is '005#'.

In the following, in syntax descriptions, reserved words appear in capital letters. Some reserved words are required, but others are optional. The required ones are underlined. The optional ones may be omitted with no change in meaning. Punctuation and operation symbols shown are required. Other syntactical units are shown in lower-case letters enclosed in < and >.

In keypunching COBOL programs, division headers, section names, paragraph names, and the highest level numbers of any structure start in column 8, and everything else starts in column 12. Continuation of statements simply starts in column 12. Blank cards may appear anywhere except before continuation cards. If a character-string constant must be continued, it is indicated by a minus sign in column 7, a quote mark in column 12, and it is assumed to follow immediately the last non-blank column on the preceding card.

The name of a paragraph starts in column 8 and is followed by a period followed by a space. A paragraph consists of one or more sentences starting in or after column 12 on the same card or the next card. The sentences end with periods.

Comments start with the key word NOTE. If that is the first word of a paragraph, then the whole paragraph is considered to be a comment. Otherwise it is only one sentence, i.e., to the first period. Note the possibility for a program bug: If you start a paragraph with a comment, following with COBOL statements, COBOL will think these statements are all comments.

The program starts with IDENTIFICATION DIVISION., which starts with the entry

```
PROGRAM-ID. <program name>.
```

The <program name> is a name enclosed in quotes. Nothing else is required, but optionally, any or all of the following may be included, in this order:

```
AUTHOR.
INSTALLATION.
DATE-WRITTEN.
DATE-COMPILED.
SECURITY.
REMARKS.
```

and each may be followed by a paragraph of information that serves as documentation only.

The second part of the program is the ENVIRONMENT DIVISION. Its first section is the CONFIGURATION SECTION, which contains two paragraphs,

```
SOURCE-COMPUTER.  source-computer entry.

OBJECT-COMPUTER.  object-computer entry.
```

describing the computer on which the program is being compiled and the computer on which it will be run, respectively. The exact form of the entry is implementation-dependent, of course. On the IBM COBOL compiler, these are treated as comments except when the programmer requests that the program be segmented because it is too large to fit in the computer, and omission is allowed. The configuration section may also contain a paragraph called SPECIAL-NAMES. This may include a sentence specifying that commas be used in place of periods as decimal points or that another character replace the dollar sign. It may also include an association of user-chosen names for certain machine- or implementation-dependent functions. For example, in the second example program, the sentence C01 IS NEWPAGE appears. In the IBM/360–370 COBOL, C01 means "skip to column 1 on the printer carriage control tape," which by convention means the start of a new page. We chose the name NEWPAGE for that function in our program.

The next section of the ENVIRONMENT DIVISION is the INPUT-OUTPUT SECTION. This contains a paragraph called FILE-CONTROL, which contains one sentence with a number of clauses for each file. The two required clauses are SELECT followed by the file name in the COBOL program and ASSIGN TO followed by the external designation. The external designation depends on the particular computer and operating system. For the IBM/360–370, for the purposes of our simple problems, the following is adequate:

```
UT-S-<ddname>
```

UT means utility, with DA (mass storage) and UR (unit record) as alternatives; S means sequential, with D (direct) as an alternative. Following is an example of a complete ASSIGN sentence:

```
SELECT DAN ASSIGN TO UT-S-TOM.
```

This starts in or after column 12. It associates the file name DAN in the COBOL program with an external file designated TOM. (The names may be the same.) In the IBM/360–370, TOM is the dd-name, i.e., the name on a job-control card which contains enough information for the system to either locate or allocate or assign the desired file or device to the name TOM.

Next is the DATA DIVISION, which contains the declarations of variables and structures. Every variable or structure name must be declared in this division. The DATA DIVISION is divided into three sections, the FILE SECTION, the WORKING-STORAGE SECTION, and the REPORT SECTION. Since all input-output is similar to PL/I record I/O, the record format for every file must be described by a structure. This is done in the file section. The record description for each file begins with one of the two-letter codes, FD, SD, or RD. FD is for an ordinary file, SD is for a sort file, and RD is for a report description. Because sorting and report production are important parts of business data processing, it is not surprising to find them integrated into the language. The report-writer feature of COBOL simplifies producing reports with neat titles and page headings, and it also automatically numbers the pages. It includes facilities for totalling certain numbers, and it generally specifies the format of the report. In this brief description of COBOL, however, we will not include either the sort feature or the report writer.

The two-letter code FD appears in columns 8 and 9, and the file name follows it in column 12. Following that are a number of clauses that provide information about that file:

RECORD CONTAINS <integer> CHARACTERS. (This is optional.)
BLOCK CONTAINS <integer> RECORDS. (This is necessary if and only if a block contains more than one record.)
LABEL RECORD IS OMITTED or
LABEL RECORD IS STANDARD whichever is appropriate for the file. (The LABEL RECORD clause is required in every FD.)
DATA RECORD IS <data-name> or
DATA RECORDS ARE <data-name>, <data-name>, ...

The above are clauses. The entire FD is one sentence, and there is a period at the end. There must be one FD sentence for each file.

For data records, the record format must be described by a structure whose name is given in the DATA RECORD clause. The level indicators for COBOL are always two digits, 01 to 49, and the 01 appears in column 8, followed by the structure name. Other level indicators start in or after column 12. Each entry starting with a level indicator is a sentence with a period at the end. All of the elementary items are declared by pictures. In place of a data name for an elementary item, the word FILLER may be used either to designate an elementary item that is never referred to or to indicate blank or unused positions (in an input record, for example).

The DATA DIVISION is divided into two sections. The first is the FILE SECTION, which contains file-description (FD) entries for each file, each followed by the structure definition of its records. After that is the WORKING-STORAGE SECTION, which contains structure and variable declarations that are not file records themselves. Elementary items that are not part of a structure and that are used as working storage are put in this section and given the level number 77, which must appear in column 8. Structures may be defined in this section, also, and are given 01 level numbers. All 01 level entries must follow all 77 level entries.

There is a clause REDEFINES that allows referring to the same data with different names and possibly different pictures. For example, consider the following:

```
01  A.
       02   B  PICTURE X(12).
       02   C  REDEFINES B.
          03  D PICTURE 9999.
          03  E PICTURE 9999.
          03  F PICTURE 9999.
       02   G  PICTURE 9(8).
       02   H  REDEFINES G PICTURE X(8).
```

Here, if we refer to B, we are referring to the same 12 characters that make up D, E, and F, and, similarly, if we refer to G or to H, we are referring to the same characters in memory. There are various uses. Input data may have different formats on different records, and after the record is in memory, the variables matching the record can be used.

The level numbers of both names in the REDEFINES clause must be the same, and the REDEFINES clause must immediately follow the definition of the variable being redefined.

When more than one data record are listed for a file, they occupy the same part of memory. Thus, it is just the same as if all the others redefined the first by REDEFINES clauses. Therefore, the REDEFINES clause is not allowed at the 01 level for data records. Applications of this appear in both example programs. In the first, three data records are defined for the input file DATAIN to match the three different kinds of input data expected. In the second, two records are defined for the output file MREPORT: (1) REPORT-LINE, for the ordinary lines, which contain only whole numbers printed with no decimal points, and (2) AVERAGES, in which the averages are printed with one digit to the right of the decimal point.

When variables are referred to, only enough qualification is needed to make the reference unambiguous, the same as in PL/I. If qualification is used, it is written using either the word IN or the word OF, as in the following examples:

```
G OF A
F IN C
E IN C IN A
```

Lists and tables are set up in COBOL using the OCCURS clause. For example,

```
02   A OCCURS 15 TIMES PICTURE 9(5).
```

defines a list of 15 numbers. The numbers are referred to by putting the subscript in parentheses, as A(T). Note that there must be a space to the left of the left parenthesis. The subscript T must be a numeric variable or constant with an integer value, and it must not be subscripted itself. Expressions are not allowed as subscripts. The OCCURS clause may not be used with a level 01 or level 77 entry.

There may be a maximum of three subscripts. An example of such a declaration follows:

```
01  X.
  02  A OCCURS 3 TIMES.
    03  B OCCURS 5 TIMES.
      04  C OCCURS 4 TIMES PICTURE 999.
```

Individual elements are referred to by putting the subscripts together separated by commas in parentheses, as C(I,J,K). If qualification is used, the subscripts come after the qualification:

```
C IN B IN A (I,J,K).
```

Actually, COBOL has another way of handling tables, called indexing, indicated by an INDEXED BY clause in the declaration. Indexing is less flexible than subscripting in that the index variables are a special type that cannot be used in arithmetic statements with ordinary variables. The intent appears to have been to provide a subscripting scheme that could be implemented with maximum efficiency. Indexing will not be described in this chapter.

A USAGE clause may be used. The two choices are

```
USAGE IS COMPUTATIONAL
USAGE IS DISPLAY.
```

If the clause is not inserted, DISPLAY is assumed. DISPLAY means that the value is stored in characters. If a DISPLAY variable is numeric, it can be used in calculations, but then it must be converted. USAGE IS COMPUTATIONAL implies that the numbers will be coded in the machine in the most convenient form for calculations, whereas all USAGE IS DISPLAY items are coded in standard character code. In the IBM/360-370 American Standard COBOL compiler, COMPUTATIONAL variables are stored in binary. The clause USAGE IS COMPUTATIONAL is never needed, but with variables that enter into many computations, such as the total of a number of input data items, declaring USAGE IS COMPUTATIONAL will save conversions and hence time. There is absolutely no conversion done when reading or writing in COBOL. Therefore, on all records defined for input from cards or output to the printer, every item must be DISPLAY. For reading from tape or disc, the record must match the record written; if an item was declared DISPLAY when written, it must be DISPLAY when read, and if it was COMPUTATIONAL in the written record, it must be COMPUTATIONAL in the input record.

Initial values are assigned by a VALUE IS clause:

```
01      A.
        02      B PICTURE 999 VALUE ZERO.
        02      C PICTURE 99  VALUE IS 12.
        02      D PICTURE 99V99 VALUE IS 2.5.
        02      E PICTURE A(6) VALUE IS "ANSWER".
```

The VALUE IS clause cannot be used in the declaration of file records.

Procedure Division

The basic unit of the procedure division is the statement, which starts with a verb that acts as a key word for the statement. A sentence consists of one or more statements, which may be separated by semicolons or by no punctuation at all. In many cases, it doesn't matter how statements are grouped into a sentence, but in conditional sentences, the grouping is important, as we shall see. The end of a sentence is marked by a period. A paragraph consists of an identifier, which serves as the paragraph name, followed by a period, followed by one or more sentences. Execution begins with the first statement in the procedure division.

Arithmetic expressions similar to FORTRAN expressions can be used, with the operators +, −, *, /, and **. Parentheses may be used. A minus sign (but not a plus sign) may be used as a unary operator preceding an operand or left parenthesis. The operands must be either numeric constants or elementary items defined by numeric pictures. In expressions, blanks must surround operators, except that a blank is needed only on the left of a unary minus sign. There must be a blank at the left but not at the right of a left parenthesis, and similarly, there must be a blank at the right but not at the left of a right parenthesis.

An operand used in an arithmetic operation must be either a numeric constant or a data name defined by a numeric picture. In the following description of syntax, we will refer to such a syntactical unit as an `<operand>`. The result may be sent to a data name which may be defined by either a numeric picture or an edited numeric picture. We will refer to such a syntactical unit as an `<answer>`. If a data item serves both as an operand and as the place where the answer goes, it must be defined by a numeric picture. We will call such an item a `<variable>`. An `<operand list>` is simply a list of `<operand>`'s separated by spaces or commas.

Following are the principal arithmetic statements:

```
ADD <operand list> GIVING <answer>
ADD <operand list> TO <variable>
SUBTRACT <operand list> FROM <variable>
SUBTRACT <operand list> FROM <operand> GIVING <answer>
MULTIPLY <operand> BY <variable>
MULTIPLY <operand> BY <operand> GIVING <answer>
DIVIDE <operand> INTO <variable>
DIVIDE <operand> INTO <operand> GIVING <answer>
DIVIDE <operand> BY <operand> GIVING <answer>
COMPUTE <answer> = <expression>
```

The results can be made rounded by inserting the word ROUNDED after

<answer> in the COMPUTE statement, or at the end of any other statement. The remainder can be found in the DIVIDE statement, by writing REMAINDER <answer> at the end of the statement. Any of these statements can be followed by the clause ON SIZE ERROR followed by a *sentence* to be executed if a size or overflow error occurs. If the error occurs, the data items where the result should go are not changed.

For all these arithmetic statements except COMPUTE, there is no need for intermediate results, and a good compiler can avoid intermediate result problems. For COMPUTE, however, it is still a problem to such an extent that many data processing centers prohibit their programmers from using the COMPUTE statement.

Here are some examples of arithmetic statements in a short program:

```
IDENTIFICATION DIVISION.
PROGRAM-ID. 'EXAMPLES'.
ENVIRONMENT DIVISION.
CONFIGURATION SECTION.
SOURCE-COMPUTER. IBM-360-J65.
OBJECT-COMPUTER. IBM-360-J65.
DATA DIVISION.
WORKING-STORAGE SECTION.
77  X PICTURE 999 VALUE IS 11.
77  Y PICTURE 999 VALUE IS 22.
77  Z PICTURE 999.
77  W PICTURE 99V999 VALUE IS 11.
77  U PICTURE S99.
77  V PICTURE S99.
77  R PICTURE +++9.99.
77  S PICTURE +++9.99.

PROCEDURE DIVISION.

    ADD 3 7 X Y GIVING S.
    DISPLAY 'A--X=' X ' Y=' Y ' S=' S

    SUBTRACT 7 FROM Y GIVING Z
    DISPLAY 'B--Y=' Y ' Z=' Z

    ADD Y TO Z
    DISPLAY 'C--Y=' Y ' Z=' Z

    SUBTRACT 5 X X FROM Z
    DISPLAY 'D--X=' X ' Z=' Z

    MULTIPLY 3 BY 3 GIVING Z
    DISPLAY 'E--Z=' Z

    MULTIPLY 4 BY Z
    DISPLAY 'F--Z=' Z
```

```
    DIVIDE 13 INTO 23 GIVING R REMAINDER S
    DISPLAY 'G--DIVIDE 13 INTO 23 GIVES ' R ' REMAINDER ' S

    DIVIDE 23 BY 13 GIVING R REMAINDER S
    DISPLAY 'H--DIVIDE 23 BY 13 GIVES ' R ' REMAINDER ' S

    DIVIDE 6 INTO X ROUNDED
    DIVIDE 6 INTO W ROUNDED
    DISPLAY 'I--X=' X ' W=' W

    MOVE 11 TO U
    MOVE 22 TO V
    DISPLAY 'J--U=' U ' V=' V

    SUBTRACT 22 FROM U
    SUBTRACT 44 FROM V
    DISPLAY 'K--U=' U ' V=' V

    STOP RUN.


PRINTED OUTPUT:



A--X=011 Y=022 S= +43.00
B--Y=022 Z=015
C--Y=022 Z=037
D--X=011 Z=010
E--Z=009
F--Z=036
G--DIVIDE 13 INTO 23 GIVES    +1.76 REMAINDER    +0.12
H--DIVIDE 23 BY 13 GIVES    +1.76 REMAINDER    +0.12
I--X=002 W=01833
J--U=1A V=2B
K--U=1J V=2K
```

The first eight lines are straightforward. Line I illustrates rounding and the fact that a 99V999 representation has no decimal point. The assumed value of W is 1.833. Lines J and K reflect the representation of signed numeric pictures in the memory of the IBM/360-370—the values of U and V are +11 and +22 in line J, −11 and −22 in line K.

The IF statement has the following form:

```
    <statement list> ::= <statement> | <statement list>
                         <statement>
  <IF statement> ::= IF <condition> <statement list> ELSE
                         <statement list>
```

It means that if the condition is true, all the statements in the first statement list are to be executed, but if the condition is false, all the statements in the second will be executed. If in either case an empty statement list is desired, the words NEXT SENTENCE replace the <statement list>. If the words ELSE NEXT SENTENCE are followed by a period, they may be omitted. Note that it is possible to put one IF statement in the <statement list> of another, but if it is in the first one, the ELSE cannot be omitted. Note also that if the <condition> is true, after the first <statement list> is executed, execution skips to the end of the second <statement list> and starts from there. The end of the first <statement list> must be marked either by its matching ELSE or by the period if there is no ELSE. The end of the second <statement list> must be marked by either a period or an ELSE from another IF statement that contains this IF statement in its first <statement list>. Some good examples of nested IF's appear in the second program example.

Here is syntax covering the more important conditions, in BNF. First, simple conditions can be combined by NOT, AND, and OR in the usual way, with precedence in that order, as is the usual case:

```
<logical product> ::= <simple condition> |
                      NOT <simple condition> |
                      <logical product> AND <simple
                                  condition> |
                      <logical product> AND NOT <simple
                                  condition>
<condition> ::= <logical product> |
                <condition> OR <logical product>
<simple condition> ::= ( <condition> ) |
                       <relation> |
                       <class condition> |
                       <condition-name>
```

The most important <simple condition> is the <relation>, which in COBOL isn't necessarily simple.

```
<relation sign> ::= > | < | = | GREATER THAN | LESS THAN |
            EQUAL TO
<relation operator> ::= IS <relation sign> | IS NOT
            <relation sign>
```

The relation operator is said to have a subject, which precedes it, and an object, which follows it, and one subject may be used with several relation operators, and one operator with several objects:

```
<logical connective> ::= AND | OR | AND NOT | OR NOT
<relation> ::= <data name> <relation operator> <data name> |
    <relation> <logical connective> <relation operator>
            <data name> |
    <relation> <logical connective> <data name>
```

It means that each object (i.e., each data name, except the first) is associated with the nearest relation operator to its left, and each relation operator is associated with the subject. Thus,

```
A IS LESS THAN B AND C OR EQUAL TO D AND NOT E
```

is acceptable and means

```
(A IS LESS THAN B AND A IS LESS THAN C) OR (A IS EQUAL TO D
AND A IS NOT EQUAL TO E).
```

Two items to be compared either must both be declared COMPUTATIONAL or must both be DISPLAY (by either being declared DISPLAY or declared by a picture and not declared COMPUTATIONAL). In the case of COMPUTATIONAL, they are compared as numbers. In the case of DISPLAY, they are compared as character strings with characters in the following order from low to high: space, special characters, letters A to Z, and digits 0 to 9.

```
<class condition> ::= <identifier> IS NUMERIC |
                      <identifier> IS ALPHABETIC |
                      <identifier> IS NOT NUMERIC |
                      <identifier> IS NOT ALPHABETIC
```

For class conditions, the identifier must represent DISPLAY type data.

The <condition name> is something else. Each <condition name> must be declared in the data division under the declaration of an elementary item. The <condition name> has the level number 88 and must have a VALUE IS clause with a value compatible with the picture for the elementary item with which it is associated. For example, in

```
07   AAA   PICTURE X.
      88   TTT VALUE IS "#".
      88   UUU VALUE IS "P".
      88   VVV VALUE IS "8".
```

TTT, UUU, and VVV are condition names associated with AAA, and TTT is equivalent to (AAA IS EQUAL TO "#"), UUU is equivalent to (AAA IS EQUAL TO "P"), and VVV is equivalent to (VVV IS EQUAL TO "8").

The idea behind condition names is to show clearly in the program the meaning of coded data. Thus, for example, we might have hair color coded in a card column with 1 for black, 2 for brown, 3 for blonde, and 4 for red. This could be declared as follows:

```
02    HAIR-COLOR PICTURE 9.
      88   BLACK-HAIR VALUE IS 1.
      88   BROWN-HAIR VALUE IS 2.
      88   BLONDE-HAIR VALUE IS 3.
      88   RED-HAIR VALUE IS 4.
```

and then in the program, such statements as this could be written:

```
IF RED-HAIR PERFORM Q.
IF BLACK-HAIR AND AGE LESS THAN 25 GO TO A.
```

Other examples of condition names appear in both program examples.

There is a simple GO TO statement, with the words GO TO followed by a paragraph name. There is also a computed GO TO like that in FORTRAN or BASIC, for example,

```
GO TO AAA BBB CCC DDD DEPENDING ON NNN
```

The value of the data name NNN must be an integer. If it is 1, it will cause control to proceed to paragraph AAA; if it is 2, control will proceed to paragraph BBB, etc. If NNN does not have the value 1, 2, 3, or 4, control will proceed to the statement following the GO TO.

With GO TO statements, after the designated paragraph is completely executed, control proceeds to the paragraph following that paragraph. This is in contrast to the PERFORM statement,

```
PERFORM <paragraph name>
```

or

```
PERFORM <paragraph name> THRU <paragraph name>.
```

In this case, after the designated paragraph or paragraphs are executed, control returns to the statement following the PERFORM statement. Thus, a paragraph may be a part of a program executed in the normal manner at one time, and that same paragraph may be used as a subroutine at another time by calling it from a PERFORM statement.

The PERFORM verb also serves the functions of **for** in ALGOL and DO in PL/I in forming loops. The PERFORM statement may be followed by the clause <operand> TIMES for simple repetition or by the clause UNTIL <condition> for something like the PL/I DO WHILE statement. Here are some examples:

```
PERFORM A 17 TIMES
PERFORM A THRU J N TIMES
PERFORM ITERATION UNTIL R IS LESS THAN 0.01.
```

where A, J, and ITERATION are paragraph names.

Finally, it is possible to combine into one PERFORM statement the equivalent of one, two, or three nested DO or FOR loops, as illustrated by the following examples:

```
PERFORM A VARYING X FROM ZERO BY 0.1 UNTIL X > 10
PERFORM A THRU E VARYING N FROM 1 BY 1 UNTIL N > 10 AFTER
   K FROM 1 BY 1 UNTIL K > N AFTER I FROM 1 BY 1 UNTIL I > J.
```

The equivalent of the first of these in PL/I is

```
DO X = 0 BY 0.1 TO 10;
   A:---------
END;
```

and the approximate equivalent of the second is

```
DO N=1 TO 10;
   DO K=1 TO N;
      DO I=1 TO J;
         A:....
         ....
         ....
         E:...
      END;
   END;
END;
```

Note that for each VARYING data name you must include BY step size and UNTIL, followed by a *condition*. Execution will continue until the condition becomes true, and the PERFORM will *not* be done for the case when the condition is true. There is a fine point in the definition of languages that causes confusion and incompatibility. Are the values of items like increments and test values which are given as expressions or variables in a statement to be taken at the time the statement is entered or at the time they are used? As far as I know, this point is not clearly defined for either BASIC or FORTRAN. For ALGOL60, it is the value at the time of use. For PL/I, it is not consistent. For COBOL, the ANSI Standards seem to imply the value at the time of use. Their clearest statement of the meaning of the PERFORM statement

```
PERFORM P1 THRU P2
   VARYING D1 FROM D2 BY D3 UNTIL C1
   AFTER   D4 FROM D5 BY D6 UNTIL C2
   AFTER   D7 FROM D8 BY D9 UNTIL C3
```

is given by the flowchart in Fig. 7.1, which is taken from the ANSI Standard.

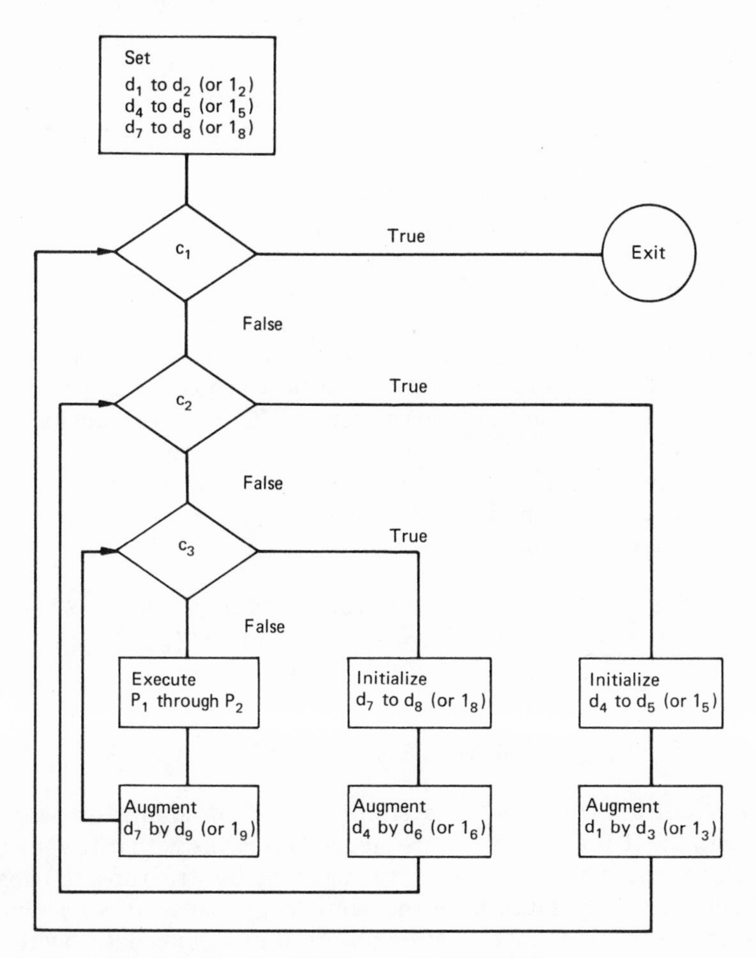

Figure 7.1. Flowchart for COBOL nested PERFORM statement.

Notice that the PERFORM statement leads to programs of a different form from our previous languages because the calculation to be done is specified elsewhere in the program, not in the PERFORM statement. Thus, in PL/I, the loop for the square-root subroutine is written

```
DO WHILE (ABS(S - R) > 0.000001);
   R = S;
   S = (R * R + X)/(2*R);
END;
```

In COBOL, this might be written

```
     PERFORM CALC UNTIL S - R < 0.000001 AND S - R > -0.000001
     ...
     ...
     ...
CALC. MOVE S TO R; COMPUTE S = (R * R + X) / (2 * R).
```

It is not permitted to PERFORM a paragraph that is already in the process of being performed, i.e., recursive use of PERFORM is specifically prohibited in ANSI COBOL.

There is a statement EXIT which must be the only statement in a paragraph, i.e., there must be only a paragraph name, followed by a period, followed by the word EXIT, followed by a period. This paragraph does nothing except provide a way of labeling a point between two paragraphs. It is sometimes needed with the PERFORM statement in situations analogous to those which require the CONTINUE statement in FORTRAN.

The statement STOP RUN causes execution of a program to terminate.

The MOVE statement is used to move data from one area of storage to another. It has the form

```
<identifier list>::=<identifier>|<identifier list><identifier>
          MOVE <identifier> TO <identifier list>
```

or

```
MOVE <constant> TO <identifier list>
```

where <identifier list> is simply a list of identifiers with spaces as punctuation. If the identifiers are single data items with different pictures or usage, conversion is done. The identifiers may be structures or substructures, in which case they must have the same length, and *no conversion is done*. There are restrictions that must be observed in moving data. Table 7.2 shows the permitted conversions.

TABLE 7.2. **Permissible COBOL MOVE combinations.**

Source \ Destination	Numeric	Numeric edited	Alphabetic	Alpha-numeric	Alpha-numeric edited
Numeric	Yes	Yes	No	Yes	Yes
Numeric edited	No	No	No	Yes	Yes
Alphabetic	No	No	Yes	Yes	Yes
Alphanumeric	Yes	Yes	Yes	Yes	Yes
Alphanumeric edited	No	No	Yes	Yes	Yes
Character constant	Yes	Yes	Yes	Yes	Yes
Numeric constant	Yes	Yes	No	Yes	Yes

Note that even some of these yes cases can lead to errors unless the data are acceptable for the destination. For example, it is possible to move alphanumeric data to numeric variables, but an error will occur as soon as they are used in arithmetic if the data are not actually arithmetic.

There is a statement EXAMINE which has the following forms:

```
EXAMINE <identifier> REPLACING ALL <character> BY
        <character>
EXAMINE <identifier> REPLACING LEADING <character> BY
        <character>
EXAMINE <identifier> REPLACING FIRST <character> BY
        <character>
EXAMINE <identifier> REPLACING UNTIL FIRST <character> BY
        <character>
```

Here <character> means a single-character character constant. For example, if AA is the string **10**, then

```
EXAMINE AA REPLACING LEADING "*" BY "#"
```

would result in AA taking the value ##10**

```
EXAMINE AA REPLACING UNTIL FIRST "0" BY "#"
```

would result in AA taking the value ###0**. This statement has a very important use. Often input data cards will have leading blanks on numbers or blanks replacing zero or inapplicable cases. An attempt to use such data in arithmetic operations will result in errors—all data used in arithmetic must be pure numeric. The EXAMINE statement can be used to replace the blanks by zeros. The <identifier> in the EXAMINE statement must be DISPLAY type, which means it must be declared by a picture but not declared COMPUTATIONAL.

Every file must be opened by an OPEN statement

```
OPEN INPUT <file name>
OPEN OUTPUT <file name>
OPEN I-O <file name>
```

The READ statement has the form

```
READ <file name> RECORD AT END <sentence>
```

Note that the AT END clause is required and specifies action to be taken if a READ is executed after all input data are used. Note that <sentence> means everything up to the next period.

The WRITE statement has the form

```
WRITE <record name>
WRITE <record name> AFTER ADVANCING <operand> LINES
WRITE <record name> BEFORE ADVANCING <operand> LINES
```

Here <operand> means an identifier or constant. Note that the word LINES is optional, but it must be plural if you use it, even if you want to advance only one line, and AFTER ADVANCING 1 LINE is not understandable to the compiler. Also, if one WRITE statement has the ADVANCING option, then every WRITE statement for that file must also have it.

For skipping to a new page or suppressing spacing, it is necessary to use "function names." The IBM function names for "skip to a new page" and "suppress spacing" are C01 or CSP, respectively. First, in the CONFIGURATION SECTION there must be a SPECIAL-NAMES paragraph with entries of the form

```
<function name> IS <identifier>
```

and then that <identifier> is used in the WRITE statement

```
WRITE <record-name> AFTER ADVANCING <identifier>
```

For example, if we choose the <identifier> NEWPAGE for skipping to a new page, then we must include the following in the CONFIGURATION SECTION:. SPECIAL-NAMES.

```
C01 IS NEWPAGE.
```

Then, the WRITE statement is written

```
WRITE PPP AFTER ADVANCING NEWPAGE.
```

Note also that the record name, i.e., the name of the structure defining the form of the output record, is used in the WRITE statement, but the file name is used in the READ statement.

There is another simple output statement

```
<item list>::=<constant>|<identifier>|
              <item list> <constant>|
              <item list> <identifier>
DISPLAY <item list>
```

This causes the items listed to be printed. They may be any type of variables and constants. For example,

```
DISPLAY "X IS" X
```

will cause X IS followed by the value of X to be printed.

Execution-time error messages furnished by the IBM/360-370 COBOL compilers are virtually useless. The message COMPLETION CODE 0C7 (DATA) means that one of the operands used in arithmetic was not truly numeric, but there is no hint given as to which one or where. I recommend inserting enough DISPLAY statements in your program so that you can tell where your program is getting into trouble. Make each DISPLAY statement print something unique, for example, A, B, C, etc., so that you can tell from the printout exactly which DISPLAY statements were executed, and in what order. Doing this *before* you ever run your program the first time will save you time in the long run. There are some debugging statements in the second program example, and part of the printed output from them is included with the output.

PART III
CHARACTER-STRING PROCESSING

Probably the greatest use of character-string processing now is in compilers, the computer programs that translate higher-level languages like those presented in this book into the actual language of the computer itself, machine language. Linguistics research, natural language translation, and information retrieval are other areas requiring extensive use of character-string processing techniques.

Although only a minority of programmers are involved in projects that are primarily character-string processing, every programmer will have occasional opportunities to have the computer assist him with an otherwise tedious problem in handling character-strings if he is familiar with these techniques. Here are some examples of common applications:

1. Text editing with easy error correction, flexible formatting, and right and left justification is possible. Some computers are now equipped with the ability to print upper- and lower-case letters.
2. Automated letter writing can be implemented.
3. Compiling, sorting, and formatting an index, bibliography, glossary, or dictionary can make effective use of character-string processing.
4. Pre-editing data, perhaps detecting and/or correcting errors and reformatting into a form suitable for another program can be done by computer. Checking for certain types of errors in and/or reformatting computer programs is often helpful.
5. When a computer program, either higher-language, machine, or assembly language, is repetitive in nature, it is often easier to write a computer program to produce that program, a so-called program generator.
6. For on-line systems, i.e., systems that use keyboard terminals connected to the computer, it is helpful to allow the terminal user some freedom and flexibility in what he types. Then, character-string processing techniques are useful in analyzing the user-typed message for meaning and errors.

PL/I for Character-String Processing Chapter 8

This third of the four chapters on PL/I presents a number of character-string processing facilities. The most important are: (1) the concatenation operation, for putting strings together to make bigger strings; (2) the sub-string function, for taking strings apart to make smaller strings; (3) the length function, for determining the length of a string; and (4) the index function, for searching one string for the occurrence of another. These features and some less important ones are described, and several program examples are presented to illustrate their use.

Character-string Functions and Operations

Usually, we declare strings specifying their length as follows:

```
DECLARE A CHARACTER(5) INITIAL ('ALICE');
DECLARE B CHARACTER(5);
DECLARE C CHARACTER(10) INITIAL ('YAMAMOTO');
DECLARE D CHARACTER(10);
```

These always have length exactly what is specified. In fact, C will actually have the value 'YAMAMOTO ', with two blanks inserted to make its length ten. The assignments

```
B = C; D = A;
```

will result in the value 'YAMAM' for B, with the last five characters of C truncated, and the value 'ALICE' for D, with five blanks inserted to make the total length ten.

We may also declare a string to be of varying length:

```
DECLARE E CHARACTER(20) VARYING;
```

The specified length is the maximum, and each time a character string is assigned to E, the length is stored with it. Thus, E = A; results in the value 'ALICE' and length five for E, and E = C; results in the value 'YAMAMOTO ' and length ten for E.

There is a built-in function LENGTH that gives the length of character strings. It can be used in expressions. In the above examples, LENGTH(A) has the value five, LENGTH(D) has the value ten, while E = C; I = LENGTH(E); will result in the value ten for I.

The operation *concatenation* means putting two character strings together to make a single character string. In PL/I, the symbol || is used.

```
E = A||C;
```

results in the value 'ALICEYAMAMOTO ' with length fifteen for E.

```
E = A||' '||C;
```

results in the value 'ALICE YAMAMOTO '.

There is a function SUBSTR (meaning "substring") that can be used in either of two ways.

```
SUBSTR(S,I,J)
```

where S is a character string and I and J are numbers means the substring of S starting from the Ith character and having length J. Thus, with the character strings used in the preceding examples, SUBSTR(C,3,3) has the value 'MAM', while SUBSTR(A,1,3) has the value 'ALI'.

SUBSTR can also be used without the third parameter:

```
SUBSTR(S,I)
```

means the substring of S starting from the Ith character and going to the end. Thus SUBSTR(C,5) has the value 'MOTO ', while SUBSTR(A,2) has the value 'LICE'.

There is a function

```
INDEX(S,T)
```

where S and T are character strings. This causes the computer to search string S for a substring equal to T. If one is found, the value of INDEX(S,T) is the starting position of the first such substring, but if one is not found, the value of the function is zero. Here are some examples, assuming the values A='ALICE' and C='YAMAMOTO   ' as before.

```
INDEX(A,'E')     has the value 5
INDEX(C,A)       has the value 0
INDEX(C,'A')     has the value 2
INDEX(C,'AM')    has the value 2
```

Note that in the fourth example, the substring 'AM' occurs both in position 2 and position 4, but the answer is 2.

These functions can be used in expressions, and, of course, expressions can be used as their arguments. Here are examples:

```
SUBSTR(S,LENGTH(S)/2+1)
```

is the last half of the string S, while

```
SUBSTR(S,1,LENGTH(S)/2)
```

is the first half.

```
SUBSTR(S,INDEX(S,' '))
```

will give the substring of S starting from the first blank and going to the end, while

```
SUBSTR(S,1,INDEX(S,' ') - 1)
```

will give a substring that goes from the beginning of S up to the first blank. (This will be valid only if S has at least one blank.)

```
S = SUBSTR(S,1,I)||'*'||SUBSTR(S,I + 1);
```

inserts a * into S after the Ith character, increasing the length of S by 1, while

```
DO WHILE(INDEX(S, ' ')¬= 0);
     I = INDEX(S,' ');
     S = SUBSTR(S,1,I - 1)||SUBSTR(S,I + 1);
END;
```

will remove all blanks from S.

SUBSTR can also be used as the destination of an assignment, i.e., either in a GET statement or on the left of the equal sign in an assignment statement. In that case, the designated substring is replaced. For example,

```
DECLARE (X,Y) CHARACTER(20) VARYING;
X = 'DISCRETE DATA';
Y = 'EET';
SUBSTR(X,6,3) = Y;
```

will result in X having the value 'DISCREET DATA', i.e., the substring of X starting at position 6 and having length three, 'ETE', is replaced in X by 'EET'.

There is a function TRANSLATE that replaces individual characters.

```
TRANSLATE(S,T,U)
```

has as its value a character string of the same length as S. T and U must be character strings of the same length. Every occurrence in S of the first character in U is replaced by the first character in T, and every occurrence in S of the second character in U is replaced by the second character in T, etc. For example,

```
TRANSLATE(S,'GAR','BEL')
```

will replace every 'B' in S by 'G', every 'E' by 'A', and every 'L' by 'R'. If S = 'PROBLEM', the result is 'PROGRAM'.

```
TRANSLATE(S,',.','.,')
```

will replace every period in S by a comma and every comma by a period.

```
TRANSLATE(S,'     ','AEIOU')
```

will replace each vowel in S by a blank.

If the third argument is omitted, then a string of all 256 possible bytes in order of their binary code is assumed. Then, the second argument should be a list of 256 characters to indicate what each of the 256 possible bytes should translate into. Use of this requires knowing what each byte normally represents. This is shown in Figure 8.1. The use of TRANSLATE is included in an example later in this chapter.

Figure 8.1 shows the most important characters. If a printer is equipped to print additional characters, they are assigned other codes. Many printers

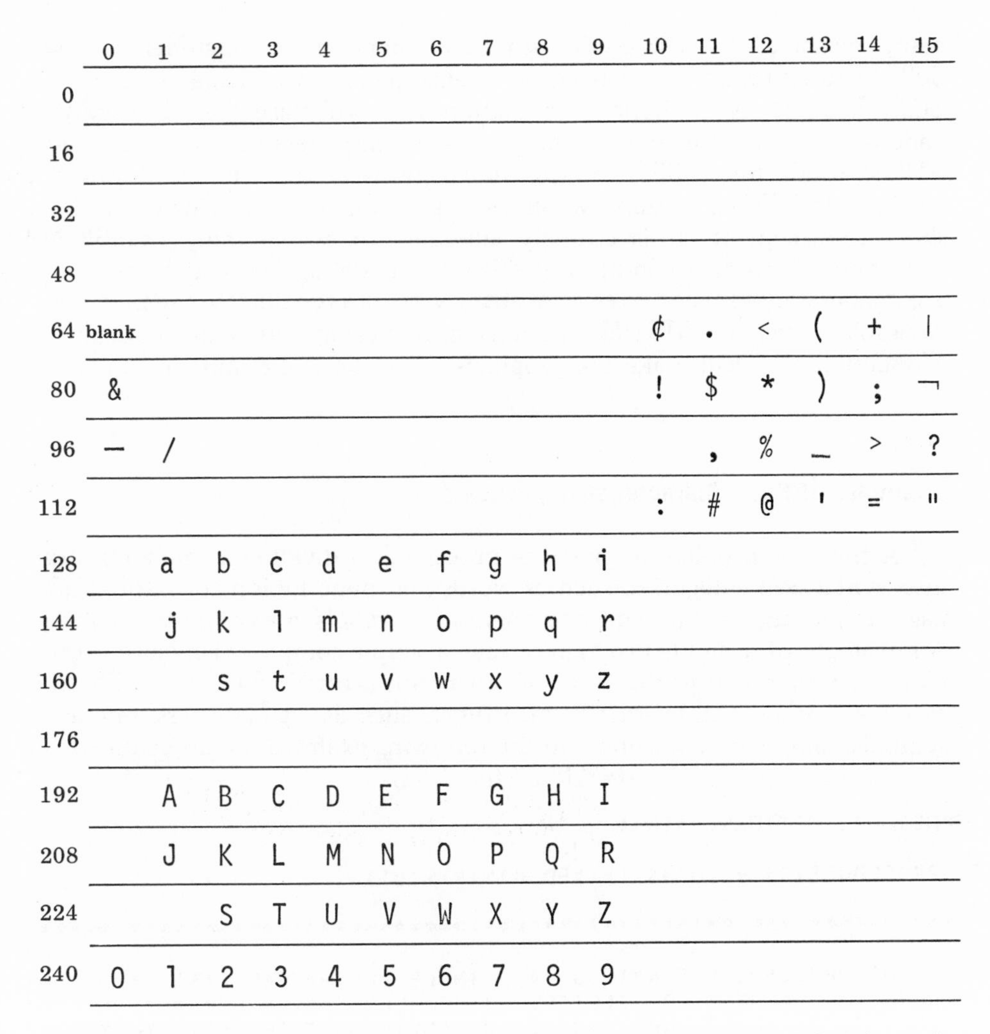

	0	1	2	3	4	5	6	7	8	9	10	11	12	13	14	15
0																
16																
32																
48																
64	blank										¢	.	<	(	+	|
80	&										!	$	*	)	;	¬
96	–	/										,	%	_	>	?
112											:	#	@	'	=	"
128		a	b	c	d	e	f	g	h	i						
144		j	k	l	m	n	o	p	q	r						
160			s	t	u	v	w	x	y	z						
176																
192		A	B	C	D	E	F	G	H	I						
208		J	K	L	M	N	O	P	Q	R						
224			S	T	U	V	W	X	Y	Z						
240	0	1	2	3	4	5	6	7	8	9						

Figure 8.1. EBCDIC character code. The 256 characters are listed in order by their code, row by row. Any blank space means that there is no printer character assigned.

don't print all these, in which case a blank is usually printed, although sometimes a printer with no lower-case letters is programmed to print the corresponding upper-case letters in their place.

There are several other functions of less importance that we will simply mention. STRING(X) combines elements of an array or structure into a single character string, or vice versa. VERIFY(S,T) searches string S for a character *not* in T. REPEAT(S,I) consists of I + 1 copies of S concatenated.

There are two ON-conditions provided for work with strings, both normally disabled. STRINGRANGE is raised whenever the arguments in the SUBSTR function are inconsistent. For example, if S is a string of length ten, SUBSTR(S,20) is an impossible request and will raise the STRINGRANGE conditions. Unfortunately, the present implementation also raises STRINGRANGE for SUBSTR(S,10), but it properly gives the null string as a result. STRINGSIZE is raised when a string is assigned to a string variable too short to accept it. It is strongly advisable to enable the STRINGRANGE condition (by using a condition prefix) during debugging, and unless strings are deliberately assigned to shorter string variables to truncate them, it is also advisable to enable STRINGSIZE during debugging. Disabling them during production runs will make the programs run faster and require less memory.

Examples of PL/I Character-string Processing

A frequent problem in language processing is dividing a character string into syntactical categories, such as words and punctuation for natural language, or identifiers, numbers, and operation symbols in a computer language. An example of a simple program to scan a simple computer language is given here. As a first step in this kind of program it is often convenient to be able to classify individual characters into types, such as digits, letters, operation symbols, and illegal characters. In the following example the procedure TYPE serves that purpose, using the INDEX function.

```
TEST: PROCEDURE OPTIONS(MAIN);

  TYPE: PROCEDURE(S) RETURNS (FIXED BINARY(15));

/**********************************************************************/
/*                                                                    */
/*       THIS PROCEDURE EXAMINES A  SINGLE  CHARACTER (S)  AND       */
/*   RETURNS THE VALUE 4 FOR DIGITS,  3 FOR LETTERS, 2 FOR ANY OF     */
/*   "()+*-/=",  1 FOR BLANKS, AND 0 FOR ANYTHING ELSE. NOTE THAT     */
/*   INDEX(X,S) SEARCHES FOR THE CHARACTER S IN THE STRING X  AND    */
/*   HAS THE VALUE ZERO IF IT IS NOT FOUND.                           */
/*                                                                    */
/**********************************************************************/

     DECLARE S CHARACTER(1);
     DECLARE A CHARACTER(26) INITIAL ('ABCDEFGHIJKLMNOPQRSTUVWXYZ');
     DECLARE D CHARACTER(10) INITIAL ('0123456789');
     DECLARE OP CHARACTER(7) INITIAL ('()+*-/=');

     IF INDEX(D,S)¬=0 THEN RETURN (4);
     ELSE IF INDEX(A,S)¬=0 THEN RETURN (3);
     ELSE IF INDEX(OP,S)¬=0 THEN RETURN (2);
     ELSE IF S=' ' THEN RETURN (1);
     ELSE RETURN (0);

  END; /*  OF PROCEDURE "TYPE"  */
```

```
/***********************************************************************/
/*                                                                     */
/*         THIS SHORT TEST PROGRAM 1) READS A CARD AND PRINTS  IT,     */
/*    2) TAKES ONE CHARACTER A T A TIME AND FINDS ITS TYPE, AND 3)     */
/*    FORMS A LINE WITH THE TYPES AND PRINTS IT SO THAT  THE  TYPE     */
/*    OF EACH CHARACTER IS PRINTED BELOW IT.  NOTE THE  USE  OF  A     */
/*    PICTURE VARIABLE AS AN  INTERMEDIATE  VALUE  FOR  CONVERTING     */
/*    NUMERIC TO CHARACTER.                                            */
/*                                                                     */
/***********************************************************************/

  DECLARE S CHARACTER(1),
          (T,U) CHARACTER(40) VARYING,
          W PICTURE '9',
          I FIXED BINARY(15);

  DO WHILE(1);   /*  UNTIL NO MORE DATA CARDS  */

     U = '';
     GET SKIP;
     GET EDIT(T)(A(40));

     DO I = 1 TO 40;
        S = SUBSTR(T,I,1);
        W = TYPE(S);
        U = U || W;
     END;

     PUT SKIP EDIT(T)(A);
     PUT SKIP EDIT(U)(A);
     PUT SKIP;

  END;  /*  OF DO WHILE(1)  */

END;  /* OF MAIN PROCEDURE  */


PRINTED OUTPUT:


X = A(5) + 3*B'
3121324212142301111111111111111111111111

TOTAL = 120*RATE + OLDTOTAL
3333312144423333121333333331111111111111

Z = A1 + A2 + ANSWER - Z100
3121341213412133333312134441111111111111
```

Here is an equivalent procedure TYPE that uses the TRANSLATE function to translate a character into a single digit which is its designated type. Both the test program and the printed output are identical to that in the previous example.

```
TEST: PROCEDURE OPTIONS(MAIN);

/***********************************************************************/
/*                                                                     */
/*        "CHARTYPE" IS A STRING OF 256 CHARACTERS. COMPARED WITH     */
/*   A STRING OF ALL POSSIBLE 256 BYTES  IN  NUMERICAL  ORDER  BY      */
/*   THEIR BINARY CODE,  "CHARTYPE  HAS  A  1  IN  THE  POSITION       */
/*   CORRESPONDING TO A BLANK, 2'S IN THE POSITIONS CORRESPONDING      */
/*   TO "()+*-/=",  3'S BY THE UPPER AND LOWER CASE LETTERS,  AND      */
/*   4'S BY THE TEN DIGITS.   TRANSLATE(S,CHARTYPE)  HAS  AS  ITS      */
/*   VALUE THE CHARACTER IN THE STRING  "CHARTYPE"  CORRESPONDING      */
/*   TO S.  SINCE FIXED BINARY IS RETURNED,  THERE IS AN  IMPLIED      */
/*   CONVERSION FROM THE ONE CHARACTER TO  FIXED  BINARY  IN  THE      */
/*   "RETURN" STATEMENT.                                               */
/*                                                                     */
/***********************************************************************/

     DECLARE CHARTYPE CHARACTER(256);
     CHARTYPE =
     (  '0000000000000000' ||
        '0000000000000000' ||
        '0000000000000000' ||
        '0000000000000000' ||
        '1000000000000220' ||
        '0000000000002200' ||
        '2200000000000000' ||
        '0000000000000020' ||
        '0333333333000000' ||
        '0333333333000000' ||
        '0033333333000000' ||
        '0000000000000000' ||
        '0333333333000000' ||
        '0333333333000000' ||
        '0033333333000000' ||
        '4444444444000000' );

  TYPE: PROCEDURE(S) RETURNS (FIXED BINARY(15));

/***********************************************************************/
/*        THIS PROCEDURE EXAMINES  A  SINGLE  CHATACTER  (S)  AND      */
/*   RETURNS THE VALUE 4 FOR DIGITS,  3 FOR LETTERS, 2 FOR ANY OF      */
/*   "()+*-/=", 1 FOR BLANKS, AND 0 FOR ANYTHING ELSE.                 */
/*                                                                     */
/***********************************************************************/


      DECLARE S CHARACTER(1);

      RETURN (TRANSLATE(S,CHARTYPE));
```

```
END; /*  OF PROCEDURE "TYPE"  */

/**********************************************************************/
/*                                                                    */
/*        THE PROCEDURE "TYPE" IN THIS EXAMPLE DOES  EXACTLY  THE     */
/*   SAME JOB AS "TYPE" IN THE PRECEDING EXAMPLE,  BUT IT DOES IT     */
/*   IN A DIFFERENT MANNER.  THIS VERSION IS PROBABLY FASTER  BUT     */
/*   REQUIRES MORE MEMORY. THE TEST PROGRAM IS IDENTICAL.             */
/*                                                                    */
/**********************************************************************/

  DECLARE S CHARACTER(1),
          (T,U) CHARACTER(40) VARYING,
          W PICTURE '9',
          I FIXED BINARY(15);

  DO WHILE(1);   /*  UNTIL NO MORE DATA CARDS   */

     U = '';
     GET SKIP;
     GET EDIT(T)(A(40));

     DO I = 1 TO 40;
        S = SUBSTR(T,I,1);
        W = TYPE(S);
        U = U || W;
     END;

     PUT SKIP EDIT(T)(A);
     PUT SKIP EDIT(U)(A);
     PUT SKIP;

  END;   /*  OF DO WHILE(1)   */

END;   /* OF MAIN PROCEDURE   */



PRINTED OUTPUT:


X = A(5) + 3*B'
3121324212142301111111111111111111111111

TOTAL = 120*RATE + OLDTOTAL
3333312144423333121333333331111111111111

Z = A1 + A2 + ANSWER - Z100
3121341213412133333312134441111111111111
```

The following example includes a procedure SCAN which scans statements and splits off syntactical symbols one by one. A typical compiler would include a procedure of this type as a first step in analyzing the source statements. The simple language assumed here includes identifiers which consist of any number of letters and digits but of which the first must be a letter. It also includes numbers having any number of digits, parentheses, equals signs, and arithmetic operators. This routine disregards blanks between symbols. It prints an error message if an illegal character appears, with a pointer indicating where the incorrect symbol is. The procedure skips to the next statement when an error is found.

```
TEST: PROCEDURE OPTIONS(MAIN);

/**************************************************************************/
/*                                                                        */
/*      THE PROCEDURE "SCAN" SCANS STATEMENTS IN A SIMPLE                 */
/*   LANGUAGE AND BREAKS THEM INTO SYNTACTICAL                            */
/*   UNITS--IDENTIFIERS, NUMBERS, AND SPECIAL SYMBOLS.                    */
/*                                                                        */
/*      THE MAIN PROCEDURE IS MERELY A SIMPLE TEST PROGRAM. IT            */
/*   INITIALIZES, PLACES A "|" AT THE END OF LINE AFTER IT IS             */
/*   READ, AND REPEATEDLY CALLS SCAN, PRINTING THE SYNTACTICAL            */
/*   UNIT FOUND BY SCAN AT EACH CALL.                                     */
/*                                                                        */
/*      "STMT" IS THE STATEMENT CURRENTLY BEING EXAMINED. "STP            */
/*   POINTS TO THE CHARACTER CURRENTLY BEING SCANNED. "TERMSYM"           */
/*   AND "SLENGTH" ARE THE LAST FOUND SYMBOL, I. E. IDENTIFIER,           */
/*   NUMBER, OR SPECIAL SYMBOL. "TOKEN" IS THE TYPE OF SYMBOL--1          */
/*   FOR NUMBERS, 2 FOR IDENTIFIERS, 3 FOR SPECIAL SYMBOLS, AND           */
/*   ZERO FOR END OF STATEMENT.                                           */
/*                                                                        */
/**************************************************************************/

  DECLARE STMT CHARACTER(81) VARYING INITIAL ('|');
  DECLARE STP FIXED BINARY(15) INITIAL (1);
  DECLARE SLENGTH FIXED BINARY(15) INITIAL(0);
  DECLARE TERMSYM CHARACTER(15) VARYING;
  DECLARE TOKEN FIXED BINARY(15);

/**************************************************************************/
/*                                                                        */
/*      THE FOLLOWING ARE USED IN A ROUTINE WHICH PRINTS ERROR            */
/*   MESSAGES.                                                            */
/*                                                                        */
/**************************************************************************/

  DECLARE  ERRMSG CHARACTER(20);
  DECLARE ERRORCOUNT FIXED BINARY(15) INITIAL (0);
  DECLARE LINE CHARACTER(80);
  DECLARE POINTER CHARACTER(60) INITIAL (
      '-----------------------------------------------------------|  ');
```

```
   DECLARE T FIXED BINARY(15);
   DECLARE S CHARACTER(1);

   ON ENDFILE STOP;

   TYPE: PROCEDURE(S) RETURNS (FIXED BINARY(15));

/*************************************************************************/
/*                                                                       */
/*        "TYPE" IS THE SAME PROCEDURE AS IN THE FIRST EXAMPLE.          */
/*                                                                       */
/*************************************************************************/

      DECLARE S CHARACTER(1);
      DECLARE A CHARACTER(26) INITIAL ('ABCDEFGHIJKLMNOPQRSTUVWXYZ');
      DECLARE D CHARACTER(10) INITIAL ('0123456789');
      DECLARE OP CHARACTER(7) INITIAL ('()+*-/=');

      IF INDEX(D,S)¬=0 THEN RETURN (4);
      ELSE IF INDEX(A,S)¬=0 THEN RETURN (3);
      ELSE IF INDEX(OP,S)¬=0 THEN RETURN (2);
      ELSE IF S=' ' THEN RETURN (1);
      ELSE RETURN (0);

   END; /*  OF PROCEDURE "TYPE"  */

   SCAN: PROCEDURE;

      DECLARE CASE(0:4) LABEL INITIAL (
            INVALID, BLANK, OPERATOR, LETTER, NUMBER);

      STP = STP+SLENGTH;    /*  MOVE PAST PREVIOUS SYMBOL.  */

      DO WHILE (SUBSTR(STMT,STP,1) = ' '); /*  PASS OVER BLANKS.  */
         STP = STP+1;
      END;

      S = SUBSTR(STMT,STP,1);
      SLENGTH = 1;

      IF S='|' THEN DO;    /*  INDICATES END OF LINE.  */
         TERMSYM = '|';
         TOKEN = 0;
         RETURN;
      END;

      GO TO CASE(TYPE(S));

   INVALID:
         ERRMSG = 'ILLEGAL CHARACTER';
         CALL ERROR;
         GO TO CASEEND;
```

```
BLANK:
      /*  THIS CASE CAN'T OCCUR--BLANKS ALREADY CUT OFF.  */

OPERATOR:
      TOKEN = 3;
      GO TO CASEEND;

LETTER:
/***********************************************************************/
/*                                                                     */
/*        SYMBOL MAY CONSIST OF ANY NUMBER OF LETTERS OR  DIGITS,      */
/*  OF WHICH THE FIRST MUST BE A LETTER.                               */
/*                                                                     */
/***********************************************************************/

     DO WHILE(TYPE(SUBSTR(STMT,STP+SLENGTH,1))>=3);
        SLENGTH = SLENGTH+1;
     END;
     TOKEN = 2;
     GO TO CASEEND;

NUMBER:
/***********************************************************************/
/*                                                                     */
/*        NUMBER MAY CONSIST OF ANY NUMBER OF DIGITS.                  */
/*                                                                     */
/***********************************************************************/

     DO WHILE(TYPE(SUBSTR(STMT,STP+SLENGTH,1))=4);
        SLENGTH = SLENGTH+1;
     END;
     TOKEN = 1;
     GO TO CASEEND;

CASEEND:
   TERMSYM = SUBSTR(STMT,STP,SLENGTH);

END;  /*  OF PROCEDURE SCAN  */

ERROR: PROCEDURE;

/***********************************************************************/
/*                                                                     */
/*        FOLLOWING WILL MAKE A POINTER LOCATE POSITION OF  ERROR      */
/*  AND PRINT AN ERROR MESSAGE.                                        */
/*                                                                     */
/***********************************************************************/

   LINE = SUBSTR(POINTER,60-STP) || ERRMSG;
   PUT EDIT (LINE) (A); PUT SKIP;
   ERRORCOUNT = ERRORCOUNT+1;
   STP = 81;  /*  THIS WILL CAUSE PROCESSING OF THIS LINE TO STOP. */

END;  /*  OF PROCEDURE ERROR  */
```

```
/**********************************************************************/
/*                                                                    */
/*        MAIN ROUTINE FOR TESTING PURPOSES                           */
/*                                                                    */
/**********************************************************************/


  DO WHILE (1);

     READ FILE (SOURCE) INTO (STMT);
     STMT = STMT || '|';      /*  TO MARK END OF STATEMENT  */
     PUT LIST (STMT); PUT SKIP;
     STP = 1;
     SLENGTH = 0;

/**********************************************************************/
/*                                                                    */
/*        NOTE--INITIALIZING STP TO 1 AND SLENGTH TO ZERO  CAUSES     */
/*   SCAN TO START WITH THE FIRST SYMBOL IN STMT.                     */
/*                                                                    */
/**********************************************************************/

     DO WHILE (STP<=80);
        CALL SCAN;
        PUT DATA (TERMSYM, TOKEN); PUT SKIP;
     END;    /*  OF DO WHILE (STP<=80)    */

  END;   /*  OF DO WHILE(1)    */

END;    /*  OF  MAIN PROCEDURE  */
```

At the end of this program is a short test procedure that reads statements and prints them, followed by a list of the individual symbols. Here is the output that it produced for two correct statements and two cards with illegal characters.

```
AREA = 6*SIDE*SIDE
TERMSYM='AREA'          TOKEN=       2;
TERMSYM='='             TOKEN=       3;
TERMSYM='6'             TOKEN=       1;
TERMSYM='*'             TOKEN=       3;
TERMSYM='SIDE'          TOKEN=       2;
TERMSYM='*'             TOKEN=       3;
TERMSYM='SIDE'          TOKEN=       2;
TERMSYM='|'             TOKEN=       0;
X = (A+B-(C*13/100))
TERMSYM='X'             TOKEN=       2;
TERMSYM='='             TOKEN=       3;
TERMSYM='('             TOKEN=       3;
TERMSYM='A'             TOKEN=       2;
TERMSYM='+'             TOKEN=       3;
TERMSYM='B'             TOKEN=       2;
```

```
TERMSYM='-'                   TOKEN=        3;
TERMSYM='('                   TOKEN=        3;
TERMSYM='C'                   TOKEN=        2;
TERMSYM='*'                   TOKEN=        3;
TERMSYM='13'                  TOKEN=        1;
TERMSYM='/'                   TOKEN=        3;
TERMSYM='100'                 TOKEN=        1;
TERMSYM=')'                   TOKEN=        3;
TERMSYM=')'                   TOKEN=        3;
TERMSYM='|'                   TOKEN=        0;
         #@#@#
--------| ILLEGAL CHARACTER
TERMSYM='|'                   TOKEN=        0;
                                       $
-----------------------------------| ILLEGAL CHARACTER
TERMSYM='|'                   TOKEN=        0;
```

The next program reads a PL/I program, scans for DO and END, and inserts labels that show which DO matches which END.

```
LABEL: PROCEDURE OPTIONS(MAIN);

/***************************************************************************/
/*                                                                         */
/*       THIS PROGRAM READS A PL/I PROGRAM  AS  INPUT  DATA  AND           */
/*   SCANS IT FOR "DO" AND "END".  IT PUTS A DIFFERENT  LABEL  IN          */
/*   FRONT OF EACH "DO" AND A MATCHING COMMENT  ON  THE   MATCHING         */
/*   END.    IT  IS  A  NAIVE  PROGRAM--IT  DOES  NOT  CHECK  FOR          */
/*   "PROCEDURE",  OR "BEGIN",  NOR DOES IT LOOK OUT FOR  WHETHER          */
/*   THE "DO" IS IN THE MIDDLE OF ANOTHER WORD, FOR EXAMPLE.               */
/*                                                                         */
/*       EACH TIME A "DO" IS MET,  IT IS LABELED,  AND THE LABEL           */
/*   NUMBER IS STACKED IN THE ARRAY S.  J IS THE POINTER  TO  THE          */
/*   TOP OF THE STACK. EACH TIME AN END IS MET, THE LABEL NUMBER           */
/*   ON THE TOP OF THE STACK IS REMOVED AND USED.  I IS THE LABEL          */
/*   NUMBER--NOTE   THE   USE   OF   A   PICTURE,   TO  ASSURE  A          */
/*   CLEARLY-DEFINED CHARACTER  AND  NUMERIC  VALUE.   K  IS  THE          */
/*   POSITION NUMBER IN THE STMT BEING EXAMINED.                           */
/*                                                                         */
/*       THE UNMODIFIED PROGRAM STATEMENTS ARE WRITTEN INTO FILE           */
/*   "A",  AND THE MODIFIED STATEMENTS ARE WRITTEN INTO FILE "B".          */
/*   BOTH ARE PRINTED, FOR COMPARISON.                                     */
/*                                                                         */
/***************************************************************************/

DECLARE STMT CHARACTER(80),
        I PICTURE '99' INITIAL (0), /*  THIS IS THE LABEL NUMBER. */
        K FIXED BINARY INITIAL (0),
        J FIXED BINARY INITIAL (0),
        S(100) CHARACTER(2);
```

```
   DO WHILE (1);

      READ FILE (SYSIN) INTO (STMT);
      WRITE FILE (A) FROM (STMT);  /* UNMODIFIED PROGRAM INTO FILE A */
      K = 1;

      DO WHILE (K<=70);

         IF SUBSTR(STMT,K,2)='DO' THEN DO;
            J = J+1;
            I = I+1;
            S(J) = I;

/*********************************************************************/
/*                                                                   */
/*          THE PREVIOUS STATEMENT  STACKS  THE  LABEL.  THE  NEXT   */
/*    STATEMENT INSERTS THE LABEL IN FRONT OF THE "DO;".             */
/*                                                                   */
/*********************************************************************/

            STMT = SUBSTR(STMT,1,K-1)||'S'||I||': '||SUBSTR(STMT,K);
            K = K+7;
         END;
         ELSE IF SUBSTR(STMT,K,4)='END;' THEN DO;
            STMT = SUBSTR(STMT,1,K+3)||'  /*  OF S'||S(J)||'  */  '||
               SUBSTR(STMT,K+4);

/*********************************************************************/
/*                                                                   */
/*          THE PREVIOUS STATEMENT INSERTS THE  COMMENT  AFTER  THE  */
/*    "END".  THE NEXT,  IN EFFECT,  REMOVES THE  LABEL  FROM  THE   */
/*    STACK.                                                         */
/*                                                                   */
/*********************************************************************/

            J = J-1;
            K = K+22;
         END;
         ELSE K = K+1;
      END;

      WRITE FILE (B) FROM (STMT); /*  MODIFIED STATEMENT INTO FILE B. */

   END;  /* OF DO WHILE (1)  */

 END;   /*  OF MAIN PROGRAM  */
```

The original program was written into file A, the modified program was written into file B, and they were printed separately. Here is the original program used for test purposes.

```
DO WHILE (1);
  IF I=1 THEN DO;
     DO I = 1 TO 10;
           J=J+1;
        END;
        ELSE DO;
        K = K+1;
     END;
     DO I = 1 TO K;
        L = L+1;
     END;
  END;
END;
```

Here is the resulting modified program.

```
S01: DO WHILE (1);
  IF I=1 THEN S02: DO;
     S03: DO I = 1 TO 10;
           J=J+1;
        END;  /*  OF S03  */
        ELSE S04: DO;
        K = K+1;
     END;  /*  OF S04  */
     S05: DO I = 1 TO K;
        L = L+1;
     END;  /*  OF S05  */
  END;  /*  OF S02  */
END;  /*  OF S01  */
```

Following is a program that reads text from cards, scans for certain words, and underlines them. This is achieved by forming another character string UNDERLINE which is made to consist of 80 blanks at the beginning of scanning one card. Each time one of the words to be underlined is found, underline marks are inserted in the corresponding positions in UNDERLINE. Finally, the original line is printed and then the UNDERLINE string is printed on the same line. This is achieved by the statement SKIP(0) which causes skip to the next line without spacing the printer, thus causing the two-character string STMT and UNDERLINE to print on the same line. (In general SKIP(I) causes a skip to the Ith line down if $I > 0$, but no spacing if $I \leqslant 0$.) Here is the program, followed by the result of running it with some text.†

†This text was taken from the very fine book by R. W. Hamming, *Numerical Methods for Scientists and Engineers*, New York: McGraw Hill Book Co. (1962), p. 400, by permission of the publisher.

```
UL: PROCEDURE OPTIONS(MAIN);

/*************************************************************************/
/*                                                                       */
/*        THIS PROGRAM SCANS ENGLISH TEXT AND UNDERLINES SELECTED        */
/*    WORDS--IF, AND, BUT, INSIGHT, AND PURPOSE.                         */
/*                                                                       */
/*        W IS THE WORD LIST, NW IS THE NUMBER  OF  WORDS,  AND L        */
/*    THEIR RESPECTIVE LENGTHS.                                          */
/*                                                                       */
/*************************************************************************/

  DECLARE NW FIXED BINARY(15) INITIAL (5);
  DECLARE W(5) CHARACTER(15) VARYING INITIAL ('IF','AND','BUT',
       'INSIGHT','PURPOSE');
  DECLARE L(5) FIXED BINARY(15) INITIAL (2,3,3,7,7);

/*************************************************************************/
/*                                                                       */
/*        STMT IS  THE  STATEMENT  BEING  SCANNED,  UNDERLINE  A         */
/*    MATCHING CHARACTER STRING WITH BLANKS AND  UNDERLINE  MARKS.       */
/*    POS IS THE PLACE BEING SCANNED.                                    */
/*                                                                       */
/*************************************************************************/

  DECLARE STMT CHARACTER(90) VARYING;
  DECLARE UNDERLINE CHARACTER(80);
  DECLARE (POS,I) FIXED BINARY(15);
  DECLARE ALPH CHARACTER(26) INITIAL ('ABCDEFGHIJKLMNOPQRSTUVWXYZ');
  DECLARE MARKS CHARACTER(15) INITIAL ('_______________');

  ON ENDFILE (IN) STOP;


  DO WHILE (1);    /* UNTIL END OF CARD DECK  */

     READ FILE (IN) INTO (STMT);
     STMT = STMT || '          ';
     UNDERLINE = ' ';
     POS = 1;

     DO WHILE (POS<80);

     /*  NEXT STATEMENT PASSES BY BLANKS.    */

        IF SUBSTR(STMT,POS,1)=' ' THEN POS = POS+1;
        ELSE DO;

     /*  NOW WE CHECK WORDS TO BE UNDERLINED.    */
```

```
                 DO I = 1 TO NW;
                    IF (SUBSTR(STMT,POS,L(I))=W(I) &
                       INDEX(ALPH,SUBSTR(STMT,POS+L(I),1))=0)
                       THEN DO;
                       SUBSTR(UNDERLINE,POS,L(I)) = MARKS;
                    END;
                 END; /*  OF DO I = 1 TO NW    */

         /*  NEXT WE MOVE PAST THE NEXT BLANK.  */

                 POS = POS+INDEX(SUBSTR(STMT,POS),' ');
              END;  /*  OF  "ELSE DO"    */

         END;  /*  OF "DO WHILE (POS<80)"    */

         PUT EDIT (STMT)(A);
         PUT SKIP(0);
         PUT EDIT(UNDERLINE)(A);
         PUT SKIP;

      END;/*  OF "DO WHILE (1)"    */

   END;  /*  OF MAIN PROCEDURE  */
```

```
  IF WE BELIEVE THAT THE PURPOSE OF COMPUTING IS INSIGHT,
NOT NUMBERS THEN  IT FOLLOWS THAT THE MAN WHO IS TO GET THE
INSIGHT MUST UNDERSTAND THE COMPUTING.  IF HE DOES NOT
UNDERSTAND WHAT IS BEING DONE, HE IS VERY UNLIKELY TO DERIVE
MUCH VALUE FROM THE COMPUTATION.  THE BARE NUMBERS HE CAN
SEE, BUT THEIR REAL MEANING MAY BE BURIED IN THE
COMPUTATION.
  EDDINGTON HAS AN ILLUMINATING STORY OF A MAN WHO WENT
FISHING WITH A  CERTAIN SIZED NET.  WHEN HE FOUND THAT THE
FISH CAUGHT HAD A MINIMUM SIZE, HE CONCLUDED THAT THIS WAS
THE MINIMUM SIZE OF THE FISH IN THE SEA; HE MADE THE MISTAKE
OF NOT UNDERSTANDING HOW THE FISHING WAS DONE.  AND SO IT IS
WITH COMPUTING; WHAT COMES OUT DEPENDS ON WHAT GOES IN AND
HOW IT IS PROCESSED.  WITHOUT AN UNDERSTANDING OF THE
PROCESSES USED, IT IS LIKELY THAT THE EFFECTS DUE TO THE
METHOD USED IN THE COMPUTING WILL BE CONFUSED WITH THE
EFFECTS OF THE MODEL ADOPTED BY THE USER WHEN HE FORMULATED
THE PROBLEM.
  IT HAS FURTHER BEEN FOUND THAT FREQUENTLY THE PROCESS OF
COMPUTING  SHEDS GREAT LIGHT ON THE MODEL BEING COMPUTED.
COMPUTING IS A TOOL THAT SUPPLIES NUMERICAL ANSWERS, BUT IT
IS ALSO AN INTELLECTUAL TOOL FOR EXAMINING THE WORLD.
```

```
   IT IS NOT LIKELY THAT GREAT PHYSICAL INSIGHTS WILL ARISE
IN THE MIND OF A  PROFESSIONAL CODER WHO ROUTINELY CODES
PROBLEMS.  IF INSIGHTS ARE TO ARISE, AND THEY ARE WHAT WE
MOST WANT, THEN IT FOLLOWS THAT THE MAN WITH THE PROBLEM
MUST COMPREHEND AND FOLLOW THE COMPUTING.  THIS DOES NOT
MEAN THAT HE MUST DO ALL THE DETAILED WORK, BUT WITHOUT A
REASONABLY THOROUGH UNDERSTANDING OF WHAT THE COMPUTER IS
DOING IT IS UNLIKELY THAT HE CAN EITHER ARRANGE HIS WORK TO
GET THE MAXIMUM BENEFIT FROM THE COMPUTER OR ACHIEVE THE
INSIGHTS WHICH CAN AND DO RESULT FROM PROPERLY ARRANGED
COMPUTATIONS.
   EXPERIENCE INDICATES THAT IT IS GENERALLY EASIER AND
BETTER TO CONVERT AN  EXPERT IN A GIVEN FIELD INTO A PARTIAL
EXPERT IN COMPUTING THAN IT IS TO TRY TO MAKE A COMPUTING
EXPERT INTO AN EXPERT IN THE GIVEN FIELD.  BUT IF WE ARE TO
REQUIRE THIS, THEN IT FALLS ON THE COMPUTING EXPERTS TO MAKE
EVERY EFFORT TO REDUCE THE BURDENS OF LEARNING AND USING THE
COMPUTER.  ARBITRARY RULES, SPECIAL JARGON, MEANINGLESS
FORMS, CHANGES IN THE METHODS AND FORM, DELAYS IN ACCESS TO
THE MACHINE, ALL SHOULD BE REDUCED TO A MINIMUM AND
CAREFULLY MONITORED TO REDUCE THEM FURTHER WHEN THE NEXT
MACHINE OFFERS NEW OPPORTUNITIES TO LIFT THE BURDEN OF THE
NONESSENTIALS OF COMPUTING FROM THE OUTSIDER.
```

Recursive techniques can often be used in character-string processing to simplify program writing. Here is one very simple example, a procedure that reverses the order of the characters in a string. The method is as follows:

1. If the string has only one character; return it—it is already reversed.
2. Otherwise remove the first character, reverse the rest, and place the removed character on the end.

```
M: PROCEDURE OPTIONS(MAIN);

/**********************************************************************/
/*                                                                    */
/*        THIS PROCEDURE WILL REVERSE A CHARACTER STRING.             */
/*                                                                    */
/**********************************************************************/
```

```
  REVERSE: PROCEDURE(S) RETURNS(CHARACTER(50) VARYING) RECURSIVE;
     DECLARE(S) CHARACTER(50) VARYING;

     IF LENGTH(S)=1 THEN RETURN(S);
     ELSE RETURN(REVERSE(SUBSTR(S,2))||SUBSTR(S,1,1));
  END;  /*  OF REVERSE  */

/**********************************************************************/
/*                                                                    */
/*          SHORT TEST PROGRAM                                        */
/*                                                                    */
/**********************************************************************/

  PUT EDIT(REVERSE('MISSISSIPPI'))(A);

END;  /*  OF MAIN ROUTINE  */
```

```
PRINTED OUTPUT:


IPPISSISSIM
```

SNOBOL was created by a research group at Bell Laboratories starting in 1962. The group was working with formula manipulation by computer, and the languages available at that time were woefully inadequate for character-string processing. The early versions were very limited in scope and were never intended for wide use. The language, however, proved to be much more interesting and useful than the developers anticipated, and it soon was being used at a number of other installations. A version known as SNOBOL3 was implemented on half a dozen different computers and used at 30 or 40 computing centers. The coming of the IBM/360 and other third-generation computers was taken by the SNOBOL developers as an opportunity to incorporate the experience gained with SNOBOL3 into a new version, SNOBOL4, which has been implemented on most of the large computers and is now widely used. It is interesting to note that no other language has achieved comparably wide use without the support of computer manufacturers.

SNOBOL4 is a relatively comprehensive language. It can do typical scientific and data-processing calculations, although not as conveniently and efficiently as the languages designed specifically for those purposes. It also has facilities that make it possible to do list processing similar to that described in Chapter 10, and for that kind of application many programmers prefer it

SNOBOL4 Chapter 9

to PL/I. Its strong point, of course, is character-string processing, for which it has no rival.

SNOBOL is very different in several ways from other computer languages, the main difference being in the "pattern matching" statement, which is very powerful. We will start by describing the statements that are similar to other languages.

Introduction to SNOBOL4 Language

In SNOBOL4, identifiers consist of one or more letters and/or digits and may include the period and/or underline character. The first character must be a letter. Identifiers are used as variable names, function names, and statement labels.

The built-in data types include character strings, patterns, integers, and real numbers. Patterns will be discussed later. Real numbers are represented internally in floating-point form, and there are fair capabilities for computations with real numbers. They will not be described here because they are not unique and they are quite unrelated to the most interesting features of SNOBOL4. As with APL, the data type of an identifier is determined by what is assigned to it. If an integer is assigned to X, it becomes an integer variable. Later in the same program a character string may be assigned to X and X becomes a character variable. Thus, there are no statements in SNOBOL4 to declare data types.

Integer constants consist of any number of digits. (The maximum size of an integer, however, is limited by the implementation. On the IBM/360-370, the limit is $2^{31} - 1$, which is about two billion.) Character-string constants are enclosed in either quote marks (") or apostrophes (') and if quote marks are used, the string may include apostrophes and vice versa.

Any statement may have a label. The label is punched starting in column 1 of the card, and if there is no label, column 1 must be left blank.

Assignment statements have the same form as FORTRAN or PL/I. Integer expressions are like FORTRAN or PL/I except that spaces must surround the equals sign and the binary operators +, -, *, /, and **, but no space may appear between the unary operator + or - and the constant or variable to which it applies. For example, if X, Y, Z, and N, are integers,

```
A1 X = (Y + Z) / (N * (N - 1))
```

is an integer assignment statement, and A1 is a statement label.

The only operation in character-string expressions is concatenation, and that uses no operation symbol, only a space between operands.

```
X = 'SENSE'
Z = "LESS"
W = X Z
T = Z ' ' X
U = ''
V =
```

results in the value 'SENSELESS' for W, 'LESS SENSE' for T, and null strings for U and V.

If an integer is used in a context that requires a string, it is converted to a character string consisting of digits with no leading zeros. Thus, the length depends on the size of the integer.

```
C = 'N' I
```

will assign 'N1' to C if I = 1, 'N100' if I = 100. Similarly, a character string consisting of digits will be converted to a numeric value if context requires it. Thus, in

```
A = '10'
N = '100'
N = N + A + 1
```

the arithmetic operator requires a numeric value, and the values of N and A are character strings. These values will be converted and the result 111 will be calculated and assigned to N. Now N is numeric, but A still has the character string value '10'.

There are three variables that provide input and output. Whenever a character string is assigned to OUTPUT, that character string is printed starting on a new line. A string assigned to PUNCH causes a card to be punched. Each new occurrence of INPUT causes a card to be read, and INPUT has as value the 80-character string read from the card. Thus, for example, each time the statement

```
X = INPUT
```

is executed, it causes the computer to read the next card and assign the 80 characters to X. The statement

```
OUTPUT = X
```

causes X to be printed.

Normally, execution proceeds from one statement to the next in sequence. The sequence can be altered after execution of any statement by including a go to part. This consists of a colon preceded by one or more blanks and followed by one of the following:

```
(<label>)
F(<label>)
S(<label>)
F(<label>)S(<label>)
S(<label>)F(<label>)
```

The first is an unconditional go to. F means to go to that label if the statement fails; S means to go that label if the statement succeeds. The simplest example of failing or succeeding is with card reading—the operation fails when there are no more cards, i.e., at end of file.

A program ends with a card with END punched starting in column 1, i.e., as a label. Any card with an asterisk in column 1 is treated as a comment.

Now we can write a complete program. The following program reads a deck of cards and prints the contents of the cards with a sequence number followed by four blanks inserted at the left.

```
1            N = 1
2 LOOP       X = INPUT                                               :F(END)
3            OUTPUT = N '    ' X
4            N = N + 1                                               :(LOOP)
5 END
```

Here is the output for a deck of fifteen input cards:

```
1         SNOBOL4 IS A COMPUTER PROGRAMMING LANGUAGE
2     CONTAINING MANY FEATURES NOT COMMONLY FOUND IN
3     OTHER PROGRAMMING LANGUAGES.  IT EVOLVED FROM
4     SNOBOL(1,2,3), A LANGUAGE FOR STRING MANIPULATION,
5     DEVELOPED AT BELL LABORATORIES, INCORPORATED, IN
6     1962.  EXTENSIONS TO SNOBOL THROUGH VARIOUS VERSIONS
7     HAVE MADE IT A USEFUL TOOL IN SUCH AREAS AS COMPILATION
8     TECHNIQUES, MACHINE SIMULATION, SYMBOLIC MATHEMATICS,
9     TEXT PREPARATION, NATURAL LANGUAGE TRANSLATION,
10     LINGUISTICS, AND MUSIC ANALYSIS.
11          THE BASIC DATA ELEMENT OF SNOBOL4 IS A
12     STRING OF CHARACTERS, SUCH AS THIS LINE OF
13     PRINTING.  THE LANGUAGE HAS OPERATIONS FOR
14     JOINING AND SEPARATING STRINGS, FOR TESTING
15     THEIR CONTENTS, AND FOR MAKING REPLACEMENTS IN THEM.
```

There are special functions called predicates that may, by definition, succeed or fail. These are six that act on numbers:

LT(X,Y)	succeeds if	$X < Y$
LE(X,Y)	" "	$X \leq Y$
EQ(X,Y)	" "	$X = Y$
NE(X,Y)	" "	$X \neq Y$
GE(X,Y)	" "	$X \geq Y$
GT(X,Y)	" "	$X > Y$

There are four other built-in primitives. INTEGER(X) succeeds if X is an integer or a character string representing an integer. INTEGER(X) succeeds for X = 17 or '17' but fails for X = 'INT' or '3.0', for example.

LGT(X,Y) compares two character strings X and Y and succeeds if X is lexically greater than Y, i.e., if X would appear after Y in a dictionary.

IDENT and DIFFER compare two data items and succeed if they are truly identical or different, respectively. For example, if we assign values to X and Y as follows

```
X = 'ABC' 'DEF'
Y = 'ABCDEF'
```

then IDENT(X,Y) succeeds because both X and Y are identical character strings. But if we assign

```
X = 17
Y = '17'
```

then IDENT(X,Y) fails because X is an integer and Y is a character string. EQ(X,Y) succeeds, however, because EQ, expecting numerical arguments, converts Y to an integer and compares the resulting values.

All predicates have the null string as their value if they succeed and can be inserted anywhere a null string could be inserted in a statement, causing tests at that point in the evaluation, but otherwise having essentially no effect. If one fails, the execution of the statement is interrupted at that point.

As an example, we will write the greatest common divisor program here in SNOBOL4. First, one way to get the remainder after dividing I by J is to subtract J from I over and over as long as I is greater than or equal to J. This can be done in one statement in SNOBOL4:

```
LOOP I = GE(I,J) I - J        :S(LOOP)
```

Following is a program that reads X and Y, each from the very left end of a separate card, and calculates the greatest common divisor:

```
1 START   X = TRIM(INPUT)                                         :F(END)
2         Y = TRIM(INPUT)
3         N1 = X
4         N2 = Y
5 LOOP1   N3 = N1
6 LOOP2   N3 = GE(N3,N2) N3 - N2                                  :S(LOOP2)
7         EQ(N3,0)                                                :S(PRINT)
8         N1 = N2
9         N2 = N3                                                 :(LOOP1)
10 PRINT  OUTPUT = 'THE GCD OF ' X ' AND ' Y ' IS ' N2 :(START)
11 END
```

Here is the printed output for four pairs of data cards.

```
THE GCD OF 91 AND 169 IS 13
THE GCD OF 4095 AND 65535 IS 15
THE GCD OF 23 AND 31 IS 1
THE GCD OF 17 AND 119 IS 17
```

The function TRIM(X) trims the trailing blanks from the character string X. Notice how easily neat output can be assembled using concatenation.

Patterns and Pattern-matching Statements

Now let us consider the pattern-matching statement. The simplest form is the following

```
A  B
```

where A is a character string called the subject and B is a pattern. The simplest example of a pattern is a character string. This statement causes a search in A for the pattern B and it succeeds if B occurs in A and fails otherwise. Thus,

```
A = 'SNOBOL4'
A     'NO'                    :S(END)
```

the second statement succeeds because the string NO occurs as a substring of A.

The next variation is

```
A  B = C
```

In this case, if the pattern match succeeds, the pattern is replaced by C. If the pattern match doesn't succeed, replacement does not take place. For example, in

```
A = 'DISCREET'
A 'ET' = 'TE'
```

the match will succeed, and ET will be replaced by TE, resulting in the value DISCRETE for A. If a pattern occurs more than once, only the first is found in one execution of the statement. Thus, in

```
X = 'MISSISSIPPI'
Y = 'ISS'
Z = '#'
X   Y = Z
```

will result in the value X = 'M#ISSIPPI'.

Now let us consider more complicated patterns. A pattern may consist of several alternatives:

```
P = 'IF' | 'AND' | 'BUT'
```

and P will match any of the three words. Here is a simple program that removes all if's, and's, and but's from text on cards, and following it is the result of applying this program to the first paragraph of the text used as an example near the end of Chapter 8.

```
1        P = 'IF' | 'AND' | 'BUT'
2 A      S = INPUT                                        :F(END)
3 B      S  P =                                           :S(B)
4        OUTPUT = S                                       :(A)
5 END
```

```
PRINTED OUTPUT:



   WE BELIEVE THAT THE PURPOSE OF COMPUTING IS INSIGHT,
 NOT NUMBERS THEN  IT FOLLOWS THAT THE MAN WHO IS TO GET THE
 INSIGHT MUST UNDERST THE COMPUTING.    HE DOES NOT
 UNDERST WHAT IS BEING DONE, HE IS VERY UNLIKELY TO DERIVE
 MUCH VALUE FROM THE COMPUTATION.  THE BARE NUMBERS HE CAN
 SEE,  THEIR REAL MEANING MAY BE BURIED IN THE
 COMPUTATION.
```

Note that as long as the statement B succeeds, it is repeated because of its go to part S(B). Thus, every IF, AND, and BUT will be removed. Note also that this simple-minded program removed the AND from UNDERSTAND.

Concatenation is also possible, and parentheses may be used. Thus,

```
P = ' ' ('IF' | 'AND' | 'BUT') (' ' | ',')
```

will match a substring of the subject that consists of a blank followed by one of the three words IF, AND, or BUT, followed by either a blank or a comma. Concatenation has the higher precedence. Thus,

```
P = A B | C D
```

has the same meaning as

```
P = (A B) | (C D)
```

Next, the "conditional assignment"

```
A B . C
```

where C is an identifier, results in assigning to C the part of A which B matches, if the match succeeds. Thus, for example,

```
1          X = 'MISSISSIPPI'
2          Y = 'MI' | 'SI' | 'PI'
3          N = 1
4  A       X Y . Z =                                          :F(END)
5          OUTPUT = 'AFTER STEP ' N ' Z=' Z ' AND X=' X
6          N = N + 1                                          :(A)
7  END
```

results in printing the following four lines

```
AFTER STEP 1 Z=MI AND X=SSISSIPPI
AFTER STEP 2 Z=SI AND X=SSSIPPI
AFTER STEP 3 Z=SI AND X=SSPPI
AFTER STEP 4 Z=PI AND X=SSP
```

Note that there must be spaces surrounding the period when it is used as a sign for conditional assignment, just as spaces must surround every operator symbol.

Here is a program that searches text read from cards for any of the five words IF, AND, BUT, INSIGHT, or PURPOSE preceded by a blank and followed by a blank, period, or comma. Whenever a match is found, quote marks are inserted around the word:

```
1          P = 'IF' | 'AND' | 'BUT' | 'INSIGHT' | 'PURPOSE'
2          Q = ' ' | '.' | ','
3  A       S = ' '  INPUT                                     :F(END)
4  B       S  ' '  P . X  Q . Y  = ' "' X '"' Y               :S(B)
5          OUTPUT = S                                         :(A)
6  END
```

and here are the results:

```
PRINTED OUTPUT:

  "IF" WE BELIEVE THAT THE "PURPOSE" OF COMPUTING IS "INSIGHT",
NOT NUMBERS THEN  IT FOLLOWS THAT THE MAN WHO IS TO GET THE
"INSIGHT" MUST UNDERSTAND THE COMPUTING.  "IF" HE DOES NOT
UNDERSTAND WHAT IS BEING DONE, HE IS VERY UNLIKELY TO DERIVE
MUCH VALUE FROM THE COMPUTATION.  THE BARE NUMBERS HE CAN
SEE, "BUT" THEIR REAL MEANING MAY BE BURIED IN THE
COMPUTATION.
```

Note that the conditional assignment assigns the word to X and the character that follows it to Y. Then, the pattern that is matched is replaced by

```
' "' X '"' Y
```

which does exactly what is required. Since the entire pattern that is matched is replaced and since that includes the character preceding and following the word, these two characters must be included on the right of the equals sign if they are to be kept.

The following program illustrates a common error.

```
1          S = 'PEAS AND QUEUES'
2          P = 'IF' | 'AND' | 'BUT'
3 A        S  P . X  = '"' X '"'                         :F(END)
4          OUTPUT = S                                    :(A)
5 END
```

and here are the first few lines of printed results, which will go on for pages.

```
PEAS "AND" QUEUES
PEAS ""AND"" QUEUES
PEAS """AND""" QUEUES
PEAS """"AND"""" QUEUES
PEAS """""AND""""" QUEUES
PEAS """"""AND"""""" QUEUES
PEAS """""""AND""""""" QUEUES
PEAS """"""""AND"""""""" QUEUES
PEAS """""""""AND""""""""" QUEUES
PEAS """"""""""AND"""""""""" QUEUES
PEAS """""""""""AND""""""""""" QUEUES
PEAS """"""""""""AND"""""""""""" QUEUES
PEAS """""""""""""AND""""""""""""" QUEUES
PEAS """"""""""""""AND"""""""""""""" QUEUES
```

The first execution of statement A finds the word AND in S and puts quotes around it. The second execution, presumably intended to find a second ocurrence of the pattern P, if one exists, finds the same AND and puts a second set of quotes on it. This continues until the allowable string size is exceeded. This does not occur in the preceding program because no match will occur unless the word is preceded by a blank.

There are a number of built-in special patterns that make certain common tasks easier and/or more efficient. The more important ones are described briefly here.

ANY(X) matches any single character that occurs in X, and NOTANY(X) matches any single character that is not in X.

A null string matches anything, even a null string. NULL is a variable that initially has the null string as its value. Following is an example of the use of NULL:

```
P = ('HONEY' | NULL)  'BEE'
S  P = 'BUG'
```

If the word 'HONEYBEE' occurs in S, it will be replaced by the word 'BUG'. If the word 'BEE' occurs, not preceded by 'HONEY', then it alone will be replaced by the word 'BUG'.

LEN(N) matches any string of length N where N is an integer. Thus, for example,

```
P = ',' LEN(3) . X ','
```

will match two commas with any three characters between them, and the three characters will be assigned to X.

FENCE matches a null string the first time it is met in the process of scanning, looking for a match. The second time, however, it causes the whole matching process to be given up. For example, the pattern

```
P = 'A ' 'DOG'
```

causes a search first for 'A '. When the first 'A ' is found, then a check is made for the word 'DOG' following it. If that fails, then the search for another 'A ' is made, and if another 'A ' is found, a check is made for whether or not it is followed by the word 'DOG', etc. However, for the pattern

```
Q = 'A ' FENCE 'DOG'
```

if the first 'A ' is not followed by 'DOG', the FENCE prevents backing up to look for a new 'A '. Thus, the search for a match to Q can succeed only if the first 'A ' is followed by 'DOG'. Similarly, the pattern match

```
Q = FENCE  ANY('0123456789')
S  Q
```

succeeds only if the first character in the subject S is a digit. The FENCE prevents retrying the pattern match in the second or any other position.

The string position that is being scanned is called the *curser position.* If @X is included in a pattern, it matches a null string the same as NULL and causes the curser position to be assigned to X. For example, after executing

```
        Q = @N  NOTANY('0123456789')
     A  S  Q
```

N will have as its value the position of the first character in S that is not a digit. The statement A will fail if S contains only digits.

TAB(N) matches all characters from the present position of the curser to position N. RTAB(N) matches up to the Nth position from the right. REM matches from the present position to the end. Suppose we want to print a number I, which is less than 1,000,000, with exactly enough leading blanks in front to use a total of six columns. We can do it as follows:

```
     ('     ' I)  RTAB(6) REM . X
```

We concatenate five blanks in front of I. RTAB(6) matches all but the last six characters, and thus REM matches exactly the last six characters. They are assigned to X, which can then be used for printing.

ARB matches any string of characters. Thus,

```
S "," ARB . X ","
```

will succeed if S contains two commas, and the characters between them will be matched by ARB and assigned to X.

```
S "(" ARB . X ")"
```

will search for the first right parenthesis following the first left parenthesis, and everything between will be assigned to X. These are not necessarily matching parentheses. For example, if S = 'A + (B + (C + D))', then 'B + (C + D' will be assigned to X.

BAL will match any character string in which parentheses are properly balanced. Thus, it will match, for example, 'A + B', 'XYZ.3', '(A + B)', 'XYZ(A)(CD#)' , or '()', but not '(ABC' , '(A))', or ')('.

Two very useful patterns are SPAN and BREAK. SPAN(X) matches as long as possible a string of the characters of X. As a pattern, it fails if it does not find even one character of X. Thus, for example,

```
     A  S  SPAN('0123456789') . N
```

starts by examining the first character of S. If it is a digit, then the second character is examined, etc., until a non-digit is found, and SPAN matches the string of digits. If the first character is not a digit, then the pattern fails, and another attempt to match is attempted starting from the second character, etc. Thus, the above statement will fail completely only if S contains no digits at all. If S contains at least one digit, then the pattern matches as long as possible a run of digits starting at the first digit in S. The statement

```
A  S  '$'  SPAN('0123456789')
```

will succeed only if S contains a '$' followed by at least one digit, and SPAN will match the first string of digits found following a '$'. If S = '123$XYZ$11ABC$200', then SPAN will match the '11'.

BREAK(X) similarly matches from the curser position up to but not including the first character in X. It fails as a pattern if the first character found is in X. As an example, suppose S consists of a list of words separated by commas. Then, in

```
S  BREAK(',') . N ',' =
```

BREAK(',') would match up to the first comma, and this would be assigned to N. The ',' would match the comma and cause it to be thrown away with the first word by the replacement caused by the equals sign.

ARBNO(P) matches an arbitrary number of patterns P in succession. It matches as few as possible. Thus,

```
S = 'MISSISSIPPI'
S   ('M' ARBNO('ISS') 'I') . X
```

will match, with ARBNO('ISS') being *no* copies of 'ISS', with 'M' matching the first letter of S and 'I' the second. Then, the value of X is 'MI'. However,

```
S  ('M' ARBNO('ISS') 'IPPI') . X
```

tries and fails with ARBNO representing no copies of 'ISS' and one copy. With two copies, however, it succeeds, and X = 'MISSISSIPPI'.

As one more example of pattern matching, here is a program that reads text and underlines the words 'IF', 'AND', 'BUT', 'INSIGHT', and 'PURPOSE'. Statement B searches for one of those words preceded by a blank and followed by a blank, comma, or period. It replaces the word by '#'. The next two statements replace the # by a number of underline marks equal to the length of the word. This is repeated until all of these words are removed from S. Then, all other characters in S except underline characters are changed to blanks by statement C, done repeatedly. Then string S, which contains appropriate underlining, and string 7, a copy of the original text, are printed on the same line. This latter is accomplished by defining a new output with carriage control character +. IBM/360-370 SNOBOL4 uses the FORTRAN I/O routines, and the function

```
OUTPUT(X, Y, Z)
```

defines a new output variable whose name is the value of X, using FORTRAN I/O unit Y and FORTRAN FORMAT statement *Z*. The output is identical to that produced by the last program of Chapter 8.

```
 1       OUTPUT("OVERPRINT",6,"('+',132A1)")
 2       UL = '__________'
 3       P = 'IF' | 'AND' | 'BUT' | 'INSIGHT' | 'PURPOSE'
 4       P = ' ' . X  P . Y  (' ' | '.' | ',') . Z
 5 A     S = ' '  INPUT                                      :F(END)
 6       T = S
 7 B     S  P  =  X '#' Z                                    :F(C)
 8       UL  LEN(SIZE(Y)) . W
 9       S  '#'  = W                                         :(B)
10 C     S  NOTANY('_ ')  =  ' '                             :S(C)
11       OUTPUT = T
12       OVERPRINT = S                                       :(A)
13 END
```

PRINTED OUTPUT:

```
 IF WE BELIEVE THAT THE PURPOSE OF COMPUTING IS INSIGHT, NOT NUMBERS THEN
IT FOLLOWS THAT THE MAN WHO IS TO GET THE INSIGHT MUST UNDERSTAND THE
COMPUTING.  IF HE DOES NOT UNDERSTAND WHAT IS BEING DONE, HE IS VERY
UNLIKELY TO DERIVE MUCH VALUE FROM THE COMPUTATION.  THE BARE NUMBERS
HE CAN SEE, BUT THEIR REAL MEANING MAY BE BURIED IN THE COMPUTATION.
```

The following discussion on SNOBOL4 statement syntax may be helpful. Suppose A is a label and B, C, D, E, and F are expressions. Then, the statement

```
A B
```

causes the expression B to be evaluated. The purpose may be to determine whether or not it fails or to evaluate a function that serves some purpose other than simply returning a value.

```
A B C
```

causes a search for pattern C in subject B. In

```
A B C D E F
```

B is the subject and C D E F is interpreted as a pattern whose parts C, D, E, and F are to be concatenated. Similarly, if A is a label, B is an identifier, and C, D, E, and F are expressions,

```
A B = C
```

is a simple assignment statement,

```
A B C = D
```

is a pattern-matching statement with subject B and pattern C to be replaced by D if a match occurs. In

```
A B C D = E F
```

A is a label, B is the subject, C D is interpreted as the pattern, and E F will replace the pattern if pattern matching succeeds. Of course, the label always may be omitted, in which case column 1 is left blank.

Indirect Reference

If A has as its value the character string 'B', then $A used in SNOBOL as a variable is the same as B. In general, the symbol $ means that the expression following is to be evaluated and used as a variable name, and reference should be made to that variable. This idea has a number of uses. One of the simplest is that it provides a way to do a calculated go to.

As an illustration, let us do the water bill problem once more. Let us assume that I, the type of calculation, is punched in column 1 of a card, NGAL in columns 2 to 7, and the name in 8 to 27. Here is the program.

```
 1 START  L = INPUT                                       :F(END)
 2        OUTPUT = L
 3        L LEN(1) . I  LEN(6) . NGAL  LEN(20) . NAME :($('F' I))
 4 F1     BILL = NGAL / 200                               :(PRINT)
 5 F2     BILL = 20 + NGAL / 250                          :(PRINT)
 6 F3     BILL = LE(NGAL,25000) 1000                      :S(PRINT)
 7        BILL = 1000 + (NGAL - 25000) / 400              :(PRINT)
 8 F4     BILL = GT(NGAL,5000) 3000                       :S(PRINT)
 9        BILL = GT(NGAL,3000) 2000                       :S(PRINT)
10        BILL = 1000                                     :(PRINT)
11 PRINT  OUTPUT = 'BILL=$' BILL ' FOR ' NAME             :(START)
12 END
```

```
PRINTED OUTPUT:


1002000JONES
BILL=$10 FOR JONES
3000100YAMAMOTO
BILL=$1000 FOR YAMAMOTO
4004000LEE
BILL=$2000 FOR LEE
2005000SMITH
BILL=$40 FOR SMITH
```

The go to `S($('F' I))` will cause a go to `F1`, `F2`, `F3`, or `F4` according to the value of `I` because the value of the character-string expression following the `$` is `F1`, `F2`, `F3`, or `F4`.

There is an interesting way of defining arrays in SNOBOL4 using indirect reference. We simply generate a name for each element in an expression and use it with indirect reference. For example, we might have a list of elements called `A1`, `A2`, `A3`, `A4`, etc. To reference the `I`th element, we simply use `$('A' I)` because, for example, if `I` has the value 100, then the expression in parentheses is `A100`, and the reference `$('A100')` is the same as the reference `A100`.

Here is a SNOBOL4 program for labeling all `DO`'s and placing comments on the matching `END`'s. Statement `B` searches for the first remaining `DO` or `END`. The next statement determines whether it was `'DO'` or `'END'`. If it was a `DO`, then the stack counter `J` is increased, and `'S' I`, the label, is stored as the value of `$('T' J)`, i.e., the value of `T1`, `T2`, `T3`, or `T4`, etc. Then, the label `'S' I ':'` is inserted in front of the `DO`. In the case of an `END`, the comment `' /* OF ' $('T' J) ' */ '`, which includes the last label on the stack, is inserted, and then the stack counter `J` is decreased by one. Note that at each step the part of the statement that is processed is removed from `Z` and moved to `SOUT`, so that a statement has been completely processed when no more `DO`'s or `END`'s are found in `Z`.

```
1        I = 1
2        J = 0
3 A      Z = INPUT                                             :F(END)
4        SOUT = ''
5 B      Z    ARB . X   ('DO' | 'END;') . Y   REM . Z          :F(D)
6        J = IDENT(Y,'DO')   J + 1                             :F(C)
7        $('T' J) = 'S' I
8        SOUT = SOUT X 'S' I ': DO'
9        I = I + 1                                             :(B)
10 C     SOUT = SOUT X 'END;   /*   OF '   $('T' J)   '        */   '
11       J = J - 1                                             :(B)
12 D     OUTPUT = SOUT Z                                       :(A)
13 END
```

Here are the printed results using the same input as was used in Chapter 8 for the same problem.

```
S1: DO WHILE (1);
  IF I=1 THEN S2: DO;
     S3: DO I = 1 TO 10;
            J=J+1;
        END;  /*  OF S3  */    ELSE S4: DO;
        K = K+1;
     END;  /*  OF S4  */
     S5: DO I = 1 TO K;
        L = L+1;
     END;  /*  OF S5  */
  END;  /*  OF S2  */
END;  /*  OF S1  */
```

Function Definition in SNOBOL4

A function definition in SNOBOL4 includes two parts:

(1) a call to a function DEFINE which indicates the prototype for the function being defined and its entry point and

(2) the SNOBOL language procedure.

DEFINE has two arguments. The first is a character string showing the prototype. It includes the function name followed by the list of formal parameters enclosed in parentheses and separated by commas. Following that is a list of local variables separated by commas. The second argument is the name of the entry point.

```
DEFINE('F(X,Y)Z, W' , FO)
```

defines a function F with two parameters X and Y and two local variables Z and W and with entry point FO. If no local variables are needed, they are simply omitted:

```
DEFINE('F(X,Y)' , FO)
```

If the entry point is omitted, it is assumed to be the same as the function name:

```
DEFINE('F(X,Y)')
```

If the function has no parameters, the parameters are omitted, but the parentheses are needed both in the definition and in the function reference:

```
DEFINE('F()')
Y = F()
```

Note that there is never a space between a function name and the left parenthesis.

In the procedure, the function value is assigned to the function name. (In SNOBOL4, it is permissible anytime to use an identifier simultaneously as a function or variable name and as a label, and, thus, it is in particular permissible to use a function name as an entry point label.)

The reserved go to name RETURN is used in the go to part in order to cause a return to the calling program. The reserved go to name FRETURN causes a return plus a failure indication that can be used with a failure go to in the main program. The programmer may use this in any way he chooses.

The program logic requires that the DEFINE statement be *executed* before the function is used. The DEFINE statement and the procedure need not be together in the program.

As a simple example of a function definition, here is a definition for the function TYPE(S) which examines a single character S and returns 4 for digits, 3 for letters, 2 for math symbols, 1 for blanks, and 0 for anything else. With it is a short test program that reads a card and examines each character, printing its type as was done in PL/I. In the printed result, the type of each character is printed below it.

```
*****************************************************************
*                                                               *
*          THE FOLLOWING  FUNCTION  HAS  ONE  PARAMETER,        *
*     WHICH IS A SINGLE CHARACTER,  AND RETURNS  AS  ITS        *
*     VALUE, THE TYPE, ACCORDING TO THIS CODE:                  *
*                                                               *
*          0 ILLEGAL                                            *
*                                                               *
*          1 BLANK                                              *
*                                                               *
*          2 OPERATION SYMBOL                                   *
*                                                               *
*          3 LETTER                                             *
*                                                               *
*          4 DIGIT                                              *
*                                                               *
*****************************************************************
*
        DEFINE('TYPE(S)')                               :(R)
TYPE    '0123456789'   S                                :F(T1)
        TYPE = 4                                        :(RETURN)
T1      'ABCDEFGHIJKLMNOPQRSTUVWXYZ'   S                :F(T2)
        TYPE = 3                                        :(RETURN)
T2      '()+*-/=' S                                     :F(T3)
        TYPE = 2                                        :(RETURN)
T3      IDENT(S,' ')                                    :F(T4)
        TYPE = 1                                        :(RETURN)
T4      TYPE = 0                                        :(RETURN)
*
```

```
***************************************************************
*                                                             *
*       THE FOLLOWING IS A SHORT PROGRAM TO CHECK THE         *
*    FUNCTION "TYPE".  IT READS A CARD,  PRINTS IT, AND       *
*    THEN FORMS A SEQUENCE CONSISTING OF ONE DIGIT, THE       *
*    TYPE,  FOR EACH CHARACTER IN THE  INPUT  SEQUENCE,       *
*    AND PRINTS THAT. THUS FOR EACH CHARACTER, THE TYPE       *
*    IS PRINTED BELOW IT.                                     *
*                                                             *
***************************************************************
*
R        Z = TRIM(INPUT)                              :F(END)
         OUTPUT = Z
         LINE = ''
L        Z  LEN(1) . C  =                             :F(P)
         LINE = LINE TYPE(C)                          :(L)
P        OUTPUT = LINE                                :(R)
END
```

Here are the printed results for two input cards.

```
X = A(5)+3*B
312132422423
AREA = 6*SIDE*SIDE
333312142333323333
```

Here is a SNOBOL version of the SCAN subroutine in Chapter 8. It divides statements into "terminal symbols" that are numbers, identifiers, or mathematical symbols, assigning the value 1, 2, or 3, respectively to TOKEN in order to indicate which type occurred. If an illegal character occurs, an error message is printed using the function ERROR. In case of an illegal symbol or end of statement, the SCAN routine does a failure return (FRETURN), and the main routine uses this to signal that the next card is to be read. In the scan routine, the SNOBOL-style calculated go to is used in the second statement in order to distinguish the five cases that may occur when a new search for a symbol is started. Those five cases correspond to the five types of characters: illegal, blank, math symbol, letter, or digit.

```
***************************************************************
*                                                             *
*       THE FUNCTION "TYPE" IS THE SAME  FUNCTION  AS         *
*   WAS DEFINED IN THE PREVIOUS EXAMPLE.                      *
*                                                             *
***************************************************************
*
         ALPH = 'ABCDEFGHIJKLMNOPQRSTUVWXYZ'
         DIGIT = '0123456789'
         DEFINE('TYPE(S)')                            :(D2)
TYPE     DIGIT S                                      :F(T1)
         TYPE = 4                                     :(RETURN)
```

```
T1      ALPH S                                          :F(T2)
        TYPE = 3                                        :(RETURN)
T2      '()+*-/=' S                                     :F(T3)
        TYPE = 2                                        :(RETURN)
T3      IDENT(S,' ')                                    :F(T4)
        TYPE = 1                                        :(RETURN)
T4      TYPE = 0                                        :(RETURN)
*
**************************************************************
*                                                            *
*        THE FOLLOWING PROCEDURE SCANS STATEMENTS IN A       *
*   SIMPLE  COMPUTER  LANGUAGE,   BREAKING  THEM  INTO       *
*   TERMINAL SYMBOLS  AND  ASSIGNING  THEM  TOKENS  AS       *
*   FOLLOWS:                                                 *
*                                                            *
*        1 NUMBERS OF ONE OR MORE DIGITS                     *
*                                                            *
*        2 IDENTIFIERS,  CONSISTING OF ANY  NUMBER  OF       *
*   LETTERS AND/OR DIGITS,  OF WHICH THE FIRST MUST BE       *
*   A LETTER                                                 *
*                                                            *
*        3 OPERATION SYMBOLS                                 *
*                                                            *
*        BLANKS   BETWEEN   TERMINAL   SYMBOLS   ARE         *
*   DISREGARDED.  AN ILLEGAL CHARACTER  CAUSES  1)  AN       *
*   ERROR MESSAGE TO BE PRINTED,  AND  2)  A  FAILURE        *
*   RETURN TO THE MAIN PROGRAM.  WHEN SCAN  IS  CALLED       *
*   AND THERE ARE NO  MORE  TERMINAL  SYMBOLS  IN  THE       *
*   INPUT STRING, THERE IS A FAILURE RETURN.                 *
*                                                            *
**************************************************************
*
D2      DEFINE('SCAN()')                                :(D3)
SCAN    STP = STP + SLENGTH
S1      P = LEN(STP - 1) LEN(1) . S
        STMT P               :S($('CASE' TYPE(S)))F(FRETURN)
CASE0   ERROR('ILLEGAL SYMBOL')                         :(FRETURN)
CASE1   STP = STP + 1                                   :(S1)
CASE2   TOKEN = 3
        TERMSYM = S
        SLENGTH = 1                                     :(RETURN)
CASE3   TOKEN = 2
        STMT LEN(STP - 1) SPAN(ALPH DIGIT) . TERMSYM
        SLENGTH = SIZE(TERMSYM)                         :(RETURN)
CASE4   TOKEN = 1
        STMT  LEN(STP - 1) SPAN(DIGIT) . TERMSYM
        SLENGTH = SIZE(TERMSYM)                         :(RETURN)
*
**************************************************************
*                                                            *
*        THIS PROCEDURE PRINTS AN ERROR MESSAGE AND  A       *
*   POINTER TO THE ERROR LOCATION.                           *
*                                                            *
**************************************************************
```

```
*
D3      DEFINE('ERROR(MESSAGE)')                              :(MAIN)
ERROR   '___________________________' LEN(STP - 1) . P
        OUTPUT = P '|   ' MESSAGE                             :(RETURN)
*
*************************************************************
*                                                           *
*          THIS IS A SHORT TEST PROCEDURE.  IT READS  AN    *
*     EXPRESSION,  CALLS SCAN REPEATEDLY, AND PRINTS THE    *
*     TERMINAL SYMBOLS AND THEIR TOKENS.                    *
*                                                           *
*************************************************************
*
MAIN    STMT = TRIM(INPUT)                     :F(END)
        OUTPUT = STMT
        STP = 1
        SLENGTH = 0
M1      SCAN()                                                :F(MAIN)
        OUTPUT = 'TOKEN=' TOKEN '  TERMSYM=' TERMSYM  :(M1)
END
```

Here is the printed output.

```
AREA = 6*SIDE*SIDE
TOKEN=2  TERMSYM=AREA
TOKEN=3  TERMSYM==
TOKEN=1  TERMSYM=6
TOKEN=3  TERMSYM=*
TOKEN=2  TERMSYM=SIDE
TOKEN=3  TERMSYM=*
TOKEN=2  TERMSYM=SIDE
X = (A+B-(C*13/100))
TOKEN=2  TERMSYM=X
TOKEN=3  TERMSYM==
TOKEN=3  TERMSYM=(
TOKEN=2  TERMSYM=A
TOKEN=3  TERMSYM=+
TOKEN=2  TERMSYM=B
TOKEN=3  TERMSYM=-
TOKEN=3  TERMSYM=(
TOKEN=2  TERMSYM=C
TOKEN=3  TERMSYM=*
TOKEN=1  TERMSYM=13
TOKEN=3  TERMSYM=/
TOKEN=1  TERMSYM=100
TOKEN=3  TERMSYM=)
TOKEN=3  TERMSYM=)
          #@#@#
__________|  ILLEGAL SYMBOL
                      $
______________________|  ILLEGAL SYMBOL
                      $
______________________|  ILLEGAL SYMBOL
```

SNOBOL4 procedures may be recursive. For example, here is a procedure to calculate binomial coefficients again using the principal of Pascal's triangle.

```
         DEFINE('B(N,K)','B1')
         OUTPUT = 'FINAL ANSWER IS ' B(6,3)            :(END)
B1       B = EQ(K,0) 1                                 :S(RETURN)
         B = EQ(K,N) 1                                 :S(RETURN)
         B = B(N - 1,K - 1) + B(N - 1,K)               :(RETURN)
END


PRINTED OUTPUT:


FINAL ANSWER IS 20
```

In Chapter 8 there is a recursive procedure for reversing a character string. The algorithm is as follows:

1. If the string has length one, return it unaltered.
2. If the string does not have length 1, take off the first character, reverse the rest, and replace the first character on the end.

Here is a SNOBOL4 version.

```
         DEFINE('REVERSE(S)X,Y')                       :(MAIN)
REVERSE  REVERSE = EQ(SIZE(S),1) S                     :S(RETURN)
         S  LEN(1) . X  REM . Y
         REVERSE = REVERSE(Y) X                        :(RETURN)
MAIN     OUTPUT = REVERSE('MISSISSIPPI')
END
```

The printed results are

```
                    IPPISSISSIM
```

Note that it is necessary to declare X and Y as local variables here because they must be stacked each time the procedure is re-entered. Only local variables are stacked. In SNOBOL4, a variable is assumed to be global unless it is specifically declared to be local.

This chapter can provide only an introduction to SNOBOL4. There are many features that haven't yet been mentioned. Probably the most important are related to pattern matching. It is possible to understand the pattern-processing process in some detail and use that knowledge to accomplish some ends more easily and quickly. Related to that are facilities for immediate assignment, which is like conditional assignment (P . X) except that it takes place as soon as that component of the pattern is matched, not when the entire pattern is matched. "Unevaluated expressions" allow a pattern expression to be calculated only immediately before it is needed. Together these allow you to determine in a single pattern match whether, for example, the same word appears twice, by assigning a word to a variable immediately and then using that variable in the pattern to look for another copy of that word. Another important facility in SNOBOL4 is "programmer-defined data types," which, in particular, give SNOBOL4 list-processing capabilities somewhat similar to those in PL/I which are described in the next chapter. In addition, there are many, many other goodies in the form of built-in patterns, functions, and key words. For anyone who has a serious interest in character-string processing, the well written *The SNOBOL4 Programming Language*† is a necessity.

†R. E. Griswold, J. F. Poage, and I. P. Polonsky, *The SNOBOL4 Programming Language* (Englewood Cliffs, N.J.: Prentice-Hall, Inc., 1968).

PART IV
LIST PROCESSING

We have studied the use of subscripted variables in every language and structures in PL/I and COBOL for representing a collection of related information. For complex interrelated information, for example, the interconnection of cities on a route map, another technique has been developed which sometimes is considerably more effective. This has come to be known as *list processing* and is the subject of this part of the book.

Sometimes list-processing techniques also turn out to make possible efficient use of storage. Thus, for example, if we had 10 lists and 100 items spread among them, with the possibility that all would be on any one list, it would seem that we would need to provide storage for 1000 items. Even though we know that 900 of the provided spaces will be vacant at any given time, we don't know which 900. List-processing techniques provide a solution that requires very little more than space for the 100 items. Because of this, list-processing techniques are especially widely used in computer operating systems, particularly in storing queues.

Although list-processing techniques are not the best solution to most problems, they are widely enough used and often useful enough so that every serious student of computer science must be familiar with them.

List Processing in PL/I Chapter 10

In this chapter the notions of based storage and pointers are introduced and their application in list processing is explained. First, the most applicable features of PL/I language will be described.

Based Storage

A pointer variable is a variable whose value is the address of some data in memory. A pointer variable can be assigned a value with the built-in function ADDR. For example

```
DECLARE P POINTER,
     X FIXED BINARY (31);
P = ADDR(X);
```

assigns to P the address of X. There is a special value NULL that is definitely not the address of any data in the computer, and that value can also be assigned to a pointer

```
P = NULL;
```

or used in tests, for example, as in

```
DO WHILE (P¬= NULL);
```

Also, pointers can be set by the ALLOCATE statement to tell where a newly allocated memory area is located. This statement will be discussed in more detail later.

Normally, a DECLARE statement performs two functions:

1. It defines the identifier and the type of data which it represents, i.e., whether it is fixed binary, decimal, floating point, or character, and the size of each item and, if it is an array, the dimensions of the array, etc.
2. It allocates storage for this data and associates the location of the storage with the identifier.

Thus, usually there is associated with each identifier (1) data characteristics and (2) a fixed assigned-memory area.

With based variables, these two functions are separated. The statement

```
DECLARE AZ CHARACTER (100) BASED;
```

says that AZ is a character variable of length 100, but memory is *not* allocated and thus AZ is not associated with any fixed place in memory. It has a size, 100 bytes. When you use AZ, you must tell separately where it is, and for that purpose you use a pointer. The notation used in PL/I is a little strange:

```
P -> AZ
```

means the variable AZ at address P. (The symbol -> is read "points to," but this expression should be read, "The AZ that P points to.") It is possible to have more than one data item referred to as AZ. By changing the pointer value appropriately we can refer to any one of them in much the same manner as a subscripted variable has many values, and we can refer to any one by choosing the subscript properly.

To serve the function (2) above there is a statement ALLOCATE:

```
ALLOCATE AZ SET (P);
```

This statement allocates storage suitable for AZ and sets the pointer P to its address. It can be done many times, and each time a new memory area will be allocated, and P will be assigned the address of the new memory area. If all the values of P are saved in some way, any of the allocated memory areas can be referred to and used.

If a certain area of allocated storage is no longer needed, it can be freed. The statement

```
FREE P -> AZ;
```

frees the memory allocated to AZ at address P, and that memory can then be allocated at a later time to AZ again or to some other variable.

It is possible to designate a pointer in the declaration of a based variable:

```
DECLARE V CHARACTER (80) BASED (T);
```

Then, in any use of V, if no pointer is explicitly written, the pointer T is assumed.† Thus, with the above declaration,

```
GET EDIT (V)(A(80));
```

is equivalent to

```
GET EDIT (T -> V)(A(80));
```

but it is still possible to write

```
GET EDIT (P -> V)(A(80));
```

i.e., to override the designation of T.

There are a couple of problems that might well be mentioned here. First, there are many, many kinds of errors you can commit when using based variables that are not checked in the PL/I implementation. For example, there is no check when you use P -> AZ that P really points to memory allocated to AZ or even to anything of the same size as AZ. The following statements illustrate this kind of error:

```
DECLARE AZ CHARACTER (100) BASED,
        P POINTER,
        X(10) DECIMAL FLOAT (14);
P = ADDR(X);
P -> AZ = ' ';
```

will cause 100 blank characters to be stored in memory starting at location

†The IBM PL/I F compiler requires this form of declaration. Furthermore, with PL/I F P(I) —> V and A.P —> V are *not* allowed. The pointer must be a simple pointer variable. The newer "optimizing compiler" does not have these restrictions.

X. This will entirely fill the array X with data that are meaningless as floating-decimal data, and since X requires 10 eight-byte variables (a total of 80 characters), 20 more blank characters will be stored in memory assigned to something else. Errors can result unpredictably. Unpredictable errors can also result from the statement

```
FREE P -> AZ;
```

unless P really points to a memory area actually allocated to AZ.

Another problem is memory fragmentation. After repeated allocating and freeing of various-sized memory areas, the memory available for allocation may consist of many small segments scattered widely, and even though more than enough memory may be available, it may be impossible to allocate to a variable because no adequate single segment of contiguous storage is available.

A third warning is that in most large computers multi-programming is used—several programs are put in the computer memory at the same time. There is no assurance that a program will be placed in any specific place in memory. Since pointers are actual memory addresses, they have meaning in one computer run, but, generally, the pointer values assigned in one computer run will point to the wrong area of memory on the next run and, thus, they will be totally meaningless. For that reason, there is no provision for printing pointer values and, generally, there is no purpose in writing pointers to tape or disk units. (There is another similar concept in PL/I called "offset" which gives the location of data in an area relative to the beginning of an area. Since these relative locations can be the same on successive runs, it may make sense to save offset values from one computer run to the next.)

For the purpose of understanding what is really happening in list processing, we would like to print pointer values. Printing pointer values can also serve as a debugging aid. Unless we can print pointers and locations, we can't confirm directly that they are being set up in the manner which we have planned. In the IBM/360-370, a pointer is four bytes, the same as FIXED BINARY (31). Probably the easiest solution is simply to print the pointer as FIXED BINARY (31), but if the PL/I processor thinks that it is dealing with a pointer, it will refuse to print it. One possible solution is to use the following procedure.

```
LIE: PROCEDURE (X) RETURNS (FIXED BINARY (31));
   DECLARE X POINTER;
   RETURN (UNSPEC(X));
END;
```

UNSPEC is a built-in machine-dependent function that converts its argument to the bit string representation used in the computer. Actually, no conversion need take place. It is only necessary that the computer consider the result as a bit string instead of a pointer. Then, the bit string is converted to fixed binary because of the RETURNS clause in the PROCEDURE statement. Again, no conversion is really necessary. It is only necessary that the computer consider the result to be FIXED BINARY (31). This procedure returns exactly what it received, but since the PL/I processor considers the result a binary integer instead of a pointer, it is willing to print it.

List-processing Concepts

There is a technique for representing a collection of related information in memory using pointers, known as "list processing," although it is by no means the only way to process information structures such as ordinary lists. In fact, it is the best way only in a minority of cases. Yet, since there are important practical applications, it should be understood by every serious student of computer science.

Let us consider a simple sequential list consisting of the nine words of the sentence, "The quick brown fox jumped over the lazy dog." There will be nine items on the list. Each item might consist of one word and a pointer to the next item, as in Fig. 10.1. Usually, a pointer to the first item on the list will be stored somewhere. HP serves that purpose in the diagram.

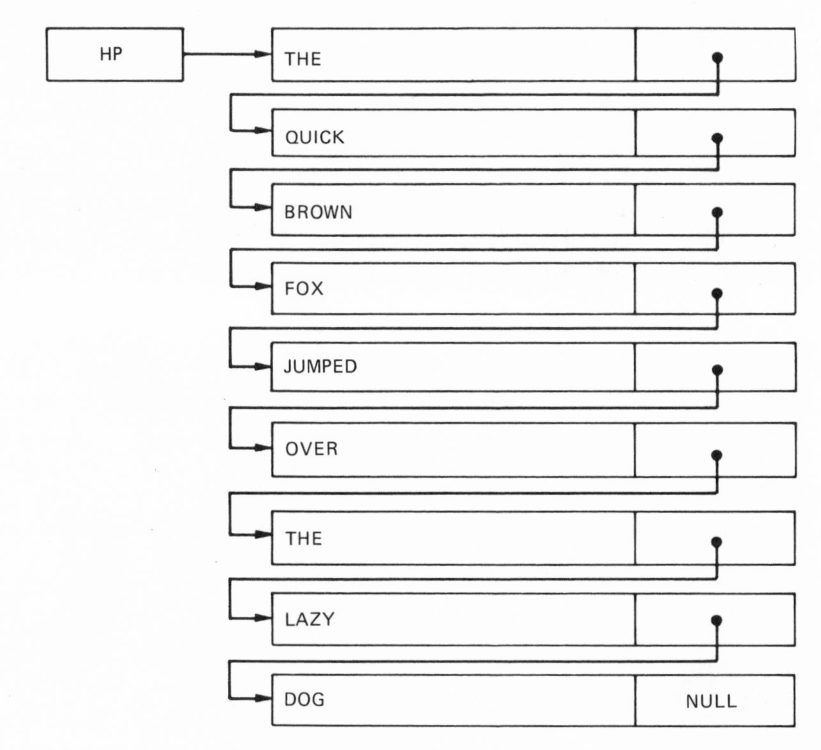

Figure 10.1. A Linked List.

Here is a printout of such a list from the memory, with pointers printed. (This was printed by the procedures on pages (261 and 262) and the main program on page (266).)

```
ORIGINAL LIST
THE QUICK BROWN FOX JUMPED OVER THE LAZY DOG

VALUE OF HP IS       1492554
    LOCATION       WORD                 POINTER
     1492554       THE                  1492530
     1492530       QUICK                1492506
     1492506       BROWN                1492482
     1492482       FOX                  1492458
     1492458       JUMPED               1492434
     1492434       OVER                 1492410
     1492410       THE                  1492386
     1492386       LAZY                 1492362
     1492362       DOG               2130706432
```

Note that NULL prints as 2130706432 which, in binary, is 01111111000000 000000000000000000.† The value of NULL is not the same in all implementations.

The declarations for this list might be

```
DECLARE 1 ITEM BASED,
          2 WORD CHARACTER (12) VARYING,
          2 P POINTER;
```

The list would be set up by reading in the sentence and somehow dividing it into words. For example, if the words are punched on a card in the form 'THE ' 'PURPOSE ' 'OF ' 'COMPUTING ' 'IS ' 'INSIGHT ',then successive words can be read by the statement

```
GET LIST (W);
```

Next, you must allocate memory for an item

```
ALLOCATE ITEM SET (Q);
```

Then, you can move the word just read into the newly allocated structure by the statement

```
Q -> WORD = W;
```

†Actually, the value is 11111111000000000000000000000000. The first 1, the sign, is lost in conversion in LIE.

If this is the first item on the list, you should set the pointer HP to point to this item:

```
HP = Q;
```

If this is not the first item, then the pointer on the previous item should be set to point to this one. If R points to the previous item, then this can be accomplished by the statement

```
R -> P = Q;
```

If this is the last item on the list, you should make its pointer null:

```
Q -> P = NULL;
```

Otherwise, you must wait until another item is allocated and then set the pointer in this item to point to the new item.

Following are a complete procedure to set up this list in memory and a procedure to print it out:

```
      MAKELIST: PROCEDURE(HP);

/***********************************************************************/
/*                                                                     */
/*         THIS PROCEDURE READS WORDS FROM CARDS, MAKES A THREADED     */
/*    LIST FROM THEM, AND SETS HP TO POINT TO THE FIRST WORD.          */
/*                                                                     */
/***********************************************************************/

      DECLARE (HP, Q, R) POINTER,
               W CHARACTER(12) VARYING,
               FIRST BIT(1) INITIAL ('1'B),
               PAU BIT(1) INITIAL('0'B),
               TRUE BIT(1) INITIAL('1'B),
               FALSE BIT(1) INITIAL ('0'B);

      ON ENDFILE PAU = TRUE;

      DO WHILE(¬PAU);

         GET LIST (W);

         IF ¬PAU THEN DO;

            ALLOCATE ITEM SET (Q);
            Q->WORD = W;

            IF FIRST THEN DO;
               HP = Q;
```

```
            FIRST = FALSE;
         END;

         ELSE R->P = Q;
         Q->P = NULL;    /* WILL BE CHANGED IF NOT LAST  */
         R = Q;   /*  SET R FOR NEXT TIME THRU LOOP   */

      END;   /*  OF IF ¬PAU THEN DO   */

   END;   /*  OF DO WHILE(¬PAU)   */

END;   /*  OF PROCEDURE MAKELIST   */


  LIST: PROCEDURE(X);

/**********************************************************************/
/*                                                                    */
/*         THIS PROCEDURE PRINTS A LIST OF WORDS. THE PARAMETER IS    */
/*    A POINTER TO THE FIRST ITEM ON THE LIST.                        */
/*                                                                    */
/*         THE FIRST LOOP PRINTS THE WORDS, ONE AFTER THE OTHER ON    */
/*    ONE LINE. THE SECOND LOOP PRINTS ONE WORD PER LINE, WITH THE    */
/*    LOCATION AND POINTER VALUE.                                     */
/*                                                                    */
/**********************************************************************/


     DECLARE (X,T) POINTER;

     T = X;

     DO WHILE(T¬=NULL);
        PUT EDIT(T->WORD,' ')(A,A);
        T = T->P;
     END;

     PUT SKIP(2) EDIT('VALUE OF HP IS',LIE(HP))(A,F(12));
     PUT SKIP;
     PUT EDIT('    LOCATION    WORD                 POINTER')(A);
     PUT SKIP;

     Q = X;

     DO WHILE (Q¬=NULL);
        PUT EDIT(LIE(Q), '    ', Q->WORD, LIE(Q->P))
                (F(12),  A(4),   A(12),   F(12)   );
        PUT SKIP;
        Q = Q->P;   /* GET POINTER TO NEXT ITEM   */
     END;   /* OF DO WHILE   */

  END;   /*  OF LIST   */
```

What can you do with a list like this? You can sort it, for example,

```
SORTED LIST
BROWN DOG FOX JUMPED LAZY OVER QUICK THE THE

VALUE OF HP IS      1492554
    LOCATION      WORD                 POINTER
      1492506     BROWN                1492362
      1492362     DOG                  1492482
      1492482     FOX                  1492458
      1492458     JUMPED               1492386
      1492386     LAZY                 1492434
      1492434     OVER                 1492530
      1492530     QUICK                1492554
      1492554     THE                  1492410
      1492410     THE               2130706432
```

(This was sorted using the procedure on page (265).)

Note that every item is in the same place as it was before. Sorting was accomplished by changing the values of HP and the other pointers. It is also possible to insert an item in a list or delete an item by simply changing pointers but without moving any items. Here is an example. (It was made by the procedure on page (264).)

```
LIST WITH "LARGE" INSERTED
BROWN DOG FOX JUMPED LARGE LAZY OVER QUICK THE THE

VALUE OF HP IS      1492554
    LOCATION      WORD                 POINTER
      1492506     BROWN                1492362
      1492362     DOG                  1492482
      1492482     FOX                  1492458
      1492458     JUMPED               1492338
      1492338     LARGE                1492386
      1492386     LAZY                 1492434
      1492434     OVER                 1492530
      1492530     QUICK                1492554
      1492554     THE                  1492410
      1492410     THE               2130706432
```

It is not difficult to write ordinary procedures to do sorting, inserting, and deleting with lists like this if you use the techniques used in the MAKELIST and LIST procedures. It is a good exercise. For example, using the method of stepping through the list in LIST, you might make a procedure INSERT that searches for the place in which a new item must be placed and then changes the pointers. You might sort by taking items off the unsorted list and inserting them one by one into a new initially empty list using INSERT.

These computer printouts, however, were produced by a pair of recursive procedures. These procedures illustrate well the recursive style of thinking.

Recursive procedures for inserting and sorting by the same method using LISP are presented in the next chapter.

First, we define a procedure INSERT that inserts one item in proper sequence in a sorted list. The method is as follows:

1. If the sorted list is empty, make a list with the one new item.
2. If the new item precedes the first element in the sorted list, place that element on the front of the list.
3. Otherwise, remove the first item from the list, using INSERT insert the new item in the rest of the list, and then place the removed item back on the front of the list.

Here is a listing of INSERT.

```
  INSERT: PROCEDURE(X,Y) RECURSIVE RETURNS(POINTER);

/************************************************************************/
/*                                                                      */
/*        THIS PROCEDURE INSERTS THE ITEM THAT  Y  POINTS  TO  IN       */
/*   SEQUENCE INTO THE LIST  THAT  X  POINTS  TO  AND  RETURNS  A       */
/*   POINTER TO THE RESULTING LIST.                                     */
/*                                                                      */
/************************************************************************/

     DECLARE (X,Y) POINTER;

/************************************************************************/
/*                                                                      */
/*        IF THE LIST IS EMPTY,  RETURN A LIST WITH THIS ONE  NEW       */
/*   ELEMENT.                                                           */
/*                                                                      */
/************************************************************************/

     IF X=NULL THEN DO;
        Y->P = NULL;
        RETURN(Y);
     END;

/************************************************************************/
/*                                                                      */
/*        IF THE NEW ITEM PRECEDES THE FIRST ITEM  ON  THE  LIST,       */
/*   PUT IT ON THE FRONT OF THE LIST AND RETURN POINTER TO IT.          */
/*                                                                      */
/************************************************************************/


       IF Y->WORD<=X->WORD THEN DO;
          Y->P = X;
          RETURN(Y);
       END;
```

```
/*********************************************************************/
/*                                                                   */
/*         OTHERWISE REMOVE FIRST ITEM FROM LIST, INSERT NEW ITEM,   */
/*    AND REPLACE FIRST ITEM.  NOTE THAT X->P POINTS TO  THE  LIST   */
/*    WITH THE FIRST ITEM REMOVED.                                   */
/*                                                                   */
/*********************************************************************/

      X->P = INSERT(X->P,Y);
      RETURN(X);
   END;  /*  OF INSERT  */
```

Next, we define SORT, which has a pointer to an unsorted list as a parameter and returns a pointer to the sorted list.

1. If the list has only one item, then return the original list—it is already sorted.
2. Otherwise, remove the first item from the list, sort the rest of the list (using SORT), and finally insert the removed item in the sorted list (using INSERT).

Here is a listing for SORT.

```
  SORT: PROCEDURE(X) RECURSIVE RETURNS(POINTER);
     DECLARE X POINTER;

/*********************************************************************/
/*                                                                   */
/*         THIS PROCEDURE SORTS THE LIST  THAT  X  POINTS  TO  AND   */
/*    RETURNS A POINTER TO THE RESULTING LIST.                       */
/*                                                                   */
/*         IF THERE IS ONLY ONE ITEM, RETURN THE ORIGINAL LIST.      */
/*                                                                   */
/*********************************************************************/

      IF X->P=NULL THEN RETURN(X);

/*********************************************************************/
/*                                                                   */
/*         OTHERWISE, REMOVE THE FIRST ITEM, SORT THE REST OF THE    */
/*    LIST, AND INSERT THE ITEM IN THE RESULT.                       */
/*                                                                   */
/*********************************************************************/

      RETURN(INSERT(SORT(X->P),X));

   END;  /*  OF SORT  */
```

Here is a computer listing for the main procedure that produced the listings in the preceding discussion.

```
M: PROCEDURE OPTIONS (MAIN);

/***********************************************************************/
/*                                                                     */
/*        THIS PROGRAM MAKES A THREADED LIST OF WORDS,  AND  THEN      */
/*   USES THE RECURSIVE PROCEDURES "INSERT" AND  "SORT"  TO  SORT      */
/*   THE LIST AND INSERT ONE ITEM IN THE SORTED LIST.                  */
/*                                                                     */
/*        "ITEM" IS THE NODE STRUCTURE,  HP POINTS TO THE HEAD OF      */
/*   THE LIST,  AND W IS THE INPUT WORD.  WHEN THE LIST IS  BEING      */
/*   SET UP,  Q POINTS TO THE  NEW  ITEM  AND  R  PCINTS  TO  THE      */
/*   PREVIOUS ITEM.  FIRST IS TRUE UNTIL THE FIRST ITEM HAS  BEEN      */
/*   SET UP. PAU IS SET TRUE ON END OF FILE ON INPUT.                  */
/*                                                                     */
/***********************************************************************/

  DECLARE 1 ITEM BASED,
            2 WORD CHARACTER(12) VARYING,
            2 P POINTER;

  DECLARE (HP,Q,R) POINTER,
          (NULL,UNSPEC) BUILTIN;

  LIE: PROCEDURE(X) RETURNS (FIXED BINARY(31));
     DECLARE X POINTER;

/***********************************************************************/
/*                                                                     */
/*        THE PROCEDURE LIE ACTUALLY DOES NOTHING BUT  MAKE  PL/I      */
/*   THINK THAT THE POINTER IS FIXED BINARY(31) SO IT WILL PRINT.      */
/*                                                                     */
/***********************************************************************/

     RETURN (UNSPEC(X));

  END;  /*  OF LIE  */

/***********************************************************************/
/*                                                                     */
/*        NOTE: THE PROCEDURES "MAKELIST", "PRINTLIST", "INSERT",      */
/*   AND "SORT" WERE INSERTED HERE WHEN THE PROGRAM WAS RUN.           */
/*                                                                     */
/***********************************************************************/

   PUT SKIP EDIT('ORIGINAL LIST')(A);
   PUT SKIP;
   CALL MAKELIST(HP);
   CALL LIST(HP);


   PUT SKIP(3) EDIT('SORTED LIST')(A);
   PUT SKIP;
   R = SORT(HP);
   CALL LIST(R);
```

```
 PUT SKIP(3) EDIT('LIST WITH "LARGE" INSERTED')(A);
 PUT SKIP;
 ALLOCATE ITEM SET(Q);
 Q->WORD = 'LARGE';
 R = INSERT(R,Q);
 CALL LIST(R);

ND;  /* OF MAIN PROCEDURE  */
```

This kind of list is more complicated than an ordinary subscripted vari-ble. Does it have any advantages? Probably not in most cases, but in some ases it definitely does. Inserting an item into an ordinary list requires mov-ng all items beyond the new one—inserting is definitely easier in a pointer ist. Frequently, pointer lists permit more efficient use of storage. For ex-mple, if we have 100 items, any or all of which may be on any of 10 lists, rdinary techniques require space for 100 items on each list, a total of 1000 paces. For pointer lists, you need space only for the 100 items. Another nteresting idea is to include several pointers with each item and use one to equence the list in one way, another to sequence it in another way. Thus, ointer lists have a great deal of flexibility.

Let us now consider a couple of rather different examples. Figure 10.2 hows a maze. We can represent its structure in the computer by using list tructures in the following way: For the entrance, exit, each dead end, and ach point where there is a fork in the road, we will store a data item. In this naze, there is no node where four or more paths meet. We have chosen to nake all data items consist of the node name, three pointers, and one num-er, which we will use later to keep track of how many times we pass a node vhile wandering around in the maze.

```
DECLARE 1 NODE,
          2 NAME CHARACTER(4),
          2 POINTERS(3) POINTER,
          2 COUNT FIXED BINARY(15);
```

Now, we describe a node by putting its name in the data item. For ordinary odes where three paths meet, we put pointers to the three nodes that will e met first if we go on those three paths. We will arrange them in clockwise rder, although this is unimportant. For dead-end nodes, the pointer to the earest node is stored as POINTER(1), and the other two pointers are NULL. The input node is stored with the next node as the second pointer, with the irst and third null, which is more convenient.

The required input data for this maze is shown beside the maze. For each ode the node name followed by the names of the nodes to which the pointer nust point—or NULL—is shown. These data were punched into cards, and hese were used as input data for the program MAZE, which sets up the maze

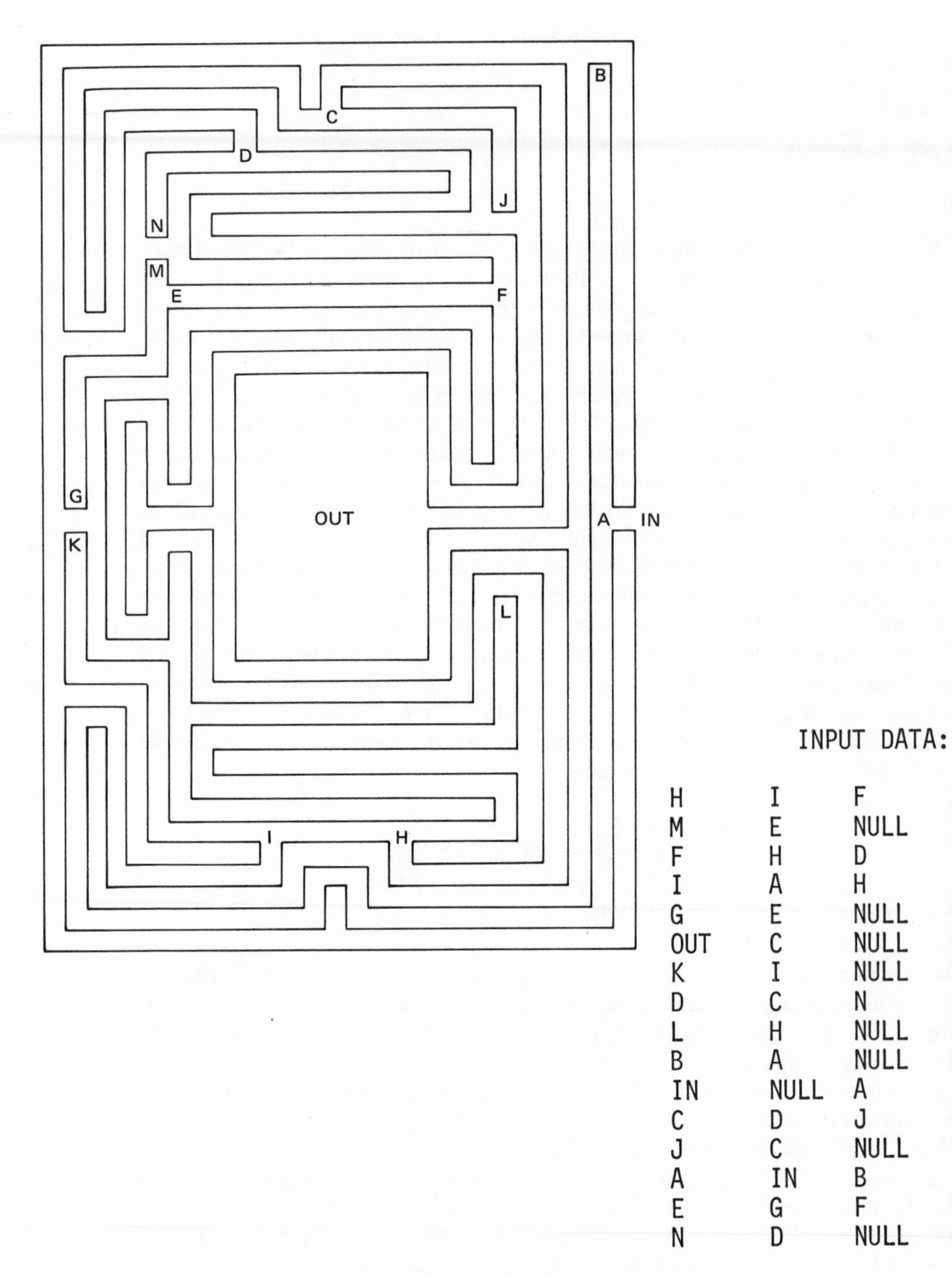

Figure 10.2. Maze example.

as a list structure in memory, and then searches for a path from the entrance to the exit. The program listing is on page (270).

SETUP is the procedure that makes the list structure. PTABLE is a table of pointers. Each time a node is allocated, its pointer is entered in this table. For each card read, for the node name and for each of the non-NULL pointers, a check is made by searching PTABLE to see whether or not a NODE structure has been allocated for that node, and if it has not, it is allocated at this time. Then, all pointers in the node represented by this card can be filled in. Thus, for example, the first card reads H I F L. Storage is immediately allocated for all four nodes, but the pointers are filled in only for the one allocated to H. The third card is F H D E. When it is read, storage is allocated for E and D. F and H have already been allocated and are found in the table. Then the pointers for F are filled in. When the input node is met, its pointer is stored as the value of IN. Each time a card is read, the corresponding node is completed, and one line is printed showing the values of the pointers. The printed table is shown following the program listing.

The procedure SOLVE actually finds a path through the maze. It uses the strategy of simply taking the first path to the right at every intersection and turning about face at every dead end. In this procedure, TAIL is the pointer to the node we are leaving, HEAD the pointer to the node we are going to. We start by making TAIL equal NULL and making HEAD point to the input node.

The essential statements in the procedure SOLVE are the following: (The complete procedure listing is on page (273).)

```
L:  DO WHILE(1);
    P=HEAD;
    IF P->POINTERS(2)=NULL & P->POINTERS(3)=NULL THEN DO;
          HEAD = TAIL;
          TAIL = P;
    END;
    ELSE DO;
          DO I=1 TO 3 WHILE (P->POINTERS(I)=TAIL);
          END;
          I = I+1;
          IF I>3 THEN I=I-3;
          HEAD = P->POINTERS(I);
          TAIL = P;
    END;
END; /* OF DO WHILE(1) */
```

The third statement determines whether or not the node that HEAD points to is a dead end. If it is, the combination of the three statements P = HEAD; HEAD = TAIL; TAIL = P; results in an about face. If the node that HEAD points to is not a dead end, then the statements DO I=1 TO 3 WHILE(P->POINTERS(I)>=TAIL); END; locate in the list of pointers the one that points to the node we just came from. The next three statements make HEAD take as its value the next pointer down the list, or the first if TAIL matches the last. This points to the node we will go to if we turn right. Making HEAD take that value and making TAIL the pointer to this node means turning right at this corner.

In the actual program there are a few more statements. One checks whether or not we have arrived at the node named OUT. The others simply print a running account of where we go as we go through the maze. The printed results follow the program listings.

Note that in this program the main program consists of the two statements CALL SETUP(IN,OUT); and CALL SOLVE(IN);.

```
MAZE: PROCEDURE OPTIONS(MAIN);

/***********************************************************************/
/*                                                                     */
/*       THIS PROGRAM  CONTAINS  A  PROCEDURE  TO  MAKE  A  LIST       */
/*   STRUCTURE FOR A MAZE,  AND A PROCEDURE TO FIND A SOLUTION TO      */
/*   THE MAZE.                                                         */
/*                                                                     */
/***********************************************************************/


   DECLARE (IN,OUT) POINTER,
           (NULL,UNSPEC) BUILTIN;

   LIE: PROCEDURE(X) RETURNS(FIXED BINARY(31));


/***********************************************************************/
/*                                                                     */
/*       "LIE" MAKES IT POSSIBLE TO PRINT POINTERS.                    */
/*                                                                     */
/***********************************************************************/


      DECLARE X POINTER;
      RETURN(UNSPEC(X));
   END;  /*  OF LIE  */


   SETUP: PROCEDURE(IN,OUT);
```

```
/*********************************************************************/
/*                                                                   */
/*      THIS PROCEDURE MAKES THE LIST STRUCTURE  FOR  THE  MAZE     */
/*   AND PRINTS A TABLE TO SHOW ITS STRUCTURE.  IN  AND  OUT  ARE   */
/*   POINTERS TO THE ENTRANCE AND EXIT.                              */
/*                                                                   */
/*      NODE IS THE STRUCTURE FOR EACH CORNER IN THE MAZE,  AND     */
/*   IN IS THE POINTER TO THE ENTRANCE NODE.  IN NODE,  POINTERS    */
/*   POINT TO THE THREE NEAREST NEIGHBORS,  EXCEPT IN THE CASE OF   */
/*   A DEAD END,  POINTERS(2) AND POINTERS(3) ARE NULL.  COUNT IS   */
/*   USED IN THIS PROBLEM TO COUNT THE NUMBER OF TIMES THIS  NODE   */
/*   IS PASSED.                                                      */
/*                                                                   */
/*      BRANCH IS THE STRUCTURE INTO WHICH INPUT DATA IS  READ.     */
/*   BRANCH.NAME(1) IS THE NODE NAME, AND THE OTHER NAMES ARE THE   */
/*   NAMES TO WHICH IT IS CONNECTED DIRECTLY.  (DEAD END HAS  TWO   */
/*   "NULLS".) PTABLE IS A LIST  OF  POINTERS  TO  NODES  ALREADY   */
/*   CREATED, AND NUM IS THE NUMBER OF NODES SO FAR ON THAT LIST.   */
/*   WE MAKE P POINT TO THE NAME WE ARE LOOKING AT AND Q  TO  THE   */
/*   FIRST NAME ON THAT CARD,  I.  E.  THIS NODE NAME. PAU IS SET   */
/*   TRUE AT END OF FILE. NODE.COUNT IS USED TO KEEP TRACK OF THE   */
/*   NUMBER OF TIMES THIS NODE IS PASSED.                            */
/*                                                                   */
/*********************************************************************/

    DECLARE (IN,OUT) POINTER;
    DECLARE 1 NODE BASED(P),
              2 NAME CHARACTER(4),
              2 POINTERS(3) POINTER,
              2 COUNT FIXED BINARY(31);

    DECLARE 1 BRANCH,
              2 NAME(4) CHARACTER(4),
              2 FILLER CHARACTER(64),   /* TO MAKE FULL CARD  */
            PTABLE(100) POINTER,
            (NUM,I,J) FIXED BINARY(31),
            (P,Q) POINTER,
            PR BIT(1),
            PAU BIT(1) INITIAL('0'B),
            TRUE BIT(1) INITIAL('1'B);

    PUT SKIP EDIT('GRAPH STRUCTURE')(X(20),A);
    PUT SKIP EDIT('NAME','P','1','2','3')(5 A(11));
    PUT SKIP(2);
    ON ENDFILE(SYSIN) PAU = TRUE;
    NUM = 0;

/*********************************************************************/
/*                                                                   */
/*      MAIN LOOP                                                    */
/*                                                                   */
/*********************************************************************/
```

```
      DO WHILE(1);
         READ FILE(SYSIN) INTO (BRANCH),
         IF PAU THEN RETURN;

/***********************************************************************/
/*                                                                     */
/*          EXAMINE THE FOUR NAMES, ALLOCATING FOR ANY NOT FOUND IN    */
/*    THE TABLE, AND FILLING IN THE POINTERS FOR THE FIRST NAME.       */
/*                                                                     */
/***********************************************************************/

         DO J = 1 TO 4;
            IF BRANCH.NAME(J)='NULL' THEN P=NULL;

/***********************************************************************/
/*                                                                     */
/*          SEARCH FOR NAME IN TABLE.                                  */
/*                                                                     */
/***********************************************************************/

            ELSE DO;
               PR = TRUE;
               I = 1;
               DO WHILE(PR & I<=NUM);
                  P = PTABLE(I);
                  PR = (BRANCH.NAME(J)¬=P->NODE.NAME);
                  IF PR THEN I = I+1;
               END;

               IF I>NUM THEN DO;

/***********************************************************************/
/*                                                                     */
/*          NOT FOUND--MAKE ALLOCATION AND ENTRY IN TABLE.             */
/*                                                                     */
/***********************************************************************/

                  NUM = NUM+1;
                  ALLOCATE NODE SET(P);
                  P->NODE.NAME = BRANCH.NAME(J);
                  PTABLE(NUM) = P;
               END;  /*  OF IF I>NUM  */

            END;  /*  OF ELSE DO  */

/***********************************************************************/
/*                                                                     */
/*          NOW P POINTS TO THE BRANCH WHOSE  NAME  IS  BRANCH.NAME    */
/*    AND THIS HAS BEEN ENTERED IN THE TABLE.                          */
/*                                                                     */
/*          IF THIS IS THE FIRST NODE NAME,  THEN SET Q TO POINT TO    */
/*    IT.  OTHERWISE INSERT P AS POINTER(J-1) FOR THIS NODE, I. E.     */
/*    THE ONE THAT Q POINTS TO.                                        */
/*                                                                     */
/***********************************************************************/
```

```
      IF J=1 THEN DO;
         Q = P;
         P->COUNT = 0;
         IF P->NODE.NAME='IN  ' THEN IN = P;
         IF P->NODE.NAME='OUT ' THEN OUT = P;
      END;

      ELSE Q->POINTERS(J-1) = P;

   END;  /*  OF DO J=1 TO 4  */

   PUT SKIP EDIT(Q->NODE.NAME,LIE(Q),(LIE(Q->POINTERS(J))
        DO J = 1 TO 3),Q->NODE.COUNT)(A(4),4 F(11));

  END;  /*  OF DO WHILE(TRUE)  */

END;  /*  OF PROCEDURE SETUP  */


SOLVE: PROCEDURE(IN);
/*************************************************************************/
/*                                                                       */
/*        THIS PROCEDURE SEARCHES THE MAZE FOR A WAY OUT. NODE IS        */
/*   DEFINED IN SETUP.  IN IS THE POINTER TO THE  ENTRANCE  NODE.        */
/*   HEAD AND TAIL POINT TO THE NODE WE ARE GOING TO  AND  COMING        */
/*   FROM RESPECTIVELY.  P POINTS TO THE NODE WE ARE AT.  I IS  A        */
/*   TEMPORARY.                                                          */
/*                                                                       */
/*************************************************************************/

   DECLARE 1 NODE BASED(P),
              2 NAME CHARACTER(4),
              2 POINTERS(3) POINTER,
              2 COUNT FIXED BINARY(31),
           (P,IN,HEAD,TAIL) POINTER,
           I FIXED BINARY(15),
           NULL BUILTIN,
           TRUE BIT(1) INITIAL('1'B);

  PUT SKIP(3);
  HEAD = IN;
  TAIL = NULL;

  DO WHILE(1); /*  REALLY UNTIL "OUT" OR "IN" IS FOUND  */

     P = HEAD;
     P->COUNT = P->COUNT+1;
     IF P¬=NULL THEN PUT EDIT(P->NODE.NAME)(X(5),A(4));

     IF P->NODE.NAME='OUT ' THEN DO;
        PUT SKIP(2) LIST('WE HAVE FOUND THE WAY OUT OF THE MAZE');
        RETURN;
     END;
```

```
      IF HEAD=NULL THEN DO;  /*  WE ARE BACK AT THE "IN" NODE.  */
         PUT SKIP(2) LIST('THERE IS NO WAY OUT OF THIS MAZE');
         RETURN;
      END;

      IF P->POINTERS(2)=NULL & P->POINTERS(3)=NULL THEN DO;
         PUT SKIP LIST('THIS IS A DEAD END. RETURN TO ');
         HEAD = TAIL;
         TAIL = P;
      END;

      ELSE DO;  /*  TURN RIGHT AT THIS CORNER  */
         DO I=1 TO 3 WHILE(P->POINTERS(I)¬=TAIL);
         END;
         I = I+1;
         IF I>3 THEN I = I-3;
         HEAD = P->POINTERS(I);
         TAIL = P;
         IF P->COUNT=3 THEN
           PUT SKIP LIST('WE HAVE EXHAUSTED THIS POSSIBILITY.  LET US
 GO BACK TO ');
         ELSE PUT SKIP LIST('WE NOW BRANCH TO ');
      END;

    END;  /*  OF DO WHILE(1)  */

  END;  /*  OF SOLVE  */


/***********************************************************************/
/*                                                                     */
/*         MAIN PROGRAM                                                */
/*                                                                     */
/***********************************************************************/

  CALL SETUP(IN,OUT);
  CALL SOLVE(IN);

END;  /*  OF MAIN PROCEDURE  */
```

GRAPH STRUCTURE

NAME	P	1	2	3
H	1492536	1492512	1492488	1492464
M	1492440	1492416	2130706432	2130706432
F	1492488	1492536	1492392	1492416
I	1492512	1492368	1492536	1492344
G	1492320	1492416	2130706432	2130706432
OUT	1492296	1492272	2130706432	2130706432
K	1492344	1492512	2130706432	2130706432
D	1492392	1492272	1492248	1492488
L	1492464	1492536	2130706432	2130706432
B	1492224	1492368	2130706432	2130706432

```
IN        1492200 2130706432    1492368 2130706432
C         1492272    1492392    1492176    1492296
J         1492176    1492272 2130706432 2130706432
A         1492368    1492200    1492224    1492512
E         1492416    1492320    1492488    1492440
N         1492248    1492392 2130706432 2130706432


        IN
WE NOW BRANCH TO            A
WE NOW BRANCH TO            B
THIS IS A DEAD END. RETURN TO          A
WE NOW BRANCH TO            I
WE NOW BRANCH TO            H
WE NOW BRANCH TO            F
WE NOW BRANCH TO            D
WE NOW BRANCH TO            C
WE NOW BRANCH TO            J
THIS IS A DEAD END. RETURN TO          C
WE NOW BRANCH TO            OUT

WE HAVE FOUND THE WAY OUT OF THE MAZE
```

Another example of the use of lists is the analysis of languages. For example, simple expressions can be represented as a kind of graph called a tree, with two kinds of nodes:

1. A variable or constant with no branches going out—a kind of dead end.
2. An operation with branches going out to the operands.

Figure 10.3 shows some examples.

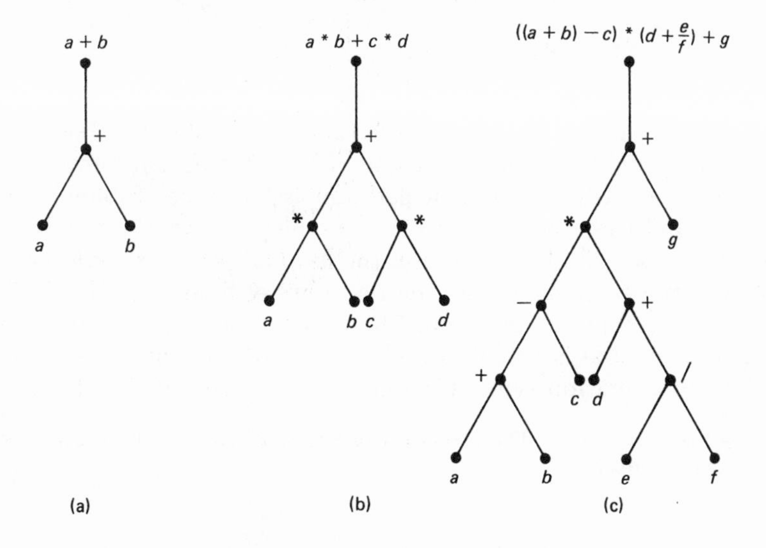

Figure 10.3 Examples of graphs for expressions.

Another representation of expressions is the so-called Polish notation. For it you write the two operands followed by the operator. For example, $a + b$ is written $ab+$.† If the operands are expressions, they both precede the operation. For example, in $a * b + c * d$, $a * b$ and $c * d$ are the operands for the +. In Polish notation, they are $ab*$ and $cd*$, and $a * b + c * d$ is written $ab * cd*+$. The expression $((a + b) - c) * (d + e/f) + g$ is written $ab + c - def/ + *g +$ in Polish notation.

Many computer language processors convert to Polish notation as an intermediate step. Polish notation isn't very clear to the eye trained to use the conventional notation, but it requires no parentheses and can be interpreted very simply by an algorithm very suitable for a computer. The algorithm uses a last-in, first-out stack for the variables. The algorithm is as follows: Working on the expression from left to right, if the next item is a variable, stack it. If it is an operation, apply that operation to the top two variables on the stack, removing them and placing the result on the stack. Here as an example is the step-by-step calculation of $5\ 3 + 4 - 7\ 9 + * = ((5 + 3) - 4) * (7 + 9)$.

TABLE 10.1.

Stack	Remaining Expression
empty	5 3 + 4 − 7 9 + *
5	3 + 4 − 7 9 + *
5 3	+ 4 − 7 9 + *
8	4 − 7 9 + *
8 4	− 7 9 + *
4	7 9 + *
4 7	9 + *
4 7 9	+ *
4 16	*
64	empty

In the program on page (277), the procedure MAKETREE takes an expression in Polish notation and constructs a tree for it. The representation of nodes uses essentially the same declaration as the maze problem. Every node has a name and three pointers. In the case of variables, the second and third pointers are made NULL. Otherwise, the second and third pointers point to the two operands. In each case, the first pointer points up. MAKETREE uses a stack called S(I) in the program. The expression is processed left to right. Each time a variable is found, a node is created and the pointer is stacked. Each time an operation symbol is met, a node is created. The first pointer of

†This is "postfix Polish." The operator could be written first, for example, $+ab$, which would be "prefix Polish."

each of the two nodes corresponding to the top of the stack is made to point to the new node—it will serve as the operand for this operation node. Then pointers to those two nodes are put in the second and third pointers of this new operation node. Finally, the top two pointers are removed from the stack, and the pointer to the new node is placed on the stack. At the end, the first pointer on the last operation is made NULL and the pointer called ROOT is made to point at that last operation used.

The procedure PRINT prints the information concerning one node. Each time a node becomes complete, it is printed, and the results are shown at the end of the program. The graph can be constructed from this listing. Results are shown for the expression of Figure 10.3c.

Now here is an interesting fact. If you start at the top of any graph of an expression and do the following, you will write a conventional expression corresponding to the graph.

1. At each variable node, write the variable name and do an about face.
2. Each time you meet an operation node, turn right. It turns out that you will meet each node three times.
    a. coming down, going right
    b. coming up from right, going down to left
    c. coming up from left and proceeding upward.

The first time, print a left parenthesis, the second time, the operation symbol, and the third time a right parenthesis.

3. Stop when you arrive at the top of the graph again.

Except for what is printed, this is exactly the same as the procedure for finding a way through the maze. The procedure SOLVE modified only in what it prints is included with the procedure MAKETREE. Here the main program consists of the two statements CALL MAKETREE; CALL SOLVE(ROOT);. At the end of the printout is the expression produced by the program.

```
M: PROCEDURE OPTIONS (MAIN);

/***********************************************************************/
/*                                                                     */
/*        THIS PROCEDURE CONTAINS PROCEDURES  FOR  (1)  MAKING  A      */
/*   TREE   CORRESPONDING   TO  AN  EXPRESSION  GIVEN  IN  POLISH      */
/*   NOTATION,  AND  (2) BY TRAVERSING  THE  TREE,  PRINTING  THE      */
/*   CONVENTIONAL FORM FOR THE EXPRESSION.                             */
/*                                                                     */
/***********************************************************************/

   DECLARE ROOT POINTER,
           NULL BUILTIN;
```

```
  DECLARE 1 NODE BASED,
             2 NAME CHARACTER(4),
             2 POINTERS(3) POINTER,
             2 COUNT FIXED BINARY(31);

LIE: PROCEDURE(X) RETURNS (FIXED BINARY(31));

/*********************************************************************/
/*                                                                   */
/*       THIS PROCEDURE MAKES IT POSSIBLE TO PRINT POINTERS.         */
/*                                                                   */
/*********************************************************************/

  DECLARE X POINTER;

  RETURN (UNSPEC(X));

END;

PRINT: PROCEDURE(X);

/*********************************************************************/
/*                                                                   */
/*       THIS PROCEDURE IS USED TO PRINT DATA ABOUT EACH NODE        */
/*                                                                   */
/*********************************************************************/

  DECLARE X POINTER;
  DECLARE (I,J,K,L) FIXED BINARY(31);

  I = LIE(X);
  J = LIE(X->POINTERS(1));
  K = LIE(X->POINTERS(2));
  L = LIE(X->POINTERS(3));

  PUT EDIT(X->NAME,I,J,K,L)(A(5),4 F(11));
  PUT SKIP;

END;    /* OF PRINT */

  MAKETREE: PROCEDURE(ROOT);

/*********************************************************************/
/*                                                                   */
/*       THE FOLLOWING PROCEDURE READS AN EXPRESSION  IN  POLISH     */
/*    FROM A CARD STORES THE ROOT POINTER IN "ROOT", AND FORMS ITS   */
/*    GRAPH AS A THREADED LIST.                                      */
/*                                                                   */
/*       POLISH IS THE INPUT EXPRESSION,  T POINTS TO  THE  NODE     */
/*    CURRENTLY BEING BUILT,  S IS  THE  STACK  AND  I  THE  STACK   */
/*    COUNTER,  C IS  THE  CHARACTER  OF  POLISH  CURRENTLY  BEING   */
/*    EXAMINED, AND Q IS A TEMPORARY.                                */
/*                                                                   */
/*********************************************************************/
```

```
DECLARE ROOT POINTER,
        POLISH CHARACTER(80) VARYING,
        (T,Q) POINTER,
        S(10) POINTER,
        I FIXED BINARY(15),
        C CHARACTER(1);

READ FILE (SYSIN) INTO (POLISH);
PUT EDIT (POLISH)(A);
PUT SKIP(2) EDIT('NODE','LOC','POINTER1','POINTER2','POINTER3')
   (A(8),4 A(11));
PUT SKIP;
I = 0;

DO WHILE (SUBSTR(POLISH,1,1)¬=' ');

/**********************************************************************/
/*                                                                    */
/*       WE ALLOCATE ONE NODE FOR  EACH  SYMBOL  IN  THE  POLISH      */
/*   EXPRESSION.                                                      */
/*                                                                    */
/**********************************************************************/

    ALLOCATE NODE SET (T);
    C = SUBSTR(POLISH,1,1);
    POLISH = SUBSTR(POLISH,2);
    T->NAME = C;
    T->COUNT = 0;

/**********************************************************************/
/*                                                                    */
/*       IF IT IS A VARIABLE NAME, WE STACK THE POINTER TO IT.        */
/*                                                                    */
/**********************************************************************/

    IF INDEX('+-*/',C)=0 THEN DO;
       T->POINTERS(2) = NULL;
       T->POINTERS(3) = NULL;
       I = I+1;
       S(I) = T;

    END;

    ELSE DO;


/**********************************************************************/
/*                                                                    */
/*       IF IT IS AN OPERATION, WE REMOVE THE TOP TWO NODES FROM      */
/*   THE STACK, PUT POINTERS TO THEM IN THIS NODE AND VICE VERSA,     */
/*   AND STACK A POINTER TO THIS NODE.                                */
/*                                                                    */
/**********************************************************************/
```

```
            Q = S(I-1);
            T->POINTERS(2) = Q;
            Q->POINTERS(1) = T;
            CALL PRINT(Q);
            Q = S(I);
            T->POINTERS(3) = Q;
            Q->POINTERS(1) = T;
            CALL PRINT(Q);
            I = I-1;
            S(I) = T;

         END;

      END;  /*  OF DO WHILE--I. E. END OF POLISH  */

      ROOT = T;
      T->POINTERS(1) = NULL;
      CALL PRINT(ROOT);

   END;  /* OF MAKETREE  */

      SOLVE: PROCEDURE(IN);

/*************************************************************************/
/*                                                                       */
/*        THIS PROCEDURE TRAVERSES THE TREE FOR AN EXPRESSION AND        */
/*   PRINTS THE CONVENTIONAL FORM OF THE EXPRESSION.  IT  IS  THE        */
/*   SAME AS THE PREVIOUS PROCEDURE "SOLVE", FOR THE MAZE, EXCEPT        */
/*   FOR WHAT IT PRINTS.  THIS PROCEDURE GOES THROUGH  THE  GRAPH        */
/*   FOR AN EXPRESSION, TURNING RIGHT AT EACH NODE, ABOUT FACE AT        */
/*   DEAD ENDS,  PRINTING "(" THE FIRST TIME, THE NAME THE SECOND        */
/*   TIME, AND ")" THE THIRD TIME FOR ORDINARY NODES, OR THE NAME        */
/*   FOR DEAD ENDS.  IN IS THE POINTER TO THE ROOT, HEAD AND TAIL        */
/*   POINT  TO  THE  NODES  WE  ARE  GOING  TO  AND  COMING  FROM        */
/*   RESPECTIVELY.  P POINTS TO THE NODE WE ARE AT,  AND I  IS  A        */
/*   TEMPORARY.                                                          */
/*                                                                       */
/*************************************************************************/

         DECLARE 1 NODE BASED(P),
                    2 NAME CHARACTER(4),
                    2 POINTERS(3) POINTER,
                    2 COUNT FIXED BINARY(31),
                 (P,IN,HEAD,TAIL) POINTER,
                 I FIXED BINARY(15),
                 TRUE BIT(1) INITIAL('1'B);

         PUT SKIP(3);
         HEAD = IN;
         TAIL = NULL;

         DO WHILE(TRUE);
```

```
        P = HEAD;

        IF HEAD=NULL THEN DO;
           PUT SKIP(2) LIST('END OF EXPRESSION');
           RETURN;
        END;

        P->COUNT = P->COUNT+1;

        IF P->POINTERS(2)=NULL & P->POINTERS(3)=NULL THEN DO;
           PUT EDIT(P->NAME)(A(1));
           HEAD = TAIL;
           TAIL = P;
        END;

        ELSE DO;  /*  PRINT AND THEN TURN RIGHT AT THIS CORNER  */

           IF P->COUNT=1 THEN PUT EDIT('(')(A);
           ELSE IF P->COUNT=2 THEN PUT EDIT(P->NAME)(A(1));
           ELSE PUT EDIT(')')(A);

           DO I=1 TO 3 WHILE(P->POINTERS(I)¬=TAIL);
           END;
           I = I+1;
           IF I>3 THEN I = I-3;

           HEAD = P->POINTERS(I);
           TAIL = P;

        END;  /*  OF ELSE DO  */

     END;  /*  OF DO WHILE(TRUE)  */

  END;  /*  OF SOLVE  */


/********************************************************************/
/*                                                                  */
/*        MAIN PROCEDURE                                            */
/*                                                                  */
/********************************************************************/


  CALL MAKETREE(ROOT);
  CALL SOLVE(ROOT);

END;  /* OF MAIN PROCEDURE  */
```

```
    AB+C-DEF/+*G+     CORRESPONDS TO (A+B-C)*(D+E/F)+G

    NODE      LOC        POINTER1    POINTER2    POINTER3
    A          1492536    1492488  2130706432  2130706432
    B          1492512    1492488  2130706432  2130706432
    +          1492488    1492440     1492536     1492512
```

```
C          1492464     1492440 2130706432 2130706432
E          1492392     1492344 2130706432 2130706432
F          1492368     1492344 2130706432 2130706432
D          1492416     1492320 2130706432 2130706432
/          1492344     1492320    1492392    1492368
-          1492440     1492296    1492488    1492464
+          1492320     1492296    1492416    1492344
*          1492296     1492248    1492440    1492320
G          1492272     1492248 2130706432 2130706432
+          1492248  2130706432    1492296    1492272

((((A+B)-C)*(D+(E/F)))+G)

END OF EXPRESSION
```

It turns out that we can write a very simple recursive version of the procedure SOLVE that we used to solve a maze and to convert an expression from graph form to conventional form. Let us consider the graph for the expression. The following algorithm does the trick:

1. If the graph consists of a variable name only, print it.
2. If the graph root is an operation node,
   a. print a left parenthesis
   b. print the expression for the left subgraph going out of this node
   c. print the operation symbol
   d. print the expression for the right subgraph going out of this node
   e. print a right parenthesis

The program listing of the recursive version of the procedure SOLVE follows. This version of SOLVE substituted for the other on page 280 gives identical results.

```
SOLVE: PROCEDURE (X) RECURSIVE;

/*************************************************************************/
/*                                                                       */
/*        THIS PROCEDURE TRAVERSES THE TREE FOR AN EXPRESSION AND        */
/*   PRINTS THE CONVENTIONAL FORM OF THE EXPRESSION.                     */
/*                                                                       */
/*        THIS IS A RECURSIVE VERSION OF  SOLVE,   THAT  PRODUCES        */
/*   EXACTLY   THE  SAME  RESULT  AS  THE  PREVIOUS  PROGRAM  FOR        */
/*   CONVERTING A GRAPH OF AN EXPRESSION TO CONVENTIONAL FORM.           */
/*                                                                       */
/*************************************************************************/

  DECLARE X POINTER;

  DECLARE 1 NODE BASED,
          2 NAME CHARACTER(4),
          2 POINTERS(3) POINTER,
          2 COUNT FIXED BINARY(31);
```

```
/*********************************************************************/
/*                                                                   */
/*          FOR A DEAD END, PRINT THE NODE NAME.                     */
/*                                                                   */
/*********************************************************************/

   IF (X->POINTERS(2)=NULL & X->POINTERS(3)=NULL) THEN DO;
      PUT EDIT (X->NAME)(A(1));
      RETURN;
   END;

/*********************************************************************/
/*                                                                   */
/*          OTHERWISE PRINT "(", SOLVE(LEFT BRANCH), THE OPERATION   */
/*    SIGN, SOLVE(RIGHT BRANCH), AND ")".                            */
/*                                                                   */
/*********************************************************************/

   PUT EDIT ('(')(A);
   CALL SOLVE(X->POINTERS(2));
   PUT EDIT (X->NAME)(A(1));
   CALL SOLVE(X->POINTERS(3));
   PUT EDIT (')')(A);

END;  /* OF SOLVE  */
```

Here is one final example to illustrate two more points:

1. You can use pointer techniques with subscripts as well as with PL/I pointer variables. Thus, you can use pointer techniques with any language, and you can take advantage of the SUBSCRIPTRANGE ON-condition in PL/I to catch many errors against which pointer variables are unprotected.
2. What you can do with pointers is limited only by your imagination.

We have one hundred items numbered 0 to 99 and each is assigned a value between 0 and 9.

```
ORIGINAL LIST
   0-8    1-4    2-2    3-6    4-9    5-9    6-0    7-6    8-9    9-8
  10-1   11-5   12-4   13-2   14-4   15-8   16-0   17-6   18-5   19-3
  20-5   21-4   22-4   23-4   24-2   25-7   26-6   27-5   28-0   29-1
  30-0   31-6   32-5   33-0   34-0   35-0   36-9   37-4   38-0   39-8
  40-4   41-3   42-5   43-3   44-0   45-5   46-3   47-3   48-9   49-1
  50-2   51-4   52-1   53-8   54-7   55-8   56-7   57-6   58-7   59-4
  60-9   61-4   62-5   63-5   64-4   65-1   66-0   67-5   68-2   69-5
  70-1   71-9   72-1   73-4   74-3   75-3   76-5   77-2   78-3   79-9
  80-2   81-2   82-6   83-8   84-4   85-1   86-6   87-9   88-7   89-0
  90-2   91-7   92-0   93-4   94-0   95-5   96-7   97-0   98-9   99-0
```

We want to sort them as follows:

```
FINAL TABULATION
VALUE 0 ITEMS:  6 16 28 30 33 34 35 38 44 66 89 92 94 97 99
VALUE 1 ITEMS: 10 29 49 52 65 70 72 85
VALUE 2 ITEMS:  2 13 24 50 68 77 80 81 90
VALUE 3 ITEMS: 19 41 43 46 47 74 75 78
VALUE 4 ITEMS:  1 12 14 21 22 23 37 40 51 59 61 64 73 84 93
VALUE 5 ITEMS: 11 18 20 27 32 42 45 62 63 67 69 76 95
VALUE 6 ITEMS:  3  7 17 26 31 57 82 86
VALUE 7 ITEMS: 25 54 56 58 88 91 96
VALUE 8 ITEMS:  0  9 15 39 53 55 83
VALUE 9 ITEMS:  4  5  8 36 48 60 71 79 87 98
```

One way is to go through the list ten times, first listing all the numbers whose value is zero, then those whose value is 1, etc. It is possible with a big computer and a small problem like this, but it would be prohibitive with numbers a hundred times larger.

A better way is to go through the list once, forming ten new lists. In the program that produced the results above, we do that. We conserve storage by using pointer lists right in the same memory space as the original lists, the only additional storage required being ten FIXED BINARY (15) numbers in the array PNT. PNT(I) is a pointer to the list of items whose value is I. If the value of PNT(I) is J, then the next pointer is put at LIST(J). If the value of LIST(J) is K, the next is at LIST(K), etc. The pointers in each case are subscript values. Here is the program.

```
TAB: PROCEDURE OPTIONS(MAIN);

/************************************************************************/
/*                                                                      */
/*        THE FIRST LOOP IN THIS PROGRAM MAKES A LIST OF 100            */
/*   NUMBERS BETWEEN 0 AND 9 USING A PSEUDO-RANDOM NUMBER               */
/*   GENERATOR. (NOTE THAT "X = X*Y" HERE PRODUCES A SEQUENCE OF        */
/*   PSEUDO-RANDOM NUMBERS BETWEEN 0 AND 2**31.  DIVIDING BY Z =        */
/*   2**31/10 GIVES A QUOTIENT BETWEEN 0 AND 9 INCLUSIVE.)              */
/*                                                                      */
/*        THE SECOND LOOP, USING SUBSCRIPTS AS POINTERS AND USING       */
/*   THE SAME MEMORY AS THE LIST ORIGINALLY OCCUPIED, MAKES A           */
/*   THREADED LIST OF THOSE ITEMS WHOSE VALUE IS J FOR EACH J           */
/*   BETWEEN 0 AND 9.  HP(J) IS THE POINTER TO THE FIRST ITEM ON        */
/*   THE LIST OF ITEMS WHOSE VALUE IS J. WE START FROM THE END OF       */
/*   THE ORIGINAL LIST, ADDING ITEMS TO THE FRONT OF THE NEW            */
/*   LISTS AS WE MEET THEM.                                             */
/*                                                                      */
/*        THE THIRD LOOP PRINTS THESE TEN THREADED LISTS, GIVING        */
/*   THE REQUIRED TABULATION.                                           */
/*                                                                      */
/************************************************************************/

  DECLARE X FIXED BINARY(31) INITIAL(1162261467),
          Y FIXED BINARY(31) INITIAL(1162261467),
```

```
          Z FIXED BINARY(31) INITIAL(214748365), /* =2**31/10 */
          LIST(0:99) FIXED BINARY(15),
          PNT(0:9) FIXED BINARY(15) INITIAL((10) -1),
          (I,J) FIXED BINARY(15);

   PUT EDIT('ORIGINAL LIST')(A);
   PUT SKIP;

   DO J = 0 TO 99 BY 10;
      DO I = J TO J+9;
         (NOFIXEDOVERFLOW): X = X*Y;
         LIST(I) = X/Z;
         PUT EDIT(I,'-',LIST(I))(F(4),A,F(1));
      END;
      PUT SKIP;
   END;

   DO I = 99 TO 0 BY -1;
      J = LIST(I);
      LIST(I) = PNT(J);
      PNT(J) = I;
   END;

   PUT SKIP(3) EDIT('FINAL TABULATION')(A);
   DO J = 0 TO 9;
      I = PNT(J);
      PUT SKIP EDIT('VALUE ',J,' ITEMS:')(A,F(1),A);
      DO WHILE(I>=0);
         PUT EDIT(I)(F(3));
         I = LIST(I);
      END;
   END;  /*  OF DO J = 0 TO 9  */


   PUT SKIP(3) EDIT('DUMP OF PNT')(A);
   PUT SKIP;
   DO I = 0 TO 9;
      PUT EDIT(I,'-',PNT(I))(F(3),A,F(2));
   END;

   PUT SKIP(3) EDIT('DUMP OF LIST')(A);
   PUT SKIP;
   DO I = 0 TO 99 BY 10;
      DO J = I TO I+10;
         PUT EDIT(J,'-',LIST(J))(F(3),A,F(2));
      END;
      PUT SKIP;
   END;

END;  /*  OF  MAIN PROCEDURE  */
```

Here is a dump of the contents of PNT and LIST at the end of the program.

```
DUMP OF PNT
  0- 6  1-10  2- 2  3-19  4- 1  5-11  6- 3  7-25  8- 0  9- 4


DUMP OF LIST
  0- 9  1-12  2-13  3- 7  4- 5  5- 8  6-16  7-17  8-36  9-15 10-29
 10-29 11-18 12-14 13-24 14-21 15-39 16-28 17-26 18-20 19-41 20-27
 20-27 21-22 22-23 23-37 24-50 25-54 26-31 27-32 28-30 29-49 30-33
 30-33 31-57 32-42 33-34 34-35 35-38 36-48 37-40 38-44 39-53 40-51
 40-51 41-43 42-45 43-46 44-66 45-62 46-47 47-74 48-60 49-52 50-68
 50-68 51-59 52-65 53-55 54-56 55-83 56-58 57-82 58-88 59-61 60-71
 60-71 61-64 62-63 63-67 64-73 65-70 66-89 67-69 68-77 69-76 70-72
 70-72 71-79 72-85 73-84 74-75 75-78 76-95 77-80 78--1 79-87 80-81
 80-81 81-90 82-86 83--1 84-93 85--1 86--1 87-98 88-91 89-92 90--1
 90--1 91-96 92-94 93--1 94-97 95--1 96--1 97-99 98--1 99--1100- 6
```

The items whose value was 5 are 11, 18, 20, . . . , 76, 95. PNT(5) = 11, LIST(11) = 18, LIST(18) = 20, . . . , LIST(76) = 95, LIST(95) = −1. The list end-marker was given the value − 1 in this program.

In about 1955 serious interest arose in programming a computer to do tasks that are generally considered to require intelligence, such as playing checkers and chess and proving theorems. This type of research soon came to be known as "artificial intelligence." Some of the principal workers in the field soon concluded that more flexible ways of storing and processing information were needed. Two languages, at least, that were developed to meet this need were widely used. One, IPL (Information Processing Language), developed by Newel, Shaw, and Simon, had list structures and handled them quite efficiently. In other respects it was quite similar to assembly language. There was a long line of development along this line, and the list-processing features of PL/I and other similar languages may be considered to be an outgrowth of that first "low-level" list-processing language.

LISP, developed by John McCarthy about 1959, in sharp contrast to IPL, is a much higher-level way of handling list structures. Note that its development is approximately concurrent with ALGOL, and thus it is earlier than any of the languages discussed in this book except ALGOL and FORTRAN. Yet it still is fairly commonly used and has a number of loyal followers.

LISP Chapter 11

The unique features of LISP include:

1. The high-level notation for lists.
2. The emphasis on recursive routines. The influence of LISP has probably done much to motivate recent workers to include recursive routines in modern languages.
3. LISP programs consist of a list of function definitions and a list of functions to be evaluated. In this way it is like APL. Unlike APL, however, in pure LISP even the function definitions are not procedures in the ordinary sense of being executed step-by-step. Instead, each function definition is in the form of an expression. There are no statements like the IF and GO TO so characteristic of programming languages. They are replaced by the strong use of recursive definitions.

It turns out that this latter approach, although elegant, is sometimes so inefficient that a procedure type of function definition has been introduced in LISP. It is called the PROG feature. Since it is like conventional languages but inferior, it is really not interesting from the point of view of this book, and we will confine our study to pure LISP, which is very interesting.

The data that a LISP program operates on and the program itself consist of a special type of list structures with pointers. One kind of data item is called an atom. There are three kinds of atoms:

Atomic symbols consist of one or more letters or digits, of which the first must be a letter, e.g., A, A2, ANEXTRALONGSTRINGOFLETTERS.

Numeric constants may take any form that is acceptable in FORTRAN, and if a number appears to be an integer, it is stored as an integer, otherwise as floating point.

Character strings may be introduced as atomic symbols if they fit that format or else with the following convention: Some character that does not appear in the character string is chosen as a "bracket." Then, the character string is entered as $$ followed by the bracket character, the character string, and another bracket character. For example, to enter the character string A+B*C we might use X as a bracket character and write $$XA+B*CX, or we might choose an apostrophe as the bracket character and write $$'A+B*C'.

In addition to atoms, the only data item in LISP is a *node* consisting of two pointers. The pointers may point to an atom or to another node.

As in PL/I, there is a special atomic symbol used to indicate the end of a list. In LISP it is called NIL. The list of six words THE PURPOSE OF COMPUTING IS INSIGHT would be represented as in Figure 11.1. This form is always used for a simple sequential list. Otherwise, the representation is left to the programmer. For example, for the graph of the expression discussed in Chapter 10, the following representation might be used: For a variable name, the atom alone, but for an operation, two nodes and the operation symbol as in Figure 11.2. The entire graph looks as shown in Figure 11.3.

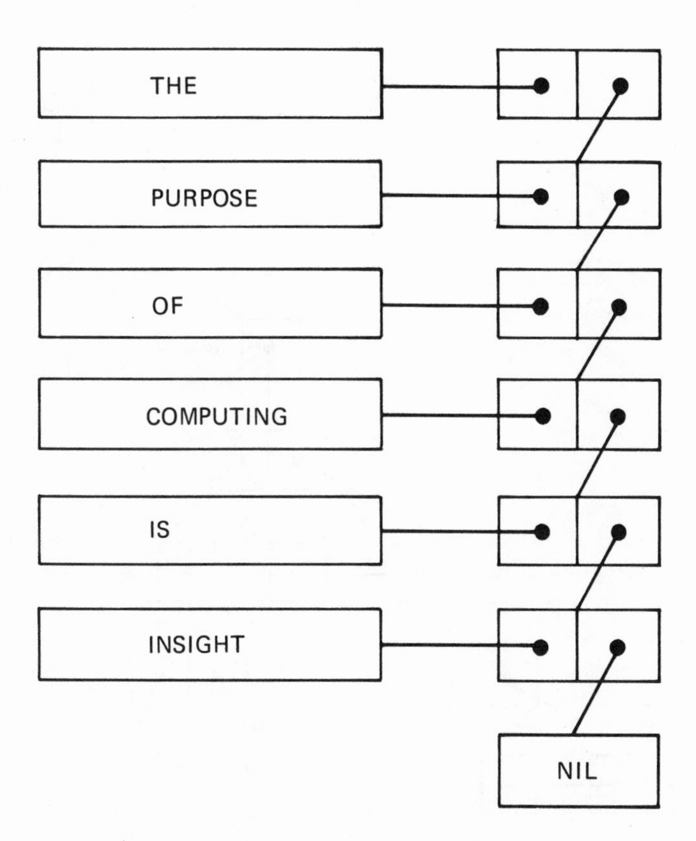

Figure 11.1. Representation of a simple list in LISP.

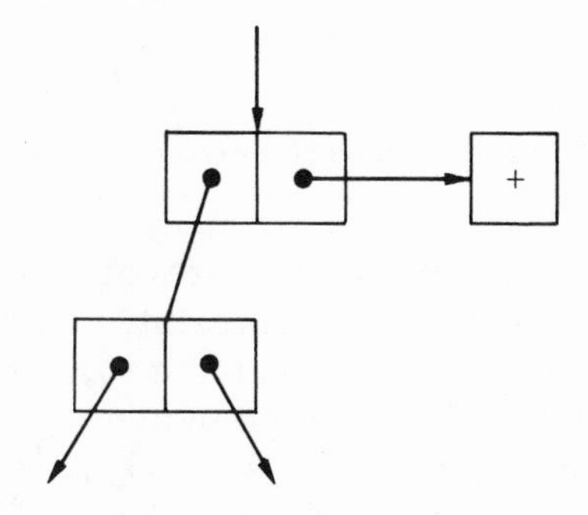

Figure 11.2. Representation of one operation node for the graph of an expression in LISP.

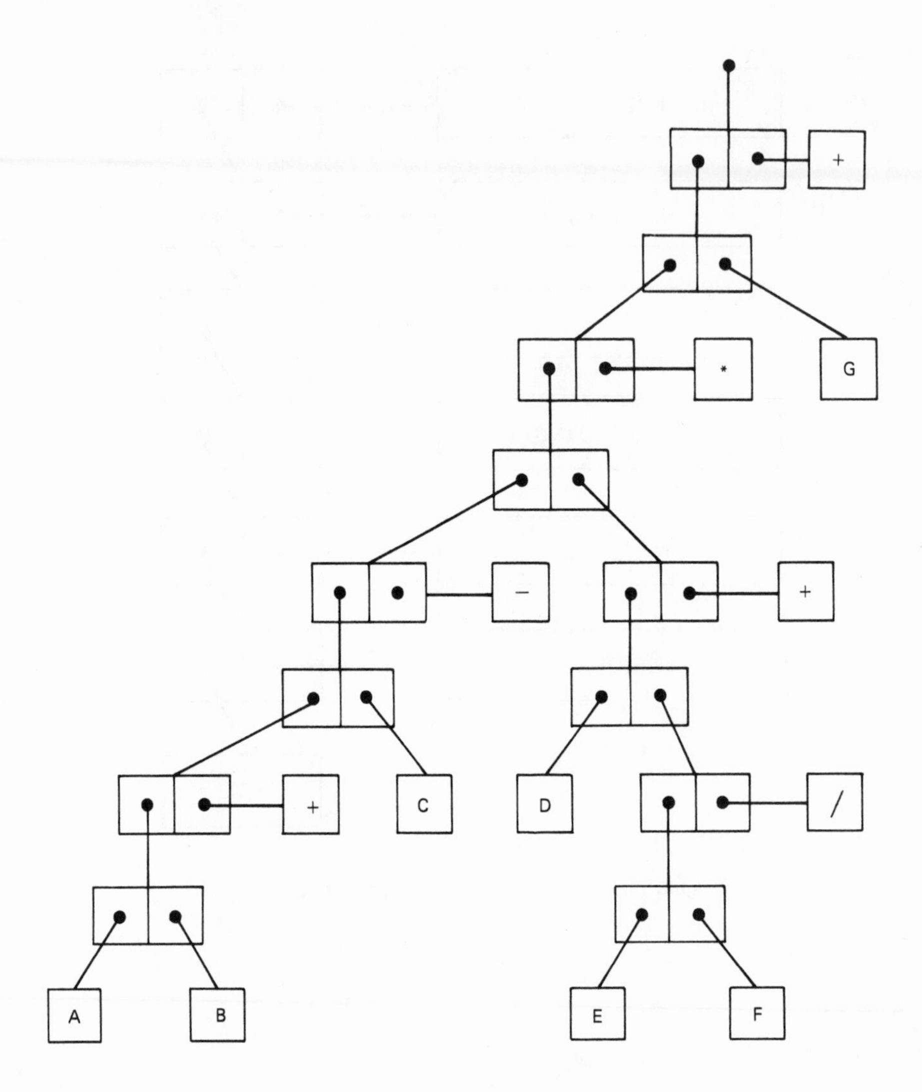

Figure 11.3. Representation of the graph of an expression in LISP.

There is a special notation for structures of this type in LISP. An atom is used to represent itself. The node is represented by a pair of parentheses containing the structures that the pointers point to, separated by a period. Thus, the graph shown in Figure 11.4 is represented by `(A . B)`, and that shown in Figure 11.5 is represented by `((A . B) . (C . D))`. The list of six words (Figure 11.1) is represented as `(THE . (PURPOSE . (OF . (COMPUTING . (IS . (INSIGHT . NIL))))))`, and the graph for the expression `(A+B-C)*(D+E/F)+G` (Figure 11.3) becomes

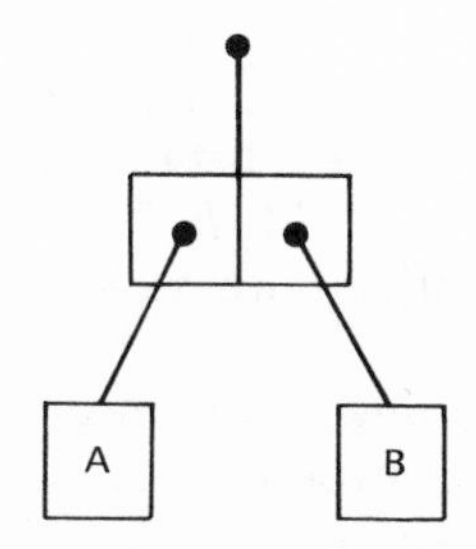

Figure 11.4 Graph for (A . B).

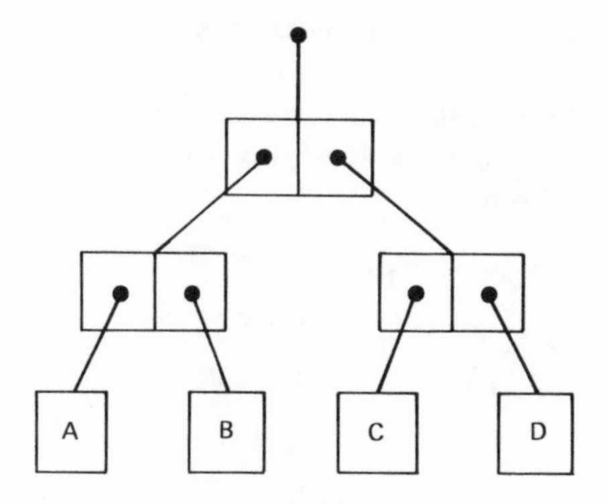

Figure 11.5 Graph for ((A . B) . (C . D)).

```
(((((((A . B) . +) . C) . -) .
                ((D . ((E . F) . /)) . +)) . *) . G) . +)
```

(Actually, since +, −, *, and / are not S-expressions, they must be written as character strings, for example, `$$'+'` for +. Some LISP processors will accept the above, however.)

These expressions are known as S-expressions. Their syntax can be expressed very simply in BNF:

<S-expression> ::= <atom> |
(<S-expression> . <S-expression>)

Ordinary sequential lists occur so frequently that a special notation is used for them. A list of S-expressions is represented by simply enclosing them in parentheses and separating them by spaces. The meaning is the same as if they were written as S-expressions. Thus, `(A B C D)` is the same as `(A . (B . (C. (D . NIL))))`. The items on the list may be S-expressions, as for example, ((A . B) C (D . (E . F))) is a list with three items (A . B), C, and (D . (E . F)). It can also be written ((A . B) . (C . ((D . (E . F)) . NIL))). Since a list represents an S-expression, it is also possible to make a list of lists, as ((A B C) (D E F) (G H)). The expression () represents a list with no items, which is NIL, and (A) represents a list with one item, (A . NIL).

Note that in LISP there is never any choice about whether or not to include parentheses. If a set of parentheses is inserted or deleted, the expression definitely changes. Thus, A is an atom, but (A) is a list. (A) is the same as (A . NIL), which is not the same as A. ((A)) is a list consisting of one item (A) which is in turn a list. ((A)) is the same as ((A) . NIL) or ((A . NIL) . NIL), which is different from (A).

A LISP program is also written as an S-expression. Thus, it corresponds to a tree and is represented in the computer using pointers. The entire program consists of function definitions—new functions are defined using existing ones. Therefore, we start by studying some of the functions built into most LISP implementations:

PLUS(X_1 X_2 . . . X_n)	$= X_1 + X_2 + \ldots + X_n$
TIMES(X_1 X_2 . . . X_n)	$= X_1 * X_2 * \ldots * X_n$
DIFFERENCE(X Y)	$= X - Y$
ADD1(X)	$= X + 1$
SUB1(X)	$= X - 1$
MAX(X_1 X_2 . . . X_n)	= the largest of its arguments
MIN(X_1 X_2 . . . X_n)	= the smallest of its arguments
QUOTIENT(X Y)	$= \frac{X}{Y}$
REMAINDER(X Y)	= remainder after dividing X by Y
EXPT(X Y)	$= X^Y$
SQRT(X)	$= \sqrt{\lvert X \rvert}$
RECIP(X)	$= \frac{1}{X}$
ABSVAL(X)	$= \lvert X \rvert$
FLOAT(X)	= floating-point representation of the argument
ENTIER(X)	= integer part of X

For all these functions except SQRT, RECIP, and the last two, if all arguments are integer, the result is integer; otherwise, the result is floating point. SQRT and RECIP always give a floating-point representation.

In addition to the above functions, which operate on numbers and give numeric answers, there are a number of functions which operate on S-expressions and give S-expressions as answers. The most fundamental are CAR(X), CDR(X), and CONS(X Y). The first two take the S-expression apart, giving the left and right sides, respectively. Thus,

```
CAR((A . B)) = A
CDR((A . B)) = B
CAR((A . B) . (C . E)) = (A . B)
CAR((A B C D)) = A
CDR((A B C D)) = (B C D)
```

The last two are derived from the S-expression form of lists—

```
(A B C D) = (A . (B . (C . (D . NIL))))
```

so that CDR((A B C D)) = (B . (C . (D . NIL))) = (B C D). CONS puts two S-expressions together:

```
CONS(A B) = (A . B)
CONS((A . B) (C . D)) = ((A . B) . (C . D))
CONS(A (B C D)) = (A B C D)
CONS((B C D) A) = ((B C D) . A)
```

Note the difference between (A . B) and CONS(A B). The first is an S-expression in which A and B are the left and right parts. CONS(A B) instructs the computer to build an S-expression with A and B as the left and right parts. The result of the operation indicated by CONS(A B) is (A . B).

Another function, LIST(X_1 X_2 . . . X_n), makes a list out of its S-expression arguments. For example,

```
LIST(A B (C . D) (E F)) = (A B (C . D) (E F))
```

Next there are a number of predicates whose values are either T (true) or NIL (false):

1. EQ(X Y) compares two *atoms* X and Y and is true if they are equal.
2. EQUAL(X Y) is more general. It compares two S-expressions and is true if they are equal. In particular, it can be used on atoms and numbers, which are a special case of atoms. It is safer to use EQUAL rather than EQ.
3. ATOM(X) is true if the value of X is an atom.
4. NUMBERP(X) is true if the value of X is a number.
5. ZEROP(X) is true if the value of X is zero.

6. ONEP(X) is true if the value of X is 1.

7. GREATERP(X Y) is true if the value of X is greater than the value of Y.

8. LESSP(X Y) is true if the value of X is less than the value of Y.

9. NULL(X) is true if the value of X is NIL.

10. MEMBER(X Y) is true if the value of X is an S-expression which is an element of the list which is the value of Y.

The LISP monitor expects to find as input a function name followed by a list of arguments. After one such item there may be another and another, and the monitor simply evaluates these functions, printing the value for each one. There is no GO TO statement—no apparent way to loop in the main program. (Actually, the equivalent of looping is achieved by defining functions that are recursive, as we shall see a little later.) Here is an example of a LISP program.

```
PLUS (5 11 17 3)
EQUAL (17 17)
GREATERP (17 17)
CAR ((A.(B.C)))
CDR ((A.(B.C)))
CONS (A (B C D))


ARGUMENTS FOR EVALQUOTE ...
  PLUS
  (5 11 17 3)

TIME        0MS,  VALUE IS ...
  36

ARGUMENTS FOR EVALQUOTE ...
  EQUAL
  (17 17)

TIME        0MS,  VALUE IS ...
  T

ARGUMENTS FOR EVALQUOTE ...
  GREATERP
  (17 17)

TIME        0MS,  VALUE IS ...
  NIL

ARGUMENTS FOR EVALQUOTE ...
  CAR
  ((A B . C))

TIME        0MS,  VALUE IS ...
  A
```

```
ARGUMENTS FOR EVALQUOTE ...
  CDR
  ((A B . C))

TIME       OMS,  VALUE IS ...
  (B . C)

ARGUMENTS FOR EVALQUOTE ...
  CONS
  (A (B C D))

TIME       OMS,  VALUE IS ...
  (A B C D)



DEFINE (( (F (LAMBDA (X Y Z)
   (PLUS X (TIMES Y Z)) )) ))

F (10 3 15)


ARGUMENTS FOR EVALQUOTE ...
  DEFINE
  (((F (LAMBDA (X Y Z) (PLUS X (TIMES Y Z))))))

TIME       OMS,  VALUE IS ...
  (F)

ARGUMENTS FOR EVALQUOTE ...
  F
  (10 3 15)

TIME       OMS,  VALUE IS ...
  55
```

The following notation is sometimes used, and examples appear above: (A B C D E . F) means (A . (B . (C . (D . (E . F))))). Note that this is the same as a list, except that something else, F in this example, replaces the NIL that usually ends a list.

For numeric constants and for the atomic symbols NIL and T (which means true), there is no doubt about their value when they appear. For example, the value of NIL is NIL and the value of 17 is 17. When an ordinary atomic symbol occurs in an expression, then rules are required to determine whether it is an alphanumeric constant, a variable, or a function name. The rules are slightly different for the top-level function calls—the functions given directly to the monitor to evaluate—and for the references to a function within an expression. Let us consider the latter case first. A function reference is written as a list, with the function name as the first item on the list, and the arguments following. Thus, PLUS (12 17 11 2) is written

(PLUS 12 17 11 2), CAR (X) is written (CAR X), CONS (A B) is written (CONS A B), etc. In general, when a list occurs in the middle of an expression, it is interpreted as a function call. Thus, when LISP finds (A B C D E) in the middle of an expression, it goes looking for a function named A, just as FORTRAN or PL/I would upon finding A(B,C,D,E) if A is not an array.

Also, in general, the atomic symbols other than the first item in a list are assumed to be variable names. Thus, in (CONS A B), A and B are assumed to be variable names and their values are retrieved, i.e., they are evaluated. In (A B C D E), A is assumed to be a function name, and B, C, D, and E are assumed to be variable names.

If you want an atomic symbol, or for that matter any S-expression, to be used as a constant, you must "quote" it. You write it as if it were the argument of a function called QUOTE. Thus, the value of (QUOTE A) is A, the value of (QUOTE (A B C D E)) is the list (A B C D E), and the value of (QUOTE (A . B)) is (A . B).

The highest-level call differs from a function reference within an expression in two ways.

1. The function name and a separate list of arguments are passed to the LISP monitor instead of the simple list used for a function reference in an expression.

2. The arguments are not evaluated by the LISP monitor. It is as if they were already quoted. Thus, to request the LISP monitor to evaluate a function F with arguments that are atomic symbols A, B, and C (treated as if they were character string constants A, B, and C), we write

```
F (A B C)
```

but to achieve the same result in the middle of an expression we must write

```
(F (QUOTE A) (QUOTE B) (QUOTE C))
```

For some reason, the creators of LISP decided that it ought to be possible to define a function without naming it. This is analogous to writing something like

```
PROCEDURE (X, Y, Z); RETURN (X + Y * Z); END;
```

in PL/I without labeling the procedure statement. (In PL/I, every procedure statement—even for the main procedure—must be labeled.) Notation used by the logician Alonzo Church was chosen. He used the Greek letter λ in place of the word PROCEDURE to designate a function definition. In LISP, the above function would be written

```
(LAMBDA (X Y Z) (PLUS X (TIMES Y Z)))
```

This is called a λ-expression. It consists of a list with three items. The first is the word LAMBDA. The second is a list of formal parameters. The third is the S-expression that defines the function.

Normally, of course, we want to name functions. This is done by using a built-in function DEFINE. The argument for define is a list of function definitions. Each function definition consists of a list of two items, the function name and its λ-expression. All that adds up to a lot of parentheses. If you go through this description extremely carefully, you can determine exactly how many; if you include too many or too few, the definition will be wrong.

Let us look at the previous example. Let us call our function F.

```
        a b c  d          e     e
DEFINE ( ( (F (LAMBDA (X Y Z)
    f        g           g f d c b a
   (PLUS X (TIMES Y Z) ) ) ) ) )
```

This is written as a top-level call to the monitor. Thus, we write the function name DEFINE followed by the list of arguments in parentheses a. The argument consists of one list, the list of functions we wish to define, enclosed in parentheses b. Each definition (the only one in this case) consists of a list of two items, the name and the λ-expression, in parentheses c. The λ-expression consists of a list enclosed by parentheses d, containing the word LAMBDA, the formal parameter list in parentheses e, and the S-expression which defines the function, which uses parentheses f and g to enclose the lists which result in a function call to PLUS and TIMES, respectively. If we run this program, we get the following results:

```
DEFINE (( (F (LAMBDA (X Y Z)
    (PLUS X (TIMES Y Z)) )) ))

F (10 3 15)


ARGUMENTS FOR EVALQUOTE ...
  DEFINE
  (((F (LAMBDA (X Y Z) (PLUS X (TIMES Y Z))))))

TIME       OMS,   VALUE IS ...
  (F)

ARGUMENTS FOR EVALQUOTE ...
  F
  (10 3 15)

TIME       OMS,   VALUE IS ...
  55
```

To make an interesting program we need one more thing—an *if* statement. In LISP, it is called a conditional form. It is written as if it were a function called COND that has an arbitrary number of arguments. Each argument is a list of two items. The first item of the first argument is evaluated, and if it is not NIL, then the second item of the first argument is evaluated and used as the value of COND. If the first argument evaluates to NIL, then the second argument is examined in the same way, etc. Thus, for example, (COND (A B) (C D) (T E)) is a conditional expression. A is evaluated and if it is not NIL, the value of B is taken as the value of this expression. Otherwise, C is evaluated and if it is not NIL, then the value of D is the value of the expression. If C is NIL also, then T is evaluated. But the value of T is T, which is not NIL; therefore, the value of the expression is the value of E in that case.

The equivalent of this expression can be written in ALGOL:

if A **then** B **else if** C **then** D **else** E.

The programmer must make sure that at least one of the arguments is not NIL, and the usual way to do that is the way shown in the above example—to make the first item of the last pair T.

Now we are in a position to define a non-trivial function. It seems that almost every non-trivial function in LISP is defined recursively. Let us start with a very simple one—factorial. The function fact(n) is defined to be 1*2*3*...*N, which is equivalent to

```
fact(0) = 1
fact(n) = n*fact(n-1)
```

which becomes, in LISP,

```
(FACT (LAMBDA (N) (COND ((ZEROP N) 1)
     (T (TIMES (FACT (SUB1 N)) N) ) ) ) )
```

In earlier chapters of this book the greatest common divisor of two numbers was found by a recursive procedure: If N is divisible by M, then the greatest common divisor is M. Otherwise, the greatest common divisor of M and N is the same as the greatest common divisor of M and the remainder after dividing N by M:

```
(GCD (LAMBDA (N M) (COND
     ((ZEROP (REMAINDER N M)) M)
     (T (GCD M (REMAINDER N M))) )))
```

Here is a computer run of these two functions together with the binomial coefficient function by the method of Pascal's triangle (a part of the printout was cut off the right side, but it was redundant anyway).

```
DEFINE ((
   (FACT (LAMBDA (N) (COND
      ((ZEROP N) 1)
      (T (TIMES (FACT (SUB1 N)) N)) )))

   (GCD (LAMBDA (N M) (COND
      ((ZEROP (REMAINDER N M)) M)
      (T (GCD M (REMAINDER N M))) )))

   (B (LAMBDA (N K)  (COND
      ((EQUAL K 0) 1)
      ((EQUAL K N) 1)
      (T (PLUS (B (SUB1 N) (SUB1 K))  (B (SUB1 N) K) )) ))) ))

FACT (6)
GCD (91 169)
B (6 3)


ARGUMENTS FOR EVALQUOTE ...
  DEFINE
  (((FACT (LAMBDA (N) (COND ((ZEROP N) 1) (T (TIMES (FACT (SUB1 N)) N)
  ((ZEROP (REMAINDER N M)) M) (T (GCD M (REMAINDER N M)))))) (B (LAMBD
  1) ((EQUAL K N) 1) (T (PLUS (B (SUB1 N) (SUB1 K)) (B (SUB1 N) K)))))

TIME      16MS,  VALUE IS ...
  (FACT GCD B)

ARGUMENTS FOR EVALQUOTE ...
  FACT
  (6)

TIME      33MS,  VALUE IS ...
  720

ARGUMENTS FOR EVALQUOTE ...
  GCD
  (91 169)

TIME       0MS,  VALUE IS ...
  13

ARGUMENTS FOR EVALQUOTE ...
  B
  (6 3)

TIME      99MS,  VALUE IS ...
  20
```

Now let us look at sorting by the method described in Chapter 10. First, we define a function INSERT with two arguments; the first X is a sorted list and the second Y is an atom. The value is the list resulting from inserting Y in X in sequence. This algorithm was used.

1. If X has no items, return a list with Y alone.

2. If Y is less than the first item of X, add it to the front of the list and return that.

3. Otherwise, remove the first item from X, insert Y in the rest, put the first item back on, and return the resulting list.

In LISP,

```
(INSERT (LAMBDA (X Y) (COND
        ((NULL X) (CONS Y NIL))
        ((GREATERP (CAR X) Y) (CONS Y X))
        (T (CONS (CAR X) (INSERT (CDR X) Y))))))
```

SORT has one parameter, a list, and returns that same list sorted. The algorithm is

1. If there is only one item, return the original list.

2. Otherwise, remove the first item, sort the rest, insert the first item, and return the result.

In LISP,

```
(SORT (LAMBDA (X) (COND
   ((NULL (CDR X)) X)
   (T (INSERT (SORT (CDR X)) (CAR X))))))
```

Here is an actual run with these two functions.

```
DEFINE ((
   (INSERT (LAMBDA (X Y) (COND
      ((NULL X) (CONS Y NIL))
      ((GREATERP (CAR X) Y) (CONS Y X))
      (T (CONS (CAR X) (INSERT (CDR X) Y))) )))

   (SORT (LAMBDA (X) (COND
      ((NULL (CDR X)) X)
      (T (INSERT (SORT (CDR X)) (CAR X))) ))) ))

INSERT ((2 6 9 12 23 31 73 97) 61)
SORT ((12 4 32 17 1 91 8 5 123 17))


ARGUMENTS FOR EVALQUOTE ...
  DEFINE
  (((INSERT (LAMBDA (X Y) (COND ((NULL X) (CONS Y NIL)) ((GREATERP (CA
  (CAR X) (INSERT (CDR X) Y))))))) (SORT (LAMBDA (X) (COND ((NULL (CDR
  X)) (CAR X))))))))
```

```
TIME        0MS,   VALUE IS ...
  (INSERT SORT)

ARGUMENTS FOR EVALQUOTE ...
  INSERT
  ((2 6 9 12 23 31 73 97) 61)

TIME        16MS,  VALUE IS ...
  (2 6 9 12 23 31 61 73 97)

ARGUMENTS FOR EVALQUOTE ...
  SORT
  ((12 4 32 17 1 91 8 5 123 17))

TIME        83MS,  VALUE IS ...
  (1 4 5 8 12 17 17 32 91 123)
```

There is a function PRINT in LISP. When it is executed, its argument is printed on a line—a new line for each use of the function. It also returns a value. In some implementations it returns the value NIL and in others it returns its argument unchanged. The latter is probably more convenient. In any case, it is easy to define a function that will return whatever you wish, and in the following example PRINTN prints and returns NIL, but PRINTI prints and returns its argument unchanged.

With this example is a program for operating on the graph of an expression and producing the expression in conventional form, except that this program prints one symbol per line. It uses the structure shown earlier in this chapter and the method used in the recursive PL/I routine—if you are at a dead-end, print the node name. Otherwise, print a left parenthesis, perform SOLVE on the expression corresponding to the left branch, print the operation symbol, perform SOLVE on the expression corresponding to the right branch, and finally print a right parenthesis. Note that since PRINTN and SOLVE always return NIL, the conditional statement always proceeds to the last line if it does not terminate on the first.

```
DEFINE ((
   (PRINTN (LAMBDA (X) (COND
      ((PRINT X) NIL)  (T NIL) )))

   (PRINTI (LAMBDA (X) (COND
      ((PRINT X) X) (T X) )))

   (SOLVE (LAMBDA (X) (COND
      ((ATOM X) (PRINTN X))
      ((PRINTN (QUOTE $$'(')) NIL)
      ((SOLVE (CAAR X)) NIL)
      ((PRINTN (CDR X)) NIL)
      ((SOLVE (CDAR X)) NIL)
      (T (PRINTN (QUOTE $$')')))  )))  ))
```

```
PRINT  ( ((A.(B.C)).D) )
PRINTN ( ((A.(B.C)).D) )
PRINTI ( ((A.(B.C)).D) )
SOLVE    (((((((((A.B).+).C).-).((D.((E.F)./)).+)).*).G).+))

ARGUMENTS FOR EVALQUOTE ...
  DEFINE
  (((PRINTN (LAMBDA (X) (COND ((PRINT X) NIL) (T NIL)))) (PRINTI (LAMB
  (T X)))) (SOLVE (LAMBDA (X) (COND ((ATOM X) (PRINTN X)) ((PRINTN (QU
  X)) NIL) ((PRINTN (CDR X)) NIL) ((SOLVE (CDAR X)) NIL) (T (PRINTN (C

TIME        OMS,  VALUE IS ...
  (PRINTN PRINTI SOLVE)

ARGUMENTS FOR EVALQUOTE ...
  PRINT
  (((A B . C) . D))
  ((A B . C) . D)

TIME        OMS,  VALUE IS ...
  NIL

ARGUMENTS FOR EVALQUOTE ...
  PRINTN
  (((A B . C) . D))
  ((A B . C) . D)

TIME        OMS,  VALUE IS ...
  NIL

ARGUMENTS FOR EVALQUOTE ...
  PRINTI
  (((A B . C) . D))
  ((A B . C) . D)

TIME        OMS,  VALUE IS ...
  ((A B . C) . D)

ARGUMENTS FOR EVALQUOTE ...
  SOLVE
  (((((((((A . B) . +) . C) . -) (D (E . F) . /) . +) . *) . G) . +))
  (
  (
  (
  (
  A
  +
  B
  )
  -
  C
  )
  *
  (
```

This is the conventional form of the expression

((((A+B)-C)*(D+(E/F)))+G)

```
    D
    +
    (
    E
    /
    F
    )
    )
    )
    +
    G
    )

 TIME       149MS,   VALUE IS ...
    NIL
*** END OF DATA
```

It requires a combination of cleverness, thought, and practice to develop the ability to state a program recursively. When the light dawns, the programs are frequently remarkably simple—deceptively simple. It seems that for some people and some problems programs can be created more quickly and easily this way than by conventional means.

What are the relative advantages and disadvantages of the PL/I approach and LISP? In LISP, the function definitions are very concise. This encourages breaking a problem up into parts by defining simple functions, then more complex functions in terms of the ones you have, etc. Since you are also forced to break the problem into parts and to think recursively, you are frequently forced into an impressively simple description of the problem.

Low-level list processing like PL/I's, however, gives you a choice of conventional or recursive formulation. That approach also allows you to choose the form of the structures used to represent the data. Clearly, anything you can do in LISP can also be done with the low-level approach in more different ways, good and bad. (The problems in Appendix C indicate a way of handling S-expressions in PL/I.)

For a surprisingly large class of problems, the recursive formulation is surprisingly simple and concise. The cost, of course, is generally an increase in time and memory requirements associated with the recursive linkage and often with the computation itself. For small problems, the recursive formulation often yields a solution quicker than does the conventional approach. For example, when I wrote them, the non-recursive PL/I procedure SOLVE required some debugging, but the recursive version is so simple that it worked immediately, and thus was more economical of my time. For the simple examples given here, the recursive procedure itself is so short that most of the execution time is in the linkage. For more complex programs, if recursive procedures are used at higher, less trivial levels, then the linkage would not be so important in relation to the rest of the computation, and the computational and memory overhead of recursive procedures might be quite tolerable.

Suggested References Appendix A

Generally, one who has studied one computer language quite thoroughly should find that this book adequately gives him the basic ideas for each new language. In doing a problem, however, he is likely to want more detailed information about some aspect of the language. For that purpose the best source is the documentation for the language processor actually being used, and the best source for that is his own computing center. There is no point in even attempting to list that kind of material.

If one wants introductory material, in general, for each language there are a number of books available, each with its good points. It is impossible in most cases to choose the best and equally impossible to list them all. I will list one or two for each language.

BASIC

Since the following book was written by the creators of BASIC, it has a bit of authenticity. The examples are interesting, and the material is presented well for learning. It would be a much more useful book if it had a good index.

Kemeny, John G., and Thomas E. Kurtz, *BASIC Programming.* New York: John Wiley & Sons, Inc., 1967.

FORTRAN

There are more than one hundred books available. Here is one:

Peterson, W. Wesley, and Jean Holz, *FORTRAN and the IBM 360*. New York: McGraw-Hill Book Company, 1971.

ALGOL60

I have not seen a book on ALGOL60 that I would recommend. There is an excellent introductory set of notes on ALGOLW by R. W. Floyd available from the Computer Science Department of Stanford University.

PL/I

The following book enjoys an unusually good reputation:

Bates, Frank, and Mary L. Douglas, *Programming Language/One*. Englewood Cliffs, N. J.: Prentice-Hall, Inc., 1967.

APL

The first of the following two books concentrates on the details needed for using APL; the second deals more with the concepts and techniques of programming.

Katzan, Harry, Jr., *APL User's Guide*. New York: Van Nostrand Reinhold, 1971.

Katzan, Harry, Jr., *APL Programming and Computer Techniques*. New York: Van Nostrand Reinhold, 1971.

COBOL

Because COBOL is so widely used, a great variety of books is available. One good one is:

McCracken, D., *A Guide to COBOL Programming*. New York: John Wiley & Sons, Inc., 1970.

SNOBOL4

There is one standard, very excellent book, by three people intimately involved in the development of SNOBOL4:

Griswold, R. E., J. F. Poage, and I. P. Polonsky, *The SNOBOL4 Programming Language*. Englewood Cliffs, N. J.: Prentice-Hall, Inc., 1968.

It may also be useful to know about the following:

Griswold, Ralph E., and Madge T. Griswold, *A SNOBOL4 Primer.* Englewood Cliffs, N. J.: Prentice-Hall, Inc., 1973.

LISP

The following is a truly remarkable book because it really succeeds in making LISP easy to understand.

Weissman, Clark, *LISP 1.5 Primer.* Belmont, Calif.: Dickenson Publishing Co., 1967.

GENERAL REFERENCES

The following is a remarkable piece of scholarly work. It covers about 120 languages with a thorough coverage of history and bibliography as well as characteristics and sample programs.

Sammet, Jean E., *Programming Languages: History and Fundamentals.* Englewood Cliffs, N. J.: Prentice-Hall, Inc., 1969.

The following contains a collection of interesting, important early research papers and, in particular, gives background on FORTRAN, COBOL, ALGOL, and PL/I.

Rosen, Saul, *Programming Systems and Languages.* New York: McGraw-Hill Book Company, 1967.

Although it is not the primary objective of this book, the problem of writing good programs came in for some discussion. On that topic, the following books are relevant:

Metzger, Phillip W., *Managing a Software Project.* Englewood Cliffs, N. J.: Prentice-Hall, Inc., 1973.

Revised Report on the Algorithmic Language ALGOL 60

PETER NAUR (*Editor*)

J. W. BACKUS, C. KATZ, H. RUTISHAUSER, J. H. WEGSTEIN

F. L. BAUER, J. McCARTHY, K. SAMELSON, A. VAN WIJNGAARDEN

J. GREEN, A. J. PERLIS, B. VAUQUOIS, M. WOODGER

Dedicated to the Memory of WILLIAM TURANSKI

SUMMARY

The report gives a complete defining description of the international algorithmic language ALGOL 60. This is a language suitable for expressing a large class of numerical processes in a form sufficiently concise for direct automatic translation into the language of programmed automatic computers.

The introduction contains an account of the preparatory work leading up to the final conference, where the language was defined. In addition, the notions, reference language, publication language and hardware representations are explained.

In the first chapter, a survey of the basic constituents and features of the language is given, and the formal notation, by which the syntactic structure is defined, is explained.

The second chapter lists all the basic symbols, and the syntactic units known as identifiers, numbers and strings are defined. Further, some important notions such as quantity and value are defined.

The third chapter explains the rules for forming expressions and the meaning of these expressions. Three different types of expressions exist: arithmetic, Boolean (logical) and designational.

The fourth chapter describes the operational units of the language, known as statements. The basic statements are: assignment statements (evaluation of a formula), go to statements (explicit break of the sequence of execution of statements), dummy statements, and procedure statements (call for execution of a closed process, defined by a procedure declaration). The formation of more complex structures, having statement character, is explained. These include: conditional statements, for statements, compound statements, and blocks.

In the fifth chapter, the units known as declarations, serving for defining permanent properties of the units entering into a process described in the language, are defined.

The report ends with two detailed examples of the use of the language and an alphabetic index of definitions.

CONTENTS

INTRODUCTION
1. STRUCTURE OF THE LANGUAGE
   1.1. Formalism for syntactic description
2. BASIC SYMBOLS, IDENTIFIERS, NUMBERS, AND STRINGS. BASIC CONCEPTS.
   2.1. Letters
   2.2. Digits. Logical values.
   2.3. Delimiters
   2.4. Identifiers
   2.5. Numbers
   2.6. Strings
   2.7. Quantities, kinds and scopes
   2.8. Values and types
3. EXPRESSIONS
   3.1. Variables
   3.2. Function designators
   3.3. Arithmetic expressions
   3.4. Boolean expressions
   3.5. Designational expressions
4. STATEMENTS
   4.1. Compound statements and blocks
   4.2. Assignment statements
   4.3. Go to statements
   4.4. Dummy statements
   4.5. Conditional statements
   4.6. For statements
   4.7. Procedure statements
5. DECLARATIONS
   5.1. Type declarations
   5.2. Array declarations
   5.3. Switch declarations
   5.4. Procedure declarations
EXAMPLES OF PROCEDURE DECLARATIONS
ALPHABETIC INDEX OF DEFINITIONS OF CONCEPTS AND SYNTACTIC UNITS

INTRODUCTION

Background

After the publication of a preliminary report on the algorithmic language ALGOL,[1,2] as prepared at a conference in Zürich in 1958, much interest in the ALGOL language developed.

As a result of an informal meeting held at Mainz in November 1958, about forty interested persons from several European countries held an ALGOL implementation conference in Copenhagen in February 1959. A "hardware group" was formed for working cooperatively right down to the level of the paper tape code. This conference also led to the publication by Regnecentralen, Copenhagen, of an *ALGOL Bulletin*, edited by Peter Naur, which served as a forum for further discussion. During the June 1959 ICIP Conference in Paris several meetings, both formal and informal ones, were held. These meetings revealed some misunderstandings as to the intent of the group which was primarily responsible for the formulation of the language, but at the same time made it clear that there exists a wide appreciation of the effort involved. As a result of the discussions it was decided to hold an international meeting in January 1960 for improving the ALGOL language and preparing a final report. At a European ALGOL Conference in Paris in November 1959 which was attended by about fifty people, seven European representatives were selected to attend the January 1960 Conference, and they represent the following organizations: Association Française de Calcul, British Computer Society, Gesellschaft für Angewandte Mathematik und Mechanik, and Nederlands Rekenmachine Genootschap. The seven representatives held a final preparatory meeting at Mainz in December 1959.

Meanwhile, in the United States, anyone who wished to suggest changes or corrections to ALGOL was requested to send his comments to the *Communications of the ACM*, where they were published. These comments then became the basis of consideration for changes in the ALGOL language. Both the SHARE and USE organizations established ALGOL working groups, and both organizations were represented on the ACM Committee on Programming Languages. The ACM Committee met in Washington in November 1959 and considered all comments on ALGOL that had been sent to the ACM *Communications*. Also, seven representatives were selected to attend the January 1960 international conference. These seven representatives held a final preparatory meeting in Boston in December 1959.

January 1960 Conference

The thirteen representatives,[3] from Denmark, England, France, Germany, Holland, Switzerland, and the United States, conferred in Paris from January 11 to 16, 1960.

Prior to this meeting a completely new draft report was worked out from the preliminary report and the recommendations of the preparatory meetings by Peter Naur and the conference adopted this new form as the basis for its report. The Conference then proceeded to work for agreement on each item of the report. The present report represents the union of the Committee's concepts and the intersection of its agreements.

April 1962 Conference [Edited by M. Woodger]

A meeting of some of the authors of ALGOL 60 was held on April 2–3, 1962 in Rome, Italy, through the facilities and courtesy of the International Computation Centre. The following were present:

Authors	*Advisers*	*Observer*
F. L. Bauer	M. Paul	W. L. van der Poel (Chairman, IFIP TC 2.1 Working Group ALGOL)
J. Green	R. Franciotti	
C. Katz	P. Z. Ingerman	
R. Kogon (representing J. W. Backus)		
P. Naur		
K. Samelson	G. Seegmüller	
J. H. Wegstein	R. E. Utman	
A. van Wijngaarden		
M. Woodger	P. Landin	

The purpose of the meeting was to correct known errors in, attempt to eliminate apparent ambiguities in, and otherwise clarify the ALGOL 60 Report. Extensions to the language were not considered at the meeting. Various proposals for correction and clarification that were submitted by interested parties in response to the Questionnaire in *ALGOL Bulletin* No. 14 were used as a guide.

This report* constitutes a supplement to the ALGOL 60 Report which should resolve a number of difficulties therein. Not all of the questions raised concerning the original report could be resolved. Rather than risk hastily drawn conclusions on a number of subtle points, which might create new ambiguities, the committee decided to report only those points which they unanimously felt could be stated in clear and unambiguous fashion.

Questions concerned with the following areas are left for further consideration by Working Group 2.1 of IFIP, in the expectation that current work on advanced pro-

* [EDITOR'S NOTE. The present edition follows the text which was approved by the Council of IFIP. Although it is not clear from the Introduction, the present version is the original report of the January 1960 conference modified according to the agreements reached during the April 1962 conference. Thus the report mentioned here is incorporated in the present version. The modifications touch the original report in the following sections: Changes of text: 1 with footnote; 2.1 footnote; 2.3; 2.7; 3.3.3; 3.3.4.2; 4.1.3; 4.2.3; 4.2.4; 4.3.4; 4.7.3; 4.7.3.1; 4.7.3.3; 4.7.5.1; 4.7.5.4; 4.7.6; 5; 5.3.3; 5.3.5; 5.4.3; 5.4.4; 5.4.5. Changes of syntax: 3.4.1; 4.1.1; 4.2.1; 4.5.1.]

[1] Preliminary report—International Algebraic Language. *Comm. ACM 1*, 12 (1958), 8.

[2] Report on the Algorithmic Language ALGOL by the ACM Committee on Programming Languages and the GAMM Committee on Programming, edited by A. J. Perlis and K. Samelson. *Num. Math. 1* (1959), 41–60.

[3] William Turanski of the American group was killed by an automobile just prior to the January 1960 Conference.

gramming languages will lead to better resolution:

1. Side effects of functions
2. The call by name concept
3. **own:** static or dynamic
4. For statement: static or dynamic
5. Conflict between specification and declaration

The authors of the ALGOL 60 Report present at the Rome Conference, being aware of the formation of a Working Group on ALGOL by IFIP, accepted that any collective responsibility which they might have with respect to the development, specification and refinement of the ALGOL language will from now on be transferred to that body.

This report has been reviewed by IFIP TC 2 on Programming Languages in August 1962 and has been approved by the Council of the International Federation for Information Processing.

As with the preliminary ALGOL report, three different levels of language are recognized, namely a Reference Language, a Publication Language and several Hardware Representations.

REFERENCE LANGUAGE

1. It is the working language of the committee.
2. It is the defining language.
3. The characters are determined by ease of mutual understanding and not by any computer limitations, coders notation, or pure mathematical notation.
4. It is the basic reference and guide for compiler builders.
5. It is the guide for all hardware representations.
6. It is the guide for transliterating from publication language to any locally appropriate hardware representations.
7. The main publications of the ALGOL language itself will use the reference representation.

PUBLICATION LANGUAGE

1. The publication language admits variations of the reference language according to usage of printing and handwriting (e.g., subscripts, spaces, exponents, Greek letters).
2. It is used for stating and communicating processes.
3. The characters to be used may be different in different countries, but univocal correspondence with reference representation must be secured.

HARDWARE REPRESENTATIONS

1. Each one of these is a condensation of the reference language enforced by the limited number of characters on standard input equipment.
2. Each one of these uses the character set of a particular computer and is the language accepted by a translator for that computer.
3. Each one of these must be accompanied by a special set of rules for transliterating from Publication or Reference language.

For transliteration between the reference language and a language suitable for publications, among others, the following rules are recommended.

Reference Language	*Publication Language*
Subscript bracket [ ]	Lowering of the line between the brackets and removal of the brackets
Exponentiation ↑	Raising of the exponent
Parentheses ( )	Any form of parentheses, brackets, braces
Basis of ten $_{10}$	Raising of the ten and of the following integral number, inserting of the intended multiplication sign

DESCRIPTION OF THE REFERENCE LANGUAGE

Was sich überhaupt sagen lässt, lässt
sich klar sagen; und wovon man nicht
reden kann, darüber muss man schweigen.
LUDWIG WITTGENSTEIN.

1. Structure of the Language

As stated in the introduction, the algorithmic language has three different kinds of representations—reference, hardware, and publication—and the development described in the sequel is in terms of the reference representation. This means that all objects defined within the language are represented by a given set of symbols—and it is only in the choice of symbols that the other two representations may differ. Structure and content must be the same for all representations.

The purpose of the algorithmic language is to describe computational processes. The basic concept used for the description of calculating rules is the well-known arithmetic expression containing as constituents numbers, variables, and functions. From such expressions are compounded, by applying rules of arithmetic composition, self-contained units of the language—explicit formulae—called assignment statements.

To show the flow of computational processes, certain nonarithmetic statements and statement clauses are added which may describe, e.g., alternatives, or iterative repetitions of computing statements. Since it is necessary for the function of these statements that one statement refer to another, statements may be provided with labels. A sequence of statements may be enclosed between the statement brackets **begin** and **end** to form a compound statement.

Statements are supported by declarations which are not themselves computing instructions but inform the translator of the existence and certain properties of objects appearing in statements, such as the class of numbers taken on as values by a variable, the dimension of an array of numbers, or even the set of rules defining a function. A sequence of declarations followed by a sequence of statements and enclosed between **begin** and **end** constitutes a block. Every declaration appears in a block in this way and is valid only for that block.

A program is a block or compound statement which is not contained within another statement and which makes no use of other statements not contained within it.

In the sequel the syntax and semantics of the language will be given.[4]

1.1. Formalism for Syntactic Description

The syntax will be described with the aid of metalinguistic formulae.[5] Their interpretation is best explained by an example

⟨ab⟩ ::= (| [| ⟨ab⟩ (| ⟨ab⟩⟨d⟩

Sequences of characters enclosed in the brackets ⟨ ⟩ represent metalinguistic variables whose values are sequences of symbols. The marks ::= and | (the latter with the meaning of **or**) are metalinguistic connectives. Any mark in a formula, which is not a variable or a connective, denotes itself (or the class of marks which are similar to it). Juxtaposition of marks and/or variables in a formula signifies juxtaposition of the sequences denoted. Thus the formula above gives a recursive rule for the formation of values of the variable ⟨ab⟩. It indicates that ⟨ab⟩ may have the value (or [or that given some legitimate value of ⟨ab⟩, another may be formed by following it with the character (or by following it with some value of the variable ⟨d⟩. If the values of ⟨d⟩ are the decimal digits, some values of ⟨ab⟩ are:

[(((1(37(
(12345(
(((
[86

In order to facilitate the study, the symbols used for distinguishing the metalinguistic variables (i.e. the sequences of characters appearing within the brackets ⟨ ⟩ as ab in the above example) have been chosen to be words describing approximately the nature of the corresponding variable. Where words which have appeared in this manner are used elsewhere in the text they will refer to the corresponding syntactic definition. In addition some formulae have been given in more than one place.

Definition:

⟨empty⟩ ::=
(i.e. the null string of symbols).

[4] Whenever the precision of arithmetic is stated as being in general not specified, or the outcome of a certain process is left undefined or said to be undefined, this is to be interpreted in the sense that a program only fully defines a computational process if the accompanying information specifies the precision assumed, the kind of arithmetic assumed, and the course of action to be taken in all such cases as may occur during the execution of the computation.

[5] Cf. J. W. Backus, The syntax and semantics of the proposed international algebraic language of the Zürich ACM-GAMM conference. Proc. Internat. Conf. Inf. Proc., UNESCO, Paris, June 1959.

2. Basic Symbols, Identifiers, Numbers, and Strings. Basic Concepts.

The reference language is built up from the following basic symbols:

⟨basic symbol⟩ ::= ⟨letter⟩|⟨digit⟩|⟨logical value⟩|⟨delimiter⟩

2.1. Letters

⟨letter⟩ ::= *a|b|c|d|e|f|g|h|i|j|k|l|m|n|o|p|q|r|s|t|u|v|w|x|y|z|*
A|B|C|D|E|F|G|H|I|J|K|L|M|N|O|P|Q|R|S|T|U|V|W|X|Y|Z

This alphabet may arbitrarily be restricted, or extended with any other distinctive character (i.e. character not coinciding with any digit, logical value or delimiter).

Letters do not have individual meaning. They are used for forming identifiers and strings[6] (cf. sections 2.4 Identifiers, 2.6. Strings).

2.2.1. Digits

⟨digit⟩ ::= 0|1|2|3|4|5|6|7|8|9

Digits are used for forming numbers, identifiers, and strings.

2.2.2. Logical Values

⟨logical value⟩ ::= **true**|**false**

The logical values have a fixed obvious meaning.

2.3. Delimiters

⟨delimiter⟩ ::= ⟨operator⟩|⟨separator⟩|⟨bracket⟩|⟨declarator⟩|
⟨specificator⟩
⟨operator⟩ ::= ⟨arithmetic operator⟩|⟨relational operator⟩|
⟨logical operator⟩|⟨sequential operator⟩
⟨arithmetic operator⟩ ::= +|−|×|/|÷|↑
⟨relational operator⟩ ::= <|≦|=|≧|>|≠
⟨logical operator⟩ ::= ≡|⊃|∨|∧|¬
⟨sequential operator⟩ ::= **go to**|**if**|**then**|**else**|**for**|**do**[7]
⟨separator⟩ ::= ,|.|₁₀|:|;|:=|␣|**step**|**until**|**while**|**comment**
⟨bracket⟩ ::= (|)|[|]|‘|’|**begin**|**end**
⟨declarator⟩ ::= **own**|**Boolean**|**integer**|**real**|**array**|**switch**|
procedure
⟨specificator⟩ ::= **string**|**label**|**value**

Delimiters have a fixed meaning which for the most part is obvious or else will be given at the appropriate place in the sequel.

Typographical features such as blank space or change to a new line have no significance in the reference language. They may, however, be used freely for facilitating reading.

For the purpose of including text among the symbols of

[6] It should be particularly noted that throughout the reference language underlining [in typewritten copy; boldface type in printed copy—Ed.] is used for defining independent basic symbols (see sections 2.2.2 and 2.3). These are understood to have no relation to the individual letters of which they are composed. Within the present report [not including headings—Ed.], boldface will be used for no other purpose.

[7] **do** is used in for statements. It has no relation whatsoever to the *do* of the preliminary report, which is not included in ALGOL 60.

program the following "comment" conventions hold:

The sequence of basic symbols:	*is equivalent to*
omment ⟨any sequence not containing ;⟩;	;
gin comment ⟨any sequence not containing ;⟩;	**begin**
d ⟨any sequence not containing **end** or ; or **else**⟩	**end**

y equivalence is here meant that any of the three strucres shown in the left-hand column may be replaced, in y occurrence outside of strings, by the symbol shown on e same line in the right-hand column without any ect on the action of the program. It is further understood at the comment structure encountered first in the text hen reading from left to right has precedence in being placed over later structures contained in the sequence.

2.4. IDENTIFIERS

2.4.1. Syntax

lentifier⟩ ::= ⟨letter⟩|⟨identifier⟩⟨letter⟩|⟨identifier⟩⟨digit⟩

2.4.2. Examples

q
Soup
V17a
a34kTMNs
MARILYN

2.4.3. Semantics

Identifiers have no inherent meaning, but serve for the entification of simple variables, arrays, labels, switches, d procedures. They may be chosen freely (cf., however, ction 3.2.4. Standard Functions).

The same identifier cannot be used to denote two fferent quantities except when these quantities have sjoint scopes as defined by the declarations of the proam (cf. section 2.7. Quantities, Kinds and Scopes, and ction 5. Declarations).

2.5. NUMBERS

2.5.1. Syntax

nsigned integer⟩ ::= ⟨digit⟩|⟨unsigned integer⟩⟨digit⟩
nteger⟩ ::= ⟨unsigned integer⟩|+⟨unsigned integer⟩|
 −⟨unsigned integer⟩
ecimal fraction⟩ ::= .⟨unsigned integer⟩
xponent part⟩ ::= $_{10}$⟨integer⟩
ecimal number⟩ ::= ⟨unsigned integer⟩|⟨decimal fraction⟩|
 ⟨unsigned integer⟩⟨decimal fraction⟩
nsigned number⟩ ::= ⟨decimal number⟩|⟨exponent part⟩|
 ⟨decimal number⟩⟨exponent part⟩
umber⟩ ::= ⟨unsigned number⟩|+⟨unsigned number⟩|
 −⟨unsigned number⟩

2.5.2. Examples

0	−200.084	−.083$_{10}$−02
177	+07.43$_{10}$8	−$_{10}$7
.5384	9.34$_{10}$+10	$_{10}$−4
+0.7300	2−$_{10}$4	+$_{10}$+5

2.5.3. Semantics

Decimal numbers have their conventional meaning. he exponent part is a scale factor expressed as an integral wer of 10.

2.5.4. Types

Integers are of type **integer.** All other numbers are of type **real** (cf. section 5.1. Type Declarations).

2.6. STRINGS

2.6.1. Syntax

⟨proper string⟩ ::= ⟨any sequence of basic symbols not containing
 ' or '⟩|⟨empty⟩
⟨open string⟩ ::= ⟨proper string⟩|'⟨open string⟩'|
 ⟨open string⟩⟨open string⟩
⟨string⟩ ::= '⟨open string⟩'

2.6.2. Examples

'5k,,−'[[['∧=/:'Tt''
'.. This ␣ is ␣ a ␣ 'string''

2.6.3. Semantics

In order to enable the language to handle arbitrary sequences of basic symbols the string quotes ' and ' are introduced. The symbol ␣ denotes a space. It has no significance outside strings.

Strings are used as actual parameters of procedures (cf. sections 3.2. Function Designators and 4.7. Procedure Statements).

2.7. QUANTITIES, KINDS AND SCOPES

The following kinds of quantities are distinguished: simple variables, arrays, labels, switches, and procedures.

The scope of a quantity is the set of statements and expressions in which the declaration of the identifier associated with that quantity is valid. For labels see section 4.1.3.

2.8. VALUES AND TYPES

A value is an ordered set of numbers (special case: a single number), an ordered set of logical values (special case: a single logical value), or a label.

Certain of the syntactic units are said to possess values. These values will in general change during the execution of the program. The values of expressions and their constituents are defined in section 3. The value of an array identifier is the ordered set of values of the corresponding array of subscripted variables (cf. section 3.1.4.1).

The various "types" (**integer, real, Boolean**) basically denote properties of values. The types associated with syntactic units refer to the values of these units.

3. Expressions

In the language the primary constituents of the programs describing algorithmic processes are arithmetic, Boolean, and designational expressions. Constituents of these expressions, except for certain delimiters, are logical values, numbers, variables, function designators, and elementary arithmetic, relational, logical, and sequential operators. Since the syntactic definition of both variables and function designators contains expressions, the definition of expressions, and their constituents, is necessarily recursive.

⟨expression⟩ ::= ⟨arithmetic expression⟩|⟨Boolean expression⟩|
 ⟨designational expression⟩

3.1. Variables

3.1.1. Syntax

⟨variable identifier⟩ ::= ⟨identifier⟩
⟨simple variable⟩ ::= ⟨variable identifier⟩
⟨subscript expression⟩ ::= ⟨arithmetic expression⟩
⟨subscript list⟩ ::= ⟨subscript expression⟩|⟨subscript list⟩,
  ⟨subscript expression⟩
⟨array identifier⟩ ::= ⟨identifier⟩
⟨subscripted variable⟩ ::= ⟨array identifier⟩[⟨subscript list⟩]
⟨variable⟩ ::= ⟨simple variable⟩|⟨subscripted variable⟩

3.1.2. Examples

epsilon
detA
a17
Q[7,2]
x[*sin*(*n*×*pi*/2),*Q*[3,*n*,4]]

3.1.3. Semantics

A variable is a designation given to a single value. This value may be used in expressions for forming other values and may be changed at will by means of assignment statements (section 4.2). The type of the value of a particular variable is defined in the declaration for the variable itself (cf. section 5.1. Type Declarations) or for the corresponding array identifier (cf. section 5.2. Array Declarations).

3.1.4. Subscripts

3.1.4.1. Subscripted variables designate values which are components of multidimensional arrays (cf. section 5.2. Array Declarations). Each arithmetic expression of the subscript list occupies one subscript position of the subscripted variable, and is called a subscript. The complete list of subscripts is enclosed in the subscript brackets [ ]. The array component referred to by a subscripted variable is specified by the actual numerical value of its subscripts (cf. section 3.3. Arithmetic Expressions).

3.1.4.2. Each subscript position acts like a variable of type **integer** and the evaluation of the subscript is understood to be equivalent to an assignment to this fictitious variable (cf. section 4.2.4). The value of the subscripted variable is defined only if the value of the subscript expression is within the subscript bounds of the array (cf. section 5.2. Array Declarations).

3.2. Function Designators

3.2.1. Syntax

⟨procedure identifier⟩ ::= ⟨identifier⟩
⟨actual parameter⟩ ::= ⟨string⟩|⟨expression⟩|⟨array identifier⟩|
  ⟨switch identifier⟩|⟨procedure identifier⟩
⟨letter string⟩ ::= ⟨letter⟩|⟨letter string⟩⟨letter⟩
⟨parameter delimiter⟩ ::= ,|)⟨letter string⟩:(
⟨actual parameter list⟩ ::= ⟨actual parameter⟩|
  ⟨actual parameter list⟩⟨parameter delimiter⟩
  ⟨actual parameter⟩
⟨actual parameter part⟩ ::= ⟨empty⟩|(⟨actual parameter list⟩)
⟨function designator⟩ ::= ⟨procedure identifier⟩
  ⟨actual parameter part⟩

3.2.2. Examples

sin(*a*−*b*)
J(*v*+*s*,*n*)
R
S(*s*−5)Temperature:(*T*)Pressure:(*P*)
Compile(' := ')Stack:(*Q*)

3.2.3. Semantics

Function designators define single numerical or logic values, which result through the application of given se of rules defined by a procedure declaration (cf. section 5. Procedure Declarations) to fixed sets of actual parar eters. The rules governing specification of actual parar eters are given in section 4.7. Procedure Statements. N every procedure declaration defines the value of a functic designator.

3.2.4. Standard functions

Certain identifiers should be reserved for the standa functions of analysis, which will be expressed as procedure It is recommended that this reserved list should contai

abs(E)	for the modulus (absolute value) of the value of t expression E
sign(E)	for the sign of the value of E(+1 for E>0, 0 for E= −1 for E<0)
sqrt(E)	for the square root of the value of E
sin(E)	for the sine of the value of E
cos(E)	for the cosine of the value of E
arctan(E)	for the principal value of the arctangent of the val of E
ln(E)	for the natural logarithm of the value of E
exp(E)	for the exponential function of the value of E (e^E).

These functions are all understood to operate indifferent on arguments both of type **real** and **integer**. They wi all yield values of type **real**, except for *sign*(E) which wi have values of type **integer**. In a particular representa tion these functions may be available without explic declarations (cf. section 5. Declarations).

3.2.5. Transfer functions

It is understood that transfer functions between an pair of quantities and expressions may be defined. Amon the standard functions it is recommended that there b one, namely,

entier(E),

which "transfers" an expression of real type to one c integer type, and assigns to it the value which is th largest integer not greater than the value of E.

3.3. Arithmetic Expressions

3.3.1. Syntax

⟨adding operator⟩ ::= +|−
⟨multiplying operator⟩ ::= ×|/|÷
⟨primary⟩ ::= ⟨unsigned number⟩|⟨variable⟩|
  ⟨function designator⟩|(⟨arithmetic expression⟩)
⟨factor⟩ ::= ⟨primary⟩|⟨factor⟩↑⟨primary⟩
⟨term⟩ ::= ⟨factor⟩|⟨term⟩⟨multiplying operator⟩⟨factor⟩
⟨simple arithmetic expression⟩ ::= ⟨term⟩|
  ⟨adding operator⟩⟨term⟩|⟨simple arithmetic expressio
  ⟨adding operator⟩⟨term⟩
⟨if clause⟩ ::= **if** ⟨Boolean expression⟩**then**
⟨arithmetic expression⟩ ::= ⟨simple arithmetic expression
  ⟨if clause⟩⟨simple arithmetic expression⟩**else**
  ⟨arithmetic expression⟩

3.3.2. Examples

Primaries:

$7.394_{10}-8$
sum
$w[i+2,8]$
$cos(y+z\times 3)$
$(a-3/y+vu\uparrow 8)$

Factors:

$omega$
$sum\uparrow cos(y+z\times 3)$
$7.394_{10}-8\uparrow w[i+2,8]\uparrow(a-3/y+vu\uparrow 8)$

Terms:

U
$omega\times sum\uparrow cos(y+z\times 3)/7.394_{10}-8\uparrow w[i+2,8]\uparrow$
$(a-3/y+vu\uparrow 8)$

Simple arithmetic expression:

$U-Yu+omega\times sum\uparrow cos(y+z\times 3)/7.394_{10}-8\uparrow w[i+2,8]\uparrow$
$(a-3/y+vu\uparrow 8)$

Arithmetic expressions:

$w\times u-Q(S+Cu)\uparrow 2$
if $q>0$ **then** $S+3\times Q/A$ **else** $2\times S+3\times q$
if $a<0$ **then** $U+V$ **else if** $a\times b>17$ **then** U/V **else if**
$k\neq y$ **then** V/U **else** 0
$a\times sin(omega\times t)$
$0.57_{10}12\times a[N\times(N-1)/2,\ 0]$
$(A\times arctan(y)+Z)\uparrow(7+Q)$
if q **then** $n-1$ **else** n
if $a<0$ **then** A/B **else if** $b=0$ **then** B/A **else** z

3.3.3. Semantics

An arithmetic expression is a rule for computing a umerical value. In case of simple arithmetic expressions is value is obtained by executing the indicated arithetic operations on the actual numerical values of the rimaries of the expression, as explained in detail in ection 3.3.4 below. The actual numerical value of a rimary is obvious in the case of numbers. For variables is the current value (assigned last in the dynamic sense), nd for function designators it is the value arising from ne computing rules defining the procedure (cf. section .4.4. Values of Function Designators) when applied to ne current values of the procedure parameters given in ne expression. Finally, for arithmetic expressions enlosed in parentheses the value must through a recursive nalysis be expressed in terms of the values of primaries f the other three kinds.

In the more general arithmetic expressions, which inlude if clauses, one out of several simple arithmetic exressions is selected on the basis of the actual values of the oolean expressions (cf. section 3.4. Boolean Expressions). his selection is made as follows: The Boolean expressions f the if clauses are evaluated one by one in sequence from ft to right until one having the value **true** is found. The alue of the arithmetic expression is then the value of he first arithmetic expression following this Boolean he largest arithmetic expression found in this position is understood). The construction:

else ⟨simple arithmetic expression⟩

is equivalent to the construction:

else if true then ⟨simple arithmetic expression⟩

3.3.4. Operators and types

Apart from the Boolean expressions of if clauses, the constituents of simple arithmetic expressions must be of types **real** or **integer** (cf. section 5.1. Type Declarations). The meaning of the basic operators and the types of the expressions to which they lead are given by the following rules:

3.3.4.1. The operators $+$, $-$, and $\times$ have the conventional meaning (addition, subtraction, and multiplication). The type of the expression will be **integer** if both of the operands are of **integer** type, otherwise **real**.

3.3.4.2. The operations ⟨term⟩/⟨factor⟩ and ⟨term⟩ $\div$ ⟨factor⟩ both denote division, to be understood as a multiplication of the term by the reciprocal of the factor with due regard to the rules of precedence (cf. section 3.3.5). Thus for example

$$a/b\times 7/(p-q)\times v/s$$

means

$$((((a\times(b^{-1}))\times 7)\times((p-q)^{-1}))\times v)\times(s^{-1})$$

The operator / is defined for all four combinations of types **real** and **integer** and will yield results of **real** type in any case. The operator $\div$ is defined only for two operands both of type **integer** and will yield a result of type **integer**, mathematically defined as follows:

$$a\div b= sign\ (a/b)\times entier(abs(a/b))$$

(cf. sections 3.2.4 and 3.2.5).

3.3.4.3. The operation ⟨factor⟩↑⟨primary⟩ denotes exponentiation, where the factor is the base and the primary is the exponent. Thus, for example,

$$2\uparrow n\uparrow k \qquad \text{means} \qquad (2^n)^k$$

while

$$2\uparrow(n\uparrow m) \qquad \text{means} \qquad 2^{(n^m)}$$

Writing i for a number of **integer** type, r for a number of **real** type, and a for a number of either **integer** or **real** type, the result is given by the following rules:

$a\uparrow i$ If $i>0$, $a\times a\times\ \ldots\ \times a$ (i times), of the same type as a.
If $i=0$, if $a\neq 0$, 1, of the same type as a.
if $a=0$, undefined.
If $i<0$, if $a\neq 0$, $1/(a\times a\times\ \ldots\ \times a)$ (the denominator has $-i$ factors), of type **real**.
if $a=0$, undefined.

$a\uparrow r$ If $a>0$, $exp(r\times ln(a))$, of type **real**.
If $a=0$, if $r>0$, 0.0, of type **real**.
if $r\leq 0$, undefined.
If $a<0$, always undefined.

3.3.5. Precedence of operators

The sequence of operations within one expression is

generally from left to right, with the following additional rules:

3.3.5.1. According to the syntax given in section 3.3.1 the following rules of precedence hold:

```
first:  ↑
second: ×/÷
third:  +−
```

3.3.5.2. The expression between a left parenthesis and the matching right parenthesis is evaluated by itself and this value is used in subsequent calculations. Consequently the desired order of execution of operations within an expression can always be arranged by appropriate positioning of parentheses.

3.3.6. Arithmetics of **real** quantities

Numbers and variables of type **real** must be interpreted in the sense of numerical analysis, i.e. as entities defined inherently with only a finite accuracy. Similarly, the possibility of the occurrence of a finite deviation from the mathematically defined result in any arithmetic expression is explicitly understood. No exact arithmetic will be specified, however, and it is indeed understood that different hardware representations may evaluate arithmetic expressions differently. The control of the possible consequences of such differences must be carried out by the methods of numerical analysis. This control must be considered a part of the process to be described, and will therefore be expressed in terms of the language itself.

3.4. Boolean Expressions

3.4.1. Syntax

```
⟨relational operator⟩ ::= <|≦|=|≧|>|≠
⟨relation⟩ ::= ⟨simple arithmetic expression⟩
    ⟨relational operator⟩⟨simple arithmetic expression⟩
⟨Boolean primary⟩ ::= ⟨logical value⟩|⟨variable⟩|
    ⟨function designator⟩|⟨relation⟩|(⟨Boolean expression⟩)
⟨Boolean secondary⟩ ::= ⟨Boolean primary⟩|¬⟨Boolean primary⟩
⟨Boolean factor⟩ ::= ⟨Boolean secondary⟩|
    ⟨Boolean factor⟩∧⟨Boolean secondary⟩
⟨Boolean term⟩ ::= ⟨Boolean factor⟩|⟨Boolean term⟩
    ∨⟨Boolean factor⟩
⟨implication⟩ ::= ⟨Boolean term⟩|⟨implication⟩⊃⟨Boolean term⟩
⟨simple Boolean⟩ ::= ⟨implication⟩|
    ⟨simple Boolean⟩≡⟨implication⟩
⟨Boolean expression⟩ ::= ⟨simple Boolean⟩|
    ⟨if clause⟩⟨simple Boolean⟩ else ⟨Boolean expression⟩
```

3.4.2. Examples

```
x = −2
Y>V ∨ z<q
a+b > −5 ∧ z−d > q↑2
p∧q ∨ x≠y
g≡¬a∧b∧¬c∨d∨e⊃¬f
if k<1 then s>w else h≦c
if if if a then b else c then d else f then g else h<k
```

3.4.3. Semantics

A Boolean expression is a rule for computing a logical value. The principles of evaluation are entirely analogous to those given for arithmetic expressions in section 3.3.3.

3.4.4. Types

Variables and function designators entered as Boolean primaries must be declared **Boolean** (cf. section 5.1 Type Declarations and section 5.4.4. Values of Functio Designators).

3.4.5. The operators

Relations take on the value **true** whenever the corre sponding relation is satisfied for the expressions involve otherwise **false**.

The meaning of the logical operators ¬ (not), ∧ (and ∨ (or), ⊃ (implies), and ≡ (equivalent), is given by th following function table.

b1	false	false	true	true
b2	false	true	false	true
¬b1	true	true	false	false
b1∧b2	false	false	false	true
b1∨b2	false	true	true	true
b1⊃b2	true	true	false	true
b1≡b2	true	false	false	true

3.4.6. Precedence of operators

The sequence of operations within one expression generally from left to right, with the following addition rules:

3.4.6.1. According to the syntax given in section 3.4. the following rules of precedence hold:

```
first: arithmetic expressions according to section 3.3.5.
second:  <≦=≧>≠
third:   ¬
fourth:  ∧
fifth:   ∨
sixth:   ⊃
seventh: ≡
```

3.4.6.2. The use of parentheses will be interpreted in the sense given in section 3.3.5.2.

3.5. Designational Expressions

3.5.1. Syntax

```
⟨label⟩ ::= ⟨identifier⟩|⟨unsigned integer⟩
⟨switch identifier⟩ ::= ⟨identifier⟩
⟨switch designator⟩ ::= ⟨switch identifier⟩[⟨subscript expression
⟨simple designational expression⟩ ::= ⟨label⟩|⟨switch designator
    (⟨designational expression⟩)
⟨designational expression⟩ ::= ⟨simple designational expression
    ⟨if clause⟩⟨simple designational expression⟩ else
    ⟨designational expression⟩
```

3.5.2. Examples

```
17
p9
Choose[n−1]
Town[if y<0 then N else N+1]
if Ab<c then 17 else q[if w≦0 then 2 else n]
```

3.5.3. Semantics

A designational expression is a rule for obtaining a labe of a statement (cf. section 4. Statements). Again th principle of the evaluation is entirely analogous to that c arithmetic expressions (section 3.3.3). In the general cas the Boolean expressions of the if clauses will select simple designational expression. If this is a label th desired result is already found. A switch designator refer to the corresponding switch declaration (cf. section 5.3

witch Declarations) and by the actual numerical value f its subscript expression selects one of the designational xpressions listed in the switch declaration by counting hese from left to right. Since the designational expression hus selected may again be a switch designator this evaluaion is obviously a recursive process.

3.5.4. The subscript expression

The evaluation of the subscript expression is analogous o that of subscripted variables (cf. section 3.1.4.2). The alue of a switch designator is defined only if the subscript xpression assumes one of the positive values 1, 2, 3, . . . , n, here n is the number of entries in the switch list.

3.5.5. Unsigned integers as labels

Unsigned integers used as labels have the property that eading zeros do not affect their meaning, e.g. 00217 enotes the same label as 217.

. Statements

The units of operation within the language are called tatements. They will normally be executed consecutively s written. However, this sequence of operations may be roken by go to statements, which define their successor xplicitly, and shortened by conditional statements, which may cause certain statements to be skipped.

In order to make it possible to define a specific dynamic uccession, statements may be provided with labels.

Since sequences of statements may be grouped together nto compound statements and blocks the definition of tatement must necessarily be recursive. Also since declarations, described in section 5, enter fundamentally into he syntactic structure, the syntactic definition of statements must suppose declarations to be already defined.

4.1. Compound Statements and Blocks

4.1.1. Syntax

⟨unlabelled basic statement⟩ ::= ⟨assignment statement⟩|
    ⟨go to statement⟩|⟨dummy statement⟩|⟨procedure statement⟩
⟨basic statement⟩ ::= ⟨unlabelled basic statement⟩|⟨label⟩:
    ⟨basic statement⟩
⟨unconditional statement⟩ ::= ⟨basic statement⟩|
    ⟨compound statement⟩|⟨block⟩
⟨statement⟩ ::= ⟨unconditional statement⟩|
    ⟨conditional statement⟩|⟨for statement⟩
⟨compound tail⟩ ::= ⟨statement⟩ **end** |⟨statement⟩ ;
    ⟨compound tail⟩
⟨block head⟩ ::= **begin**⟨declaration⟩|⟨block head⟩ ;
    ⟨declaration⟩
⟨unlabelled compound⟩ ::= **begin** ⟨compound tail⟩
⟨unlabelled block⟩ ::= ⟨block head⟩ ; ⟨compound tail⟩
⟨compound statement⟩ ::= ⟨unlabelled compound⟩|
    ⟨label⟩:⟨compound statement⟩
⟨block⟩ ::= ⟨unlabelled block⟩|⟨label⟩:⟨block⟩
⟨program⟩ ::= ⟨block⟩|⟨compound statement⟩

This syntax may be illustrated as follows: Denoting arbitrary statements, declarations, and labels, by the letters S, D, and L, respectively, the basic syntactic units take the forms:

Compound statement:

L: L: ... **begin** S ; S ; ... S ; S **end**

Block:

L: L: ... **begin** D ; D ; .. D ; S ; S ; ...S ;
    S **end**

It should be kept in mind that each of the statements S may again be a complete compound statement or block.

4.1.2. Examples

Basic statements:

a := *p*+*q*
go to *Naples*
START: *CONTINUE*: *W* := 7.993

Compound statement:

begin *x* := 0 ; **for** *y* := 1 **step** 1 **until** *n* **do**
    x := *x*+*A*[*y*] ;
    if *x*>*q* **then go to** *STOP* **else if** *x*>*w*−2 **then**
        go to *S* ;
    Aw: *St*: *W* := *x*+*bob* **end**

Block:

Q: **begin integer** *i*, *k* ; **real** *w* ;
    for *i* := 1 **step** 1 **until** *m* **do**
    for *k* := *i*+1 **step** 1 **until** *m* **do**
    begin *w* := *A*[*i*, *k*] ;
        A[*i*, *k*] := *A*[*k*, *i*] ;
        A[*k*, *i*] := *w* **end** for *i* and *k*
end block *Q*

4.1.3. Semantics

Every block automatically introduces a new level of nomenclature. This is realized as follows: Any identifier occurring within the block may through a suitable declaration (cf. section 5. Declarations) be specified to be local to the block in question. This means (a) that the entity represented by this identifier inside the block has no existence outside it, and (b) that any entity represented by this identifier outside the block is completely inaccessible inside the block.

Identifiers (except those representing labels) occurring within a block and not being declared to this block will be nonlocal to it, i.e. will represent the same entity inside the block and in the level immediately outside it. A label separated by a colon from a statement, i.e. labelling that statement, behaves as though declared in the head of the smallest embracing block, i.e. the smallest block whose brackets **begin** and **end** enclose that statement. In this context a procedure body must be considered as if it were enclosed by **begin** and **end** and treated as a block.

Since a statement of a block may again itself be a block the concepts local and nonlocal to a block must be understood recursively. Thus an identifier, which is nonlocal to a block A, may or may not be nonlocal to the block B in which A is one statement.

4.2. Assignment Statements

4.2.1. Syntax

⟨left part⟩ ::= ⟨variable⟩ := |⟨procedure identifier⟩ :=
⟨left part list⟩ ::= ⟨left part⟩|⟨left part list⟩⟨left part⟩
⟨assignment statement⟩ ::= ⟨left part list⟩⟨arithmetic expression⟩|
    ⟨left part list⟩⟨Boolean expression⟩

4.2.2. Examples

```
s := p[0] := n := n+1+s
n := n+1
A := B/C−v−q×S
S[v,k+2] := 3−arctan(s×zeta)
V := Q>Y∧Z
```

4.2.3. Semantics

Assignment statements serve for assigning the value of an expression to one or several variables or procedure identifiers. Assignment to a procedure identifier may only occur within the body of a procedure defining the value of a function designator (cf. section 5.4.4). The process will in the general case be understood to take place in three steps as follows:

4.2.3.1. Any subscript expressions occurring in the left part variables are evaluated in sequence from left to right.

4.2.3.2. The expression of the statement is evaluated.

4.2.3.3. The value of the expression is assigned to all the left part variables, with any subscript expressions having values as evaluated in step 4.2.3.1.

4.2.4. Types

The type associated with all variables and procedure identifiers of a left part list must be the same. If this type is **Boolean,** the expression must likewise be **Boolean.** If the type is **real** or **integer,** the expression must be arithmetic. If the type of the arithmetic expression differs from that associated with the variables and procedure identifiers, appropriate transfer functions are understood to be automatically invoked. For transfer from **real** to **integer** type, the transfer function is understood to yield a result equivalent to

entier(E+0 5)

where E is the value of the expression. The type associated with a procedure identifier is given by the declarator which appears as the first symbol of the corresponding procedure declaration (cf. section 5.4.4).

4.3. Go To Statements

4.3.1. Syntax

```
<go to statement> ::= go to <designational expression>
```

4.3.2. Examples

```
go to 8
go to exit [n+1]
go to Town[if y<0 then N else N+1]
go to if Ab<c then 17 else q[if w<0 then 2 else n]
```

4.3.3. Semantics

A go to statement interrupts the normal sequence of operations, defined by the write-up of statements, by defining its successor explicitly by the value of a designational expression. Thus the next statement to be executed will be the one having this value as its label.

4.3.4. Restriction

Since labels are inherently local, no go to statement can lead from outside into a block. A go to statement may, however, lead from outside into a compound statement.

4.3.5. Go to an undefined switch designator

A go to statement is equivalent to a dummy statement if the designational expression is a switch designator whose value is undefined.

4.4. Dummy Statements

4.4.1. Syntax

```
<dummy statement> ::= <empty>
```

4.4.2. Examples

```
L:
begin ... ; John: end
```

4.4.3. Semantics

A dummy statement executes no operation. It may serve to place a label.

4.5. Conditional Statements

4.5.1. Syntax

```
<if clause> ::= if <Boolean expression> then
<unconditional statement> ::= <basic statement>|
    <compound statement>|<block>
<if statement> ::= <if clause> <unconditional statement>
<conditional statement> ::= <if statement>|<if statement> else
    <statement>|<if clause><for statement>|
    <label> : <conditional statement>
```

4.5.2. Examples

```
if x>0 then n := n+1
if v>u then V: q := n+m else go to R
if s<0∨P≦Q then AA: begin if q<v then a := v/s
                  else y := 2×a end
                else if v>s then a := v−q else if v>s−1
                  then go to S
```

4.5.3. Semantics

Conditional statements cause certain statements to be executed or skipped depending on the running values of specified Boolean expressions.

4.5.3.1. If statement. The unconditional statement of an if statement will be executed if the Boolean expression of the if clause is true. Otherwise it will be skipped and the operation will be continued with the next statement.

4.5.3.2. Conditional statement. According to the syntax two different forms of conditional statements are possible. These may be illustrated as follows:

```
if B1 then S1 else if B2 then S2 else S3 ; S4
```

and

```
if B1 then S1 else if B2 then S2 else if B3 then S3 ; S4
```

Here B1 to B3 are Boolean expressions, while S1 to S3 are unconditional statements. S4 is the statement following the complete conditional statement.

The execution of a conditional statement may be described as follows: The Boolean expression of the if clauses are evaluated one after the other in sequence from left to right until one yielding the value **true** is found. Then the unconditional statement following this Boolean is executed. Unless this statement defines its successor explicitly the next statement to be executed will be S4, i.e. the stateıent following the complete conditional statement. Thus ıe effect of the delimiter **else** may be described by saying ıat it defines the successor of the statement it follows to e the statement following the complete conditional :atement.

The construction

else ⟨unconditional statement⟩

ı equivalent to

else if true then ⟨unconditional statement⟩

If none of the Boolean expressions of the if clauses is ·ue, the effect of the whole conditional statement will be quivalent to that of a dummy statement.

For further explanation the following picture may be seful:

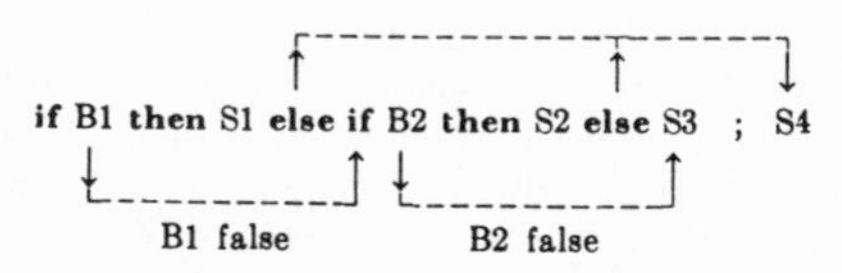

if B1 then S1 else if B2 then S2 else S3 ; S4
B1 false
B2 false

4.5.4. Go to into a conditional statement

The effect of a go to statement leading into a conditional :atement follows directly from the above explanation of ıe effect of **else**.

4.6. For Statements

4.6.1. Syntax

'or list element⟩ ::= ⟨arithmetic expression⟩|
⟨arithmetic expression⟩ **step** ⟨arithmetic expression⟩ **until**
⟨arithmetic expression⟩|⟨arithmetic expression⟩ **while**
⟨Boolean expression⟩
or list⟩ ::= ⟨for list element⟩|⟨for list⟩ , ⟨for list element⟩
'or clause⟩ ::= **for** ⟨variable⟩ := ⟨for list⟩ **do**
or statement⟩ ::= ⟨for clause⟩⟨statement⟩|
⟨label⟩: ⟨for statement⟩

4.6.2. Examples

```
for q := 1 step s until n do A[q] := B[q]
for k := 1, V1×2 while V1<N do
        for j := I+G, L, 1 step 1 until N, C+D do
            A[k,j] := B[k,j]
```

4.6.3. Semantics

A for clause causes the statement S which it precedes to e repeatedly executed zero or more times. In addition it erforms a sequence of assignments to its controlled ariable. The process may be visualized by means of the ıllowing picture:

```
Initialize ; test ; statement S ; advance ; successor
                          for list exhausted
```

n this picture the word initialize means: perform the first ssignment of the for clause. Advance means: perform the ext assignment of the for clause. Test determines if the ıst assignment has been done. If so, the execution continues with the successor of the for statement. If not, the statement following the for clause is executed.

4.6.4. The for list elements

The for list gives a rule for obtaining the values which are consecutively assigned to the controlled variable. This sequence of values is obtained from the for list elements by taking these one by one in the order in which they are written. The sequence of values generated by each of the three species of for list elements and the corresponding execution of the statement S are given by the following rules:

4.6.4.1. Arithmetic expression. This element gives rise to one value, namely the value of the given arithmetic expression as calculated immediately before the corresponding execution of the statement S.

4.6.4.2. Step-until-element. An element of the form A **step** B **until** C, where A, B, and C, are arithmetic expressions, gives rise to an execution which may be described most concisely in terms of additional Algol statements as follows:

```
    V := A  ;
L1: if (V−C)× sign(B)>0 then go to element exhausted;
    statement S  ;
    V := V+B  ;
    go to L1  ;
```

where V is the controlled variable of the for clause and *element exhausted* points to the evaluation according to the next element in the for list, or if the step-until-element is the last of the list, to the next statement in the program.

4.6.4.3. While-element. The execution governed by a for list element of the form E **while** F, where E is an arithmetic and F a Boolean expression, is most concisely described in terms of additional Algol statements as follows:

```
L3: V := E  ;
    if ¬F then go to element exhausted  ;
    Statement S  ;
    go to L3  ;
```

where the notation is the same as in 4.6.4.2 above.

4.6.5. The value of the controlled variable upon exit

Upon exit out of the statement S (supposed to be compound) through a go to statement the value of the controlled variable will be the same as it was immediately preceding the execution of the go to statement.

If the exit is due to exhaustion of the for list, on the other hand, the value of the controlled variable is undefined after the exit.

4.6.6. Go to leading into a for statement

The effect of a go to statement, outside a for statement, which refers to a label within the for statement, is undefined.

4.7. Procedure Statements

4.7.1. Syntax

⟨actual parameter⟩ ::= ⟨string⟩|⟨expression⟩|⟨array identifier⟩|
⟨switch identifier⟩|⟨procedure identifier⟩
⟨letter string⟩ ::= ⟨letter⟩|⟨letter string⟩⟨letter⟩

```
⟨parameter delimiter⟩ ::= ,|)⟨letter string⟩:(
⟨actual parameter list⟩ ::= ⟨actual parameter⟩|
    ⟨actual parameter list⟩⟨parameter delimiter⟩
    ⟨actual parameter⟩
⟨actual parameter part⟩ ::= ⟨empty⟩|
    (⟨actual parameter list⟩)
⟨procedure statement⟩ ::= ⟨procedure identifier⟩
    ⟨actual parameter part⟩
```

4.7.2. Examples

Spur (*A*)Order: (7)Result to: (*V*)
Transpose (*W*,*v*+1)
Absmax(*A*,*N*,*M*,*Yy*,*I*,*K*)
Innerproduct(*A*[*t*,*P*,*u*],*B*[*P*],10,*P*,*Y*)

These examples correspond to examples given in section 5.4.2.

4.7.3. Semantics

A procedure statement serves to invoke (call for) the execution of a procedure body (cf. section 5.4. Procedure Declarations). Where the procedure body is a statement written in ALGOL the effect of this execution will be equivalent to the effect of performing the following operations on the program at the time of execution of the procedure statement:

4.7.3.1. Value assignment (call by value)

All formal parameters quoted in the value part of the procedure declaration heading are assigned the values (cf. section 2.8. Values and Types) of the corresponding actual parameters, these assignments being considered as being performed explicitly before entering the procedure body. The effect is as though an additional block embracing the procedure body were created in which these assignments were made to variables local to this fictitious block with types as given in the corresponding specifications (cf. section 5.4.5). As a consequence, variables called by value are to be considered as nonlocal to the body of the procedure, but local to the fictitious block (cf. section 5.4.3).

4.7.3.2. Name replacement (call by name)

Any formal parameter not quoted in the value list is replaced, throughout the procedure body, by the corresponding actual parameter, after enclosing this latter in parentheses wherever syntactically possible. Possible conflicts between identifiers inserted through this process and other identifiers already present within the procedure body will be avoided by suitable systematic changes of the formal or local identifiers involved.

4.7.3.3. Body replacement and execution

Finally the procedure body, modified as above, is inserted in place of the procedure statement and executed. If the procedure is called from a place outside the scope of any nonlocal quantity of the procedure body the conflicts between the identifiers inserted through this process of body replacement and the identifiers whose declarations are valid at the place of the procedure statement or function designator will be avoided through suitable systematic changes of the latter identifiers.

4.7.4. Actual-formal correspondence

The correspondence between the actual parameters of the procedure statement and the formal parameters of the procedure heading is established as follows: The actual parameter list of the procedure statement must have the same number of entries as the formal parameter list of the procedure declaration heading. The correspondence is obtained by taking the entries of these two lists in the same order.

4.7.5. Restrictions

For a procedure statement to be defined it is evidently necessary that the operations on the procedure body defined in sections 4.7.3.1 and 4.7.3.2 lead to a correct ALGOL statement.

This imposes the restriction on any procedure statement that the kind and type of each actual parameter be compatible with the kind and type of the corresponding formal parameter. Some important particular cases of this general rule are the following:

4.7.5.1. If a string is supplied as an actual parameter in a procedure statement or function designator, whose defining procedure body is an ALGOL 60 statement (as opposed to non-ALGOL code, cf. section 4.7.8), then this string can only be used within the procedure body as an actual parameter in further procedure calls. Ultimately it can only be used by a procedure body expressed in non-ALGOL code.

4.7.5.2. A formal parameter which occurs as a left part variable in an assignment statement within the procedure body and which is not called by value can only correspond to an actual parameter which is a variable (special case of expression).

4.7.5.3. A formal parameter which is used within the procedure body as an array identifier can only correspond to an actual parameter which is an array identifier of an array of the same dimensions. In addition if the formal parameter is called by value the local array created during the call will have the same subscript bounds as the actual array.

4.7.5.4. A formal parameter which is called by value cannot in general correspond to a switch identifier or a procedure identifier or a string, because these latter do not possess values (the exception is the procedure identifier of a procedure declaration which has an empty formal parameter part (cf. section 5.4.1) and which defines the value of a function designator (cf. section 5.4.4). This procedure identifier is in itself a complete expression).

4.7.5.5. Any formal parameter may have restrictions on the type of the corresponding actual parameter associated with it (these restrictions may, or may not, be given through specifications in the procedure heading). In the procedure statement such restrictions must evidently be observed.

4.7.6. Deleted.

4.7.7. Parameter delimiters

All parameter delimiters are understood to be equivalent. No correspondence between the parameter delimiters used in a procedure statement and those used in the procedure heading is expected beyond their number being the

.me. Thus the information conveyed by using the elabo-
te ones is entirely optional.

4.7.8. Procedure body expressed in code

The restrictions imposed on a procedure statement
lling a procedure having its body expressed in non-
LGOL code evidently can only be derived from the charac-
ristics of the code used and the intent of the user and
us fall outside the scope of the reference language.

Declarations

Declarations serve to define certain properties of the
antities used in the program, and to associate them with
entifiers. A declaration of an identifier is valid for one
ock. Outside this block the particular identifier may be
ed for other purposes (cf. section 4.1.3).

Dynamically this implies the following: at the time of an
try into a block (through the **begin**, since the labels
side are local and therefore inaccessible from outside)
identifiers declared for the block assume the signifi-
nce implied by the nature of the declarations given.
these identifiers had already been defined by other
clarations outside they are for the time being given a
w significance. Identifiers which are not declared for the
ock, on the other hand, retain their old meaning.

At the time of an exit from a block (through **end**, or by
go to statement) all identifiers which are declared for
e block lose their local significance.

A declaration may be marked with the additional
clarator **own**. This has the following effect: upon a re-
try into the block, the values of own quantities will be
changed from their values at the last exit, while the
lues of declared variables which are not marked as own
e undefined. Apart from labels and formal parameters
procedure declarations and with the possible exception
those for standard functions (cf. sections 3.2.4 and
2.5), all identifiers of a program must be declared. No
entifier may be declared more than once in any one
ock head.

Syntax.

eclaration⟩ ::= ⟨type declaration⟩|⟨array declaration⟩|
⟨switch declaration⟩|⟨procedure declaration⟩

5.1. Type Declarations

5.1.1. Syntax

pe list⟩ ::= ⟨simple variable⟩|
⟨simple variable⟩ , ⟨type list⟩
pe⟩ ::= **real** | **integer** | **Boolean**
cal or own type⟩ ::= ⟨type⟩|**own** ⟨type⟩
pe declaration⟩ ::= ⟨local or own type⟩⟨type list⟩

5.1.2. Examples

integer *p,q,s*
own Boolean *Acryl,n*

5.1.3. Semantics

Type declarations serve to declare certain identifiers to
present simple variables of a given type. Real declared
riables may only assume positive or negative values
including zero. Integer declared variables may only assume
positive and negative integral values including zero.
Boolean declared variables may only assume the values
true and **false**.

In arithmetic expressions any position which can be
occupied by a real declared variable may be occupied by
an integer declared variable.

For the semantics of **own**, see the fourth paragraph of
section 5 above.

5.2. Array Declarations

5.2.1. Syntax

⟨lower bound⟩ ::= ⟨arithmetic expression⟩
⟨upper bound⟩ ::= ⟨arithmetic expression⟩
⟨bound pair⟩ ::= ⟨lower bound⟩:⟨upper bound⟩
⟨bound pair list⟩ ::= ⟨bound pair⟩|⟨bound pair list⟩,⟨bound pair⟩
⟨array segment⟩ ::= ⟨array identifier⟩[⟨bound pair list⟩]|
⟨array identifier⟩,⟨array segment⟩
⟨array list⟩ ::= ⟨array segment⟩|⟨array list⟩,⟨array segment⟩
⟨array declaration⟩ ::= **array** ⟨array list⟩|⟨local or own type⟩
array ⟨array list⟩

5.2.2. Examples

array *a, b, c*[7:*n*,2:*m*], *s*[−2:10]
own integer array *A*[**if** *c*<0 **then** 2 **else** 1:20]
real array *q*[−7:−1]

5.2.3. Semantics

An array declaration declares one or several identifiers
to represent multidimensional arrays of subscripted
variables and gives the dimensions of the arrays, the
bounds of the subscripts and the types of the variables.

5.2.3.1. Subscript bounds. The subscript bounds for
any array are given in the first subscript bracket following
the identifier of this array in the form of a bound pair list.
Each item of this list gives the lower and upper bound of a
subscript in the form of two arithmetic expressions separated by the delimiter : The bound pair list gives the
bounds of all subscripts taken in order from left to right.

5.2.3.2. Dimensions. The dimensions are given as the
number of entries in the bound pair lists.

5.2.3.3. Types. All arrays declared in one declaration
are of the same quoted type. If no type declarator is
given the type **real** is understood.

5.2.4. Lower upper bound expressions

5.2.4.1 The expressions will be evaluated in the same
way as subscript expressions (cf. section 3.1.4.2).

5.2.4.2. The expressions can only depend on variables
and procedures which are nonlocal to the block for which
the array declaration is valid. Consequently in the outer-
most block of a program only array declarations with
constant bounds may be declared.

5.2.4.3. An array is defined only when the values of all
upper subscript bounds are not smaller than those of the
corresponding lower bounds.

5.2.4.4. The expressions will be evaluated once at each
entrance into the block.

5.2.5. The identity of subscripted variables

The identity of a subscripted variable is not related to
the subscript bounds given in the array declaration. How-

ever, even if an array is declared **own** the values of the corresponding subscripted variables will, at any time, be defined only for those of these variables which have subscripts within the most recently calculated subscript bounds.

5.3. Switch Declarations

5.3.1. Syntax

⟨switch list⟩ ::= ⟨designational expression⟩|
⟨switch list⟩,⟨designational expression⟩
⟨switch declaration⟩ ::= **switch** ⟨switch identifier⟩:= ⟨switch list⟩

5.3.2. Examples

```
switch S := S1,S2,Q[m], if v>-5 then S3 else S4
switch Q :=p1,w
```

5.3.3. Semantics

A switch declaration defines the set of values of the corresponding switch designators. These values are given one by one as the values of the designational expressions entered in the switch list. With each of these designational expressions there is associated a positive integer, 1, 2, ... , obtained by counting the items in the list from left to right. The value of the switch designator corresponding to a given value of the subscript expression (cf. section 3.5. Designational Expressions) is the value of the designational expression in the switch list having this given value as its associated integer.

5.3.4. Evaluation of expressions in the switch list

An expression in the switch list will be evaluated every time the item of the list in which the expression occurs is referred to, using the current values of all variables involved.

5.3.5. Influence of scopes

If a switch designator occurs outside the scope of a quantity entering into a designational expression in the switch list, and an evaluation of this switch designator selects this designational expression, then the conflicts between the identifiers for the quantities in this expression and the identifiers whose declarations are valid at the place of the switch designator will be avoided through suitable systematic changes of the latter identifiers.

5.4. Procedure Declarations

5.4.1. Syntax

⟨formal parameter⟩ ::= ⟨identifier⟩
⟨formal parameter list⟩ ::= ⟨formal parameter⟩|
⟨formal parameter list⟩⟨parameter delimiter⟩
⟨formal parameter⟩
⟨formal parameter part⟩ ::= ⟨empty⟩|(⟨formal parameter list⟩)
⟨identifier list⟩ ::= ⟨identifier⟩|⟨identifier list⟩,⟨identifier⟩
⟨value part⟩ ::= **value**⟨identifier list⟩ ; |⟨empty⟩
⟨specifier⟩ ::= **string**|⟨type⟩|**array**|⟨type⟩**array**|**label**|**switch**|
procedure|⟨type⟩**procedure**
⟨specification part⟩ ::= ⟨empty⟩|⟨specifier⟩⟨identifier list⟩ ; |
⟨specification part⟩⟨specifier⟩⟨identifier list⟩ ;
⟨procedure heading⟩ ::= ⟨procedure identifier⟩
⟨formal parameter part⟩ ; ⟨value part⟩⟨specification part⟩
⟨procedure body⟩ ::= ⟨statement⟩|⟨code⟩
⟨procedure declaration⟩ ::=
procedure ⟨procedure heading⟩⟨procedure body⟩|
⟨type⟩ **procedure** ⟨procedure heading⟩⟨procedure body⟩

5.4.2. Examples (see also the examples at the end c the report)

```
procedure Spur(a)Order:(n)Result:(s) ; value n ;
array a ; integer n ; real s ;
begin integer k ;
s := 0 ;
for k := 1 step 1 until n do s := s+a[k,k]
end

procedure Transpose(a)Order:(n) ; value n ;
array a ; integer n ;
begin real w ; integer i, k ;
for i := 1 step 1 until n do
    for k := 1+i step 1 until n do
    begin w := a[i,k] ;
          a[i,k] := a[k,i] ;
          a[k,i] := w
    end
end Transpose

integer procedure Step (u) ; real u ;
Step := if 0≦u∧u≦1 then 1 else 0

procedure Absmax(a)size:(n,m)Result:(y)Subscripts:(i,k);
comment The absolute greatest element of the matrix
    of size n by m is transferred to y, and the subscripts of tl
    element to i and k ;
array a ; integer n, m, i, k ; real y ;
begin integer p, q ;
y := 0 ;
for p := 1 step 1 until n do for q := 1 step 1 until m do
if abs(a[p,q])>y then begin y := abs(a[p,q]) ; i := p
  k := q
end end Absmax

procedure Innerproduct(a,b)Order:(k,p)Result:(y) ; value k
integer k,p ; real y,a,b ;
begin real s ;
s := 0 ;
for p := 1 step 1 until k do s := s+a×b ;
y := s
end Innerproduct
```

5.4.3. Semantics

A procedure declaration serves to define the procedu associated with a procedure identifier. The principal cc stituent of a procedure declaration is a statement or piece of code, the procedure body, which through the u of procedure statements and/or function designators m be activated from other parts of the block in the head which the procedure declaration appears. Associated wi the body is a heading, which specifies certain identifi occurring within the body to represent formal paramete Formal parameters in the procedure body will, whenev the procedure is activated (cf. section 3.2. Functi Designators and section 4.7. Procedure Statemen be assigned the values of or replaced by actual paramete Identifiers in the procedure body which are not forn will be either local or nonlocal to the body depending whether they are declared within the body or not. Th of them which are nonlocal to the body may well be lo to the block in the head of which the procedure decla tion appears. The procedure body always acts like block, whether it has the form of one or not. Consequently the scope of any label labelling a statement within the body or the body itself can never extend beyond the procedure body. In addition, if the identifier of a formal parameter is declared anew within the procedure body (including the case of its use as a label as in section 4.1.3), it is thereby given a local significance and actual parameters which correspond to it are inaccessible throughout the scope of this inner local quantity.

5.4.4. Values of function designators

For a procedure declaration to define the value of a function designator there must, within the procedure body, occur one or more explicit assignment statements with the procedure identifier in a left part; at least one of these must be executed, and the type associated with the procedure identifier must be declared through the appearance of a type declarator as the very first symbol of the procedure declaration. The last value so assigned is used to continue the evaluation of the expression in which the function designator occurs. Any occurrence of the procedure identifier within the body of the procedure other than in a left part in an assignment statement denotes activation of the procedure.

5.4.5. Specifications

In the heading a specification part, giving information about the kinds and types of the formal parameters by means of an obvious notation, may be included In this part no formal parameter may occur more than once. Specifications of formal parameters called by value (cf. section 4.7.3.1) must be supplied and specifications of formal parameters called by name (cf. section 4.7.3.2) may be omitted.

5.4.6. Code as procedure body

It is understood that the procedure body may be expressed in non-ALGOL language. Since it is intended that the use of this feature should be entirely a question of hardware representation, no further rules concerning this code language can be given within the reference language

Examples of Procedure Declarations:

EXAMPLE 1.

```
procedure euler (fct, sum, eps, tim) ; value eps, tim ;
integer tim ; real procedure fct ; real sum, eps ;
comment euler computes the sum of fct(i) for i from zero up to
infinity by means of a suitabley refined euler transformation. The
summation is stopped as soon as tim times in succession the abso-
lute value of the terms of the transformed series are found to be
less than eps. Hence, one should provide a function fct with one
integer argument, an upper bound eps, and an integer tim. The
output is the sum sum. euler is particularly efficient in the case
of a slowly convergent or divergent alternating series ;
begin integer i, k, n, t ; array m[0:15] ; real mn, mp, ds ;
i := n := t := 0 ; m[0] := fct(0) ; sum := m[0]/2 ;
nextterm: i := i+1 ; mn := fct(i) ;
        for k := 0 step 1 until n do
            begin mp := (mn+m[k])/2 ; m[k] := mn ;
              mn := mp end means ;
            if (abs(mn)<abs(m[n]))∧(n<15) then
                begin ds := mn/2 ; n := n+1 ; m[n] :=
                  mn end accept
            else ds := mn ;
            sum := sum + ds ;
            if abs(ds)<eps then t := t+1 else t := 0 ;
            if t<tim then go to nextterm
end euler
```

EXAMPLE 2.[8]

```
procedure RK(x,y,n,FKT,eps,eta,xE,yE,fi) ; value x,y ;
integer n ; Boolean fi ; real x.eps,eta,xE ; array
y,yE ; procedure FKT ;
comment: RK integrates the system yk'=fk(x,y1,y2, ... ,yn)
(k=1,2, ... ,n) of differential equations with the method of Runge-
Kutta with automatic search for appropriate length of integration
step. Parameters are: The initial values x and y[k] for x and the un-
known functions yk(x). The order n of the system. The procedure
FKT(x,y,n,z) which represents the system to be integrated, i.e.
the set of functions fk . The tolerance values eps and eta which
govern the accuracy of the numerical integration. The end of the
integration interval xE. The output parameter yE which repre
sents the solution at x=xE. The Boolean variable fi, which must
always be given the value true for an isolated or first entry into
RK. If however the functions y must be available at several mesh-
points x0 , x1 , ... , xn , then the procedure must be called repeat-
edly (with x=xk , xE=xk+1, for k=0, 1, ... , n-1) and then the
later calls may occur with fi=false which saves computing time.
The input parameters of FKT must be x,y,n, the output parameter
z represents the set of derivatives z[k]=fk(x,y[1], y[2], ... , y[n])
for x and the actual y's. A procedure comp enters as a nonlocal
identifier ;
begin
  array z,y1,y2,y3[1:n] ; real x1,x2,x3,H ; Boolean out ;
  integer k,j ; own real s,Hs ;
  procedure RK1ST(x,y,h,xe,ye) ; real x,h,xe ; array
          y,ye ;
    comment: RK1ST integrates one single RUNGE-KUTTA
          with initial values x,y[k] which yields the output
          parameters xe=x+h and ye[k], the latter being the
          solution at xe. Important: the parameters n, FKT, z
          enter RK1ST as nonlocal entities ;
    begin
      array w[1:n], a[1:5] ; integer k,j ;
      a[1] := a[2] := a[5] := h/2 ; a[3] := a[4] := h ;
      xe := x ;
      for k := 1 step 1 until n do ye[k] := w[k] := y[k] ;
      for j := 1 step 1 until 4 do
      begin
        FKT(xe,w,n,z) ;
        xe := x+a[j] ;
        for k := 1 step 1 until n do
        begin
          w[k] := y[k]+a[j]×z[k] ;
          ye[k] := ye[k] + a[j+1]×z[k]/3
```

[8] This RK-program contains some new ideas which are related to ideas of S. GILL, A process for the step-by-step integration of differential equations in an automatic computing machine, [*Proc. Camb. Phil. Soc.* 47 (1951), 96]; and E. FRÖBERG, On the solution of ordinary differential equations with digital computing machines, [*Fysiograf. Sällsk. Lund, Förhd.* 20, 11 (1950), 136–152]. It must be clear, however, that with respect to computing time and round-off errors it may not be optimal, nor has it actually been tested on a computer.

```
            end k
         end j
      end RK1ST  ;
Begin of program:
      if fi then begin H := xE−x  ; s := 0 end else H := Hs  ;
      out := false  ;
AA: if (x+2.01×H−xE>0)≡(H>0) then
      begin Hs := H  ; out := true  ; H := (xE−x)/2
         end if  ;
      RK1ST (x,y,2×H,x1,y1)  ;
BB: RK1ST (x,y,H,x2,y2)  ; RK1ST(x2,y2,H,x3,y3)  ;
      for k := 1 step 1 until n do
            if comp(y1[k],y3[k],eta)>eps then go to CC  ;
      comment: comp(a,bc,) is a function designator, the value
         of which is the absolute value of the difference of the
         mantissae of a and b, after the exponents of these quan
         tities have been made equal to the largest of the exponent
         of the originally given parameters a,b,c  :
      x := x3  ; if out then go to DD  ;
      for k := 1 step 1 until n do y[k] := y3[k]  ;
      if s=5 then begin s := 0  ; H := 2×H end if  ;
      s := s+1  ; go to AA  ;
CC: H := 0.5×H  ; out := false  ; x1 := x2  ;
      for k := 1 step 1 until n do y1[k] := y2[k]  ;
      go to BB  ;
DD: for k := 1 step 1 until n do yE[k] := y3[k]
end RK
```

ALPHABETIC INDEX OF DEFINITIONS OF CONCEPTS AND SYNTACTIC UNITS

All references are given through section numbers. The references are given in three groups:

def Following the abbreviation "def", reference to the syntactic definition (if any) is given.

synt Following the abbreviation "synt", references to the occurrences in metalinguistic formulae are given. References already quoted in the def-group are not repeated.

text Following the word "text", the references to definitions given in the text are given.

The basic symbols represented by signs other than underlined words [in typewritten copy; boldface in printed copy—Ed.] have been collected at the beginning.

The examples have been ignored in compiling the index.

+, see: plus
−, see: minus
×, see: multiply
/, ÷, see: divide
↑, see: exponentiation
<, ≦, =, ≧, >, ≠, see: ⟨relational operator⟩
≡, ⊃, ∨, ∧, ¬, see: ⟨logical operator⟩
,, see: comma
., see: decimal point
₁₀, see: ten
:, see: colon
;, see: semicolon
:=, see: colon equal
␣, see: space
( ), see: parentheses
[ ], see: subscript brackets
‘ ’, see: string quotes

⟨actual parameter⟩, def 3.2.1, 4.7.1
⟨actual parameter list⟩, def 3.2.1, 4.7.1
⟨actual parameter part⟩, def 3.2.1, 4.7.1
⟨adding operator⟩, def 3.3.1
alphabet, text 2.1
arithmetic, text 3.3.6
⟨arithmetic expression⟩, def 3.3.1 synt 3, 3.1.1, 3.3.1, 3.4.1, 4.2.1, 4.6.1, 5.2.1 text 3.3.3
⟨arithmetic operator⟩, def 2.3 text 3.3.4
array, synt 2.3, 5.2.1, 5.4.1
array, text 3.1.4.1
⟨array declaration⟩, def 5.2.1 synt 5 text 5.2.3
⟨array identifier⟩, def 3.1.1 synt 3.2.1, 4.7.1, 5.2.1 text 2.8
⟨array list⟩, def 5.2.1
⟨array segment⟩, def 5.2.1
⟨assignment statement⟩, def 4.2.1 synt 4.1.1 text 1, 4.2.3

⟨basic statement⟩, def 4.1.1 synt 4.5.1
⟨basic symbol⟩, def 2
begin, synt 2.3, 4.1.1
⟨block⟩, def 4.1.1 synt 4.5.1 text 1, 4.1.3, 5
⟨block head⟩, def 4.1.1
Boolean, synt 2.3, 5.1.1 text 5.1.3
⟨Boolean expression⟩, def 3.4.1 synt 3, 3.3.1, 4.2.1, 4.5.1, 4.6.1 text 3.4.3
⟨Boolean factor⟩, def 3.4.1
⟨Boolean primary⟩, def 3.4.1
⟨Boolean secondary⟩, def 3.4.1
⟨Boolean term⟩, def 3.4.1
⟨bound pair⟩, def 5.2.1
⟨bound pair list⟩, def 5.2.1
⟨bracket⟩, def 2.3

⟨code⟩, synt 5.4.1 text 4.7.8, 5.4.6
colon :, synt 2.3, 3.2.1, 4.1.1, 4.5.1, 4.6.1, 4.7.1, 5.2.1
colon equal :=, synt 2.3, 4.2.1, 4.6.1, 5.3.1
comma , , synt 2.3, 3.1.1, 3.2.1, 4.6.1, 4.7.1, 5.1.1, 5.2.1, 5.3.1, 5.4.1
comment, synt 2.3
comment convention, text 2.3
⟨compound statement⟩, def 4.1.1 synt 4.5.1 text 1
⟨compound tail⟩, def 4.1.1
⟨conditional statement⟩, def 4.5.1 synt 4.1.1 text 4.5.3

⟨decimal fraction⟩, def 2.5.1
⟨decimal number⟩, def 2.5.1 text 2.5.3
decimal point . , synt 2.3, 2.5.1
⟨declaration⟩, def 5 synt 4.1.1 text 1, 5 (complete section)
⟨declarator⟩, def 2.3
⟨delimiter⟩, def 2.3 synt 2
⟨designational expression⟩, def 3.5.1 synt 3, 4.3.1., 5.3.1 text 3.5.
⟨digit⟩, def 2.2.1 synt 2, 2.4.1, 2.5.1
dimension, text 5.2.3.2
divide / ÷, synt 2.3, 3.3.1 text 3.3.4.2
do, synt 2.3, 4.6.1
⟨dummy statement⟩, def 4.4.1 synt 4.1.1 text 4.4.3

else, synt 2.3, 3.3.1, 3.4.1, 3.5.1, 4.5.1 text 4.5.3.2
⟨empty⟩, def 1.1 synt 2.6.1, 3.2.1, 4.4.1, 4.7.1, 5.4.1
end, synt 2.3, 4.1.1
entier, text 3.2.5
exponentiation ↑, synt 2.3, 3.3.1 text 3.3.4.3
⟨exponent part⟩, def 2.5.1 text 2.5.3
⟨expression⟩, def 3 synt 3.2.1, 4.7.1 text 3 (complete section

actor⟩, def 3.3.1
alse, synt 2.2.2
or, synt 2.3, 4.6.1
or clause⟩, def 4.6.1 text 4.6.3
or list⟩, def 4.6.1 text 4.6.4
or list element⟩, def 4.6.1 text 4.6.4.1, 4.6.4.2, 4.6.4.3
ormal parameter⟩, def 5.4.1 text 5.4.3
ormal parameter list⟩, def 5.4.1
ormal parameter part⟩, def 5.4.1
or statement⟩, def 4.6.1 synt 4.1.1, 4.5.1 text 4.6 (complete section)
unction designator⟩, def 3.2.1 synt 3.3.1, 3.4.1 text 3.2.3, 5.4.4

o to, synt 2.3, 4.3.1
o to statement⟩, def 4.3.1 synt 4.1.1 text 4.3.3

dentifier⟩, def 2.4.1 synt 3.1.1, 3.2.1, 3.5.1, 5.4.1 text 2.4.3
dentifier list⟩, def 5.4.1
f, synt 2.3, 3.3.1, 4.5.1
f clause⟩, def 3.3.1, 4.5.1 synt 3.4.1, 3.5.1 text 3.3.3, 4.5.3.2
f statement⟩, def 4.5.1 text 4.5.3.1
mplication⟩, def 3.4.1
nteger, synt 2.3, 5.1.1 text 5.1.3
nteger⟩, def 2.5.1 text 2.5.4

abel, synt 2.3, 5.4.1
abel⟩, def 3.5.1 synt 4.1.1, 4.5.1, 4.6.1 text 1, 4.1.3
eft part⟩, def 4.2.1
eft part list⟩, def 4.2.1
etter⟩, def 2.1 synt 2, 2.4.1, 3.2.1, 4.7.1
etter string⟩, def 3.2.1, 4.7.1
ocal, text 4.1.3
ocal or own type⟩, def 5.1.1 synt 5.2.1
ogical operator⟩, def 2.3 synt 3.4.1 text 3.4.5
ogical value⟩, def 2.2.2 synt 2, 3.4.1
ower bound⟩, def 5.2.1 text 5.2.4

inus −, synt 2.3, 2.5.1, 3.3.1 text 3.3.4.1
ultiply ×, synt 2.3, 3.3.1 text 3.3.4.1
ultiplying operator⟩, def 3.3.1

onlocal, text 4.1.3
umber⟩, def 2.5.1 text 2.5.3, 2.5.4

pen string⟩, def 2.6.1
perator⟩, def 2.3
wn, synt 2.3, 5.1.1 text 5, 2.5.5

arameter delimiter⟩, def 3.2.1, 4.7.1 synt 5.4.1 text 4.7.7
arentheses ( ), synt 2.3, 3.2.1, 3.3.1, 3.4.1, 3.5.1, 4.7.1, 5.4.1 text 3.3.5.2
lus +, synt 2.3, 2.5.1, 3.3.1 text 3.3.4.1
rimary⟩, def 3.3.1
rocedure, synt 2.3, 5.4.1
rocedure body⟩, def 5.4.1
rocedure declaration⟩, def 5.4.1 synt 5 text 5.4.3
rocedure heading⟩, def 5.4.1 text 5.4.3
rocedure identifier⟩ def 3.2.1 synt 3.2.1, 4.7.1, 5.4.1 text 4.7.5.4
rocedure statement⟩, def 4.7.1 synt 4.1.1 text 4.7.3
rogram⟩, def 4.1.1 text 1
roper string⟩, def 2.6.1

uantity, text 2.7

real, synt 2.3, 5.1.1 text 5.1.3
⟨relation⟩, def 3.4.1 text 3.4.5
⟨relational operator⟩, def 2.3, 3.4.1

scope, text 2.7
semicolon ;, synt 2.3, 4.1.1, 5.4.1
⟨separator⟩, def 2.3
⟨sequential operator⟩, def 2.3
⟨simple arithmetic expression⟩, def 3.3.1 text 3.3.3
⟨simple Boolean⟩, def 3.4.1
⟨simple designational expression⟩, def 3.5.1
⟨simple variable⟩, def 3.1.1 synt 5.1.1 text 2.4.3
space ␣, synt 2.3 text 2.3, 2.6.3
⟨specification part⟩, def 5.4.1 text 5.4.5
⟨specificator⟩, def 2.3
⟨specifier⟩, def 5.4.1
standard function, text 3.2.4, 3.2.5
⟨statement⟩, def 4.1.1, synt 4.5.1, 4.6.1, 5.4.1 text 4 (complete section)
statement bracket, see: **begin end**
step, synt 2.3, 4.6.1 text 4.6.4.2
string, synt 2.3, 5.4.1
⟨string⟩, def 2.6.1 synt 3.2.1, 4.7.1 text 2.6.3
string quotes ‘ ’, synt 2.3, 2.6.1, text 2.6.3
subscript, text 3.1.4.1
subscript bound, text 5.2.3.1
subscript brackets [ ], synt 2.3, 3.1.1, 3.5.1, 5.2.1
⟨subscripted variable⟩, def 3.1.1 text 3.1.4.1
⟨subscript expression⟩, def 3.1.1 synt 3.5.1
⟨subscript list⟩, def 3.1.1
successor, text 4
switch, synt 2.3, 5.3.1, 5.4.1
⟨switch declaration⟩, def 5.3.1 synt 5 text 5.3.3
⟨switch designator⟩, def 3.5.1 text 3.5.3
⟨switch identifier⟩, def 3.5.1 synt 3.2.1, 4.7.1, 5.3.1
⟨switch list⟩, def 5.3.1

⟨term⟩, def 3.3.1
ten ₁₀, synt 2.3, 2.5.1
then, synt 2.3, 3.3.1, 4.5.1
transfer function, text 3.2.5
true, synt 2.2.2
⟨type⟩, def 5.1.1 synt 5.4.1 text 2.8
⟨type declaration⟩, def 5.1.1 synt 5 text 5.1.3
⟨type list⟩, def 5.1.1

⟨unconditional statement⟩, def 4.1 .1, 4.5.1
⟨unlabelled basic statement⟩, def 4.1.1
⟨unlabelled block⟩, def 4.1.1
⟨unlabelled compound⟩, def 4.1.1
⟨unsigned integer⟩, def 2.5.1, 3.5.1
⟨unsigned number⟩, def 2.5.1 synt 3.3.1
until, synt 2.3, 4.6.1 text 4.6.4.2
⟨upper bound⟩, def 5 2.1 text 5.2.4

value, synt 2.3, 5.4.1
value, text 2.8, 3.3.3
⟨value part⟩, def 5.4.1 text 4.7.3.1
⟨variable⟩, def 3.1.1 synt 3.3.1, 3.4.1, 4.2.1, 4.6.1 text 3.1.3
⟨variable identifier⟩, def 3.1.1

while, synt 2.3, 4.6.1 text 4.6.4.3

END OF THE REPORT

---

eprinted from *Communications of the ACM*, Vol. 6, Jan., 1963.

This appendix has suggested computer programming exercises for self-study or class use.

Part I: Scientific Problems

1. Write a program to search by trial and error for the highest point on the hill represented by the following function:

$$H = X + 2Y + XY + 10EXP(-3((X - 0.5)^2 + (Y - 0.5)^2))$$

Limit the search to $0 \leq X \leq 1$ and $0 \leq Y \leq 1$. Note that the following calculation dictates that there is a peak somewhere in that region.

This is an excellent exercise. It can be done with a fairly short program—twenty to thirty statements are more than adequate. Yet, it requires very careful thought and a careful plan. There are many possible approaches that can lead to a correct solution. One carefully placed debugging statement can give clear information on whether or not the plan is being carried out properly by the program, and it also pretty well indicates whether or not the final answer is correct. There are opportunities to use the interesting loop-control statements of ALGOL60 and PL/I.

omputer Programming Problems Appendix C

The function given is a very simple, smooth hill, but the problem cannot be solved, even using calculus, without some trial-and-error calculation. Substituting a function with a sharper peak, and perhaps more than one peak, will make the problem more difficult.

```
100 READ X,Y
200 PRINT X;Y;X+2*Y+X*Y+10*(EXP(-3*((X-0.5)**2+(Y-0.5)**2)))
300 GO TO 100
400 DATA 0,0,0,0.5,0,1,0.5,1,1,1,1,0.5,1,0,0.5,0,0.5,0.5
500 END
RUN
EXECUTION STARTED

 0 0 2.231301601484
 0 0.5 5.72366552741
 0 1 4.231301601484
 0.5 1 7.72366552741
 1 1 6.231301601484
 1 0.5 7.22366552741
 1 0 3.231301601484
 0.5 0 5.22366552741
 0.5 0.5 11.75

LINE 100 -- OUT OF DATA
```

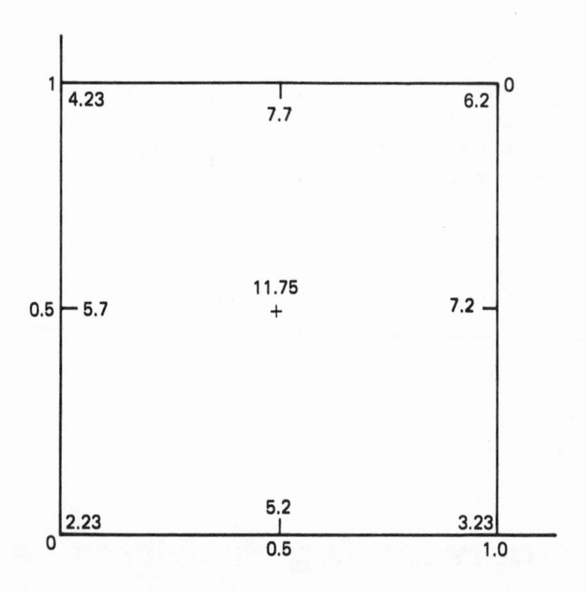

2. Write a program to generate a list of prime numbers. There are at least two very different approaches to this problem. With either one, the efficiency and speed of the program depend a great deal on how carefully the method is thought out.

3. Write a program to search for integers I, J, and K such that $I^2 + J^2 = K^2$. As refinements to this program, you might exclude all cases where I or J is zero, where J > I, and all cases for which I and J are not relatively prime. For example, include I = 4, J = 3, K = 5 because $4^2 + 3^2 = 5^2$, but do not include I = 5, J = 0, K = 5—it is too trivial. Do not include I = 3, J = 4, K = 5 or I = 8, J = 6, K = 10 because they are too easy to derive from the case I = 4, J = 3, K = 5.

Part II: Data Processing

Find some interesting data in the newspaper, an encyclopedia, or similar source and punch it into cards. From 20 to 100 cards should be adequate for this exercise. (For class use, it is interesting and convenient for the students to have the data stored in a disc file.) Write a program to prepare a report from these data which includes some interesting facts such as percentages, averages, maxima, totals, etc. For PL/I, the program should use all the features described in Chapter 6, i.e., record input-output, structures, ON-conditions, pictures, and decimal arithmetic.

Note that there are two common ways of punching decimal data into cards.

1. Sign precedes digits, and decimal point is punched, i.e., as numbers are usually seen.
2. Leading zeros punched, decimal point omitted, and sign punched in same column as last digit. This way uses fewer card columns, and it is commonly used in data processing. PL/I can handle either easily, but COBOL is not well-equipped for input with the first format—it is possible but very awkward.

Data-processing problems commonly involve incorrect data, which typically cause annoying programming problems. The data-processing exercise can be made more realistic by either including some incorrect data or by including missing data indicated by blank card columns in positions where numbers are expected.

Part III: Character-string Processing

1. Write a program to read text input from cards and print it 50 characters wide right and left justified (i.e., for each line, take as many words as possible to make the line no more than 50 characters wide and then insert extra blanks in the line so that it becomes exactly 50 characters wide.) Indent paragraphs five spaces. Double space between paragraphs. Don't attempt to right justify the last line in a paragraph. Use as data the quotation from Hamming near the end of Chapter 6.

   Right and left justification is an excellent exercise. There are many ways it can be done. It requires careful thought and a careful plan.

2. As a variation, write a simple text-editing program in which the source material contains special characters indicating editing functions. # means that what follows is to be printed as a title, centered over the text. "%" means start a paragraph of text. Right

and left justify paragraphs. Double space after each title and paragraph. Use the following as input data for test purposes:†

```
$SOME EXCERPTS FROM THE BOOK$TIMESHARING SYSTEM DESIGN CONCE
PTS$BY RICHARD W. WATSON%$INTRODUCTION TO SOFTWARE CONCEPTS%
THESE                                   POINTS ARE USEFUL FO
R THE SYSTEM DESIGNER TO KEEP IN MIND. THE DESIGNER'S FUNCTI
ON IS   TO PROVIDE A SERVICE; HIS SKILL AND KNOWLEDGE ARE US
EFUL ONLY TO THAT END AND NOT IN THEMSELVES. THE USER   PROB
ABLY CARES LITTLE FOR THE CLEVER N-DIMENSIONAL, WEB-THREADED
 SCHEDULING ALGORITHM OF WHICH THE DESIGNER IS SO PROUD
AND WHICH HE IS PLANNING TO PUBLISH, PARTICULARLY IF THE ONE
-DIMENSIONAL ONE WOULD WORK AND PROVIDE THE SAME FUNCTION AN
D COST AS SEEN BY THE USER.             IT WOULD SEEM GOOD P
RACTICE FOR THE DESIGNER TO KEEP CONCEPTUAL SIMPLICITY,
INTEGRITY, AND UNIFORMITY AS GOALS WHILE BEING AWARE OF THE
TRADEOFFS WHICH A GIVEN STATE OF TECHNOLOGY MAKES AVAILABLE
TO HIM AT EACH DESIGN STEP. THE USER, HIS INFORMATION PROCES
SING REQUIREMENTS,
  AND HIS NEED FOR PRIVACY, RELIABILITY, AND EASY
                              INTERFACE WITH THE SYSTEM SHOULD BE
 CONSTANTLY BORNE IN MIND. THESE POINTS ARE STRESSED HERE BE
CAUSE THE DESIGNER OF THE SOFTWARE SYSTEM OPERATES UNDER FEW
ER CONSTRAINTS THAN THE HARDWARE DESIGNER. THE RESULT HAS OF
TEN BEEN POOR       SOFTWARE AND HUMAN ENGINEERING.
                                        $RELIABILITY AND REC
OVERABILITY%A PRIME INTRINSIC GOAL IS RELIABLE OPERATION. TH
E USER EXPECTS THE SYSTEM TO OPERATE CORRECTLY DURING ITS SC
HEDULED AVAILABLE TIMES. IF A FAILURE SHOULD OCCUR, THE USER
 EXPECTS RECOVERY TO BE AS SMOOTH AND FAST AS POSSIBLE. THAT
 IS, RECOVERY SHOULD LEAVE THE SYSTEM AS CLOSE AS POSSIBLE T
O THE STATE IT WAS IN AT THE TIME OF THE FAILURE. THE SYSTEM
 DESIGNER MUST ASSUME THAT HARDWARE AND SOFTWARE MALFUNCTION
S WILL OCCUR IN SPITE OF ALL THE CARE TAKEN IN DESIGN AND IM
PLEMENTATION.  THEREFORE IT IS OBVIOUSLY GOOD DESIGN PRACTI
CE TH BUILD ERROR-DETECTION, ERROR-LOCATION, AND RECOVERY PR
OCEDURES INTO BOTH HARDWARE AND SOFTWARE FROM THE EARLIEST D
ESIGN STAGES.                          $SYSTEM OVERHEAD%THE
 MEASURE OF TIME SPENT IN SYSTEM FUNCTIONS HAS NO ABSOLUTE M
EANING. ONE CANNOT SAY A 20 PERCENT OVERHEAD IS GOOD OR BAD
WITHOUT EXAMINING THE SERVICES PROVIDED AND THE GIVEN STATE
OF TECHNOLOGY. OVERHEAD, HOWEVER,       CAN BE A USEFUL INDI
CATOR FOR THE DESIGNER  WHEN HE ATTEMPTS TO ASSESS THE COST
OF  HIS SOLUTIONS TO INTRINSIC AND TECHNOLOGICAL PROBLEMS AN
D TO SPOT POTENTIAL PROBLEM AREAS. ONE CERTAINLY WANTS TO MI
NIMIZE, RELATIVE TO A GIVEN LEVEL OF SERVICE PERFORMED BY TH
E SYSTEM, THE TIME THE MACHINE SPENDS ON SYSTEM FUNCTIONS, B
UT ONE MUST RECOGNIZE THE USEFULNESS OF SYSTEM FUNCTIONS IN
THE TOTAL WORK OF THE USER.
```

†This text was taken from the excellent book by Richard W. Watson, *Time-Sharing System Design Concepts*, New York: McGraw Hill Book Co. (1970), with the permission of the publisher.

The comment cards in the PL/I programs in this book were produced by a program similar to this.

3. As a simpler text-editing program, consider "%" to mean "start a new line, indenting five spaces," "@" to mean, "start a new line without indenting," and in both cases, remove all spaces except one between words and break the text into lines as long as possible but not exceeding 50 characters. Let "#" followed by an integer mean to start a new line and to insert the indicated number of spaces, i.e., "#17" means "start a new line with 17 blanks."

   Use the following as input data for testing. These quotations were used in *A Compiler Generator* by McKeeman, Horning, and Wortman.†

```
%IT IS POSSIBLE BY INGENUITY AND AT THE EXPENSE OF CLARITY .
 . . (TO DO ALMOST ANYTHING IN ANY LANGUAGE). HOWEVER, THE F
ACT THAT IT IS POSSIBLE TO PUSH A PEA UP A MOUNTAIN WITH YOU
R NOSE DOES NOT MEAN THAT THIS IS A SENSIBLE WAY OF GETTING
IT THERE. EACH OF THESE TECHNIQUES OF LANGUAGE EXTENSION SHO
ULD BE USED IN ITS PROPER PLACE.#@35CHRISTOPHER STRACHEY   #
@35NATO SUMMER SCHOOL IN PROGRAMMING     ####
%STABILITY IN LANGUAGE IS SYNONYMOUS WITH RIGOR MORTIS. #
@35ERNEST WEEKLEY#@35WORDS, ANCIENT AND MODERN####
%LANGUAGES DIE, TOO, LIKE INDIVIDUALS. . . . THEY MAY BE
EMBALMED AND PRESERVED FOR POSTERITY, CHANGELESS AND STATIC,
   LIFE-LIKE IN APPEARANCE BUT UNENDOWED WITH THE BREATH OF
LIFE.   WHILE THEY LIVE, HOWEVER, THEY CHANGE.#
@35MARIO PEI#@35THE STORY OF LANGUAGE###
%"EXPLAIN ALL THAT," SAID THE MOCK TURTLE.  %"NO, NO.  THE A
DVENTURES FIRST," SAID THE GRYPHON IN AN IMPATIENT TONE: "EX
PLANATIONS TAKE SUCH DREADFUL TIME."#@35LEWIS CARROLL#@35ALI
CE'S ADVENTURES IN WONDERLAND####
%"WOULD YOU TELL ME, PLEASE, WHICH WAY I OUGHT TO GO FROM HE
RE?"#"THAT DEPENDS A GOOD DEAL ON WHERE YOU WANT TO GET TO,"
 SAID THE CAT.#"I DON'T MUCH CARE WHERE--" SAID ALICE.#"THEN
 IT DOESN'T MATTER WHICH WAY YOU GO," SAID THE CAT.#"--SO LO
NG AS I GET SOMEWHERE," ALICE ADDED AS AN EXPLANATION.#"OH,
YOU'RE SURE TO DO THAT," SAID THE CAT, "IF ONLY YOU WALK LON
G ENOUGH."#@35LEWIS CARROLL#@35ALICE'S ADVENTURES IN WONDERL
AND####
```

4. Write a program to read a BASIC program on cards and renumber the statements 10, 20, 30, etc. The statement numbers in IF and GO TO statements must also be changed, of course. (Do not assume that line numbers, key words, etc., appear in any predetermined card columns.)

Part IV: List Processing

1. Write a PL/I program to read data of the following form and construct a list structure for the graph. (These data describe the chemical structure of aspirin.)

†W. M. McKeeman, J. J. Horning, and D. B. Wortman, *A Compiler Generator;* Englewood Cliffs, N. J.: Prentice-Hall, Inc. (1970).

Name	Label	Connected to These Nodes			
A1	C	A2	A2	A6	A7
A2	C	A1	A1	A3	A21
A3	C	A2	A4	A4	A20
A4	C	A3	A3	A5	A19
A5	C	A4	A6	A6	A18
A6	C	A5	A5	A1	A11
A7	C	A1	A8	A8	A9
A8	O	A7	A7	NULL	NULL
A9	O	A7	A10	NULL	NULL
A10	H	A9	NULL	NULL	NULL
A11	O	A6	A12	NULL	NULL
A12	C	A11	A13	A13	A14
A13	O	A12	A12	NULL	NULL
A14	C	A12	A15	A16	A17
A15	H	A14	NULL	NULL	NULL
A16	H	A14	NULL	NULL	NULL
A17	H	A14	NULL	NULL	NULL
A18	H	A5	NULL	NULL	NULL
A19	H	A4	NULL	NULL	NULL
A20	H	A3	NULL	NULL	NULL
A21	H	A2	NULL	NULL	NULL

2. Write a PL/I procedure PRINT(P) where P is a pointer to one node on a graph of the type constructed in problem 1. Make PRINT print all the key information for all the nodes that can be reached from P, including the location and the four pointers. It is interesting to make both non-recursive and recursive versions of PRINT.

3. Write a PL/I procedure COUNT(P) to count the number of nodes in the list structure that P points to. Assume a structure like that produced by problem 1, and use that list structure for testing.

4. Write a new PL/I maze-solving procedure that will be able to get out of a maze, even if it has closed loop paths. (The one in Chapter 10 will go around a loop forever and never get out under certain circumstances.)

5. Write PL/I non-recursive procedures for (1) inserting and deleting items from a list like that in the first example in Chapter 10 and (2) sorting such a list. In each case, change pointers but don't move data.

6. Write PL/I procedures L(P) to read a LISP S-expression from a card and make the corresponding list structure, assigning to P the location of the list structure, and S(P) to print the S-expression corresponding to the list structure that P points to.

The following problems can be done with LISP and, using the procedures of Problem 6, they can be done also as PL/I recursive procedures. When a problem specifies that a function parameter is an S-expression, for the PL/I procedures the parameter actually should be a pointer to the S-expression.

7. Write LISP definitions of functions

```
P(0) = 2
Q(0) = 1
P(N) = P(N - 1) + Q(N - 1)
Q(N) = P(N - 1) - Q(N - 1)
```

Here are the first few values.

N	P(N)	Q(N)
0	2	1
1	3	1
2	4	2
3	6	2
4	8	4
.	.	.
.	.	.
.	.	.

8. Write a LISP function F(N) that has as its value the Nth Fibonacci number. F(1) and F(2) are both 1, and from there on each number is defined to be the sum of the two preceding ones, i.e., F(3) = 1 + 1 = 2, F(4) = 1 + 2 = 3, F(5) = 2 + 3 = 5, etc.

9. For an arbitrary S-expression X, define the following functions:
   AC(X) is the number of atoms in X.
   NC(X) is the number of nodes in X.
   MD(X) is the maximum depth of nested parentheses in X.

10. For any S-expression Y all of whose atoms are integers, define the following functions:
    SUM(Y) is the sum of all atoms.
    MAX(Y) is the largest atom.

11. For any list L of atoms, define the following functions:
    REVERSE(L) is the same list in reverse order.
    F(L) is a list obtained from L by, wherever two successive items in L are the same, eliminating one, i.e., F((A A B C C C X)) = (A B C X).

Appendix D

In this appendix there is an example of a typical batch-processing run for a short program, a short but otherwise typical session at a terminal using a BASIC time-sharing system, and a short but otherwise typical session using APL.

The batch-processing example is also BASIC language, but it shows the essentials of a typical batch-processing job. It was run at the University of Hawaii on an IBM/360-65 using the UHBASIC processor. The program is punched in IBM cards, and a few job-control language (JCL) cards are added to inform the computer system how this program is to be processed. Here is a listing of the cards.

```
//WWP   JOB   (2337,170KR,5S,500L),PETERSON
//    EXEC    BASIC
//SYSIN   DD  *
60 INPUT X$(1),X$(2),X$(3),X$(4),X$(5),X$(6)
70 FOR I = 1 TO 6
80 FOR J = I+1 TO 6
90 IF X$(I) <= X(J) THEN 140
100 PRINT "EXCHANGE " X$(I) " AND " X$(J)
110 LET T$ = X$(J)
120 LET X$(J) = X$(I)
130 LET X$(I) = T$
140 NEXT I
150 NEXT J
160 FOR I = 1 TO 6
170 PRINT X$(I) " ";
```

```
180 NEXT I
190 PRINT
200 PRINT
999 END
RUN
THE,FOX,JUMPED,OVER,THE,DOG
BYE
//
```

All the cards that start "//" are JCL cards. The first, the JOB card, gives the job a name (WWP) that can be referred to, an account number (2337), a time limit (5S) and a limit on lines of printing (500), and the name of the person submitting it. The second card informs the system that it is to run the BASIC language processor. The third card says that the file, SYSIN, which the BASIC language processor expects, is the card deck that follows. The last card merely serves to mark the end of the deck.

These cards are submitted to the computer through a card reader. (At the University of Hawaii, for small decks like this, the user puts them through a small card reader available to all users.) The computer queues jobs on a disc unit and runs them in turn. After the results are printed, they are returned to the user. The results have at the beginning and end information on the time the program was run, accounting information, and printing information designed to make it easy for the operator to separate jobs. The rest of the results are as follows:

```
U   H   B A S I C
-   -   - - - - -
VERSION OF 7/1/73


 60 INPUT X$(1),X$(2),X$(3),X$(4),X$(5),X$(6)
 70 FOR I = 1 TO 6
 80 FOR J = I+1 TO 6
 90 IF X$(I) <= X(J) THEN 140
                  #        SYNTAX ERROR:
   >>> THE STATEMENT KEYWORD INDICATES THE "IF" STATEMENT. ANALYSIS TO TH
   >>> POINT SEEMS TO INDICATE THAT A STRING SHOULD APPEAR AT THIS POINT,
   >>> AN ERROR IN SYNTAX HAS BEEN DETECTED HERE.
 100 PRINT "EXCHANGE " X$(I) " AND " X$(J)
 110 LET T$ = X$(J)
 120 LET X$(J) = X$(I)
 130 LET X$(I) = T$
 140 NEXT I
 150 NEXT J
 160 FOR I = 1 TO 6
 170 PRINT X$(I) " ";
 180 NEXT I
 190 PRINT
 200 PRINT
 999 END
RUN
EXECUTION OMITTED
THE,FOX,JUMPED,OVER,THE,DOG
```

There was an error. The programmer must correct the error and re-run the program as many times as necessary to get a completely correct run.

Details of the form of the job-control cards differ from one computer to another, and even from one computing center to another with the same computer.

Now let us look at the same program run in a time-sharing mode. The following used UHBASIC, the same language processor as in the batch-processing example, run under the TSO time-sharing system on the University of Hawaii IBM/360-65. In the following printed output, the lower-case letters were typed by the user, the capital letters by the computer, as is the convention with TSO.

```
logon t223370/parsc
T223370 LOGON IN PROGRESS AT 11:23:10 ON JUNE 30, 1973
NO BROADCAST MESSAGES
** STARTED JOB #2337 - T223370 , APPROXIMATE BALANCE =    $942.73

U   H   B A S I C
-   -   - - - - -
VERSION OF 4/07/73
YOU MAY ENTER AN EMPTY LINE ANYTIME FOR HELP.

-60 input x$(1),x$(2),x$(3),x$(4(
60 INPUT X$(1),X$(2),X$(3),X$(4(
     SYNTAX ERROR:              #####
-60 input x$(1),x$(2),x$(3),x$(4),x$(5),x$(6)
-70 for i = 1 to 6
-80 for j = i+1 to 6
-90 if x$(i) <= x(j) then 140
90 IF X$(I) <= X(J) THEN 140
               #       SYNTAX ERROR:
-
THE STATEMENT KEYWORD INDICATES THE "IF" STATEMENT. ANALYSIS TO THIS
POINT SEEMS TO INDICATE THAT A STRING SHOULD APPEAR AT THIS POINT, AND
AN ERROR IN SYNTAX HAS BEEN DETECTED HERE.
-90 if x$(i) <= x$(j) then 140
-100 print "exchange " x$(i) " and " x$(j)
-110 let t$ = x$(j)
-120 let x$(j) = x$(i)
-130 let x$(i) = t$
-140 next i
-150 next j
-160 for i = 1 to 6
-170 print x$(i) " ";
-180 next i
-190 print
-200 print
-999 end
-run

ERROR IN LINE 140--THIS "NEXT" STMT MATCHES THE "FOR" STATEMENT IN LINE
NO. 70, BUT THE
LATER "FOR" STATEMENTS AT THE FOLLOWING LINES DO NOT HAVE MATCHING
"NEXT" STATEMENTS PRECEDING THIS ONE:  80
EXECUTION OMITTED
-140 next j
-150 next i
-run
EXECUTION STARTED
```

```
? the,fox,jumped,over,the,dog

EXCHANGE THE AND FOX
EXCHANGE FOX AND DOG
EXCHANGE THE AND JUMPED
EXCHANGE JUMPED AND FOX
EXCHANGE THE AND OVER
EXCHANGE OVER AND JUMPED
EXCHANGE THE AND OVER
DOG FOX JUMPED OVER THE THE


LINE 999 -- NORMAL END
-100
-run
EXECUTION STARTED

? the,purpose,of,computing,is,insight

COMPUTING INSIGHT IS OF PURPOSE THE


LINE 999 -- NORMAL END
-list

60    INPUT X$(1),X$(2),X$(3),X$(4),X$(5),X$(6)
70    FOR I = 1 TO 6
80       FOR J = I+1 TO 6
90          IF X$(I)<=X$(J) THEN 140
110         LET T$ = X$(J)
120         LET X$(J) = X$(I)
130         LET X$(I) = T$
140      NEXT J
150   NEXT I
160   FOR I = 1 TO 6
170      PRINT X$(I) ' ';
180   NEXT I
190   PRINT
200   PRINT
999   END

-save sort6
SORT6 SAVED ON ONE TRACK
-bye

TSO TIME JOB #2337 - T223370  ON 02E, CONNECT=  0.13.21  MUS=  0.00.10
T223370 LOGGED OFF TSO AT 11:36:35 ON JUNE 30, 1973+
```

Getting started requires "logging on," which requires typing the word LOGON followed by an account number and a password. The details differ from system to system, and even on different installations using TSO. As in batch processing, it is also necessary to tell TSO which processor is to be used. This may be done explicitly or, as in this case, by arranging for a given account number always to automatically initiate a given program.

This processor types a — as a cue that is ready to accept a statement or command. It analyzes each statement for syntax errors as it is entered (this is not done by all processors in time-sharing). If a syntax error occurs, a short error message is typed, as in line 60. If the user simply returns carriage, a more detailed message is typed. Execution is initiated by the command RUN. On the first attempt here, an error that could not be detected as statements were entered one-by-one was encountered. Note that re-entering the erroneous statements corrects them, and then the command RUN results in correct execution. Note that a ? is given by the system as a cue that input is requested.

Following that, simply entering the line number 100 results in erasing that line. The command `list` causes the system to print the program. The command `save sort6` causes the program to be saved under the name `sort6`. It can be retrieved at another time by the command `fetch sort6` or deleted by the command `scratch sort6`. Logoff is accomplished by the command `bye`.

In comparison to the batch-processing run, the corrections can be quickly and easily made and results obtained very soon. "Turn-around time" for batch processing may be as little as a few minutes for small jobs on a computer system well-adapted for handling large numbers of small jobs, as many university computing centers do. It may be 24 hours or more for computing centers that are heavily overloaded or not at all geared for small jobs. Nevertheless, batch processing uses the computer most efficiently; the cost for a run such as that shown here can be as small as a few cents.

Finally, let us look at a run on the highly interactive APL system. Log on is accomplished by typing a right parenthesis followed by an account number. For APL, as a cue that the system is ready to receive information, it moves the type ball five spaces to the right. Thus, whatever was typed indented five spaces was typed by the user, and whatever is at the left margin was typed by the computer.

```
)1023370
OPR:  JUNE 25 LATEST OF MUCH IMPORTANT NEWS..TYPE..)LOAD 1 NEWS..APLN
004) 17.07.32 06/27/73 PETERSONWW

    A P L \ 3 6 0

      ∇P N ◄────────────────────────────── Procedure definition entered
[1]    X←1                                 by user.
[2]    ⎕←X←(X , 0) + (0 , X∧
[3]    [2] ⎕ ← X ← (X , 0) + (0 , X)
[3]    →2
[4]    ∇
       P 6 ◄────────────────────────────── User invokes procedure.
1  1
1  2  1
1  3  3  1
1  4  6  4  1
1  5  10  10  5  1
1  6  15  20  15  6  1
1  7  21  35  35  21  7  1
1  8  28  56
P[3]
       ◄─────────────────────────────────── Attention key was depressed
       ∇P                                   to interrupt execution—stopped
[4]    [1] ⎕←X←1                            in statement 3.
[2]    [1.5] N←N-1
```

```
[1.6] →(N<0)/0      ◄─────── User makes changes in proce-
[1.7] [3] →1.5               dure P.
[4]    ∇
       P 4
1
1  1
DOMAIN ERROR  ◄──────────── Error in statement 5. Go to
P[5]   →1.5                  line 1.5 is not allowed.
       ∧
       ∇P
[6]    [⎕]   ◄────────────── Causes program to be listed.
     ∇ P N                   Note that statements are
[1]    ⎕←X←1                 renumbered.
[2]    N←N-1
[3]    →(N<0)/0
[4]    ⎕←X←(X,0)+(0,X)
[5]    →1.5
     ∇
[6]    [5] →2  ◄──────────── Correction.
[6]    [⎕]   ◄────────────── List program again.
     ∇ P N
[1]    ⎕←X←1
[2]    N←N-1
[3]    →(N<0)/0
[4]    ⎕←X←(X,0)+(0,X)
[5]    →2
     ∇
[6]    ∇
       P 4   ◄────────────── Execute once more.
1
1  1
1  2  1
1  3  3  1
1  4  6  4  1
       )SAVE PASCAL
  17.17.03 06/27/73
       )OFF
004   17.17.14 06/27/73 PET
CONNECTED      0.09.41  TO DATE     0.21.43
CPU TIME       0.00.01  TO DATE     0.00.01
```

There are two modes: execution and definition. You start in execution mode. You enter function definition mode by typing a function definition statement. You can always tell whether or not you are in function definition mode because the console always types a line number in brackets at the left margin if you are in function definition mode. You leave function definition mode by typing the symbol ∇ alone.

You enter statements by typing the statement alone if the console typed the correct line number. You may type the line number yourself, overriding the computer's suggestion. You can insert a statement between two statements using a decimal statement number (the computer will later renumber all statements). You may delete a statement by typing the line number in brackets, then depressing the *ATTN* key, and finally carriage return. If the system is in definition mode, entering [⎕] causes the program to be listed.

Commands are entered in execution mode.)*SAVE PASCAL* causes the work area to be saved on disc under the name *PASCAL*. It can be loaded again on another run using the same account number by the command)*LOAD PASCAL*. Individual functions, procedures, or variables can be erased by the command)*ERASE*, followed by the list of items to be erased, separated by blanks. A whole work area is erased from disc by the command)*DROP*, followed by a work area name. A work area can be copied by the command)*COPY* followed by a work area name, if you want a whole work area copied, or a work area name followed by a list of functions and/or variables separated by blanks to copy only those functions and/or variables. These are added to your work space. A session is terminated by the command)*OFF*.

Implementation of Recursive Procedures — Appendix E

```
/***********************************************************************/
/*                                                                     */
/*         IN THIS APPENDIX WE SHOW WHAT MUST BE DONE TO IMPLEMENT     */
/*    A RECURSIVE PROCEDURE BY SHOWING AN EXAMPLE WITH THE LINKAGE     */
/*    AND STACK EXPLICITLY CODED.                                      */
/*                                                                     */
/***********************************************************************/

R: PROCEDURE OPTIONS(MAIN);

/***********************************************************************/
/*                                                                     */
/*         ON ENTRY TO A RECURSIVE PROCEDURE,  THE PARAMETERS, ALL     */
/*    LOCAL VARIABLES,  AND THE RETURN ADDRESS  MUST  BE  STACKED.     */
/*    SINCE  IT  IS  NOT  POSSIBLE  TO  KNOW  THE  RETURN  ADDRESS     */
/*    EXPLICITLY   USING   THE   BUILT-IN  LINKAGE  MECHANISMS  IN     */
/*    HIGHER-LEVEL LANGUAGES, WE MUST EVEN CODE THE DETAILS OF THE     */
/*    LINKAGE AND USE GO TO STATEMENTS TO GO TO  AND  RETURN  FROM     */
/*    THE PROCEDURE.  THE EXAMPLE  IS  THE  BINOMIAL  COEFFICIENTS     */
/*    CALCULATED BY THE METHOD OF  PASCAL'S  TRIANGLE,  THE  SAME      */
/*    EXAMPLE USED FOR EVERY RECURSIVE LANGUAGE DISCUSSED IN  THIS     */
/*    BOOK,  STARTING WITH ALGOL60.  THE CHOSEN LINKAGE CONVENTION     */
/*    IS AS FOLLOWS: THERE ARE FOUR GLOBAL VARIABLES,  N AND K FOR     */
/*    THE PARAMETERS, "RETURNED_VALUE" FOR THE RETURNED VALUE, AND     */
/*    "RETURN_ADDRESS"   FOR  THE  RETURN  ADDRESS.   TO  USE  THE     */
```

```
/*   PROCEDURE,  ONE MUST ASSIGN PARAMETER VALUES TO N AND K, THE       */
/*   LABEL OF THE STATEMENT WHICH IS TO BE EXECUTED  FIRST  AFTER       */
/*   RETURN TO "RETURN_ADDRESS",  AND GO TO B. THE PROCEDURE WILL       */
/*   CALCULATE   THE   VALUE   OF   B(N,K),   ASSIGN   IT   TO          */
/*   "RETURNED_VALUE",  AND GO TO THE RETURN ADDRESS. ALL THIS IS       */
/*   NORMALLY DONE BY THE COMPILER.                                     */
/*                                                                      */
/**********************************************************************/

  DECLARE (N,K,RETURNED_VALUE) FIXED BINARY(31),
          RETURN_ADDRESS LABEL,
          (NULL,UNSPEC) BUILTIN;

/**********************************************************************/
/*                                                                      */
/*        THE FOLLOWING IS A SHORT TEST  MAIN  PROCEDURE,   WHICH       */
/*   ILLUSTRATES HOW TO LINK TO THE PROCEDURE:                          */
/*                                                                      */
/**********************************************************************/

  N = 4;
  K = 2;
  RETURN_ADDRESS = M;
  GO TO B;
M:
  PUT EDIT('FINAL RESULT: B(4,2)=',RETURNED_VALUE)(A,F(1));
  STOP;

/**********************************************************************/
/*                                                                      */
/*        FOR THE PROCEDURE TO BE RECURSIVE,  IT MUST  STACK  ALL       */
/*   PARAMETERS,  EXPLICIT AND IMPLICIT LOCAL VARIABLES,  AND THE       */
/*   RETURN ADDRESS.  THIS COULD BE DONE WITH AN ARRAY, AS IN THE       */
/*   EXAMPLE IN CHAPTERS 8 AND 9 WHICH LABELS DO'S  AND  MATCHING       */
/*   END'S. HOWEVER, USUALLY A THREADED LIST LIKE THOSE DESCRIBED       */
/*   IN CHAPTER 10 IS USED,  WITH DYNAMIC ALLOCATION.  THUS  EACH       */
/*   TIME THE PROCEDURE IS ENTERED,  STORAGE IS ALLOCATED FOR ONE       */
/*   LEVEL OF THE STACK,  "STACK_ITEM",  WHICH  CONTAINS  STACKED       */
/*   VALUES OF N,  K,  A TEMPORARY CALLED ST,  THE RETURN ADDRESS       */
/*   SRA, AND A POINTER PNT TO THE NEXT LOWER LEVEL ON THE STACK.       */
/*   P IS A POINTER TO THE TOP LEVEL ON THE STACK,  AND  Q  IS  A       */
/*   TEMPORARY POINTER.                                                 */
/*                                                                      */
/**********************************************************************/

  DECLARE 1 STACK_ITEM BASED,
              2 SN FIXED BINARY(31),
              2 SK FIXED BINARY(31),
              2 ST FIXED BINARY(31) INITIAL(-1),
              2 SRA LABEL,
              2 PNT POINTER,
            P POINTER INITIAL(NULL),
            Q POINTER;
```

```
/*********************************************************************/
/*                                                                   */
/*        IN ORDER TO SEE WHAT IS HAPPENING,  EACH TIME WE ENTER,    */
/*   AFTER STACKING THE PARAMETERS AND RETURN ADDRESS, WE PRINT A    */
/*   MESSAGE AND THE CONTENTS OF THE STACK,   AND  EACH  TIME  WE    */
/*   RETURN,  BEFORE REMOVING THE TOP LEVEL FROM THE  STACK,   WE    */
/*   PRINT A MESSAGE AND THE STACK CONTENTS. THIS IS ACCOMPLISHED    */
/*   BY THE NEXT TWO PROCEDURES:                                     */
/*                                                                   */
/*********************************************************************/

 LIE: PROCEDURE(X) RETURNS(FIXED BINARY(31));
    DECLARE X POINTER;
    RETURN(UNSPEC(X));
 END;  /*  OF LIE  */

 PRINTSTACK: PROCEDURE(X);
    DECLARE (X,Y) POINTER;
    Y = X;
    DO WHILE(Y¬=NULL);
       PUT SKIP EDIT('LOC=',LIE(Y),'  SN=',Y->SN,'  SK=',Y->SK,
          '  ST=',Y->ST)(A,F(7),A,F(1),A,F(1),A,F(2));
       IF Y->SRA=M THEN PUT EDIT('  SRA=M  PNT=')(A);
       ELSE IF Y->SRA=T THEN PUT EDIT('  SRA=T  PNT=')(A);
       ELSE IF Y->SRA=U THEN PUT EDIT('  SRA=U  PNT=')(A);
       IF Y->PNT=NULL THEN PUT EDIT('NULL--BOTTOM OF STACK')(A);
       ELSE PUT EDIT(LIE(Y->PNT))(F(7));
       Y = Y->PNT;  /* GET NEXT LOWER ITEM FROM STACK  */
    END;  /*  OF DO WHILE(Y¬=NULL)  */
    PUT SKIP(2);
 END;  /*  OF PRINTSTACK  */

/*********************************************************************/
/*                                                                   */
/*        THE REST OF THE PROGRAM IS THE PROCEDURE B.  THE  FIRST    */
/*   SEGMENT ALLOCATES A NEW LEVEL FOR THE STACK,  MAKES ITS  PNT    */
/*   POINT TO THE OLD TOP OF THE STACK,  WHICH IS  NOW  THE  NEXT    */
/*   LOWER LEVEL, AND MAKES P POINT TO THE NEW TOP LEVEL. THEN IT    */
/*   PLACES N,  K, AND THE RETURN ADDRESS ON THE STACK AND PRINTS    */
/*   A MESSAGE AND THE STACK CONTENTS.                               */
/*                                                                   */
/*********************************************************************/

 B: /* BEGINNING OF PROCEDURE B  */
    ALLOCATE STACK_ITEM SET(Q);
    Q->PNT = P;
    P = Q;
    P->SN = N;
    P->SK = K;
    P->SRA = RETURN_ADDRESS;
    PUT EDIT('ENTERED B WITH N=',N,' AND K=',K)(A,F(1),A,F(1));
    CALL PRINTSTACK(P);
```

```
/*************************************************************************/
/*                                                                       */
/*        THE NEXT SEGMENT DOES THE ACTUAL CALCULATION. NOTE THAT        */
/*   IT USES ONLY VARIABLES IN THE STACK. IT CALLS B TO CALCULATE        */
/*   B(N-1,K-1),  ASSIGNS THE RESULT TO ST,  THEN USES B AGAIN TO        */
/*   CALCULATE B(N-1,K),  WHICH IT ADDS TO ST TO GIVE THE  ANSWER        */
/*   TO BE RETURNED.  NOTE THAT WHEN IT CALLS B, ANOTHER LEVEL IS        */
/*   PLACED ON THE STACK,  AND UNTIL THAT LEVEL IS REMOVED,  THIS        */
/*   CALCULATION IS IN LIMBO.  BUT EVENTUALLY LEVELS  ABOVE  THIS        */
/*   ARE REMOVED,  AND THIS IS AGAIN THE TOP LEVEL IN  PARTICULAR        */
/*   WHEN THE END OF THIS SEGMENT OF CODE IS REACHED.                    */
/*                                                                       */
/*************************************************************************/

      IF P->SK=0 | P->SK=P->SN THEN P->ST = 1;
      ELSE DO;
         N = P->SN-1;
         K = P->SK-1;
         RETURN_ADDRESS = T;
         GO TO B;
  T:     P->ST = RETURNED_VALUE;
         N = P->SN-1;
         K = P->SK;
         RETURN_ADDRESS = U;
         GO TO B;
  U:     P->ST = P->ST + RETURNED_VALUE;
      END;

/*************************************************************************/
/*                                                                       */
/*        FINALLY WE PRINT A  MESSAGE  AND  THE  STACK  CONTENTS,        */
/*   ASSIGN ST TO "RETURNED_VALUE",  SET P TO POINT TO  THE  NEXT        */
/*   LOWER LEVEL OF THE STACK,  FREE THIS LEVEL,  AND GO  TO  THE        */
/*   RETURN ADDRESS THAT WAS ON THE TOP LEVEL OF THE STACK.              */
/*                                                                       */
/*************************************************************************/

      PUT SKIP EDIT('RETURN B(',P->SN,',',P->SK,')=',P->ST)
         (A,F(1),A,F(1),A,F(1));
      CALL PRINTSTACK(P);
      RETURNED_VALUE = P->ST;
      RETURN_ADDRESS = P->SRA;
      Q = P;
      P = P->PNT;  /*  SET P TO POINT ONE LEVEL LOWER  */
      FREE Q->STACK_ITEM;
      GO TO RETURN_ADDRESS;
   /*  END OF B  */
1
 END;  /*  OF MAIN PROCEDURE  */
```

Printed results.

```
ENTERED B WITH N=4 AND K=2
LOC=1490920  SN=4  SK=2  ST=-1  SRA=M  PNT=NULL--BOTTOM OF STACK
```

```
ENTERED B WITH N=3 AND K=1
LOC=1490688   SN=3   SK=1   ST=-1   SRA=T   PNT=1490920
LOC=1490920   SN=4   SK=2   ST=-1   SRA=M   PNT=NULL--BOTTOM OF STACK

ENTERED B WITH N=2 AND K=0
LOC=1490664   SN=2   SK=0   ST=-1   SRA=T   PNT=1490688
LOC=1490688   SN=3   SK=1   ST=-1   SRA=T   PNT=1490920
LOC=1490920   SN=4   SK=2   ST=-1   SRA=M   PNT=NULL--BOTTOM OF STACK


RETURN B(2,0)=1
LOC=1490664   SN=2   SK=0   ST= 1   SRA=T   PNT=1490688
LOC=1490688   SN=3   SK=1   ST=-1   SRA=T   PNT=1490920
LOC=1490920   SN=4   SK=2   ST=-1   SRA=M   PNT=NULL--BOTTOM OF STACK

ENTERED B WITH N=2 AND K=1
LOC=1490664   SN=2   SK=1   ST=-1   SRA=U   PNT=1490688
LOC=1490688   SN=3   SK=1   ST= 1   SRA=T   PNT=1490920
LOC=1490920   SN=4   SK=2   ST=-1   SRA=M   PNT=NULL--BOTTOM OF STACK

ENTERED B WITH N=1 AND K=0
LOC=1490640   SN=1   SK=0   ST=-1   SRA=T   PNT=1490664
LOC=1490664   SN=2   SK=1   ST=-1   SRA=U   PNT=1490688
LOC=1490688   SN=3   SK=1   ST= 1   SRA=T   PNT=1490920
LOC=1490920   SN=4   SK=2   ST=-1   SRA=M   PNT=NULL--BOTTOM OF STACK


RETURN B(1,0)=1
LOC=1490640   SN=1   SK=0   ST= 1   SRA=T   PNT=1490664
LOC=1490664   SN=2   SK=1   ST=-1   SRA=U   PNT=1490688
LOC=1490688   SN=3   SK=1   ST= 1   SRA=T   PNT=1490920
LOC=1490920   SN=4   SK=2   ST=-1   SRA=M   PNT=NULL--BOTTOM OF STACK

ENTERED B WITH N=1 AND K=1
LOC=1490640   SN=1   SK=1   ST=-1   SRA=U   PNT=1490664
LOC=1490664   SN=2   SK=1   ST= 1   SRA=U   PNT=1490688
LOC=1490688   SN=3   SK=1   ST= 1   SRA=T   PNT=1490920
LOC=1490920   SN=4   SK=2   ST=-1   SRA=M   PNT=NULL--BOTTOM OF STACK


RETURN B(1,1)=1
LOC=1490640   SN=1   SK=1   ST= 1   SRA=U   PNT=1490664
LOC=1490664   SN=2   SK=1   ST= 1   SRA=U   PNT=1490688
LOC=1490688   SN=3   SK=1   ST= 1   SRA=T   PNT=1490920
LOC=1490920   SN=4   SK=2   ST=-1   SRA=M   PNT=NULL--BOTTOM OF STACK


RETURN B(2,1)=2
LOC=1490664   SN=2   SK=1   ST= 2   SRA=U   PNT=1490688
LOC=1490688   SN=3   SK=1   ST= 1   SRA=T   PNT=1490920
LOC=1490920   SN=4   SK=2   ST=-1   SRA=M   PNT=NULL--BOTTOM OF STACK


RETURN B(3,1)=3
LOC=1490688   SN=3   SK=1   ST= 3   SRA=T   PNT=1490920
LOC=1490920   SN=4   SK=2   ST=-1   SRA=M   PNT=NULL--BOTTOM OF STACK
```

```
ENTERED B WITH N=3 AND K=2
LOC=1490688   SN=3   SK=2   ST=-1   SRA=U   PNT=1490920
LOC=1490920   SN=4   SK=2   ST= 3   SRA=M   PNT=NULL--BOTTOM OF STACK

ENTERED B WITH N=2 AND K=1
LOC=1490664   SN=2   SK=1   ST=-1   SRA=T   PNT=1490688
LOC=1490688   SN=3   SK=2   ST=-1   SRA=U   PNT=1490920
LOC=1490920   SN=4   SK=2   ST= 3   SRA=M   PNT=NULL--BOTTOM OF STACK

ENTERED B WITH N=1 AND K=0
LOC=1490640   SN=1   SK=0   ST=-1   SRA=T   PNT=1490664
LOC=1490664   SN=2   SK=1   ST=-1   SRA=T   PNT=1490688
LOC=1490688   SN=3   SK=2   ST=-1   SRA=U   PNT=1490920
LOC=1490920   SN=4   SK=2   ST= 3   SRA=M   PNT=NULL--BOTTOM OF STACK


RETURN B(1,0)=1
LOC=1490640   SN=1   SK=0   ST= 1   SRA=T   PNT=1490664
LOC=1490664   SN=2   SK=1   ST=-1   SRA=T   PNT=1490688
LOC=1490688   SN=3   SK=2   ST=-1   SRA=U   PNT=1490920
LOC=1490920   SN=4   SK=2   ST= 3   SRA=M   PNT=NULL--BOTTOM OF STACK

ENTERED B WITH N=1 AND K=1
LOC=1490640   SN=1   SK=1   ST=-1   SRA=U   PNT=1490664
LOC=1490664   SN=2   SK=1   ST= 1   SRA=T   PNT=1490688
LOC=1490688   SN=3   SK=2   ST=-1   SRA=U   PNT=1490920
LOC=1490920   SN=4   SK=2   ST= 3   SRA=M   PNT=NULL--BOTTOM OF STACK


RETURN B(1,1)=1
LOC=1490640   SN=1   SK=1   ST= 1   SRA=U   PNT=1490664
LOC=1490664   SN=2   SK=1   ST= 1   SRA=T   PNT=1490688
LOC=1490688   SN=3   SK=2   ST=-1   SRA=U   PNT=1490920
LOC=1490920   SN=4   SK=2   ST= 3   SRA=M   PNT=NULL--BOTTOM OF STACK


RETURN B(2,1)=2
LOC=1490664   SN=2   SK=1   ST= 2   SRA=T   PNT=1490688
LOC=1490688   SN=3   SK=2   ST=-1   SRA=U   PNT=1490920
LOC=1490920   SN=4   SK=2   ST= 3   SRA=M   PNT=NULL--BOTTOM OF STACK

ENTERED B WITH N=2 AND K=2
LOC=1490664   SN=2   SK=2   ST=-1   SRA=U   PNT=1490688
LOC=1490688   SN=3   SK=2   ST= 2   SRA=U   PNT=1490920
LOC=1490920   SN=4   SK=2   ST= 3   SRA=M   PNT=NULL--BOTTOM OF STACK


RETURN B(2,2)=1
LOC=1490664   SN=2   SK=2   ST= 1   SRA=U   PNT=1490688
LOC=1490688   SN=3   SK=2   ST= 2   SRA=U   PNT=1490920
LOC=1490920   SN=4   SK=2   ST= 3   SRA=M   PNT=NULL--BOTTOM OF STACK


RETURN B(3,2)=3
LOC=1490688   SN=3   SK=2   ST= 3   SRA=U   PNT=1490920
LOC=1490920   SN=4   SK=2   ST= 3   SRA=M   PNT=NULL--BOTTOM OF STACK
```

```
RETURN B(4,2)=6
LOC=1490920   SN=4   SK=2   ST= 6   SRA=M   PNT=NULL--BOTTOM OF STACK

FINAL RESULT: B(4,2)=6
```

The program examples in this book were run with the following language processors:

BASIC—UHBASIC. Information available from the author.
FORTRAN—IBM Level G FORTRAN Compiler.
ALGOL60—IBM ALGOL60 Compiler.
PL/I—all programs except the last program in Chapter 4 were run on the IBM PL/I Optimizing Compiler. The last program in Chapter 4, and many others, were run with the IBM F-level compiler, and except for minor restrictions on the use of pointers and the requirement in some cases for ENTRY declarations, I believe all will run with the F-level compiler.
APL—IBM APL/360.
COBOL—IBM ANSI COBOL Compiler.
SNOBOL4—All programs were run both with the Bell Laboratories SNOBOL4 interpreter and the Illinois Institute of Technology SPITBOL compiler, with identical results.
LISP—The University of Waterloo LISP Interpreter.

The following table is a summary of the best information I have been able to obtain on availability of language processors for various machines.

Language-Processor Availability Appendix F

	BASIC	FORTRAN	ALGOL	PL/I	APL	COBOL	SNOBOL	LISP
Burroughs	S[1]	S	S	S	D[2]	S	A[3]	N[4]
CDC 3000 Series	S	S	S	N	N	S	A[5]	A
CDC Cyber/6000 Series	S	S	S	S	S	S	A	A
DEC PDP-8	S	S	A	N	N	N	N	N
PDP-10	S	S	S	N	S	S	S	A
PDP-11	S	S	N	N	N	N	N	N
PDP-15	N	S	S	N	N	N	A	N
Honeywell Multics	S	S	N	S	S	S	N	A
Honeywell 600/6000	S	S	S	D	A	S	A	A
IBM/360-370	S	S	S	S	S	S	A	A
UNIVAC 1100 Series	S	S	S	D	S	S	A	A
Xerox Sigma 9	S	S	A	N	S	S	A	A

1. S: supported by manufacturer.
2. D: under development.
3. A: available from another source.
4. N: no information available.
5. at least on CDC3600.

Index

A FORMAT, 104
ACM, 59
ADD, 196
ADD function, 151
ADDR function, 255
Addressing, hashed, 157, 175
ADVANCING, 206
AFTER ADVANCING, 206
ALGOL60, 2, 8–10, 59–84, 86, 351
ALGOL60 report, 59, 68, 71, 309
ALGOL W, 60, 74, 306
ALLOCATE statement, 256
Allocation of storage, 76, 256
Alphabetic picture, 189
Alphanumeric data, 43
Alphanumeric edited picture, 189
Alphanumeric picture, 189
Alternative, 237
American National Standards Inst., *see* ANSI
ANSI, 42, 171, 172, 187, 351
ANY pattern, 240
APL, 2, 117–134, 306, 335, 339, 351
ARB pattern, 241
AREA attribute, 96
Array, 24, 43, 46, 96, 126–134, 245
Array expression, 99
Array operations, 133–134
Artificial intelligence, 287
Aspirin, 331
ASSIGN, 172, 192
Assigned GO TO statement, 48
Assignment
  conditional, 238
  conversion by, 152
  immediate, 252
Assignment statement, 25, 47, 71, 99, 108–111, 211–212, 232, 244
Association for Computing Machinery, 59
Atom, 288
Atomic symbol, 288
Attribute, 95–97
AT END clause, 206

B FORMAT, 104
Backus–Naur form, *see* BNF
Backus, J., 59
BAL pattern, 241
Based storage, 255–259
BASIC, 2, 13–30, 305, 335, 351
Batch, 13, 154, 335
Bates, F., 306
BEGIN block, 87, 107, 140, 141, 154
Bell Laboratories, 231, 351
Bibliography, 209
BINARY attribute, 95, 97
Binomial coefficient program, 81, 107, 125, 251, 298–299
BIT attribute, 96
Block, 61, 74–76, 78, 97, 107, 140–141
Blocks, nested, 108
BNF, 8–10, 60, 68, 119
Boolean expression, 71
Boolean variable, 69
BREAK pattern, 241–242
Built-in function, 25, 45, 120
Built-in patterns, 240
Burroughs Corp., 60, 74, 352

CALL STATEMENT, 38, 56, 106
Call by name, 57, 78–79, 106
Call by value, 78–79, 106
CAR function, 293
Card listing program, 234
Carriage control character, 149, 243
Case statement, 66–67, 92–93
CDC, 53, 352
CDR function, 293
Character
  carriage control, 149, 243
Character (*cont.*)
  drifting, 145
  insertion, 145
  zero suppression, 144
CHARACTER attribute, 96
Character code, EBCDIC, 215
Character data, 43
Character string, 232, 288
Character string constant, 187, 232
Character string expression, 213
Character string pictures, 143–144
Character string processing, 209–252, 329
Character variable, 20, 91, 148
Class condition, 200
Clause, 192
  ELSE, 100
  AT END, 206
CLOSE statement, 149
COBOL, 2, 60, 163, 171–207, 306, 351
CODASYL, 171
Comment, 24, 33, 77, 95, 191, 234
COMMON storage, 56
Comparison operator, 98
Compatibility, 32, 33
COMPLETION CODE, 207
COMPLEX attribute, 96
Complex variable, 43
Compound statement, 61, 74–76, 78, 107
Compression, 130–131
COMPUTATIONAL, 195, 200, 205
COMPUTE, 196–197
Computed GO TO statement, 20, 26, 39, 48, 201, 244
Concatenation, 98, 127, 211, 212, 232
  pattern, 237
COND function, 298
Condition, class, 200
Condition name, 173, 180, 200–201

Condition prefix, 141
Conditional assignment, 238
Conditional form, 298
Conditional replacement, 244
Conditional statement, 71–72
Configuration section, 191–192, 206
CONS function, 293
Constant, 25, 44, 69, 187, 196, 232, 288
  character, 232
  Hollerith, 53
Continuation card, 42, 190
CONTINUE statement, 50–51, 204
Control
  carriage, 149
  loop, 22
Conversational style, 117–118
Conversion, 98–99, 109, 114–115, 173, 204–205
CONVERSION, 160
Conversion by assignment, 152
CONVERSION ON-condition, 137, 138, 141, 143–144, 148, 150–151
Correction of errors, 209
Curser position, 241

DAHL, O. J., 307
Dartmouth College, 13
DATA, 103
Data, Hollerith, 43
Data division, 173, 192–195
Data processing, 136–207, 329
DATA statement, 24, 28
Data type, 95
  programmer-defined, 252
Debugging, 4, 5, 6–8, 16, 207
DEC PDP, 53, 352
DECIMAL attribute, 96, 97
Declaration, 69
  switch, 70
  procedure, 78–80
  ENTRY, 106
DECLARE statement, 211, 256, 257
DEF statement, 28
Default, 97
DEFINE function, 246, 297
Definition, of functions and procedures, 17, 19, 28, 35, 36, 55, 63, 64, 78–80, 89, 91, 105–107, 122–125, 246–251, 288
Department of Defense, 171
Designator, switch, 66
Designational expression, 71, 72
Dictionary, 209
DIFFER predicate, 235

Dijkstra, E. W., 307
DIM statement, 24, 25
Dimension statement, 24, 41, 43, 128
Disc file, 155, 157
DISPLAY statement, 180, 195, 200, 205, 207
DIVIDE, 196
DIVIDE function, 151
Division,
  data, 173, 192–195
  environment, 172, 191–193
  identification, 172, 191
  procedure, 173, 196–207
DO statement, 41, 49–50, 87, 101–102, 107, 141, 154, 224
Double-precision variable, 43
Douglas, M. L., 306
Drifting character, 145
Dyadic function, 120
Dynamic storage allocation, 76

E FORMAT, 104
EBCDIC character code, 215
EDIT, 103
Editing of text, 209, 329
Efficient use of storage, 284
ELSE clause, 100
END statement, 27, 87, 107, 224, 234
  labeled, 108
ENDFILE, 88
ENDFILE ON-condition, 137, 138, 141
ENDPAGE ON-condition, 138, 139, 141
End of file, 234
ENTRY declaration, 106, 114–115
Environment division, 172, 191–193
EQ predicate, 235
Error, 3, 6–7, 209, 248–250, 257
Error correction, 209
Error example program, 112–115
Error message, 207, 220
EVENT attribute, 96
EXAMINE statement, 205
EXIT statement, 204
Expansion, 131
Exponentiation, 25, 44, 70, 119
Expression, 44, 70, 108–111, 119–121, 196, 275
  array, 99
  Boolean, 71
  character-string, 213
  designational, 71, 72
  LAMBDA, 297
  logical, 46
  mixed, 45, 70

Expression (*cont.*)
  switch, 71
  unevaluated, 252
Extensions, language, 33
EXTERNAL, 106
External procedure, 106

F FORMAT, 104
Factorial program, 298–299
Factor, repetition, 143, 189
Fail, 234, 236
FENCE pattern, 240
Fibonacci number, 333
File
  magnetic disc, 155, 157
  master, 154
  PRINT, 149
File name, 148
File section, 192, 193
FIXED attribute, 96, 97
Fixed-decimal arithmetic, 112, 152
Fixed-decimal variable, 150–154
FIXEDOVERFLOW ON-condition, 140, 151, 154
FLOAT attribute, 96, 97
FLOW-MATIC, 172
Flowchart, 4
Floyd, R. W., 306
FNEND statement, 17, 28
FOR statement, 26–27, 62, 67, 73–74
Form, conditional, 298
Formal parameter, 78
Format item
  FORTRAN, 52–53
  PL/I, 104
FORMAT statement, 34, 52–55
FORTRAN, 2, 31–57, 86, 305, 351
FREE statement, 257, 258
FRETURN, 247, 248–250
Fully qualified, 146
Function, 17, 28, 35, 55, 63, 78–80, 89, 105–107, 122–125, 246–251, 288, 296–297
  ADD, 151
  ADDR, 255
  built-in, 25, 45, 120
  CAR, 293
  CDR, 293
  COND, 298
  CONS, 293
  DEFINE, 246, 297
  DIVIDE, 151
  dyadic, 120
  INDEX, 211, 213
  LENGTH, 211, 212
  LISP, 292
  MOD, 38, 63
  monadic, 120, 121

Function (*cont.*)
MULTIPLY, 151
OUTPUT, 243
QUOTE, 296
REPEAT, 215
step, 55
STRING, 215
SUBSTR, 211, 212, 214
TRANSLATE, 214, 217
TRIM, 236
UNSPEC, 258
VERIFY, 215
Function definition, 17, 19, 28, 35, 36, 55, 63, 64, 78–80, 89, 91, 105–107, 122–125, 246–251, 288
Function reference, 296–297
Function-type procedure, 80

GAMM, 59
GE predicate, 235
Generator, program, 209
German Assn. for Math. and Mech., 59
GET DATA, 103
GET EDIT, 92
GET LIST, 88, 103
GET SKIP, 90, 104
GET STRING, 153, 154
Glossary, 209
Go to part, 234
GO TO statement, 24, 26, 48, 66, 70, 72, 91, 100, 122, 201
computed, 20, 26, 39, 48, 201, 244
GOSUB statement, 19, 29
Government Printing Office, 171
Graph, 275
Greatest common divisor program, 18–20, 36–38, 63–65, 89–91, 123–125, 235–236, 298–299
Griswold, M. T., 306
Griswold, R. E., 252, 306
GT predicate, 235

HAMMING, R. W., 226, 229
Hashed addressing, 157, 175
High-level list processing, 287
Hoare, C. A. R., 307
Hollerith constant, 53
Hollerith data, 43
Holz, J., 306
Homework record program, 160–170, 179–187
Honeywell Corp., 172, 352
Horning, J. J., 321

I/O
record, 103, 148–150, 173
stream, 103, 104, 148
IBM, 32, 45, 59, 62, 70, 85, 86, 95, 106, 115, 117, 172, 187, 190, 206, 351
IBM/360–370, 38, 53, 54, 60, 61, 86, 89, 91, 103, 110, 141, 146, 173, 191, 195, 198, 207, 258
IBM OS/360–370 TSO, 155, 337–339
IDENT predicate, 235
Identification division, 172, 191
Identifier, 42, 95, 119, 232
IF statement, 16, 20, 26, 34, 41, 49, 54, 61, 62, 71–72, 87, 100, 141, 198–201
Illinois Institute of Technology, 351
Immediate assignment, 252
IN, 194
Index, 209
INDEX function, 211, 213
INDEXED BY, 195
INPUT, 233
INPUT statement, 19, 20, 24, 27–28
Input-output section, 192–193
Insert, 263
INSERT procedure, 264
INSERT program, 299–301
Insertion character, 145
Integer, 232
Integer arithmetic, 111
Integer variable, 38, 42, 43, 69
INTEGER predicate, 235
Intermediate result, 114–115
Iverson, K. E., 117

JCL, 335
Job control language, 335
JOSS, 118
Justification, 209

KATZAN, H., Jr., 306
Kemeny, J. G., 24, 305
Key, 154, 160, 175
Key word, 95
Knuth, D. E., 75, 157
Kurtz, T. E., 24, 305

LAMBDA EXPRESSION, 297
Language analysis, 275
Language extensions, 33
Label, 70, 95, 232
LABEL attribute, 91, 96
Label program, 224–226, 245–246
Labeled END, 108

LE predicate, 235
Leading-zero suppression character, 144
LEN pattern, 240
LENGTH function, 211, 212
LET statement, 17, 20, 25
Letter writing, 209
Level 77, 173, 193
Level 88, 200
LGT predicate, 235
LIE procedure, 258
LINPUT statement, 28
LISP, 2, 287–303, 307, 351
LISP function, 292
LISP predicate, 293–294
LISP program, 292
List, 259, 288–289
LIST, 103
List notation, 291–292
List processing, 252, 253–303, 331
high-level, 287
low-level, 287, 303
LIST procedure, 262
Local variable, 246, 251
Logical variable, 24, 41, 43, 46, 70–71, 94
Loop control, 22, 49–50, 73–74, 101–103, 201–204
Low-level list processing, 287, 303
LT predicate, 235

MAGNETIC DISC FILE, 155, 157
MAKELIST procedure, 261–262
MAKETREE procedure, 276–283
Master file, 154
Matrix operation, 29, 100, 130
Maze program, 267–275
McCracken, D., 306
McKeeman, W. M., 93, 331
Message, error, 207, 220
Metzger, P. W., 307
Mixed expression, 45, 70
MOD function, 38, 63
Monadic function, 120, 121
Money distribution program, 22–24, 39–41, 67–68, 93–94, 131–132
MOVE statement, 204–205
Multi-programming, 258
Multics, 352
MULTIPLY, 196
MULTIPLY function, 151

NAME
condition, 173, 180, 200–201
file, 148
NE predicate, 235
Nested blocks, 108
Newton's method, 16

NEXT statement, 27
NEXT SENTENCE, 199
NIL, 288
Node, 288
NOTANY pattern, 240
Notation
  Polish, 276
  list, 291–292
NOTE, 191
NULL pointer, 255, 260
Null statement, 24
Null string, 233, 235, 240
Number
  Fibonacci, 333
  statement, 42
Numeric edited picture, 189, 196
Numeric picture, 144–148, 152, 153, 189, 196, 198

OBJECT-COMPUTER, 191
OCCURS, 194
OF, 194
OFFSET attribute, 96
ON statement, 20, 26
ON-condition, 137–142, 215
  CONVERSION, 137, 138, 141, 143–144, 148, 150–151
  ENDFILE, 137, 138, 141
  ENDPAGE, 138, 139, 141
  FIXEDOVERFLOW, 140, 154
  OVERFLOW, 138, 140, 154
  SIZE, 138, 139, 140, 152, 153, 154
  STRINGRANGE, 216
  STRINGSIZE, 216
  SUBSCRIPTRANGE, 138, 139, 154
  UNDERFLOW, 138, 139, 140, 141
  ZERODIVIDE, 138, 139, 140, 154
On-line system, 154, 155, 209
ON-unit, 140
ON SIZE ERROR, 197
OPEN statement, 149, 206
Operand, 196
Operator
  comparison, 98
  logical, 98
OPTIONS, 105
Outer product, 130
OUTPUT, 233
OUTPUT function, 243
OVERFLOW ON-condition, 138, 140, 154
Overpunched sign, 145–146, 329

PAGE, 191, 206
Paragraph, 190
Parameter, 28, 55–56, 78, 105, 122, 246, 297
Partial result, 109
Pascal's triangle program, 81, 107, 125, 251, 298–299
Pass by name, 78
Pattern, 232, 236–244
  ANY, 240
  ARB, 241
  BAL, 241
  BREAK, 241–242
  built-in, 240
  FENCE, 240
  LEN, 240
  NOTANY, 240
  REM, 241
  RTAB, 241
  SPAN, 241–242
  TAB, 241
Pattern concatenation, 237
Pattern matching, 232, 236–244, 252
PDP10, 53
PEAS AND QUEUES program, 239
PERFORM statement, 173, 180, 201–204
Peterson, W. W., 306
Picture, 189
  alphabetic, 189
  alphanumeric, 189
  character-string, 143–144
  numeric, 144–148, 152, 153, 189, 196, 198
  numeric edited, 189, 196
PICTURE attribute, 96, 97
Picture specification, 143–146
Picture variable, 148
  numeric, 152
Plan, 4
PL/I, 2, 85–115, 137–170, 211–230, 255–286, 303, 306, 351
Poage, J. F., 252, 306
Polish notation, 276
Polonsky, I. P., 252, 306
Pointer, 255
  NULL, 255, 260
POINTER attribute, 96
Pointer values, printing, 258
Position, curser, 241
Procedure, 62, 97, 251
  external, 106
  function-type, 80
  INSERT, 264
  LIE, 258
  LIST, 262
  MAKELIST, 261–262
  MAKETREE, 276–283
Procedure (*cont.*)
  recursive, 80–84, 105, 107, 125, 230, 251, 263–265, 282, 288, 343
  SOLVE, 269–270, 273–274, 277, 280–283
  SORT, 265
Procedure declaration, 78–80
Procedure definition, 17, 19, 28, 35, 36, 55, 63, 64, 78–80, 89, 91, 105–107, 122–125, 246–251, 288
Procedure division, 173, 196–207
Procedure statement, 73–74
PROCEDURE statement, 87, 105, 141, 154
Processing
  batch, 154
  character-string, 209–252, 329
  data, 136–207, 329
  list, 252, 253–303, 331
  on-line, 154, 155, 209
Product
  matrix, 130
  outer, 130
PROG feature, 288
Program, 78
  binomial coefficient, 81, 107, 125, 251, 298–299
  card listing, 234
  error example, 112–115
  factorial, 298–299
  greatest common divisor, 18–20, 36–38, 63–65, 89–91, 123–125, 235–236, 298–299
  homework record, 160–170, 179–187
  INSERT, 299–301
  label, 224–226, 245–246
  LISP, 292
  maze, 267–275
  money distribution, 22–24, 39–41, 67–68, 93–94, 131–132
  Pascal's triangle, 81, 107, 125, 251, 298–299
  PEAS AND QUEUES, 239
  pseudorandom number, 141–142
  quote words, 238–239
  remove words, 237
  SCAN, 220–224, 248–250
  solution of $\exp(x) = 3 * x$, 4, 14–16, 33–35, 61–62, 87–88, 122–123
  SOLVE, 301–303
  SORT, 299–301
  Square root, 16–18, 35–36, 62–63, 88–89, 123, 204
  string reversing, 230, 251

'rogram (*cont.*)
stock price inquiry, 155–160, 174–179
student records, 160–170, 179–187
tabulation, 283–286
TYPE, 216–219, 247–248
underline, 226–229, 242–243
water bill, 20–21, 38–39, 65–67, 91–93, 244–245
'rogram generator, 209
'rogrammer-defined data type, 252
'rogramming style, 3–6, 154
'recedence, 98
'redicate
LISP, 293–294
SNOBOL4, 293–294
'refix, condition, 141
'RINT, 301–303
'RINT file, 149
'RINT statement, 20, 27
'rinting pointer values, 258
'seudorandom number program, 141–142
'UNCH, 233
'UT statement, 103
'UT DATA, 87, 103
'UT EDIT, 89, 104
'UT LIST, 103
'UT SKIP, 90, 104
'UT STRING, 153, 154

)UALIFICATION, 194, 195
)ualified, 146
)UOTE function, 296
)uote words program, 238–239

:AND CORPORATION, 118
:adin, G., 86
:andom number program, 141–142
:CA, 171
:EAD statement, 17, 20, 24, 27–28, 51–52, 54, 103, 148, 157, 206
.eal number, 232
.eal variable, 38, 42, 43, 69
:ecord I/O, 103, 148–150, 173
:ecursive, 80–84, 105, 107, 125, 230, 251, 263–265, 282, 288, 343
:EDEFINES, 193–194
.edimensioning, 30
.eduction, 129
.elation, 199
eliability of software, 3
:EM pattern, 241
.EMAINDER, 197
Remark, 24
Remove words program, 237
REPEAT function, 215
Repetition factor, 143, 189
Replacement, 236
conditional, 244
Report, 154
ALGOL60, 59, 68, 71, 309
Report section, 192
Report writer, 192
Reserved word, 187, 188, 190
RESTORE statement, 28
Result
intermediate, 114–115
partial, 109
RETURN, 19, 29, 35, 105, 140, 247
RETURNS, 105, 106
Rogoway, H. P., 86
Rosen, S., 86, 307
ROUNDED, 196
RTAB pattern, 241
Rule A, 111
Rule B, 111, 112
Rule C, 111, 112
Rule D, 152

S-EXPRESSION, 290, 332
Sammet, J. E., 2, 171, 307
SCAN program, 220–224, 248–250
Scientific computation, 11–115, 151, 327
Section
configuration, 191–192, 206
file, 192, 193
input-output, 192–193
working-storage, 192, 193
SELECT, 172, 192
Sentence, 190, 193, 196
SHARE, 32, 59, 85
SIGMA7, 352
Sign, overpunched, 145–146, 329
SIZE ON-condition, 138, 139, 140, 152, 153, 154
SKIP, 90, 104, 226
SNOBOL4, 2, 231–252, 306, 351
SNOBOL4 syntax, 243–244
Software reliability, 3
Solution, of $\exp(x) = 3 * x$ program, 4, 14–16, 33–35, 61–62, 87–88, 122–123
SOLVE procedure, 269–270, 273–274, 277, 280–283
SOLVE program, 301–303
Sort, 192, 263
SORT procedure, 265
SORT program, 299–301
SOURCE-COMPUTER, 191
SPACES, 187
SPAN pattern, 241–242
SPECIAL NAMES, 191, 206
Specification, picture, 143–146
Sperry Rand Corp., 171, 172
SPITBOL, 351
Square-root program, 16–18, 35–36, 62–63, 88–89, 123, 204
Stack, 84, 224, 245, 251, 276
Stanford University, 60, 306
Statement, 196
ALLOCATE, 256
arithmetic, 196–198
assigned GO TO, 48
assignment, 25, 47, 71, 99, 108–111, 211–212, 232, 244
BEGIN, 87, 107, 154
CALL, 38, 56, 106
case, 66–67, 92–93
CLOSE, 149
compound, 61, 74–76, 78, 107
computed GO TO, 20, 26, 39, 48, 201, 244
conditional, 71–72
CONTINUE, 50–51, 204
DATA, 24, 28
DECLARE, 211, 256, 257
DEF, 28
DIM, 24, 25
DIMENSION, 41, 43, 128
DISPLAY, 180, 207
DO, 41, 49–50, 87, 101–102, 107, 141, 154, 224
END, 27, 87, 107, 224
EXAMINE, 205
EXIT, 204
FNEND, 17, 28
FOR, 26–27, 62, 67, 73–74
FORMAT, 34, 52–55
FREE, 257, 258
GET, 103
GET LIST, 88
GET SKIP, 90
GET STRING, 153, 154
GO TO, 24, 26, 48, 66, 70, 72, 91, 100, 122, 201
GOSUB, 19, 29
IF, 16, 20, 26, 34, 41, 49, 54, 61, 62, 71–72, 87, 100, 141, 198–201
INPUT 19, 20, 24, 27–28
LET, 17, 20, 25
LINPUT, 28
MOVE, 204–205
NEXT, 27
null, 24
ON, 20, 26
OPEN, 149, 206

Statement (*cont.*)
pattern-matching, 236–244
PERFORM, 173, 180, 201–204
PRINT, 20, 27
PROCEDURE, 73–74, 87, 105, 141, 154
PUT, 103
PUT DATA, 87
PUT EDIT, 89
PUT SKIP, 90
PUT STRING, 153, 154
READ, 17, 20, 24, 27–28, 51–52, 54, 103, 148, 157, 206
RESTORE, 28
RETURN, 19, 29, 35, 105, 140
STOP, 27
STOP RUN, 204
WRITE, 34, 51–52, 54, 103, 148, 157, 206–207
Statement number, 42
Step function, 55
Stock price inquiry program, 155–160, 174–177
STOP statement, 27
STOP RUN statement, 204
Storage
COMMON, 56
based, 255–259
efficient use of, 284
Storage allocation, 76, 256
Stream I/O, 103, 104, 148
String
null, 233, 235, 240
character, 288
STRING function, 215
String reversing program, 230, 251
String variable, 20
STRINGRANGE ON-condition, 216
STRINGSIZE ON-condition, 216
Structure, 146–148
Student records program, 160–170, 179–187
Style
conversational, 117–118
programming, 3–6, 154
Subject, 236
Subroutine, 18–20, 38, 56
Subscripted variables, 22, 39
SUBSCRIPTRANGE ON-condition, 138, 139, 154, 283
Subscripts, 194, 195
SUBSTR function, 211, 212, 214
SUBTRACT, 196
Succeed, 234, 236
Switch declaration, 70
Switch designator, 66
Switch expression, 71
Switch variable, 69
Symbol, atomic, 288
SYSIN, 149
SYSPRINT, 149

TAB PATTERN, 241
Tabulation program, 283–286
TASK attribute, 96
Text editing, 209, 329
Time sharing, 13, 24, 28, 117–118, 155, 335, 337
Transaction, 154
TRANSLATE function, 214, 217
Tree, 275
TRIM function, 236
TSO, 155, 337–339
TYPE program, 216–219, 247–248

UHBASIC, 335, 351
UNDERFLOW ON-condition, 138, 139, 140, 141
Underline program, 226–229, 242–243
Unevaluated expression, 252
UNIVAC, 53
UNSPEC function, 258
USAGE, 195
UNIVAC, 352
University of Waterloo, 351

VALUE IS, 195
Value part, 78
Variable, 173, 187
Boolean, 69
character string, 20, 91, 148
complex, 43
double-precision, 43
fixed-decimal, 150–154
integer, 38, 42, 43, 69
local, 246, 251
logical, 41, 43, 46, 94
numeric picture, 152, 153
picture, 148
pointer, 255
real, 38, 42, 43, 69
subscripted, 22, 39
switch, 69
VARYING, 202
VARYING attribute, 96
Vector, 126–134
VERIFY function, 215

WATER BILL PROGRAM, 20–21, 38, 39, 65–67, 91–93, 244–24
Watson, R. W., 330
Weissman, C., 307
WHILE, 87, 101–102
Word, reserved, 187, 188, 190
Working-storage section, 192, 19
Wortman, D. B., 93, 331
WRITE statement, 34, 51–52, 5 103, 148, 157, 206–207

X FORMAT, 104
XEROX CORP., 352
XPL, 93

ZERO, 187
ZERODIVIDE ON-condition, 138, 139, 140, 154